VB Rose

Volume 9

Banri Hidaka

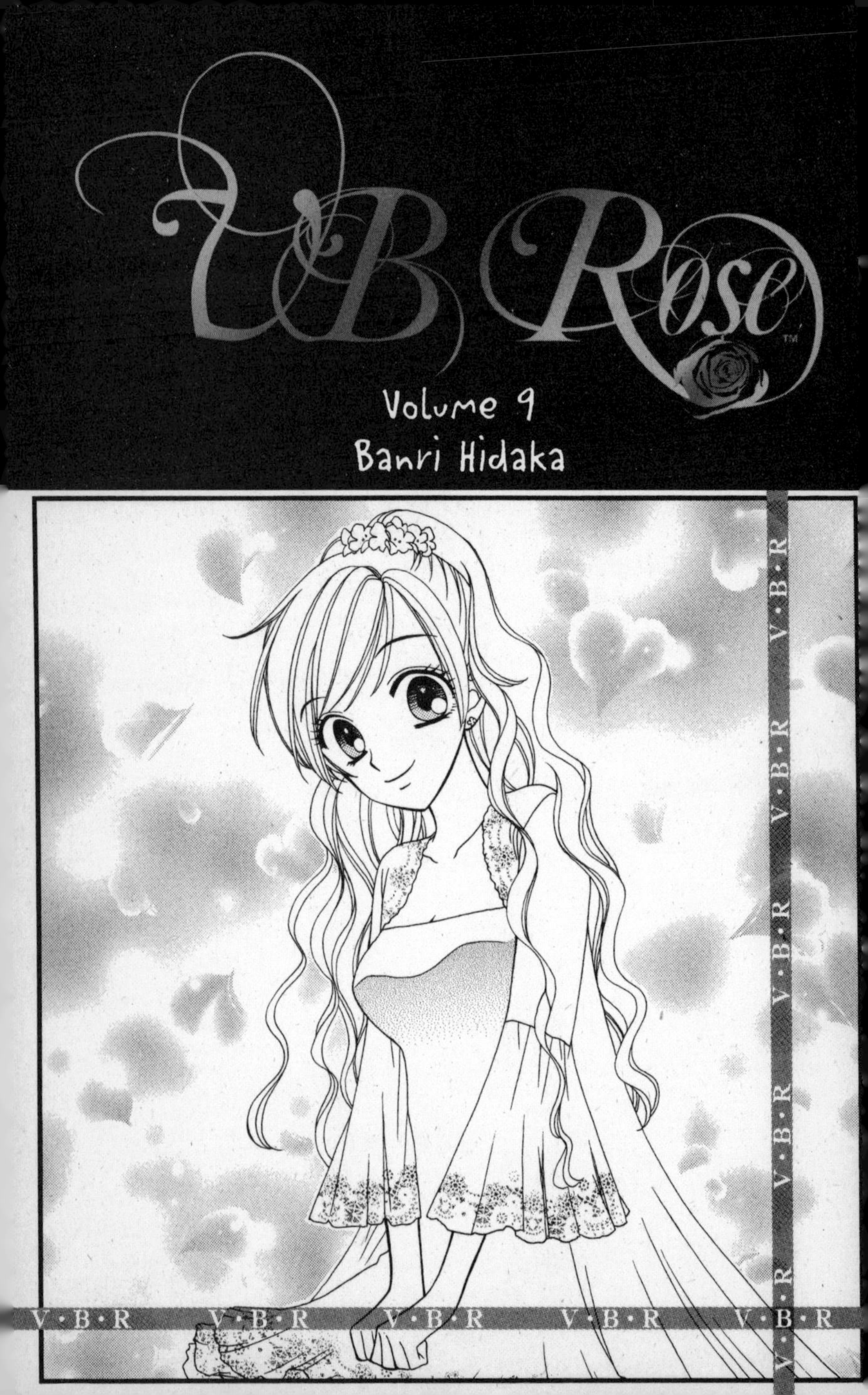
V·B·R V·B·R V·B·R V·B·R V·B·R
V·B·R V·B·R V·B·R V·B·R V·B·R

V.B. Rose Volume 9
Created by Banri Hidaka

Translation - Lori Riser
English Adaptation - Barb Lien-Cooper
Copy Editor - Noora Kamel
Retouch and Lettering - Star Print Brokers
Production Artist - Michael Paolilli
Graphic Designer - Chelsea Windlinger

Editor - Lillian Diaz-Przybyl
Print Production Manager - Lucas Rivera
Managing Editor - Vy Nguyen
Senior Designer - Louis Csontos
Art Director - Al-Insan Lashley
Director of Sales and Manufacturing - Allyson De Simone
Associate Publisher - Marco F. Pavia
President and C.O.O. - John Parker
C.E.O. and Chief Creative Officer - Stu Levy

A **TOKYOPOP** Manga

TOKYOPOP Inc.
5900 Wilshire Blvd. Suite 2000
Los Angeles, CA 90036

E-mail: info@TOKYOPOP.com
Come visit us online at www.TOKYOPOP.com

ISBN: 978-1-4278-0927-8

First TOKYOPOP printing: August 2010
10 9 8 7 6 5 4 3 2 1
Printed in the USA

VB Rose ™

Volume 9
By Banri Hidaka

HAMBURG // LONDON // LOS ANGELES // TOKYO

Contents

V.B. Rose

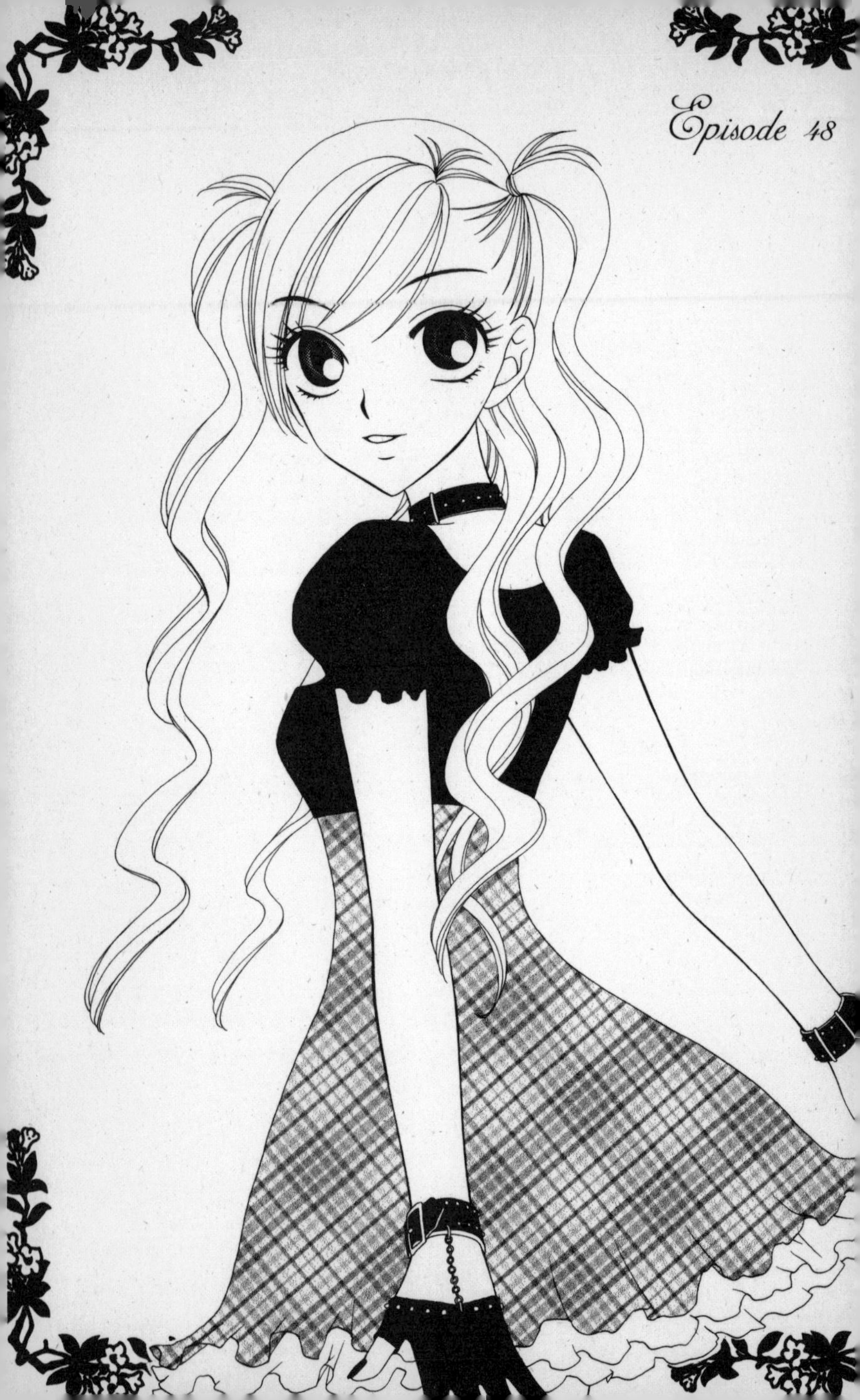
Episode 48

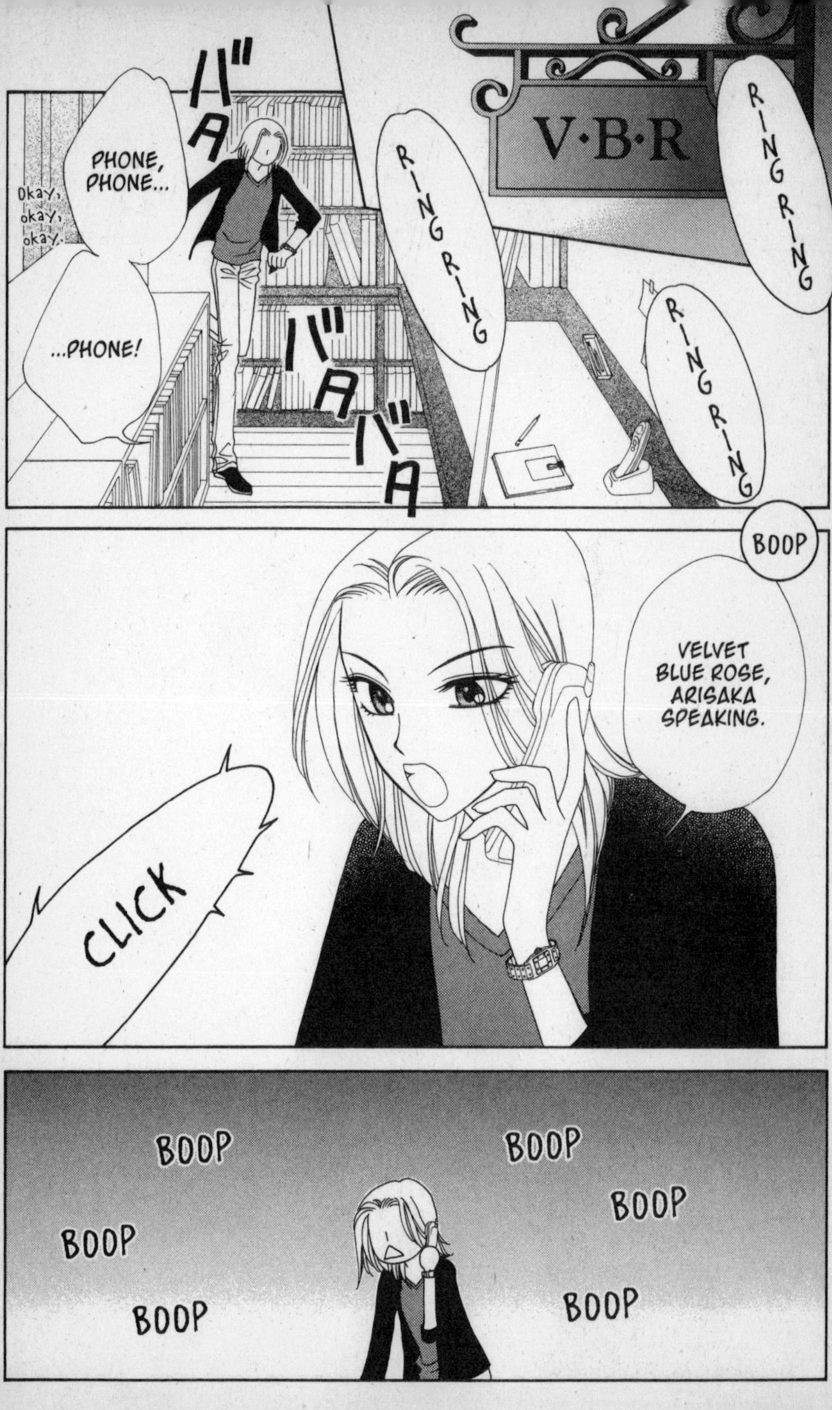
V·B·R
RING RING
RING RING
RING RING
バタバタ
バタ
PHONE, PHONE...
Okay, okay, okay.
...PHONE!
BOOP
VELVET BLUE ROSE, ARISAKA SPEAKING.
CLICK
BOOP
BOOP
BOOP
BOOP
BOOP
BOOP

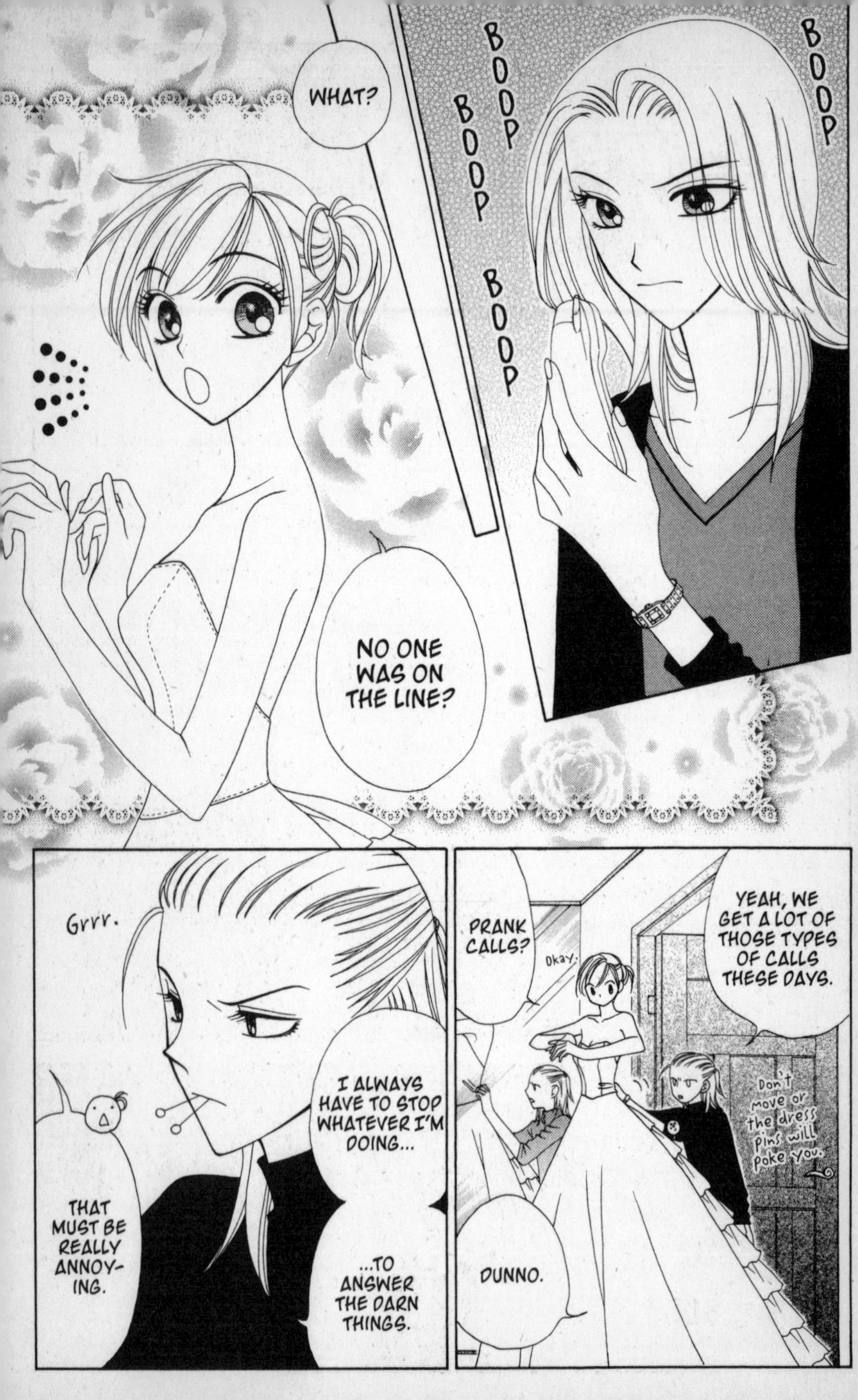
BOOP
BOOP
BOOP
BOOP
WHAT?
NO ONE WAS ON THE LINE?
YEAH, WE GET A LOT OF THOSE TYPES OF CALLS THESE DAYS.
PRANK CALLS?
Okay.
Don't move or the dress pins will poke you.
DUNNO.
I ALWAYS HAVE TO STOP WHATEVER I'M DOING...
Grrr.
...TO ANSWER THE DARN THINGS.
THAT MUST BE REALLY ANNOY-ING.

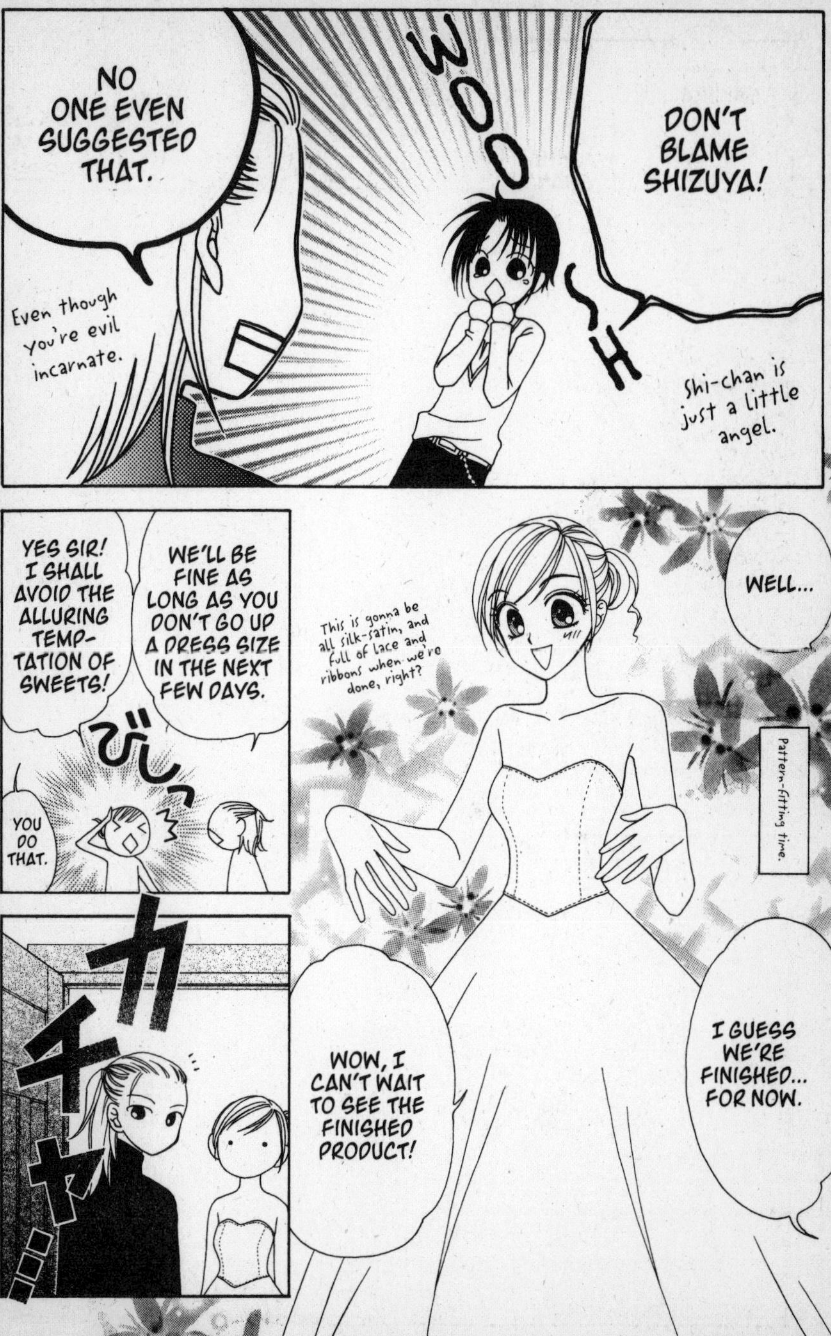
DON'T BLAME SHIZUYA!
WOOSH
Shi-chan is just a little angel.
NO ONE EVEN SUGGESTED THAT.
Even though you're evil incarnate.
WELL...
Pattern-fitting time.
This is gonna be all silk-satin, and full of lace and ribbons when we're done, right?
I GUESS WE'RE FINISHED... FOR NOW.
WOW, I CAN'T WAIT TO SEE THE FINISHED PRODUCT!
WE'LL BE FINE AS LONG AS YOU DON'T GO UP A DRESS SIZE IN THE NEXT FEW DAYS.
YES SIR! I SHALL AVOID THE ALLURING TEMPTATION OF SWEETS!
びしっ
YOU DO THAT.
カチャ…

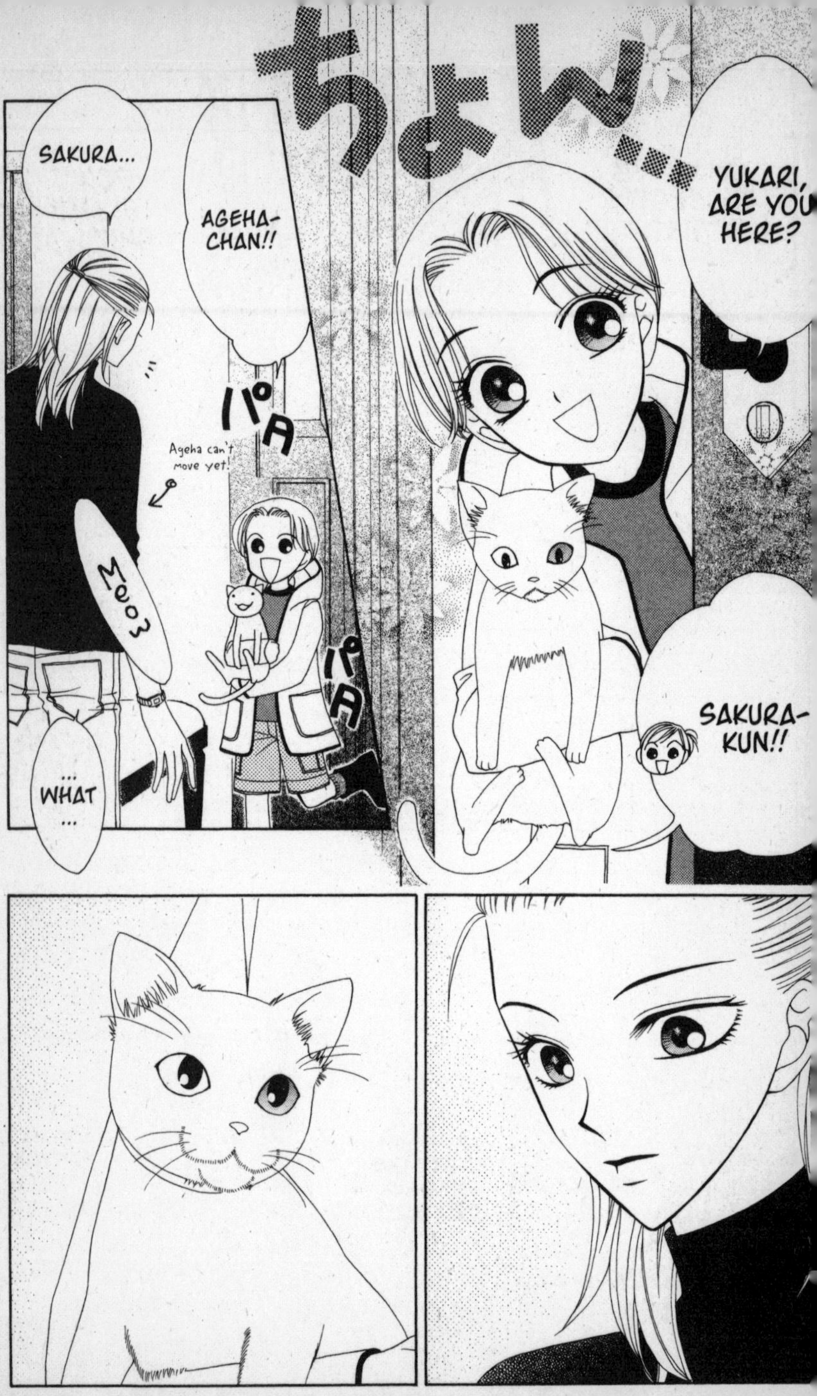
ちょん...
YUKARI, ARE YOU HERE?
SAKURA-KUN!!
AGEHA-CHAN!!
SAKURA...
パ
Ageha can't move yet!
Meow
パ
... WHAT ...

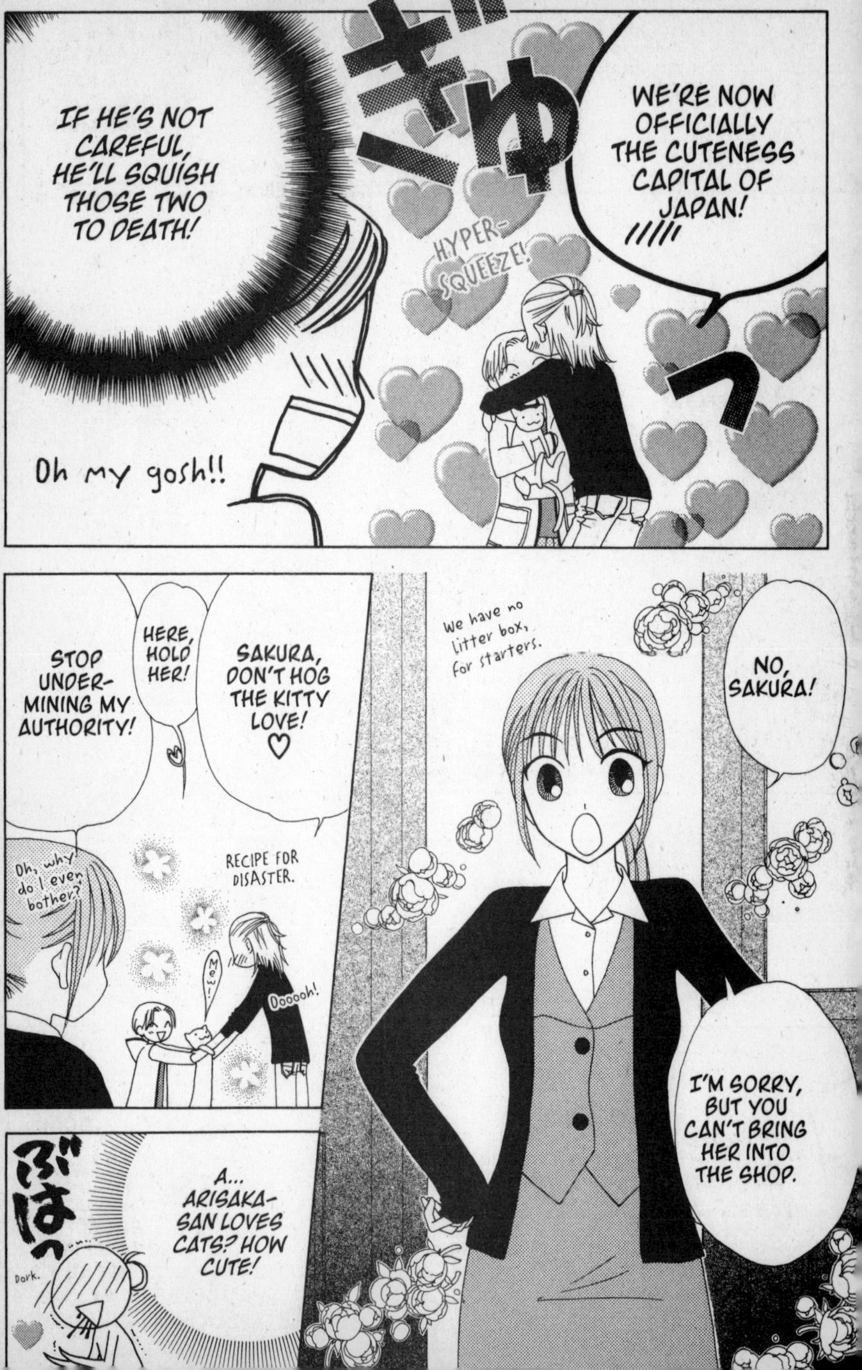
WE'RE NOW OFFICIALLY THE CUTENESS CAPITAL OF JAPAN! ////
ぎゅっ
HYPER-SQUEEZE!
IF HE'S NOT CAREFUL, HE'LL SQUISH THOSE TWO TO DEATH!
Oh my gosh!!
NO, SAKURA!
We have no litter box, for starters.
I'M SORRY, BUT YOU CAN'T BRING HER INTO THE SHOP.
SAKURA, DON'T HOG THE KITTY LOVE! ♡
HERE, HOLD HER!
STOP UNDER-MINING MY AUTHORITY!
RECIPE FOR DISASTER.
Mew-!
Ooooh!
Oh, why do I even bother?
A... ARISAKA-SAN LOVES CATS? HOW CUTE!
ぶはっ
Dork.

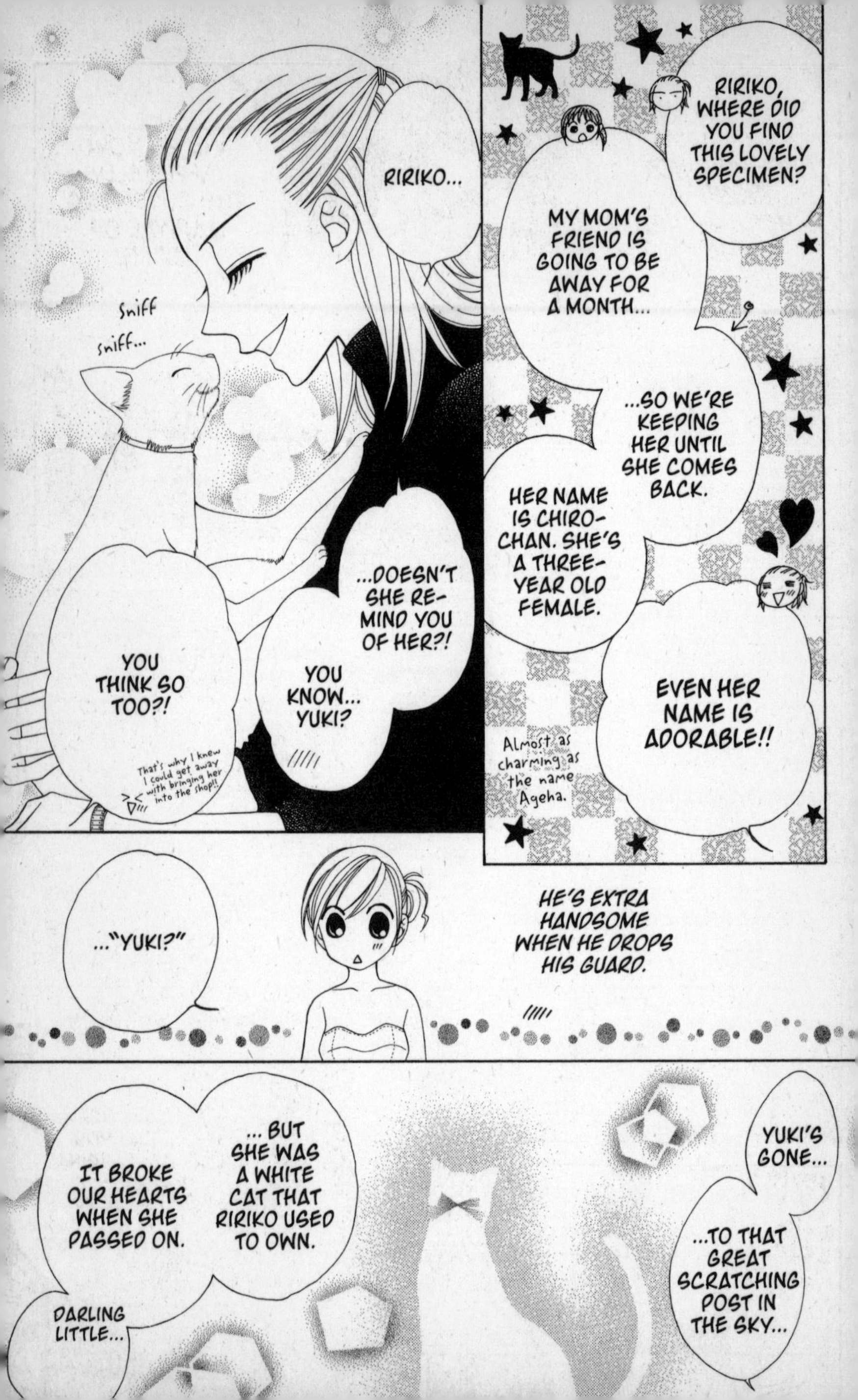
RIRIKO, WHERE DID YOU FIND THIS LOVELY SPECIMEN?
MY MOM'S FRIEND IS GOING TO BE AWAY FOR A MONTH...
...SO WE'RE KEEPING HER UNTIL SHE COMES BACK.
HER NAME IS CHIRO-CHAN. SHE'S A THREE-YEAR OLD FEMALE.
EVEN HER NAME IS ADORABLE!!
Almost as charming as the name Ageha.
RIRIKO...
...DOESN'T SHE RE-MIND YOU OF HER?!
YOU KNOW... YUKI?
YOU THINK SO TOO?!
That's why I knew I could get away with bringing her into the shop!!
Sniff sniff...
HE'S EXTRA HANDSOME WHEN HE DROPS HIS GUARD.
..."YUKI?"
YUKI'S GONE...
...TO THAT GREAT SCRATCHING POST IN THE SKY...
... BUT SHE WAS A WHITE CAT THAT RIRIKO USED TO OWN.
IT BROKE OUR HEARTS WHEN SHE PASSED ON.
DARLING LITTLE...

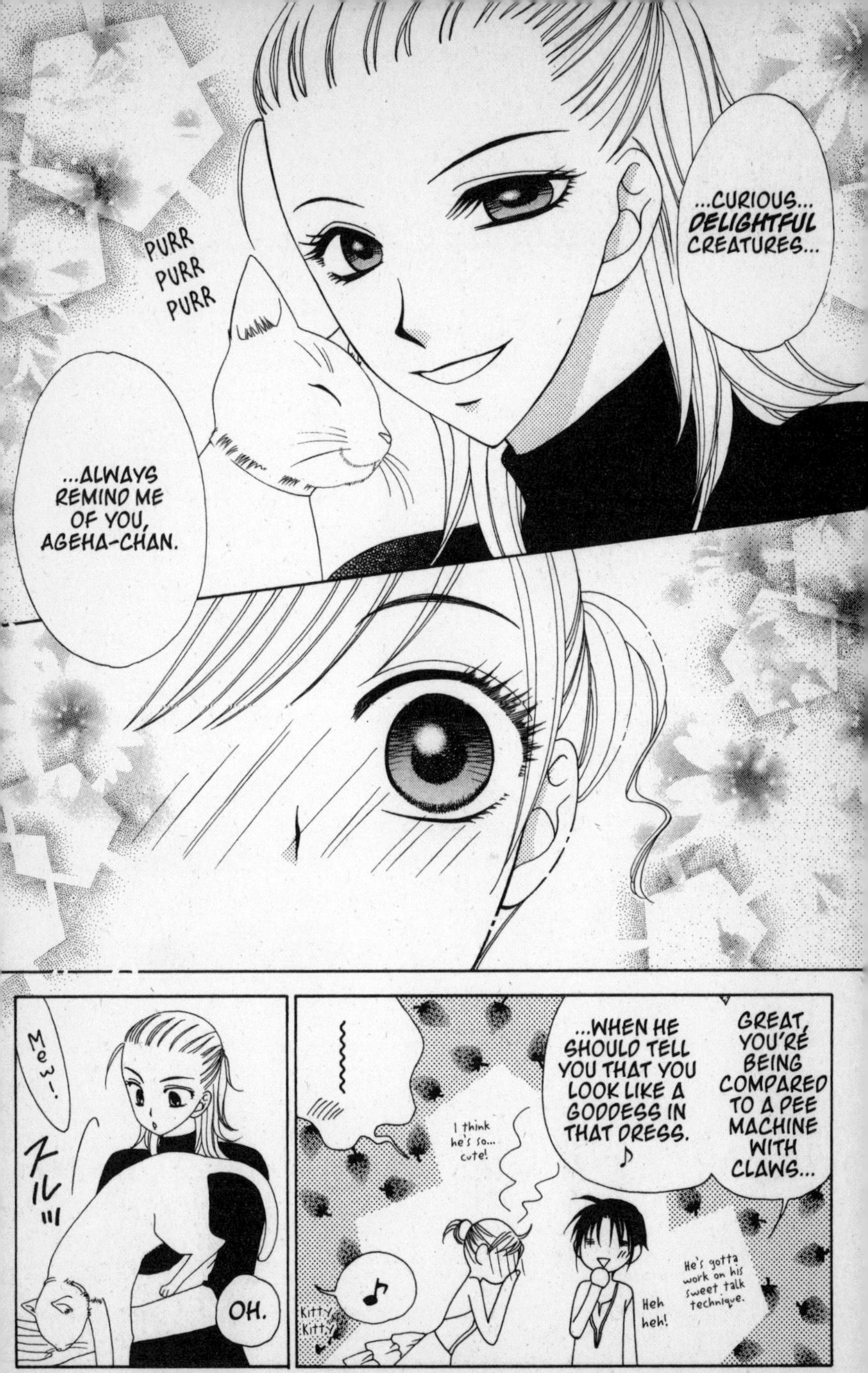
...CURIOUS... **DELIGHTFUL** CREATURES...
PURR PURR PURR
...ALWAYS REMIND ME OF YOU, AGEHA-CHAN.
GREAT, YOU'RE BEING COMPARED TO A PEE MACHINE WITH CLAWS...
...WHEN HE SHOULD TELL YOU THAT YOU LOOK LIKE A GODDESS IN THAT DRESS. ♪
I think he's so... cute!
He's gotta work on his sweet talk technique.
Heh heh!
♪
Kitty Kitty
Mew!
ズル
OH.

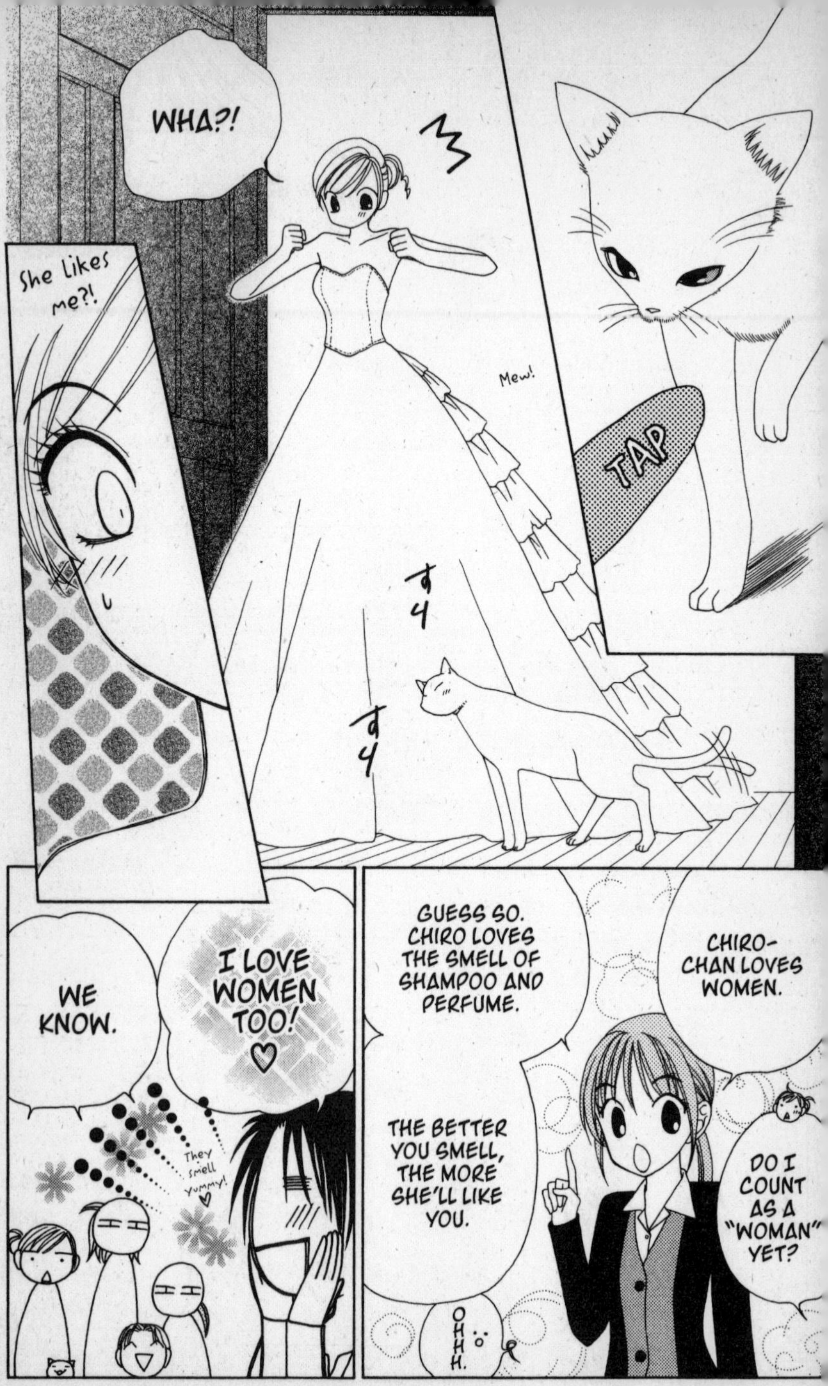
TAP
Mew!
すり
すり
WHA?!
She likes me?!
CHIRO-CHAN LOVES WOMEN.
GUESS SO. CHIRO LOVES THE SMELL OF SHAMPOO AND PERFUME.
DO I COUNT AS A "WOMAN" YET?
THE BETTER YOU SMELL, THE MORE SHE'LL LIKE YOU.
OHHH.
I LOVE WOMEN TOO! ♥
WE KNOW.
They smell yummy! ♥

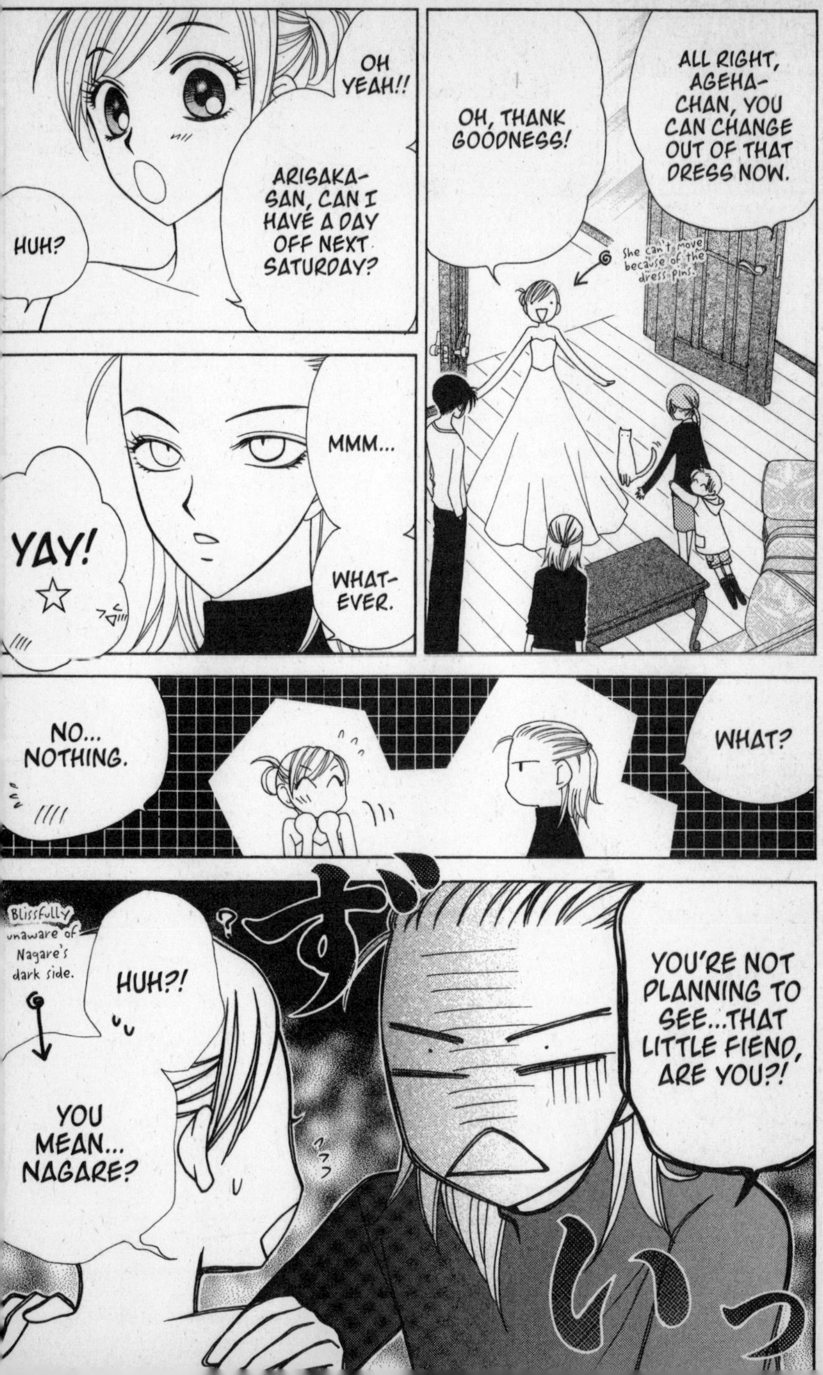
ALL RIGHT, AGEHA-CHAN, YOU CAN CHANGE OUT OF THAT DRESS NOW.
OH, THANK GOODNESS!
She can't move because of the dress pins.
OH YEAH!!
ARISAKA-SAN, CAN I HAVE A DAY OFF NEXT SATURDAY?
HUH?
MMM...
WHAT-EVER.
YAY! ☆
WHAT?
NO... NOTHING.
YOU'RE NOT PLANNING TO SEE...THAT LITTLE FIEND, ARE YOU?!
HUH?!
YOU MEAN... NAGARE?
Blissfully unaware of Nagare's dark side.

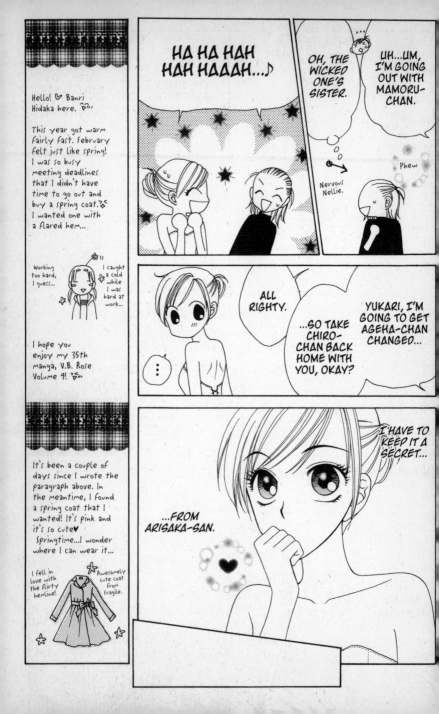

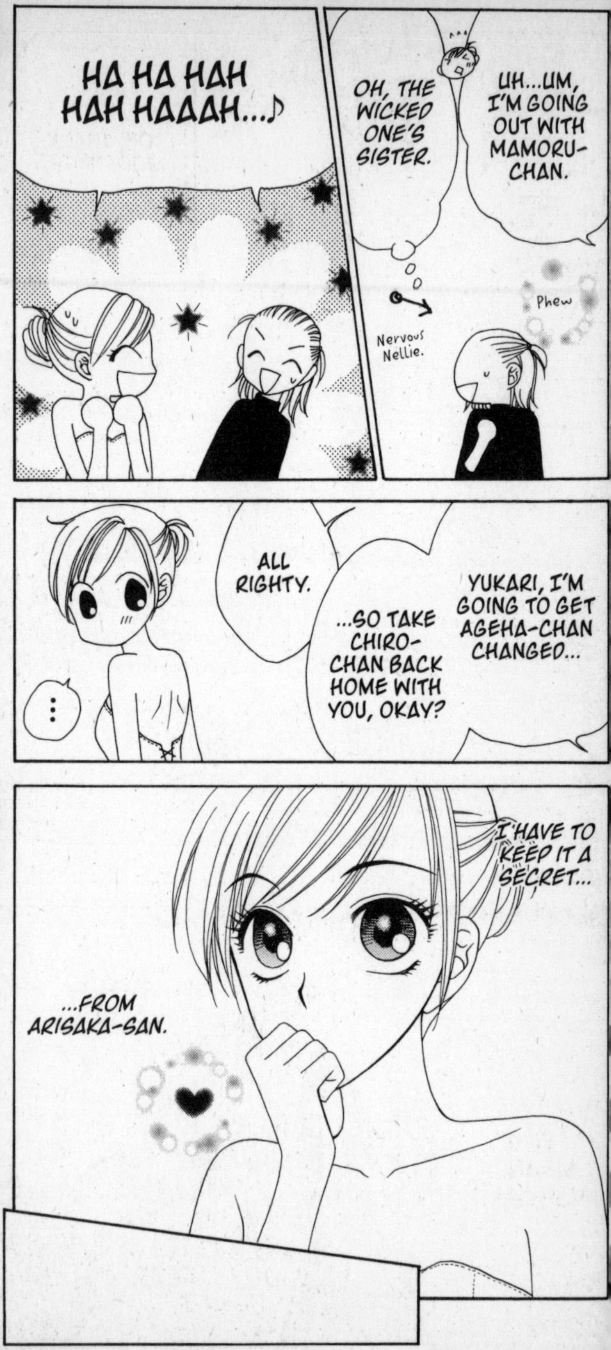
UH...UM, I'M GOING OUT WITH MAMORU-CHAN.
OH, THE WICKED ONE'S SISTER.
Phew
Nervous Nellie.
HA HA HAH HAH HAAAH...♪
YUKARI, I'M GOING TO GET AGEHA-CHAN CHANGED...
...SO TAKE CHIRO-CHAN BACK HOME WITH YOU, OKAY?
ALL RIGHTY.
...
I HAVE TO KEEP IT A SECRET...
...FROM ARISAKA-SAN.

Hello! ♡ Banri Hidaka here.

This year got warm fairly fast. February felt just like spring! I was so busy meeting deadlines that I didn't have time to go out and buy a spring coat. I wanted one with a flared hem...

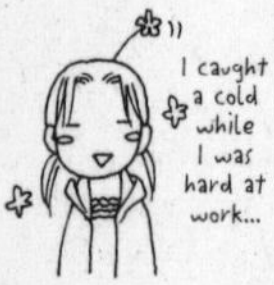
Working too hard, I guess...
I caught a cold while I was hard at work...

I hope you enjoy my 35th manga, V.B. Rose Volume 9!

It's been a couple of days since I wrote the paragraph above. In the meantime, I found a spring coat that I wanted! It's pink and it's so cute♥ Springtime...I wonder where I can wear it...

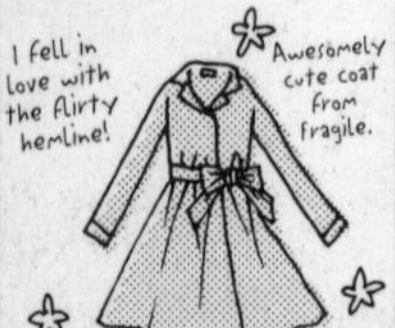
I fell in love with the flirty hemline!
Awesomely cute coat from Fragile.

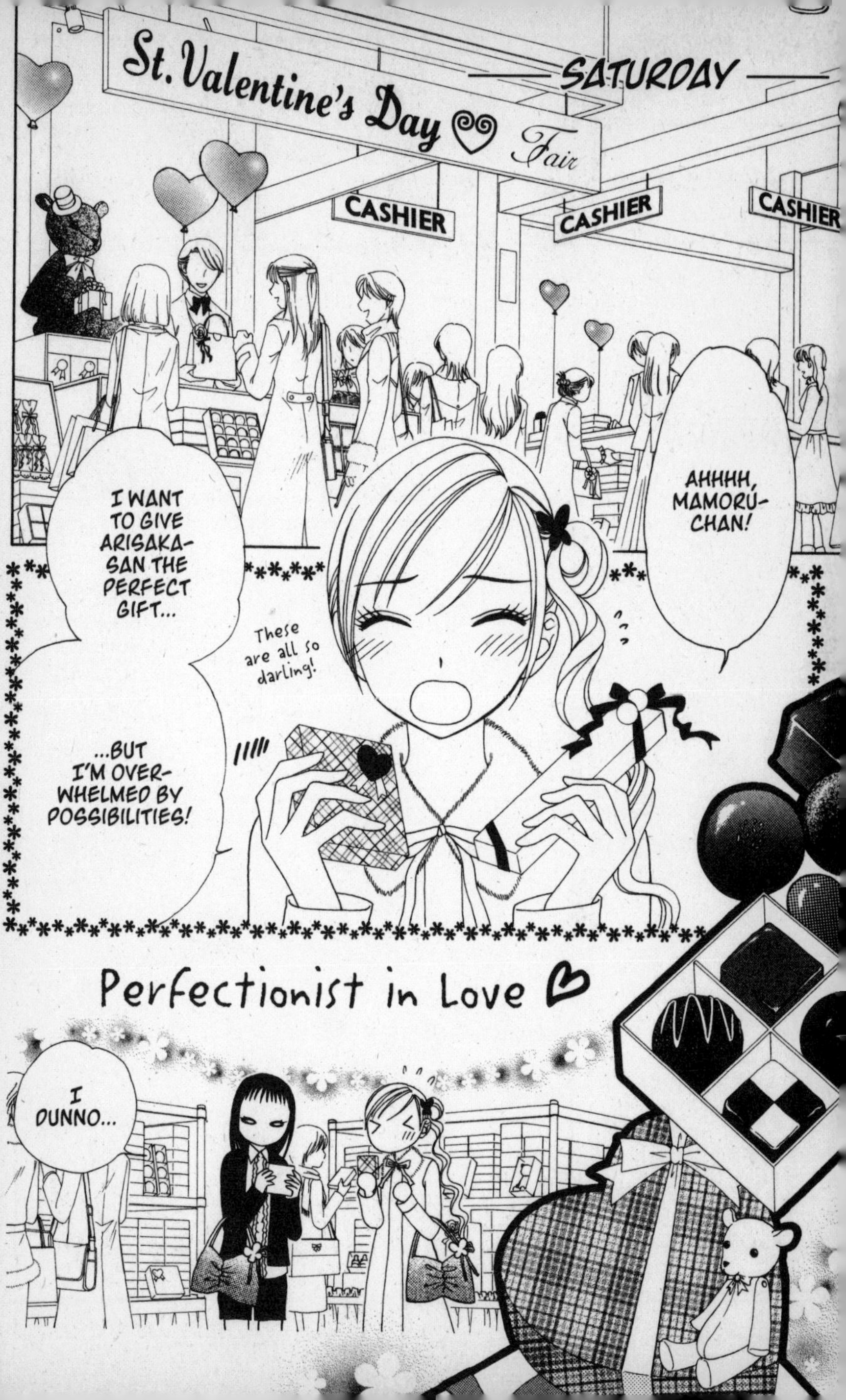
SATURDAY
St. Valentine's Day Fair
CASHIER
CASHIER
CASHIER
AHHHH, MAMORU-CHAN!
These are all so darling!
I WANT TO GIVE ARISAKA-SAN THE PERFECT GIFT...
...BUT I'M OVER-WHELMED BY POSSIBILITIES!
Perfectionist in Love
I DUNNO...

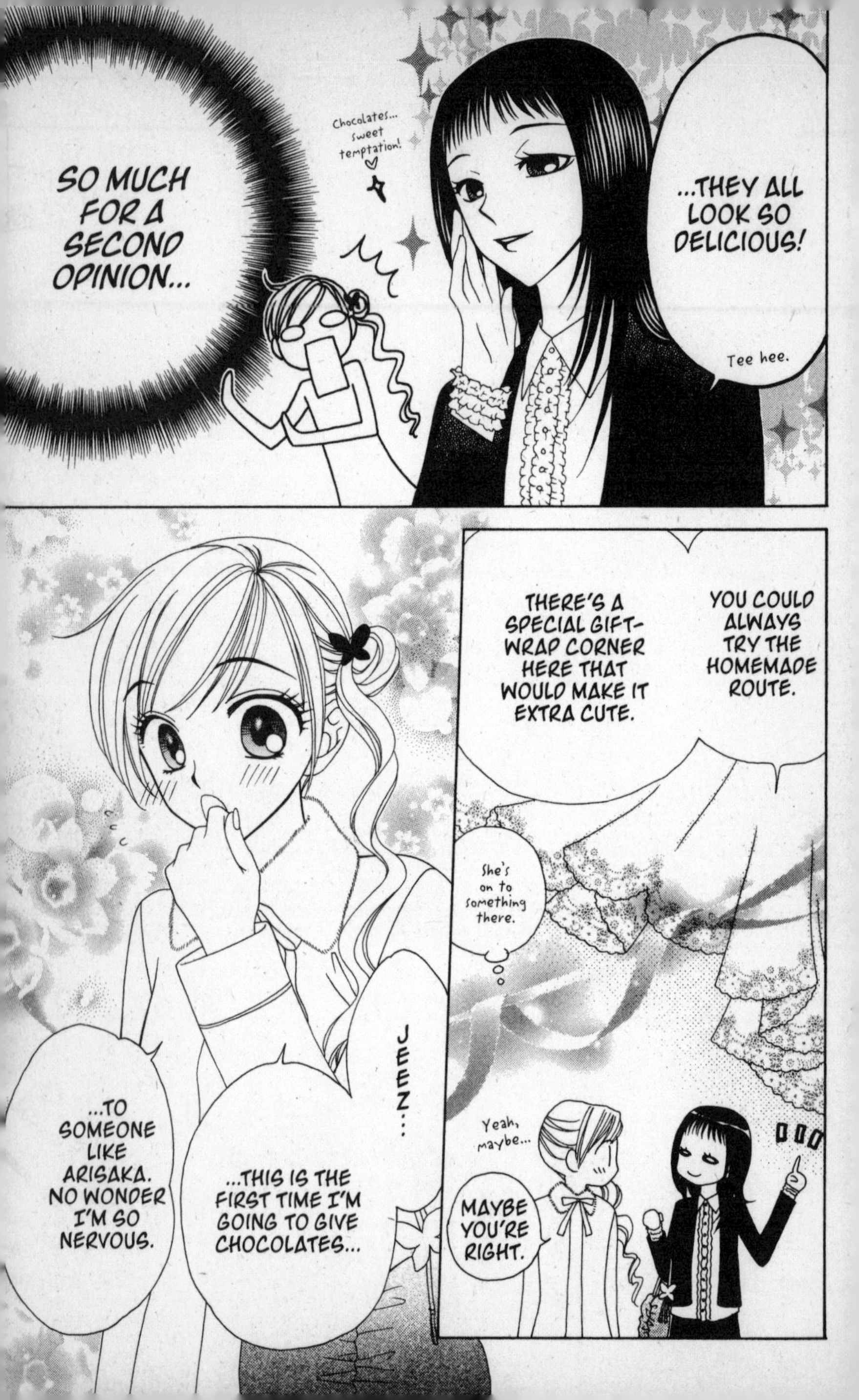
...THEY ALL LOOK SO DELICIOUS!
Tee hee.
Chocolates... sweet temptation!
SO MUCH FOR A SECOND OPINION...
YOU COULD ALWAYS TRY THE HOMEMADE ROUTE.
THERE'S A SPECIAL GIFT-WRAP CORNER HERE THAT WOULD MAKE IT EXTRA CUTE.
She's on to something there.
Yeah, maybe...
MAYBE YOU'RE RIGHT.
JEEZ...
...THIS IS THE FIRST TIME I'M GOING TO GIVE CHOCOLATES...
...TO SOMEONE LIKE ARISAKA. NO WONDER I'M SO NERVOUS.

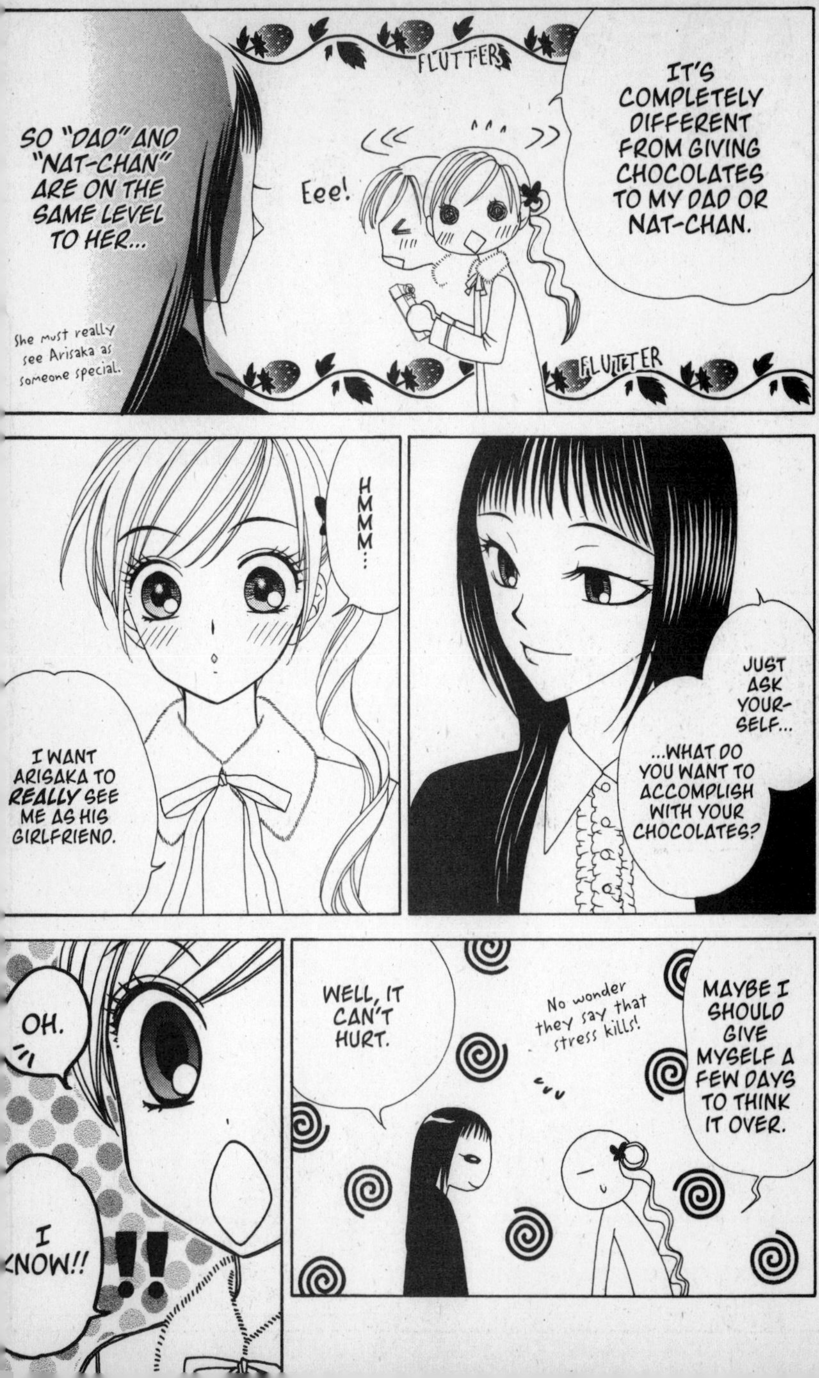
IT'S COMPLETELY DIFFERENT FROM GIVING CHOCOLATES TO MY DAD OR NAT-CHAN.
FLUTTER
SO "DAD" AND "NAT-CHAN" ARE ON THE SAME LEVEL TO HER...
Eee!
She must really see Arisaka as someone special.
FLUTTER
JUST ASK YOURSELF...
...WHAT DO YOU WANT TO ACCOMPLISH WITH YOUR CHOCOLATES?
HMMM...
I WANT ARISAKA TO REALLY SEE ME AS HIS GIRLFRIEND.
MAYBE I SHOULD GIVE MYSELF A FEW DAYS TO THINK IT OVER.
No wonder they say that stress kills!
WELL, IT CAN'T HURT.
OH.
I KNOW!!

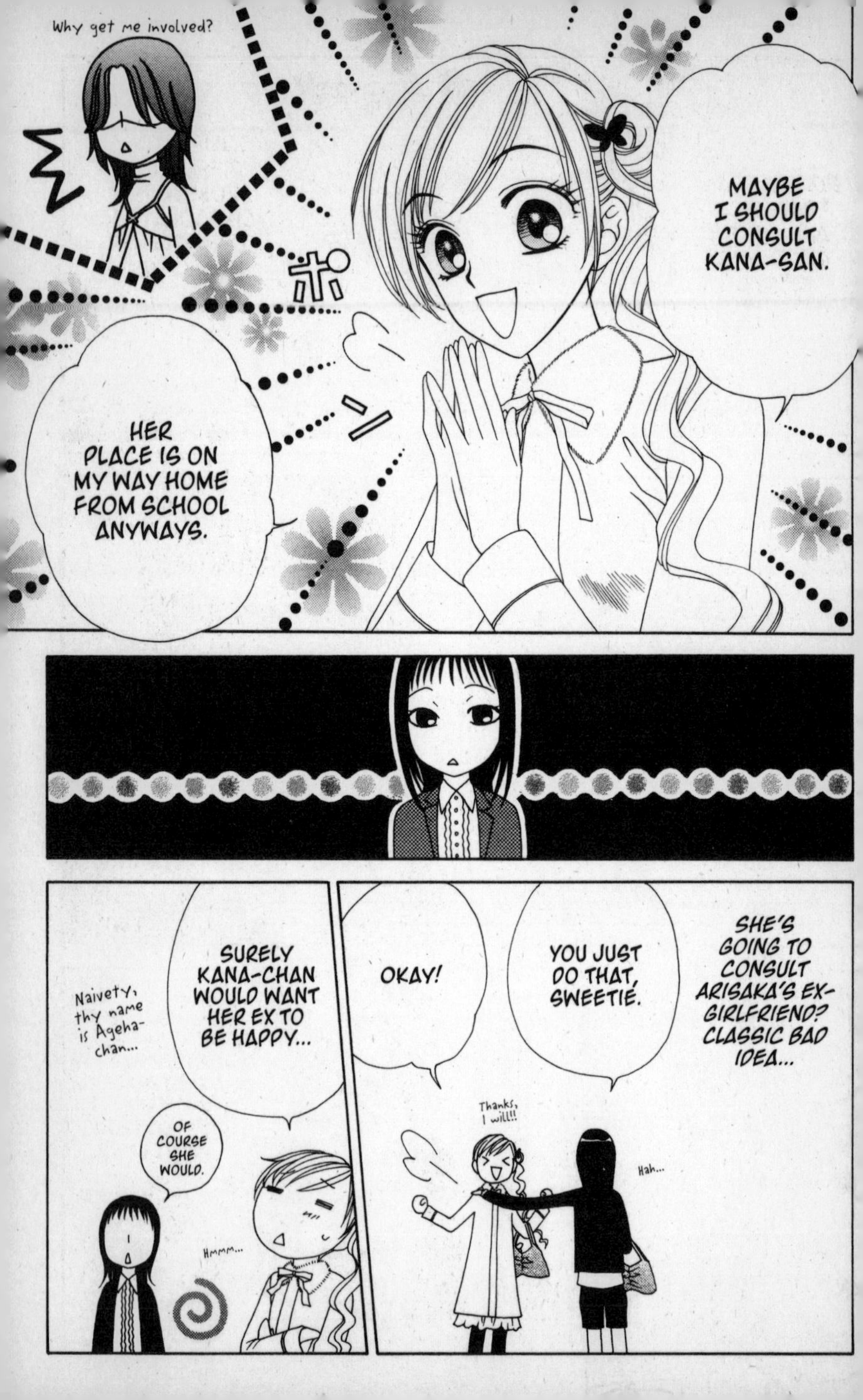
MAYBE I SHOULD CONSULT KANA-SAN.
ポ
ン
HER PLACE IS ON MY WAY HOME FROM SCHOOL ANYWAYS.
Why get me involved?
SHE'S GOING TO CONSULT ARISAKA'S EX-GIRLFRIEND? CLASSIC BAD IDEA...
YOU JUST DO THAT, SWEETIE.
OKAY!
Thanks, I will!!
Hah...
SURELY KANA-CHAN WOULD WANT HER EX TO BE HAPPY...
Naivety, thy name is Ageha-chan...
OF COURSE SHE WOULD.
Hmmm...

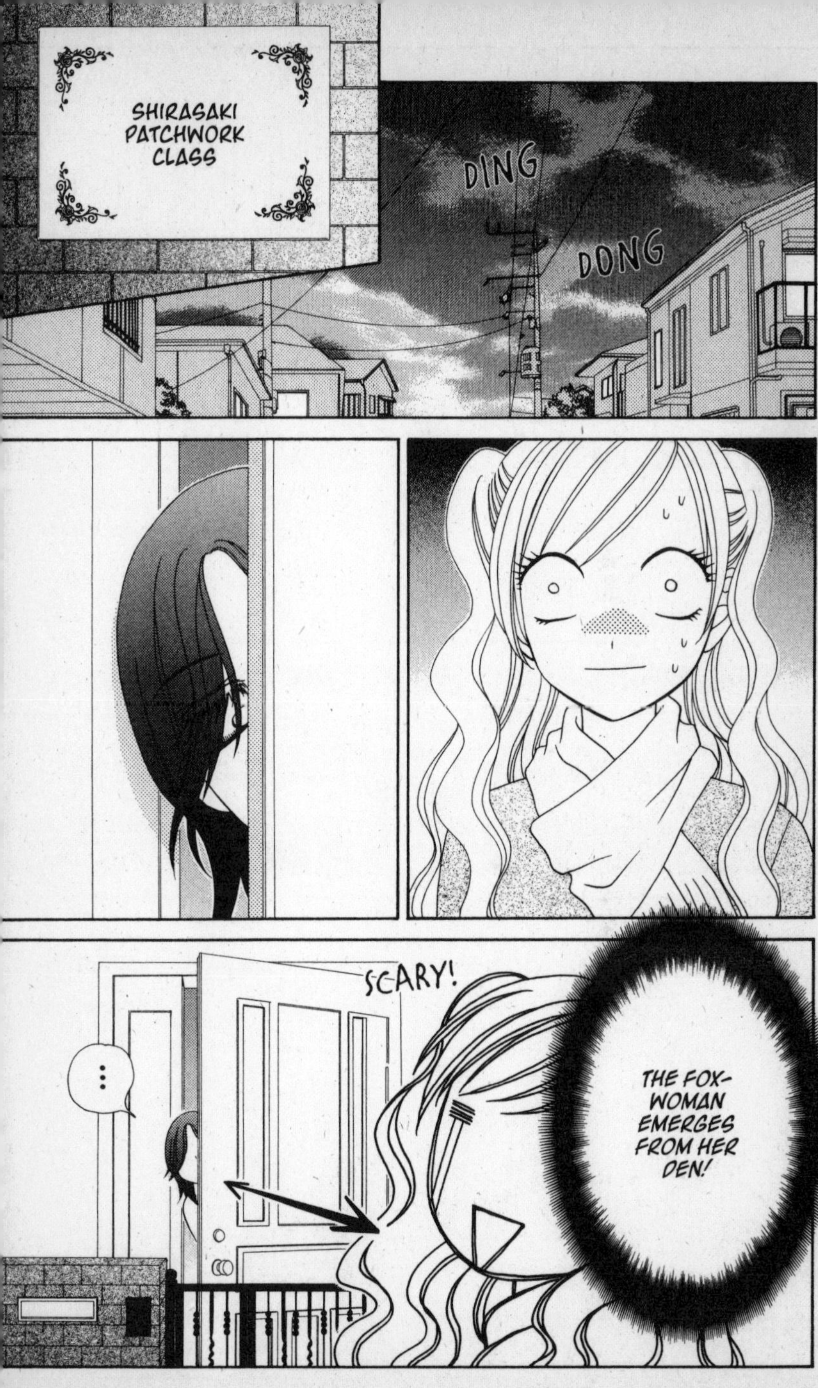
SHIRASAKI PATCHWORK CLASS
DING
DONG
SCARY!
THE FOX-WOMAN EMERGES FROM HER DEN!
...

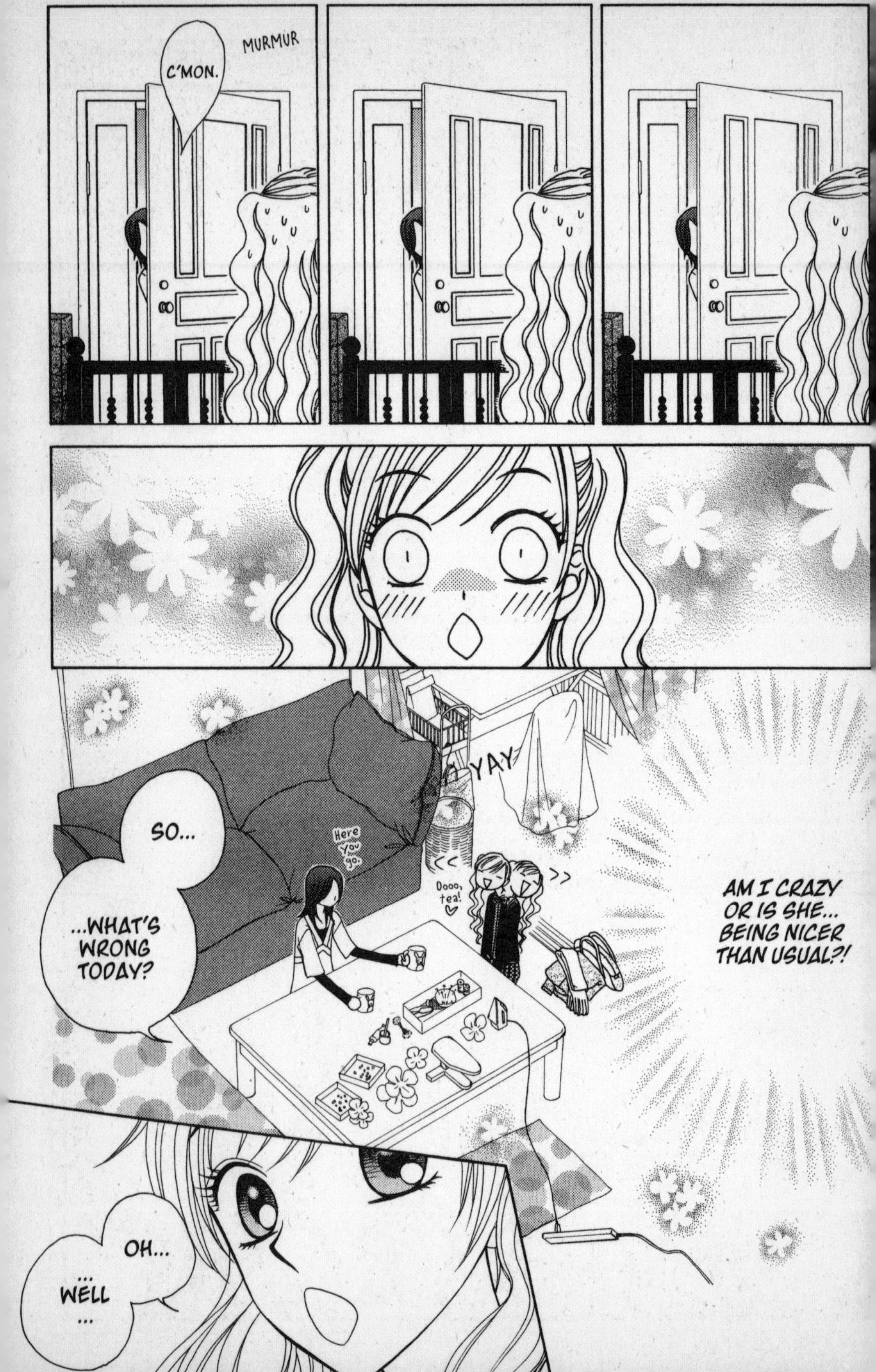

C'MON.
MURMUR
SO...
...WHAT'S WRONG TODAY?
Here you go.
YAY
Oooo, tea! ♥
AM I CRAZY OR IS SHE... BEING NICER THAN USUAL?!
OH...
... WELL ...

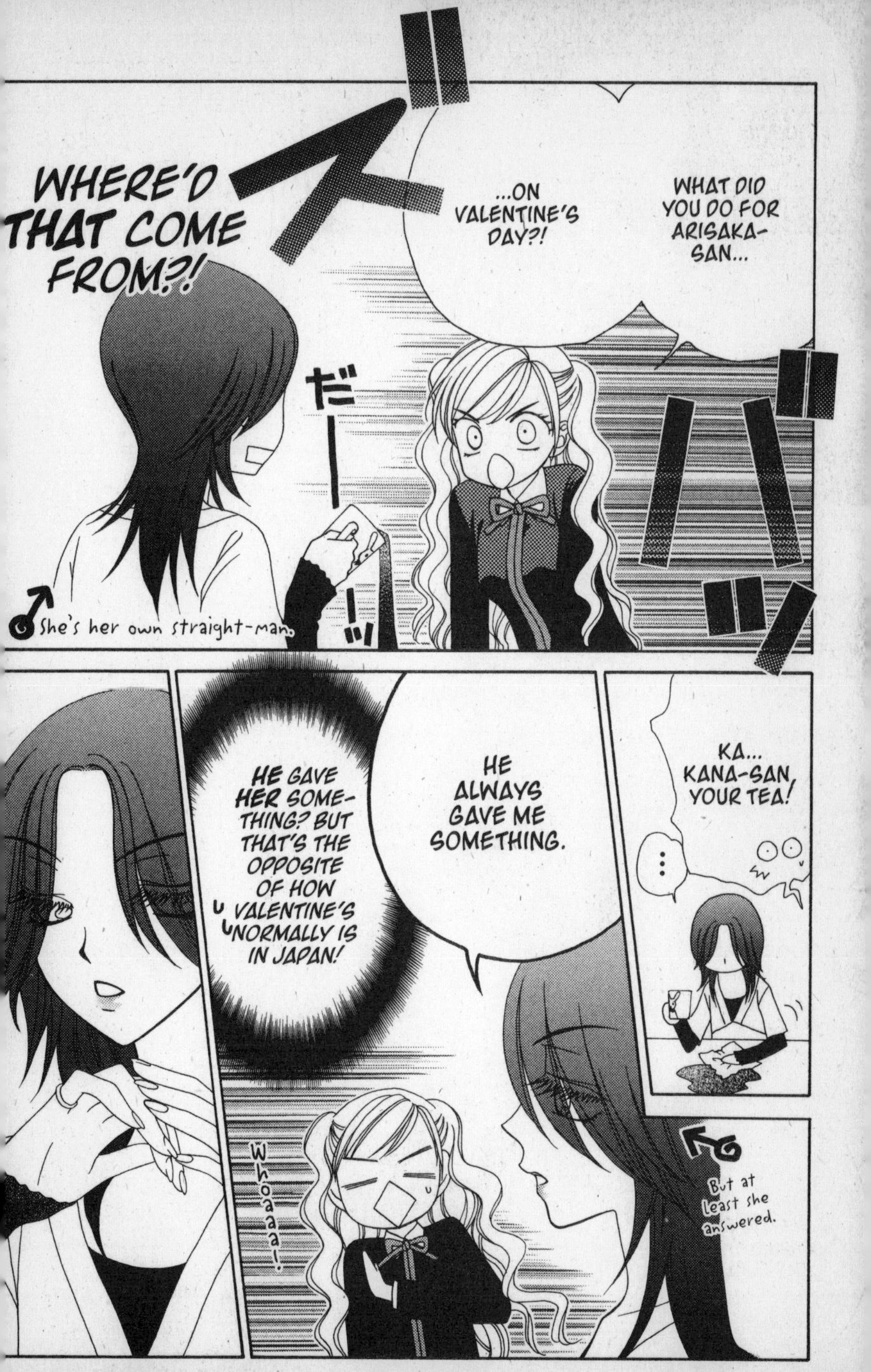
WHAT DID YOU DO FOR ARISAKA-SAN...
...ON VALENTINE'S DAY?!
WHERE'D THAT COME FROM?!
She's her own straight-man.
KA... KANA-SAN, YOUR TEA!
...
But at least she answered.
HE ALWAYS GAVE ME SOMETHING.
HE GAVE HER SOMETHING? BUT THAT'S THE OPPOSITE OF HOW VALENTINE'S NORMALLY IS IN JAPAN!
Whoaaaa!

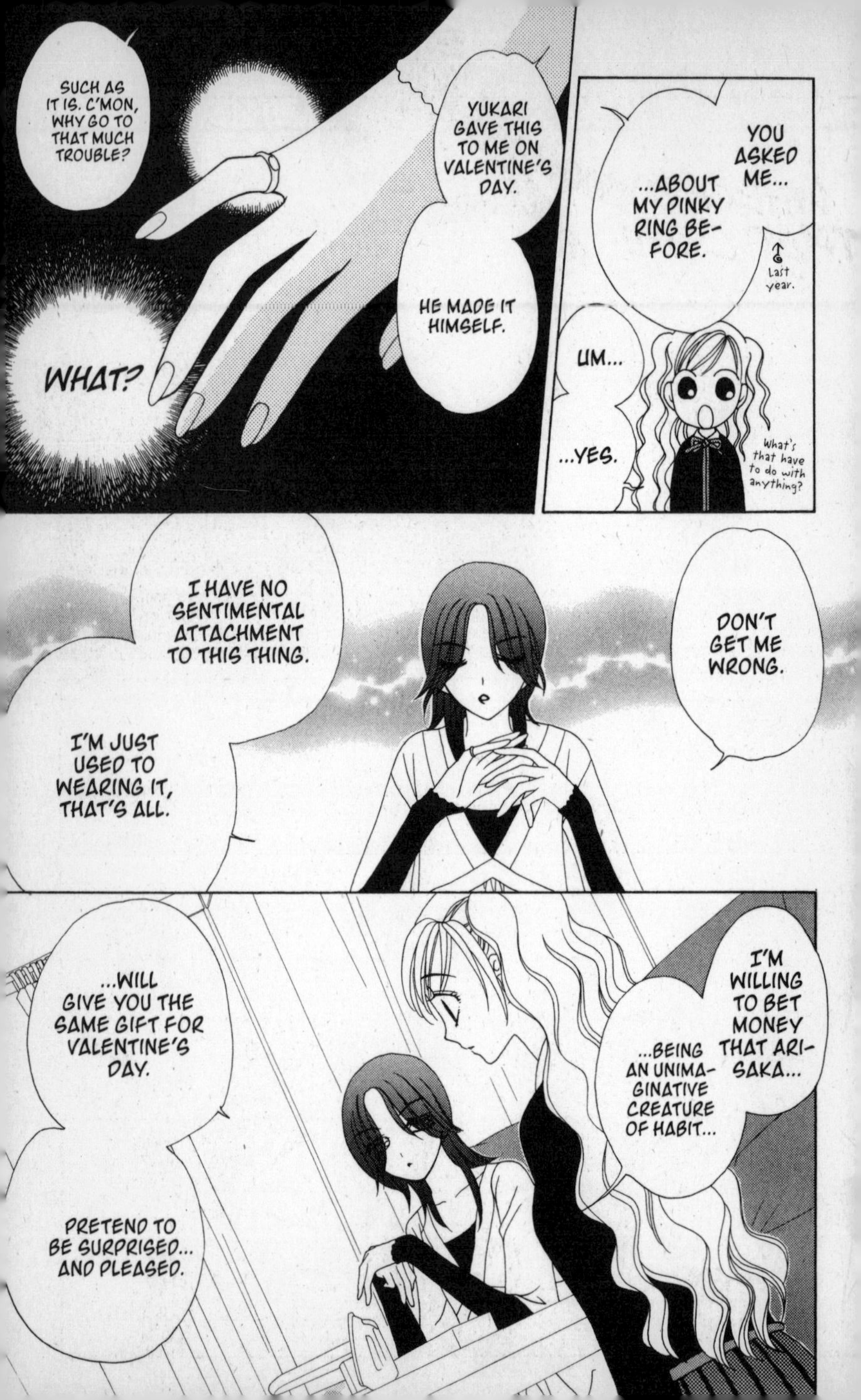
YOU ASKED ME...
...ABOUT MY PINKY RING BE-FORE.
Last year.
UM...
...YES.
What's that have to do with anything?
YUKARI GAVE THIS TO ME ON VALENTINE'S DAY.
HE MADE IT HIMSELF.
WHAT?
SUCH AS IT IS. C'MON, WHY GO TO THAT MUCH TROUBLE?
DON'T GET ME WRONG.
I HAVE NO SENTIMENTAL ATTACHMENT TO THIS THING.
I'M JUST USED TO WEARING IT, THAT'S ALL.
I'M WILLING TO BET MONEY THAT ARI-SAKA...
...BEING AN UNIMA-GINATIVE CREATURE OF HABIT...
...WILL GIVE YOU THE SAME GIFT FOR VALENTINE'S DAY.
PRETEND TO BE SURPRISED... AND PLEASED.

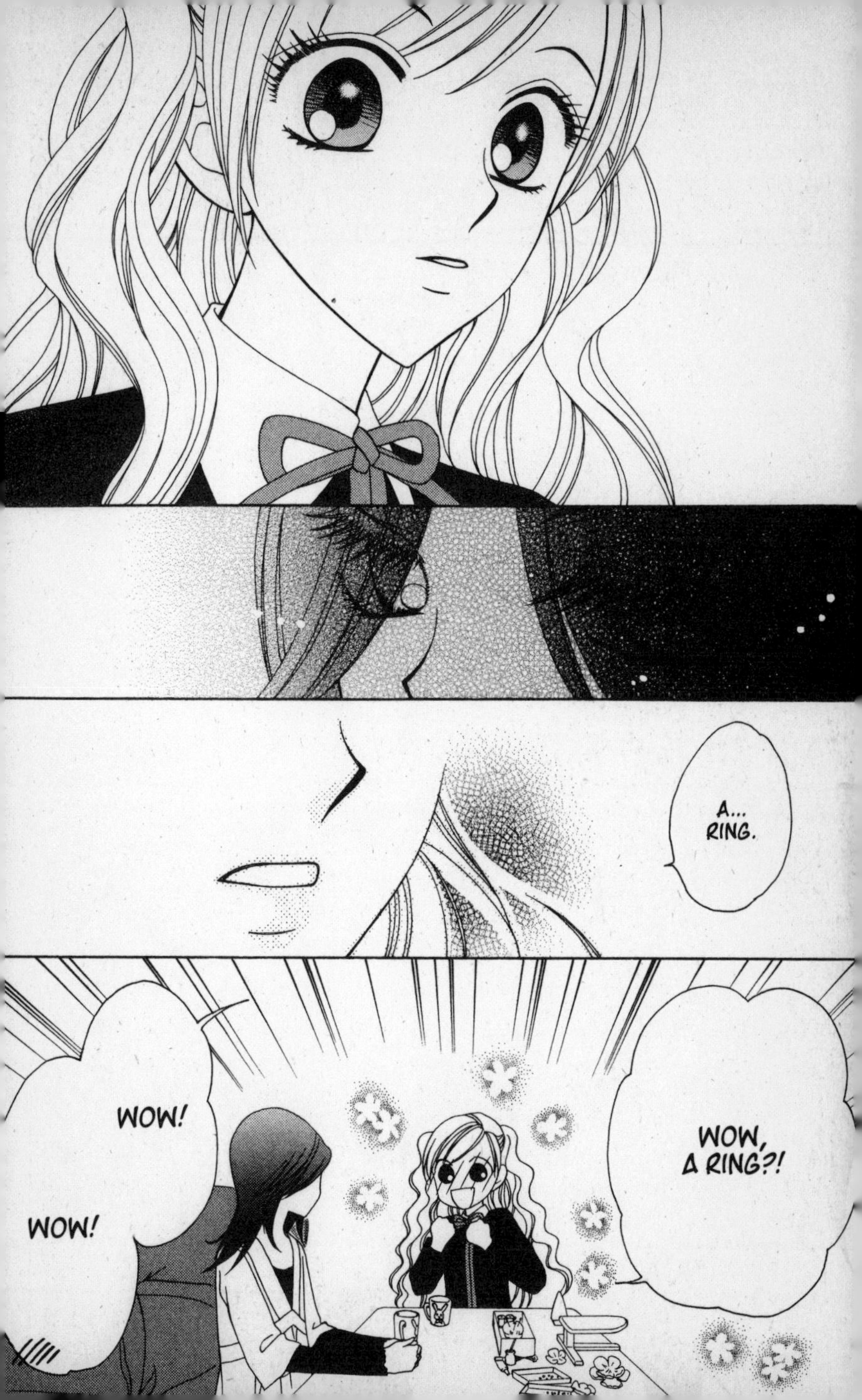
A... RING.
WOW, A RING?!
WOW!
WOW!

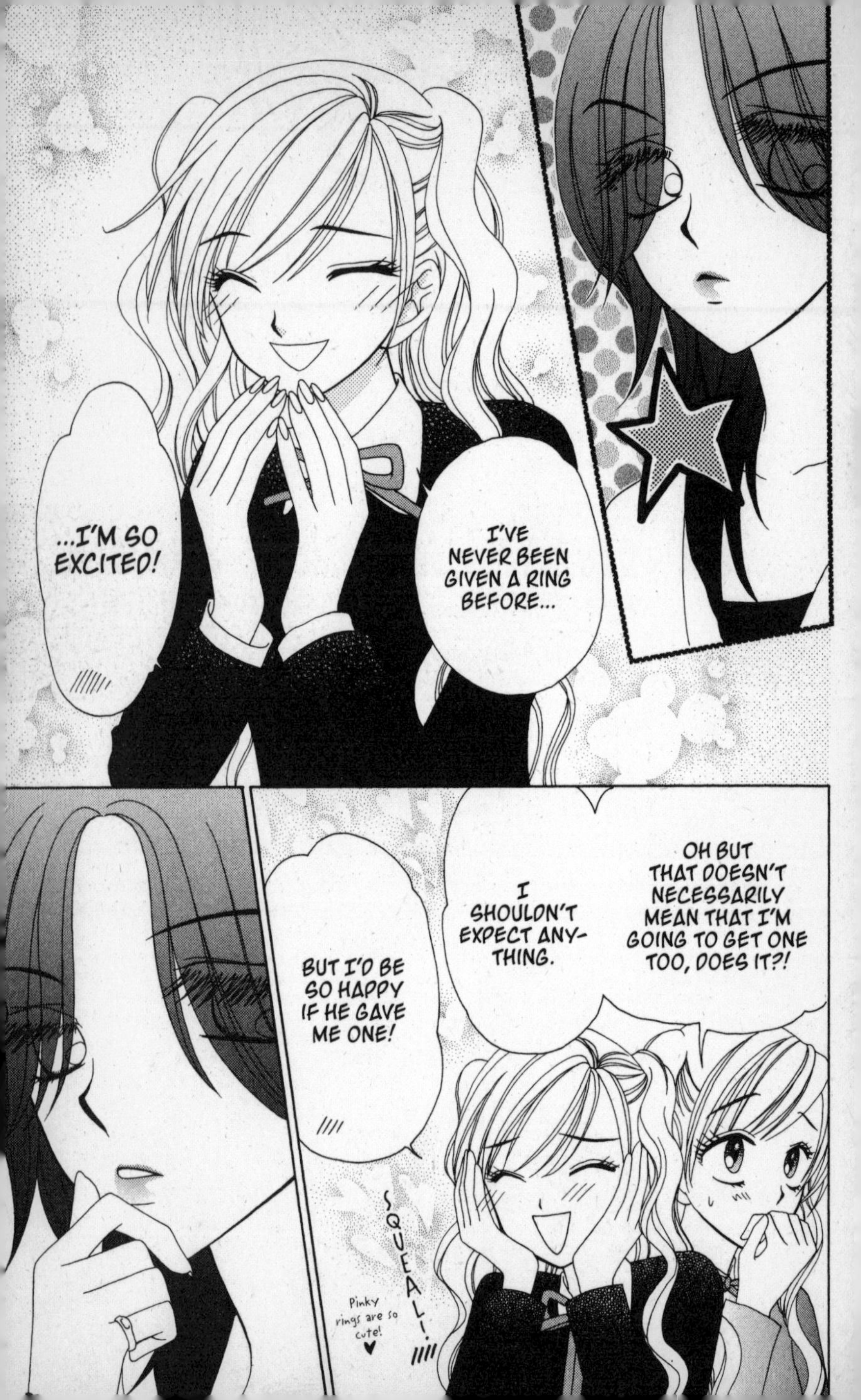
I'VE NEVER BEEN GIVEN A RING BEFORE...
...I'M SO EXCITED!
OH BUT THAT DOESN'T NECESSARILY MEAN THAT I'M GOING TO GET ONE TOO, DOES IT?!
I SHOULDN'T EXPECT ANY-THING.
BUT I'D BE SO HAPPY IF HE GAVE ME ONE!
SQUEAL!
Pinky rings are so cute! ♥

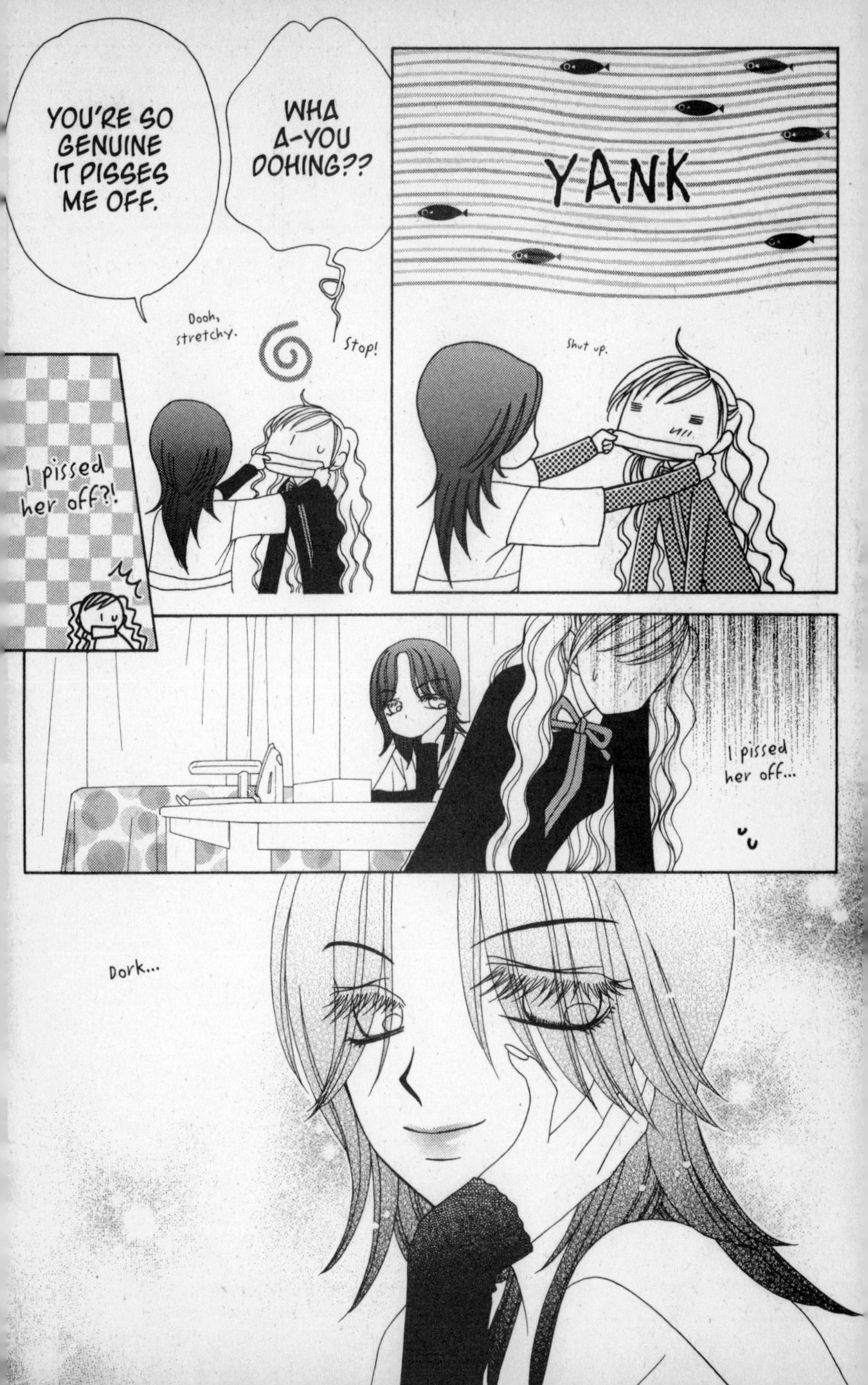
YANK
Shut up.
WHA A-YOU DOHING??
YOU'RE SO GENUINE IT PISSES ME OFF.
Stop!
Oooh, stretchy.
I pissed her off?!
I pissed her off...
Dork...

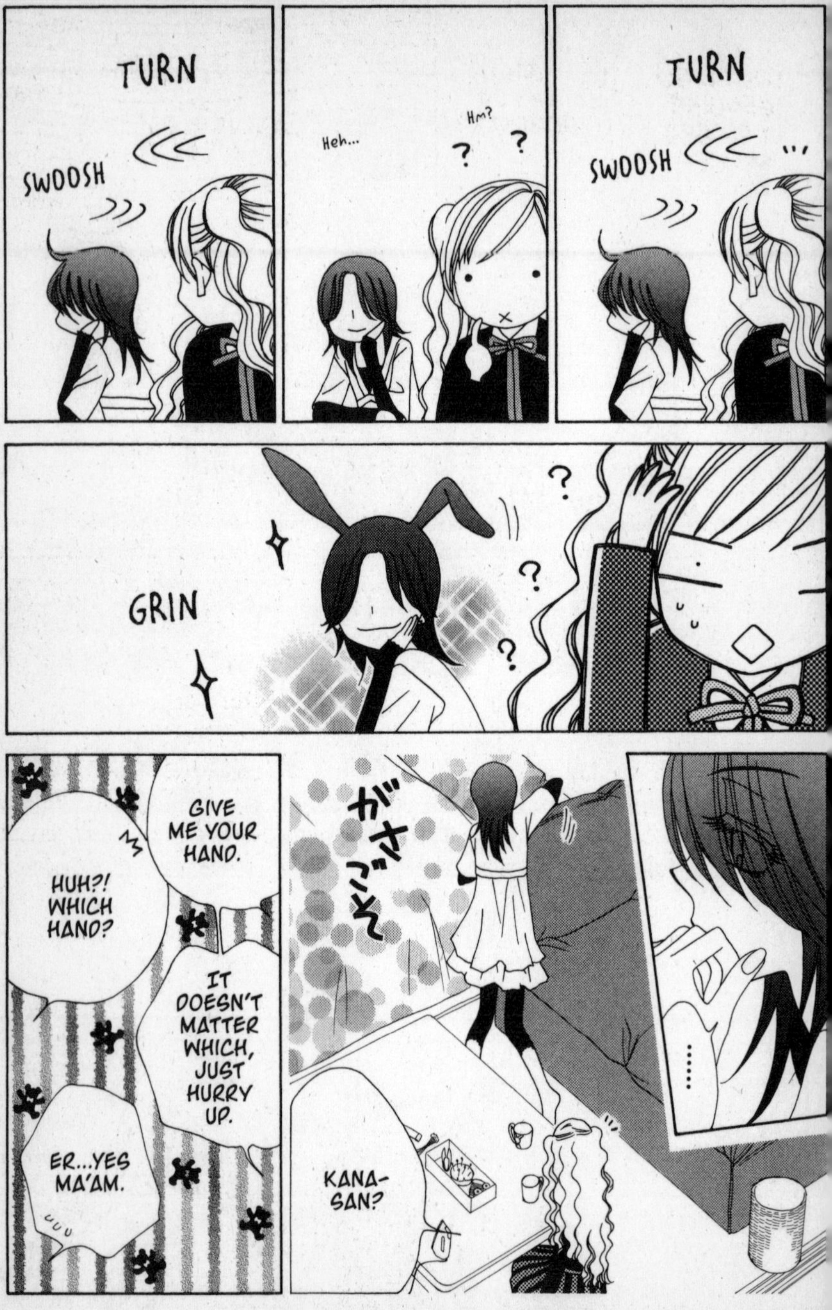
TURN
SWOOSH
Hm?
Heh...
TURN
SWOOSH
GRIN
......
がさごそ
KANA-SAN?
GIVE ME YOUR HAND.
HUH?! WHICH HAND?
IT DOESN'T MATTER WHICH, JUST HURRY UP.
ER...YES MA'AM.

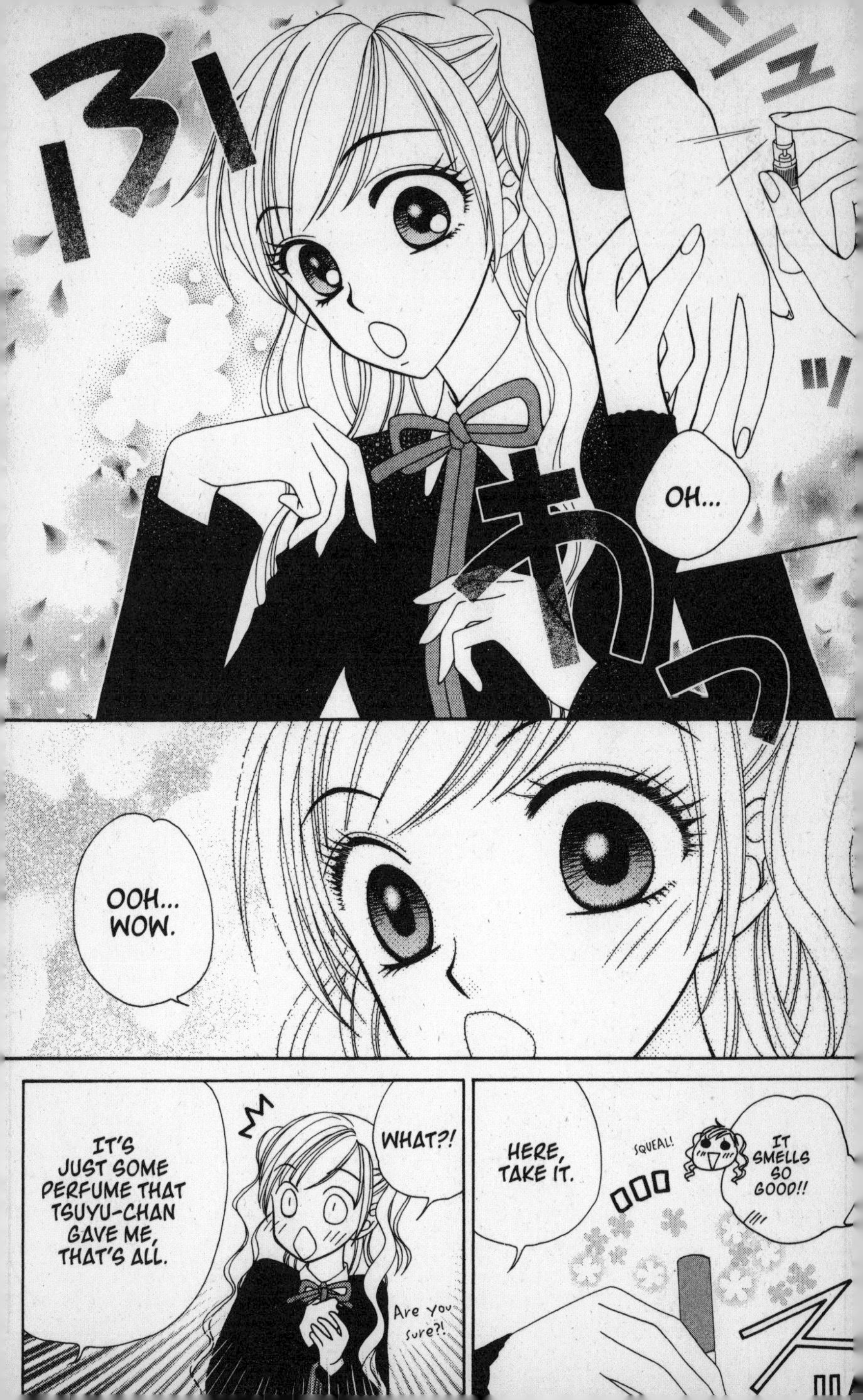
OH...
OOH... WOW.
IT SMELLS SO GOOD!!
SQUEAL!
HERE, TAKE IT.
WHAT?!
IT'S JUST SOME PERFUME THAT TSUYU-CHAN GAVE ME, THAT'S ALL.
Are you sure?!

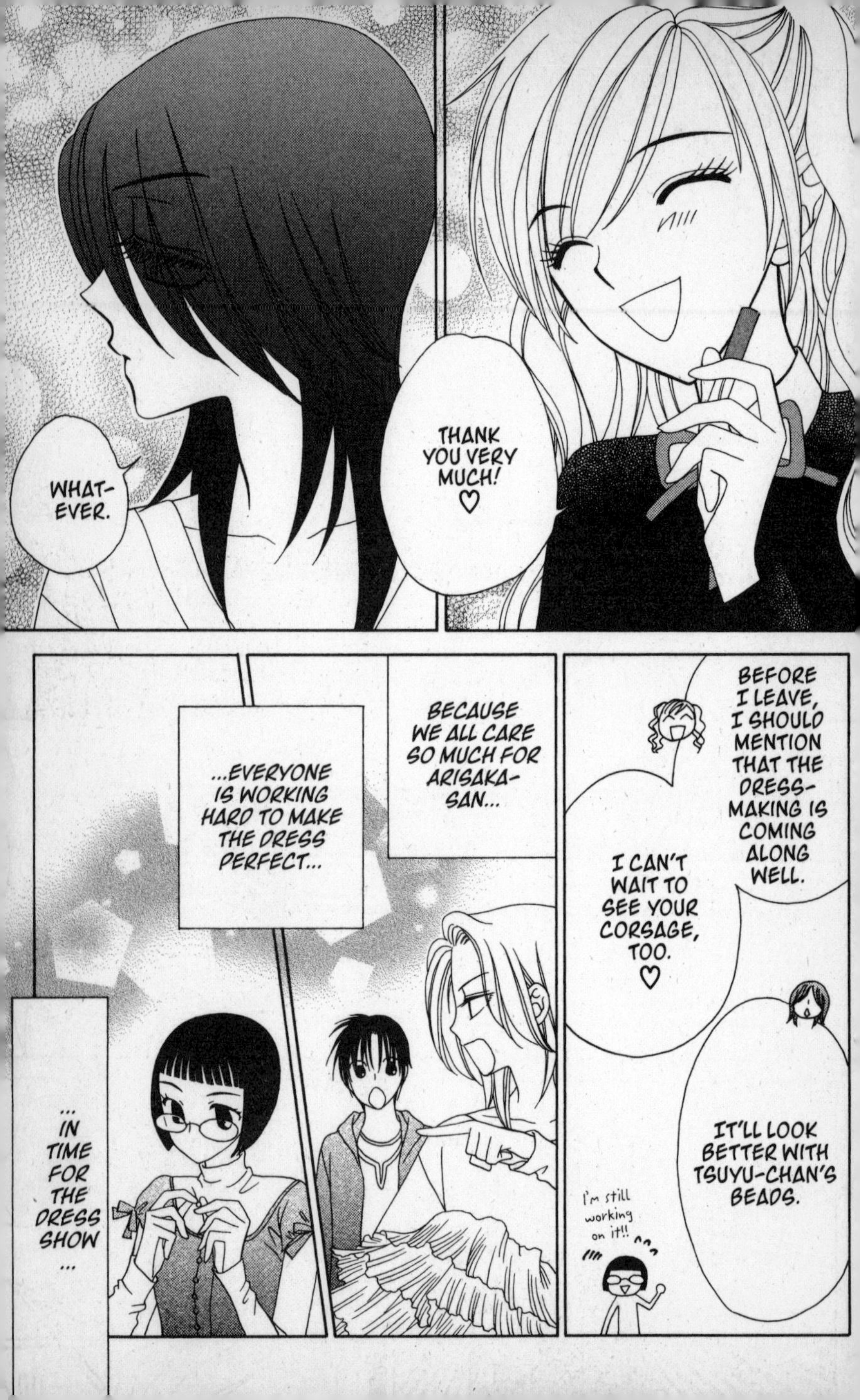
THANK YOU VERY MUCH! ♡
WHAT-EVER.
BEFORE I LEAVE, I SHOULD MENTION THAT THE DRESS-MAKING IS COMING ALONG WELL.
I CAN'T WAIT TO SEE YOUR CORSAGE, TOO. ♡
IT'LL LOOK BETTER WITH TSUYU-CHAN'S BEADS.
I'm still working on it!!
BECAUSE WE ALL CARE SO MUCH FOR ARISAKA-SAN...
...EVERYONE IS WORKING HARD TO MAKE THE DRESS PERFECT...
... IN TIME FOR THE DRESS SHOW ...

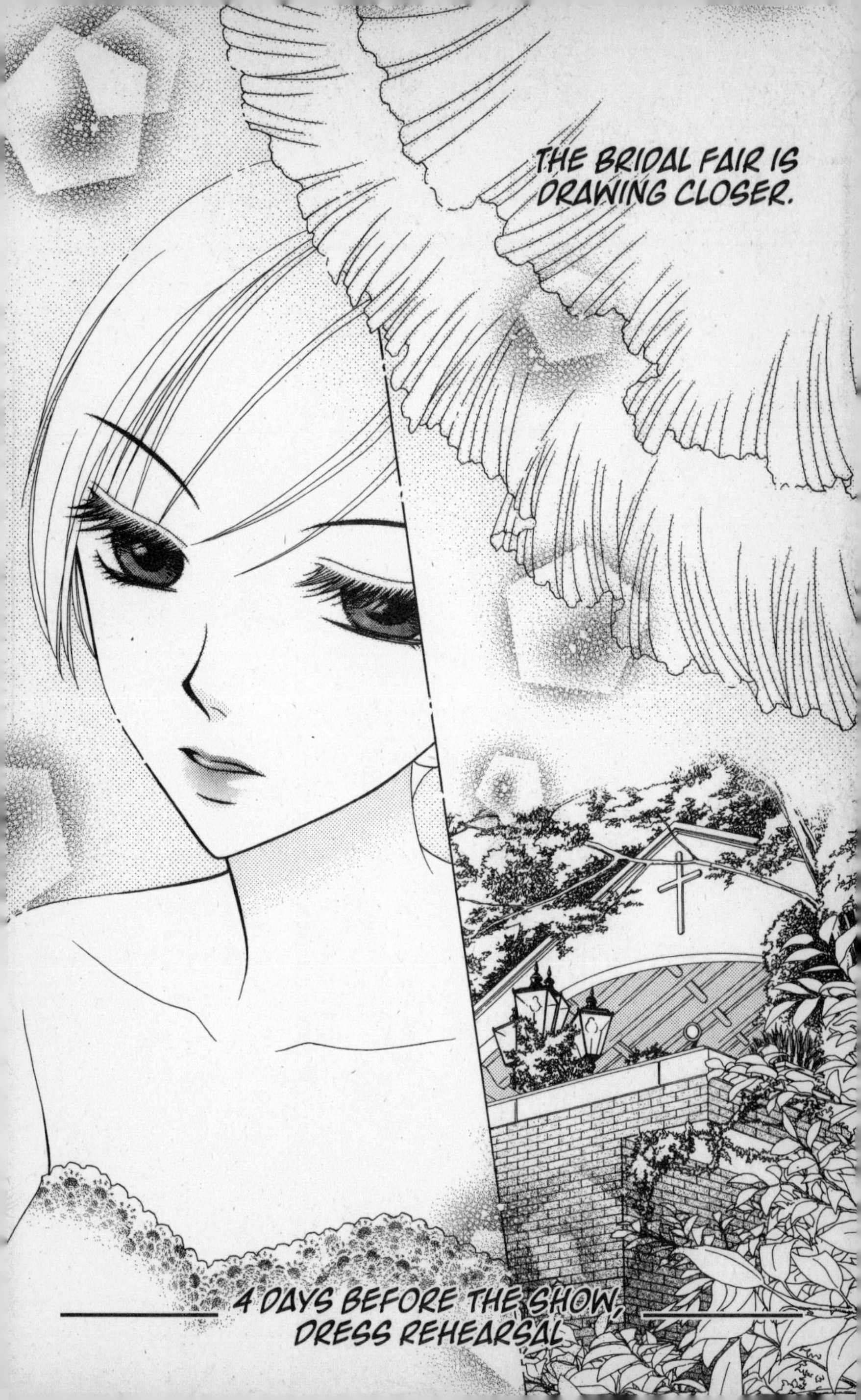
THE BRIDAL FAIR IS DRAWING CLOSER.
4 DAYS BEFORE THE SHOW, DRESS REHEARSAL

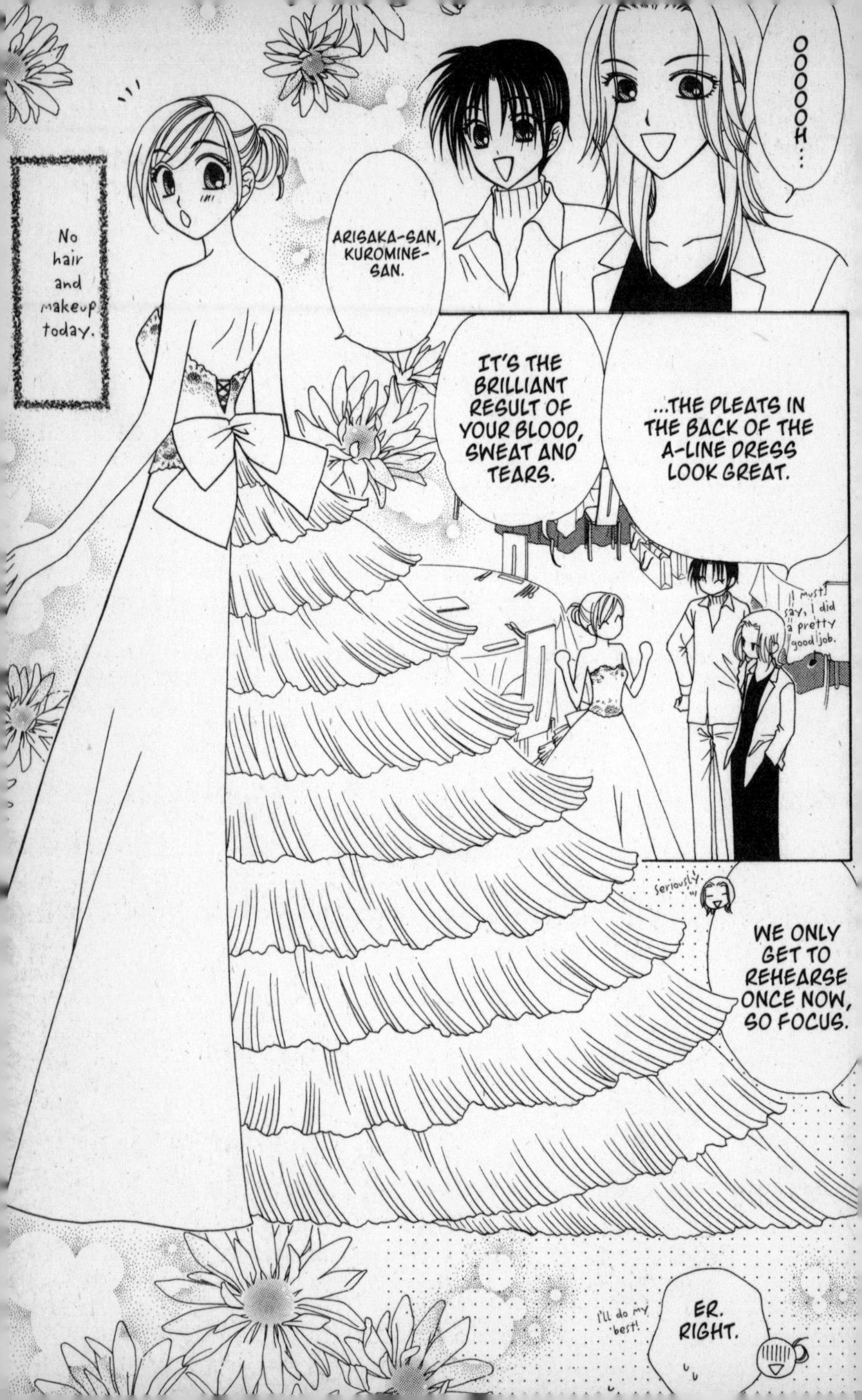
OOOOOH...
ARISAKA-SAN, KUROMINE-SAN.
No hair and makeup today.
...THE PLEATS IN THE BACK OF THE A-LINE DRESS LOOK GREAT.
IT'S THE BRILLIANT RESULT OF YOUR BLOOD, SWEAT AND TEARS.
I must say, I did a pretty good job.
seriously.
WE ONLY GET TO REHEARSE ONCE NOW, SO FOCUS.
ER. RIGHT.
I'll do my best!

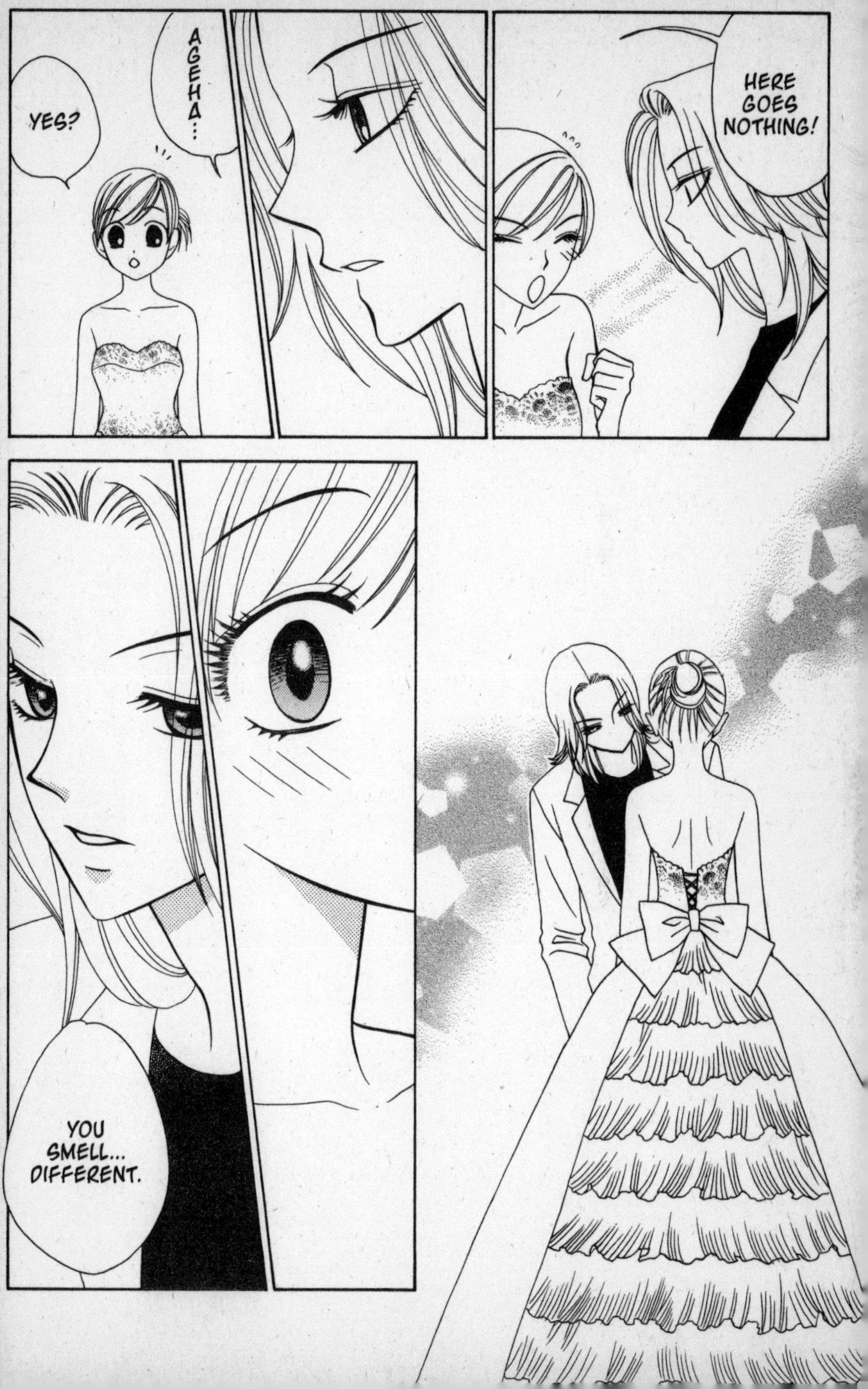
HERE GOES NOTHING!
AGEHA...
YES?
YOU SMELL... DIFFERENT.

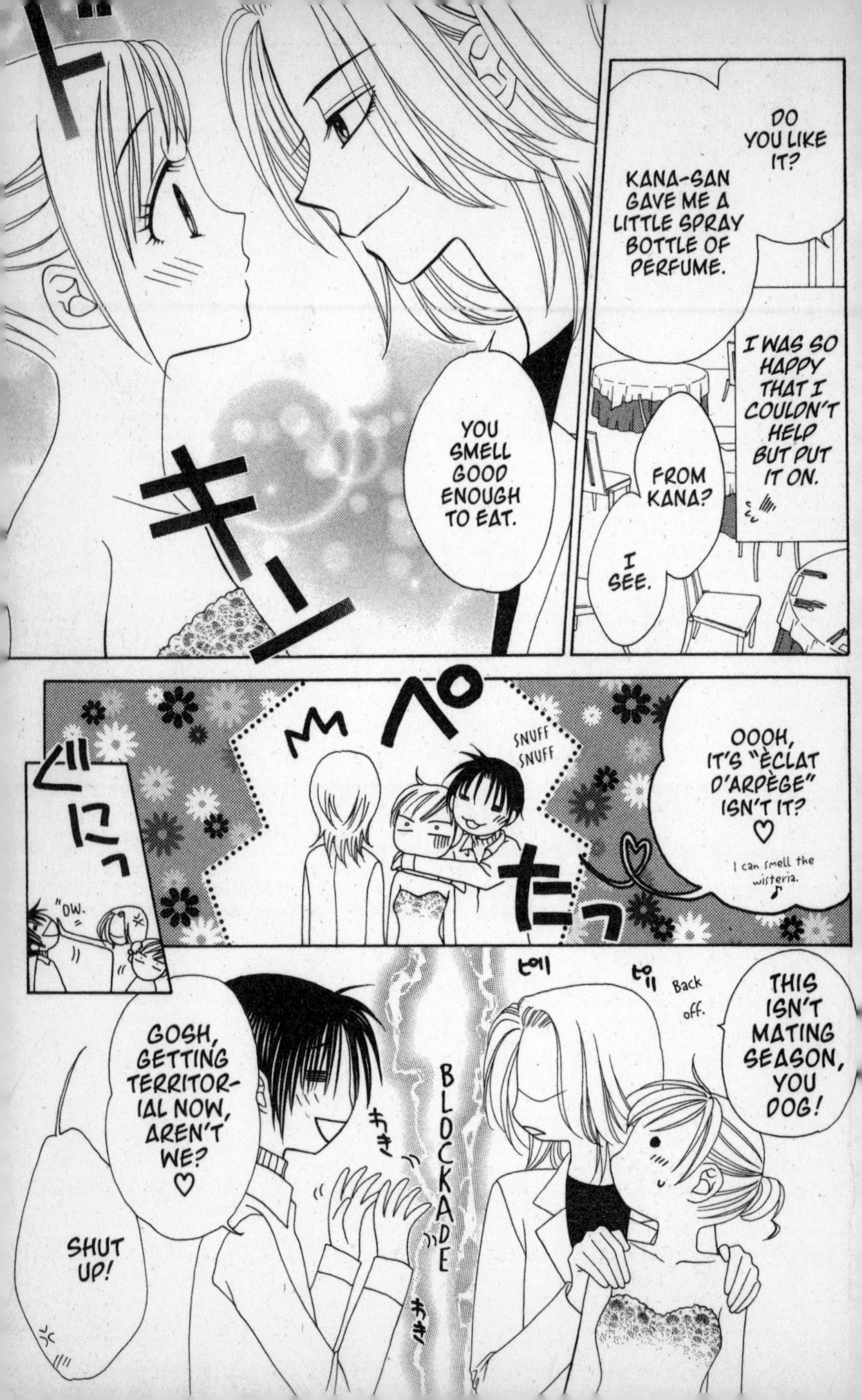
DO YOU LIKE IT?
KANA-SAN GAVE ME A LITTLE SPRAY BOTTLE OF PERFUME.
I WAS SO HAPPY THAT I COULDN'T HELP BUT PUT IT ON.
FROM KANA?
I SEE.
YOU SMELL GOOD ENOUGH TO EAT.
キーン
OOOH, IT'S "ÈCLAT D'ARPÈGE" ISN'T IT? ♡
I can smell the wisteria. ♪
SNUFF SNUFF
ぺ
たっ
ぐにっ
"OW.
THIS ISN'T MATING SEASON, YOU DOG!
Back off.
BLOCKADE
GOSH, GETTING TERRITORIAL NOW, AREN'T WE? ♡
SHUT UP!

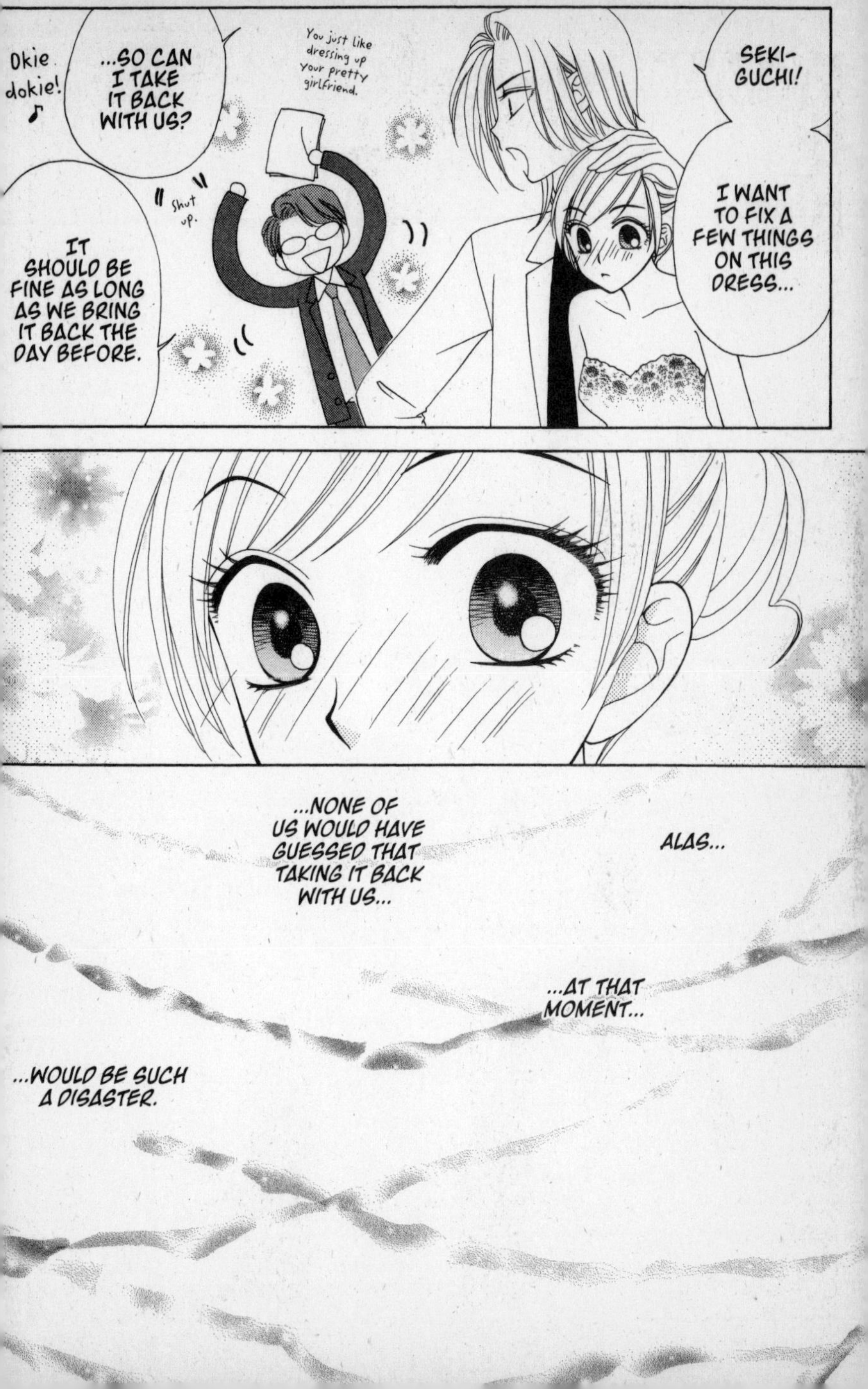
SEKI-GUCHI!
I WANT TO FIX A FEW THINGS ON THIS DRESS...
You just like dressing up your pretty girlfriend.
...SO CAN I TAKE IT BACK WITH US?
Okie dokie! ♪
Shut up.
IT SHOULD BE FINE AS LONG AS WE BRING IT BACK THE DAY BEFORE.
ALAS...
...NONE OF US WOULD HAVE GUESSED THAT TAKING IT BACK WITH US...
...AT THAT MOMENT...
...WOULD BE SUCH A DISASTER.

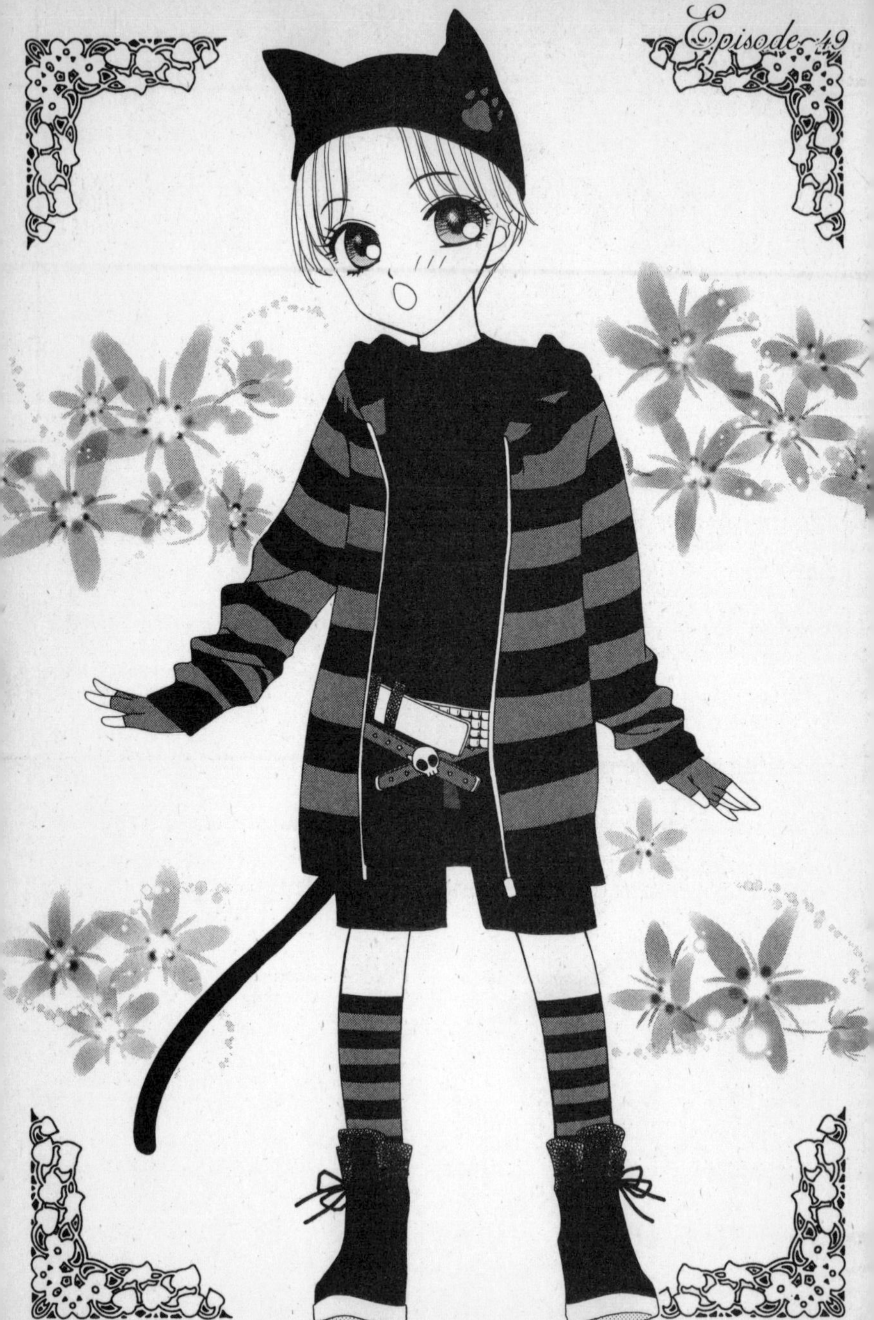Episode 49

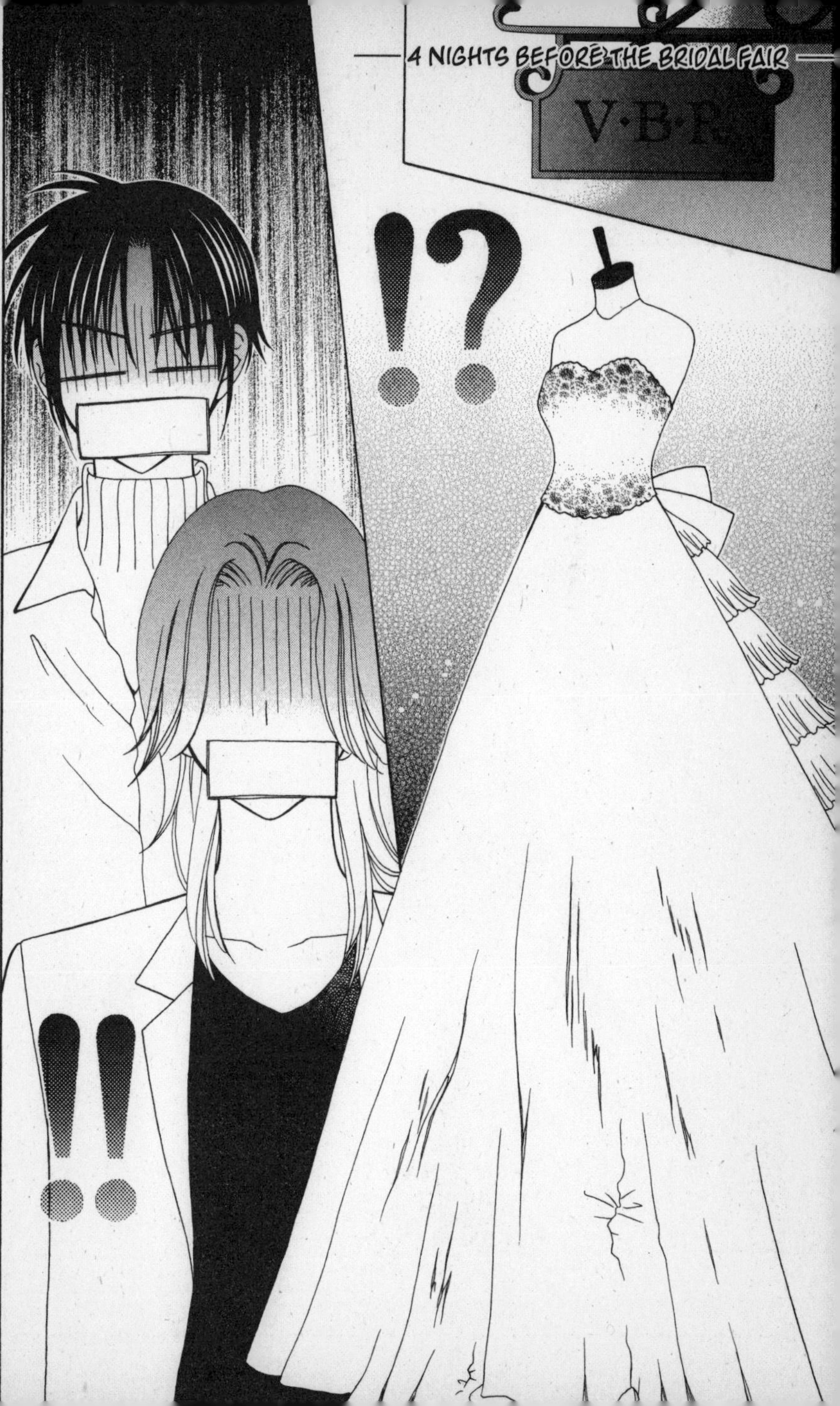

—4 NIGHTS BEFORE THE BRIDAL FAIR—
V·B·R.
!?
!!

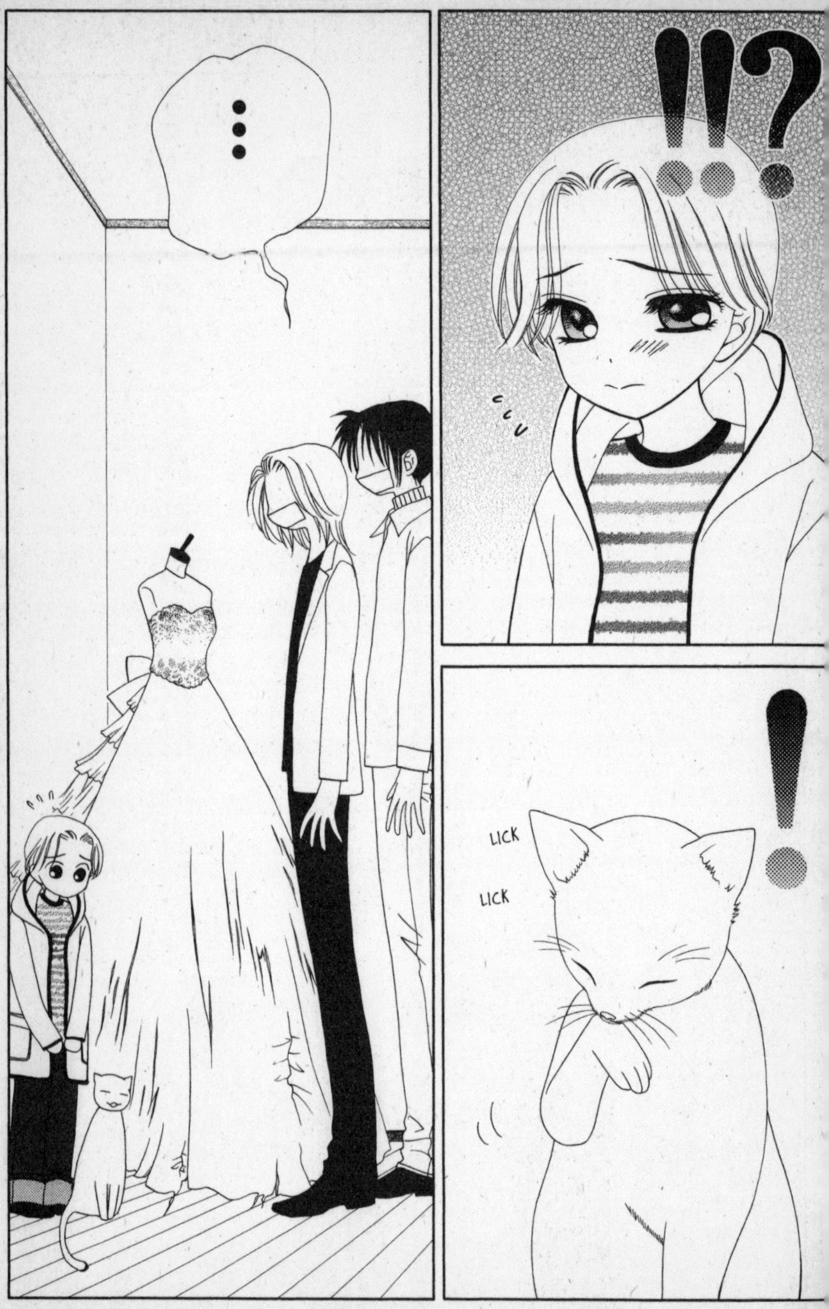
!!?
!
LICK
LICK
...

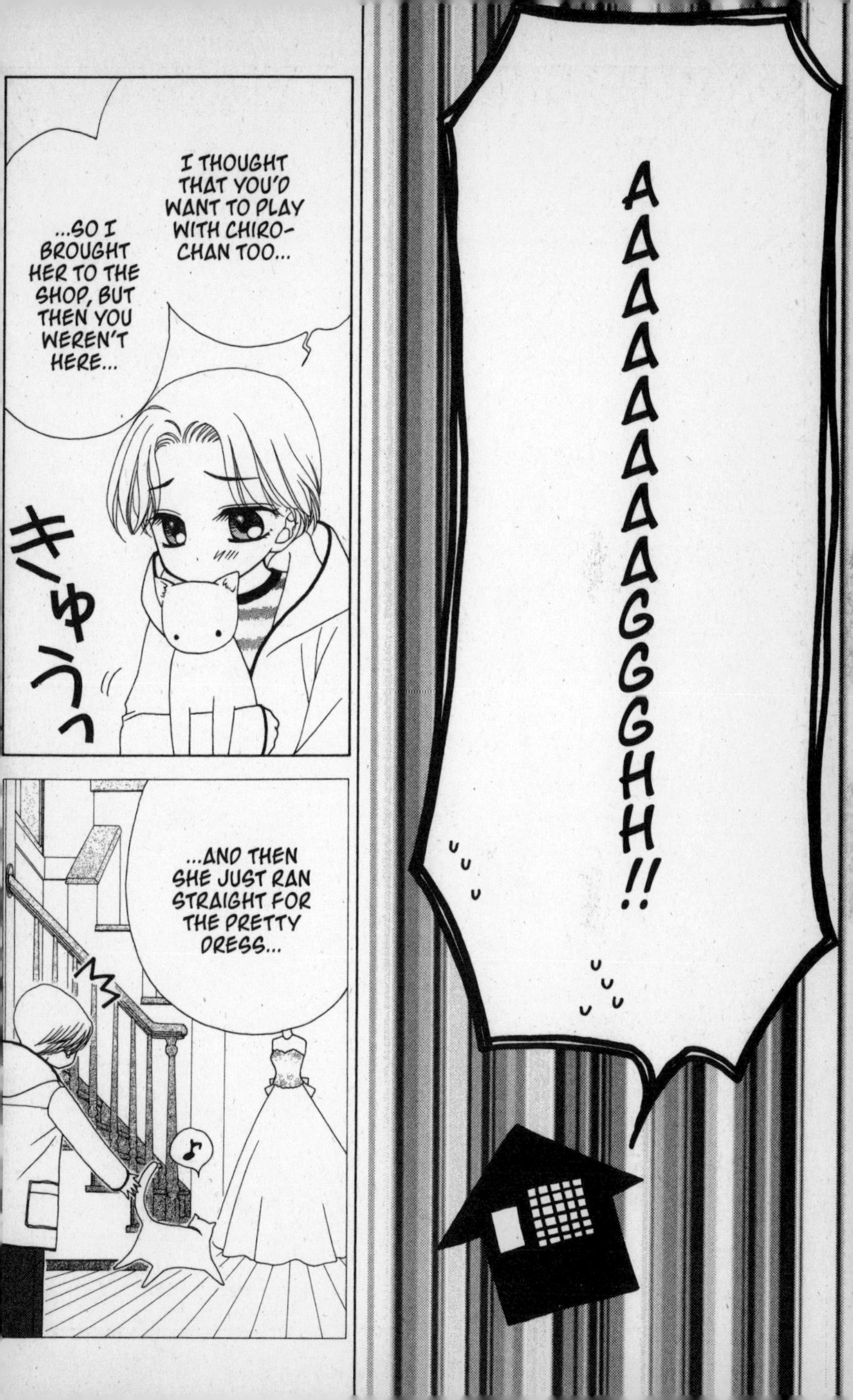
AAAAAAAAGGGHH!!
I THOUGHT THAT YOU'D WANT TO PLAY WITH CHIRO-CHAN TOO...
...SO I BROUGHT HER TO THE SHOP, BUT THEN YOU WEREN'T HERE...
きゅうっ
...AND THEN SHE JUST RAN STRAIGHT FOR THE PRETTY DRESS...

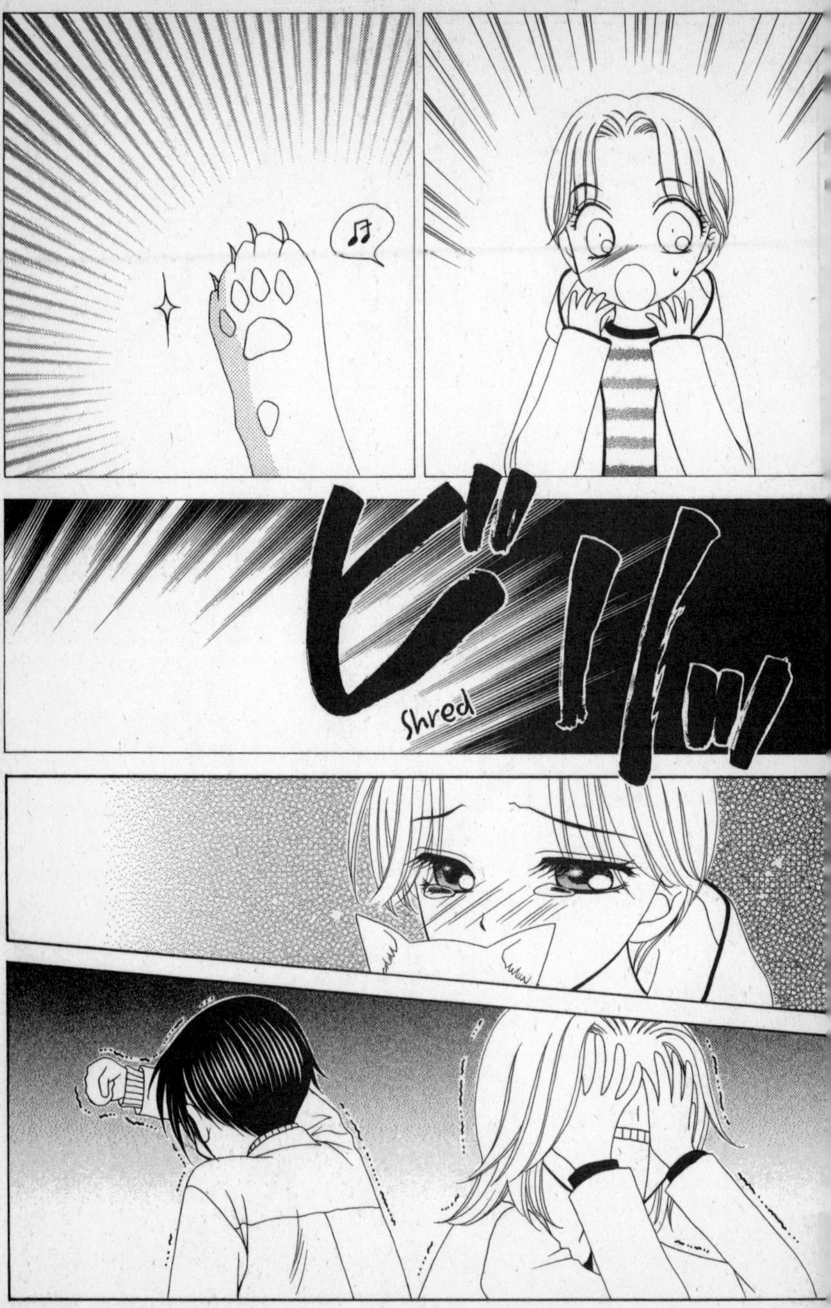
♬
ビリッ
Shred

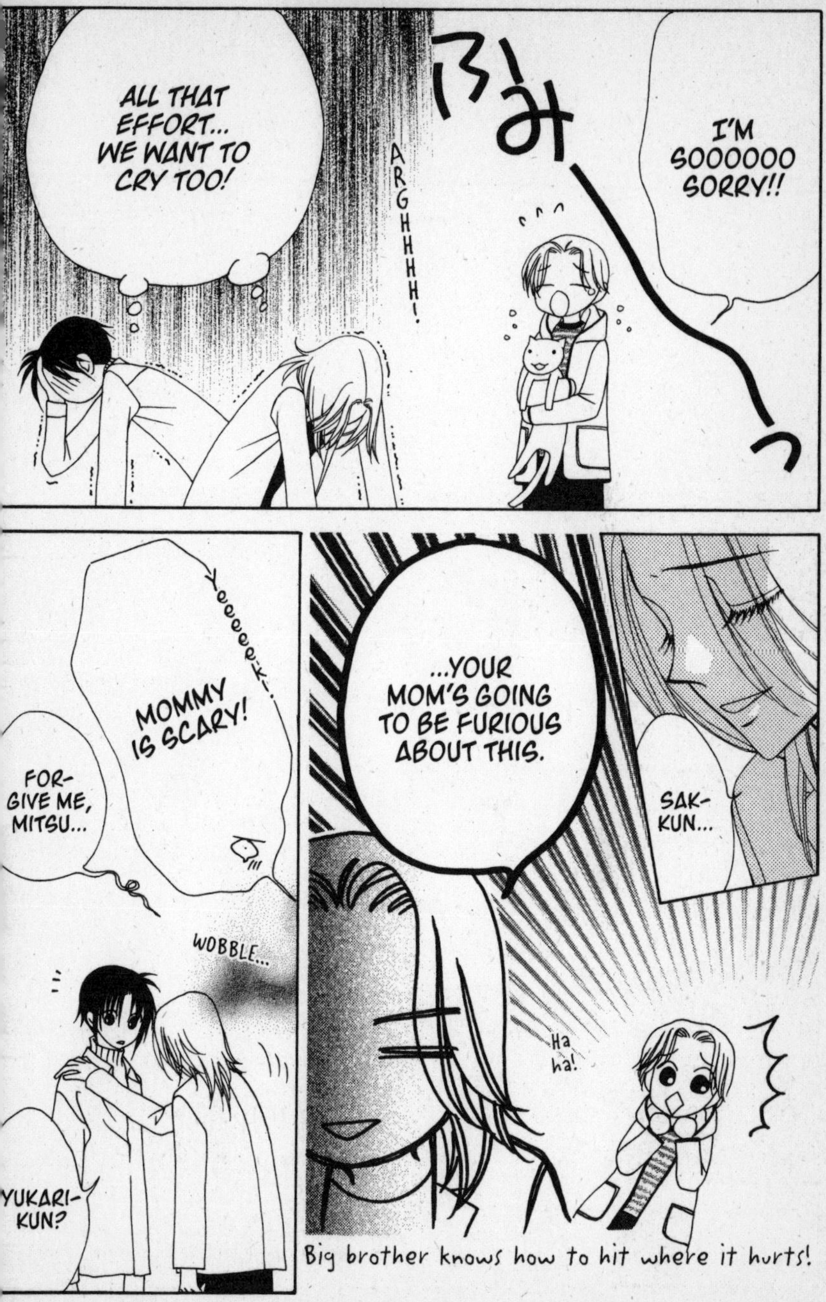
I'M SOOOOOO SORRY!!
ARGHHHH!
ALL THAT EFFORT... WE WANT TO CRY TOO!
SAK-KUN...
...YOUR MOM'S GOING TO BE FURIOUS ABOUT THIS.
Ha ha!
Yeeeeek!
MOMMY IS SCARY!
FOR-GIVE ME, MITSU...
WOBBLE...
YUKARI-KUN?
Big brother knows how to hit where it hurts!

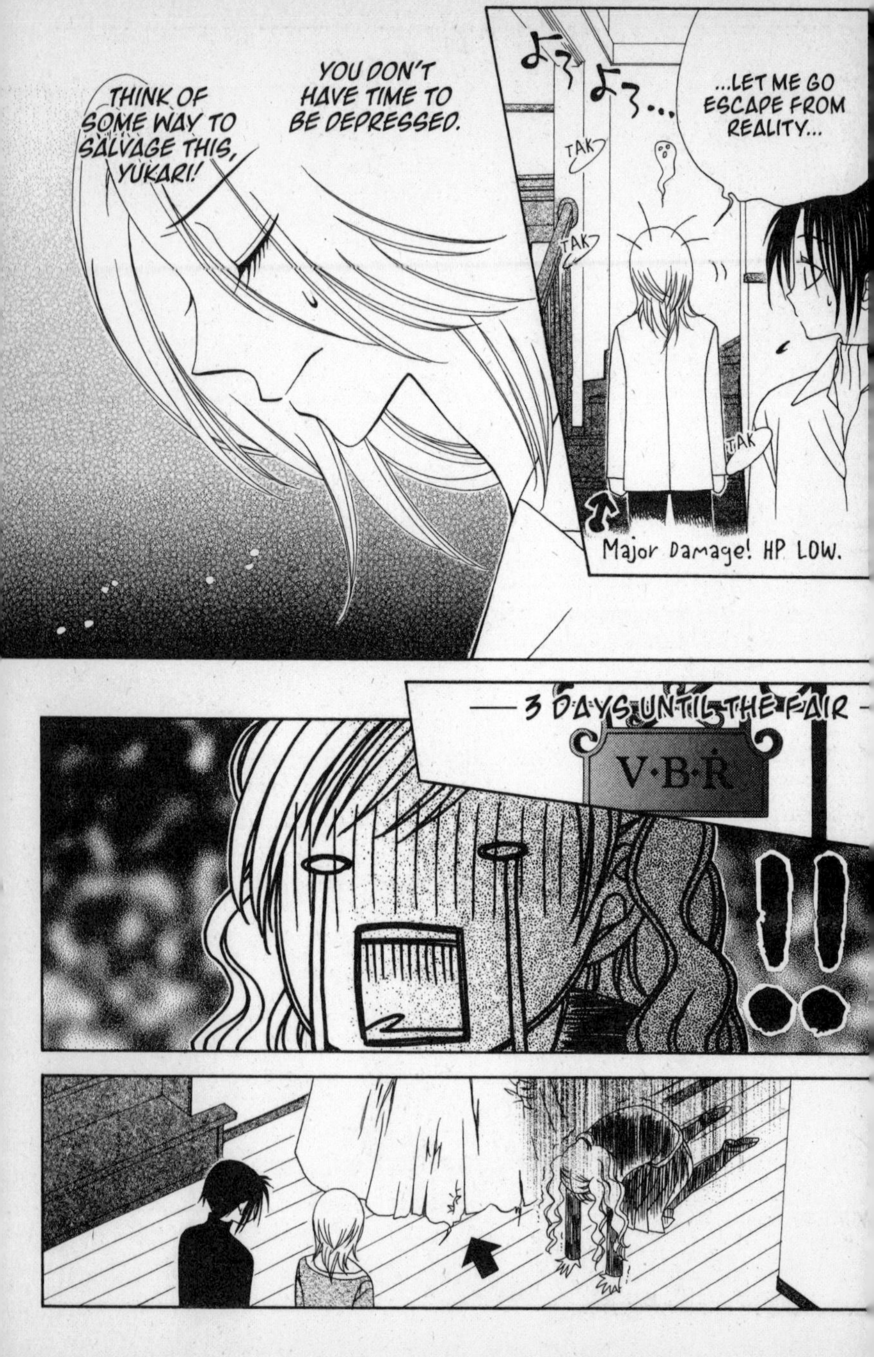
よろよろ...
...LET ME GO ESCAPE FROM REALITY...
TAK
TAK
TAK
Major Damage! HP LOW.
YOU DON'T HAVE TIME TO BE DEPRESSED.
THINK OF SOME WAY TO SALVAGE THIS, YUKARI!
—3 DAYS UNTIL THE FAIR—
V·B·R
!!

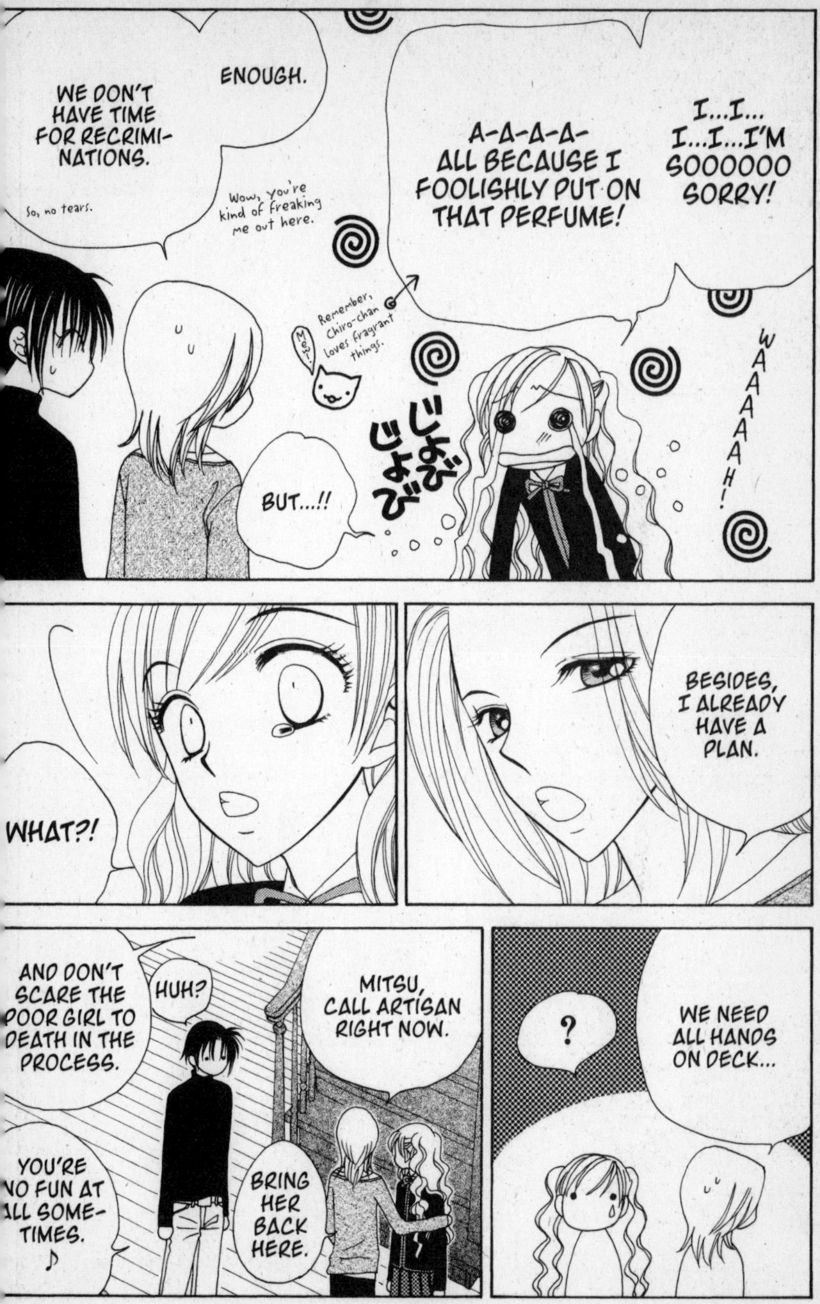
I...I...
I...I...I'M SOOOOOO SORRY!
WAAAAAAH!
A-A-A-A-
ALL BECAUSE I FOOLISHLY PUT ON THAT PERFUME!
Remember, Chiro-chan loves fragrant things.
Mew!
じょびじょび
BUT...!!
ENOUGH.
Wow, you're kind of freaking me out here.
WE DON'T HAVE TIME FOR RECRIMI-NATIONS.
So, no tears.
BESIDES, I ALREADY HAVE A PLAN.
WHAT?!
WE NEED ALL HANDS ON DECK...
?
MITSU, CALL ARTISAN RIGHT NOW.
BRING HER BACK HERE.
HUH?
AND DON'T SCARE THE POOR GIRL TO DEATH IN THE PROCESS.
YOU'RE NO FUN AT ALL SOME-TIMES. ♪

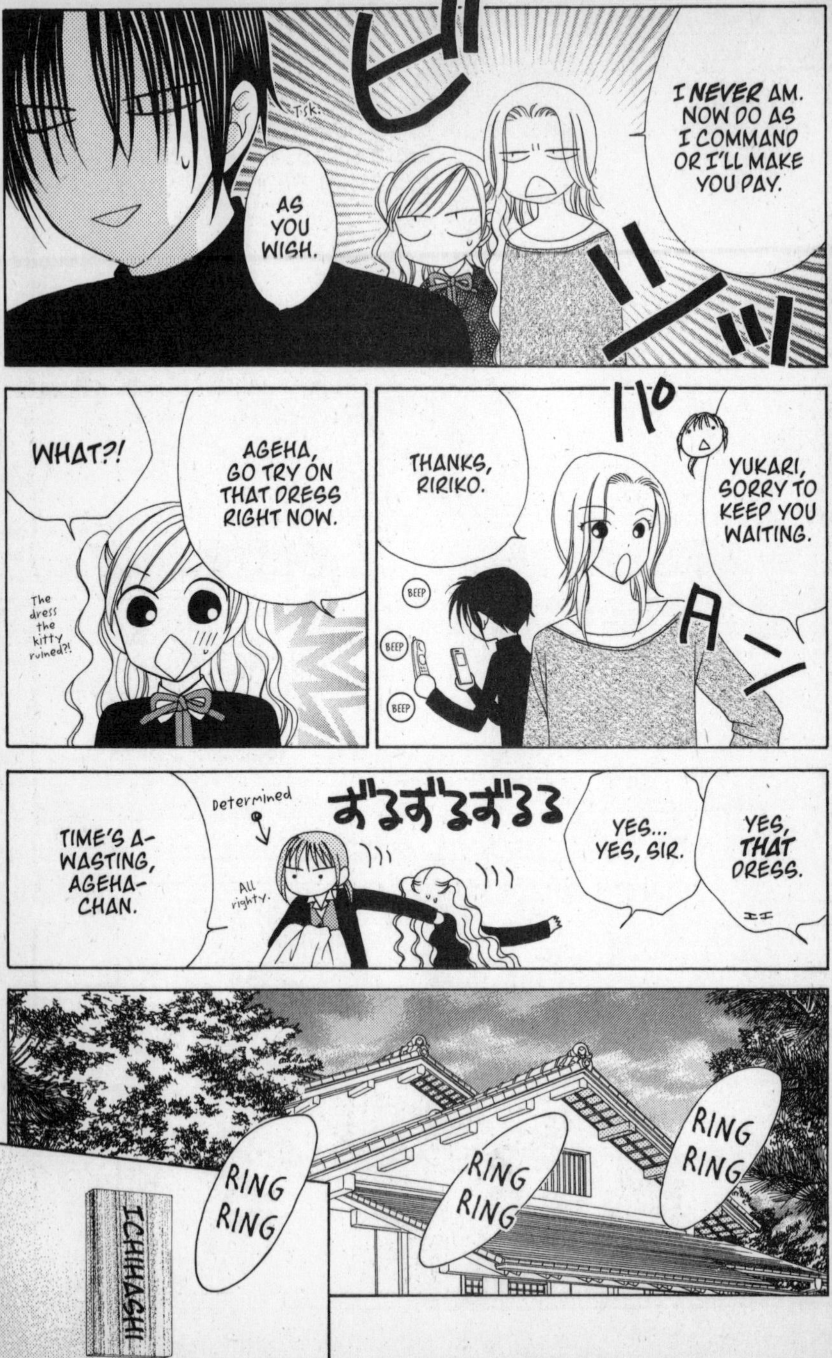
I NEVER AM. NOW DO AS I COMMAND OR I'LL MAKE YOU PAY.
Tsk.
AS YOU WISH.
パ
YUKARI, SORRY TO KEEP YOU WAITING.
THANKS, RIRIKO.
BEEP
BEEP
BEEP
AGEHA, GO TRY ON THAT DRESS RIGHT NOW.
WHAT?!
The dress the kitty ruined?!
YES, THAT DRESS.
YES... YES, SIR.
ずるずるずるる
Determined
All righty.
TIME'S A-WASTING, AGEHA-CHAN.
RING RING
RING RING
RING RING
ICHIHASHI

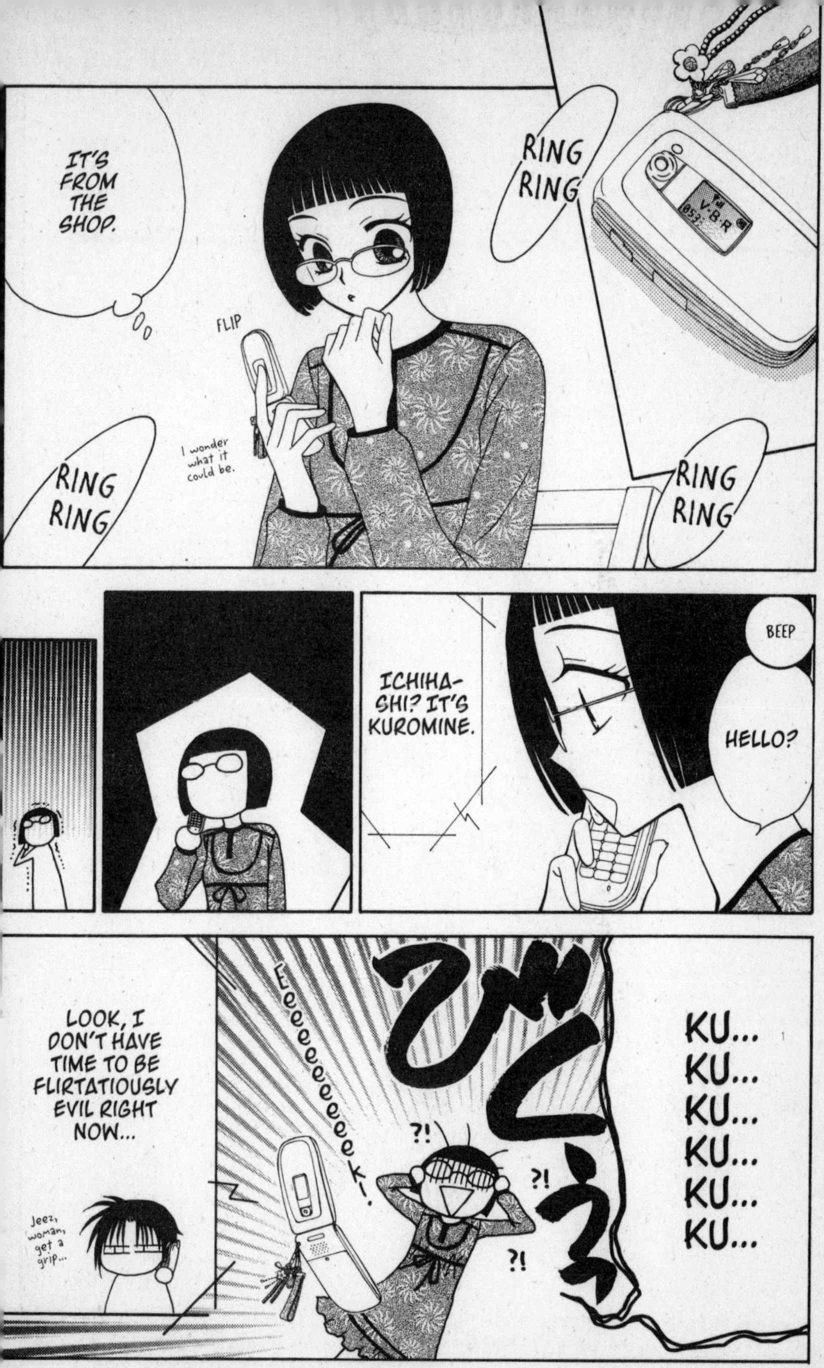
RING RING
RING RING
IT'S FROM THE SHOP.
FLIP
I wonder what it could be.
RING RING
BEEP
HELLO?
ICHIHASHI? IT'S KUROMINE.
KU... KU... KU... KU... KU... KU...
びくぅ
Eeeeeeeeeeek!
?!
?!
?!
LOOK, I DON'T HAVE TIME TO BE FLIRTATIOUSLY EVIL RIGHT NOW...
Jeez, woman, get a grip...

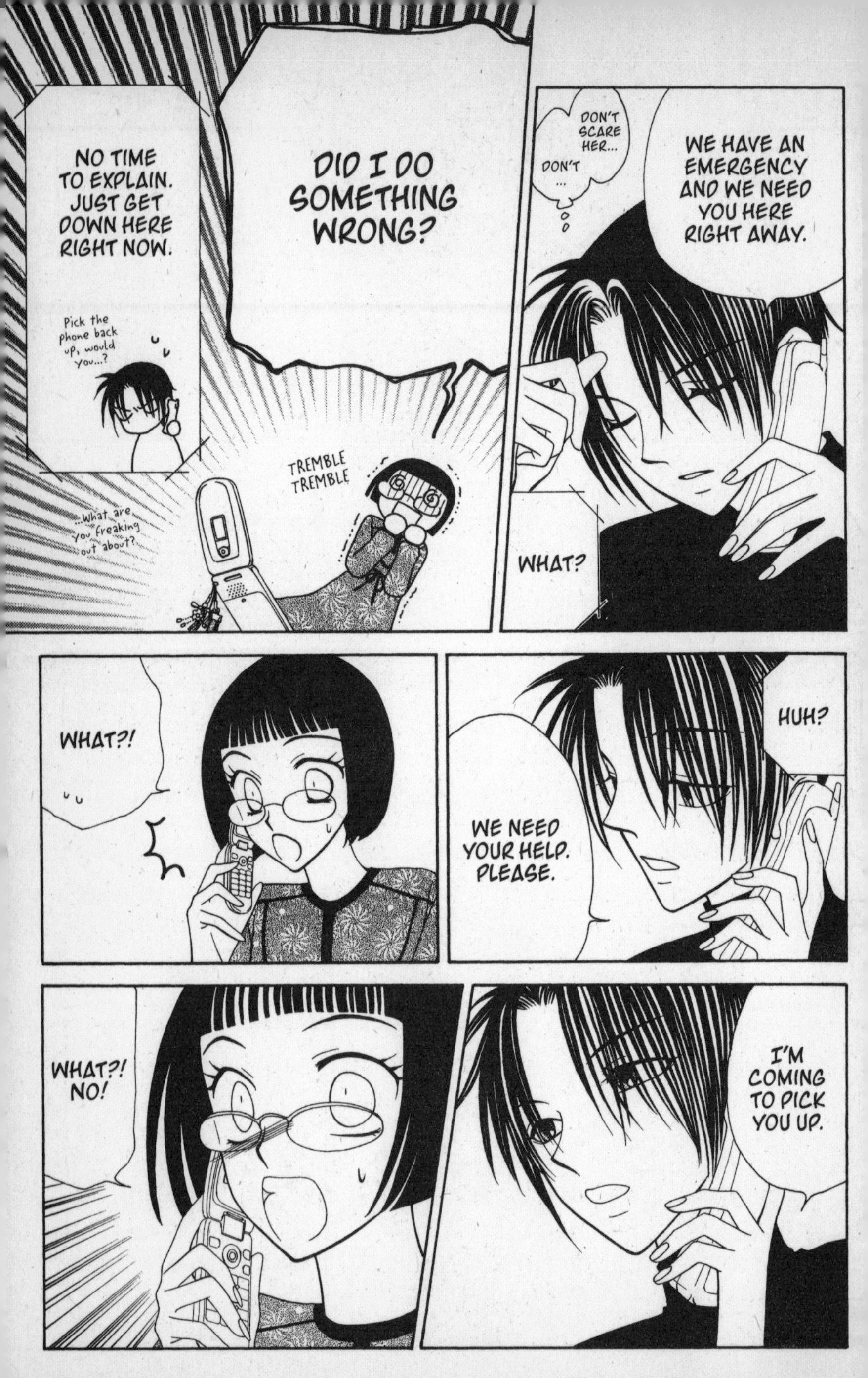
WE HAVE AN EMERGENCY AND WE NEED YOU HERE RIGHT AWAY.
DON'T SCARE HER... DON'T ...
WHAT?
DID I DO SOMETHING WRONG?
TREMBLE TREMBLE
...What are you freaking out about?
NO TIME TO EXPLAIN. JUST GET DOWN HERE RIGHT NOW.
Pick the phone back up, would you...?
HUH?
WE NEED YOUR HELP. PLEASE.
WHAT?!
I'M COMING TO PICK YOU UP.
WHAT?! NO!

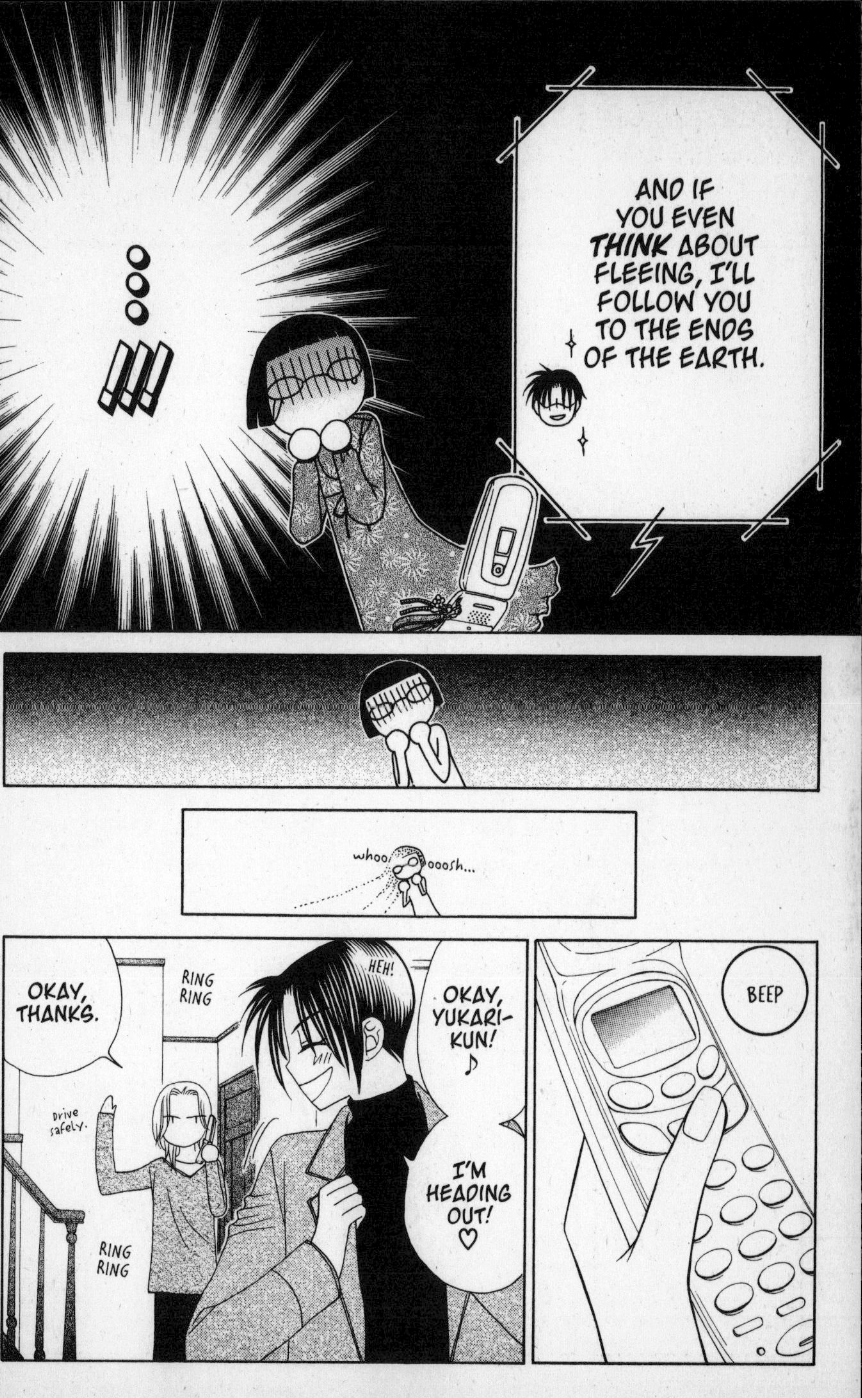
AND IF YOU EVEN *THINK* ABOUT FLEEING, I'LL FOLLOW YOU TO THE ENDS OF THE EARTH.
...!!!
whoooooosh...
BEEP
HEH!
OKAY, YUKARI-KUN! ♪
I'M HEADING OUT! ♡
RING RING
OKAY, THANKS.
Drive safely.
RING RING

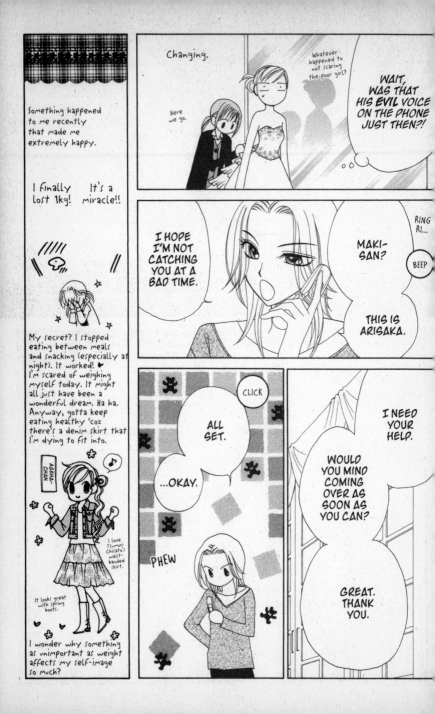

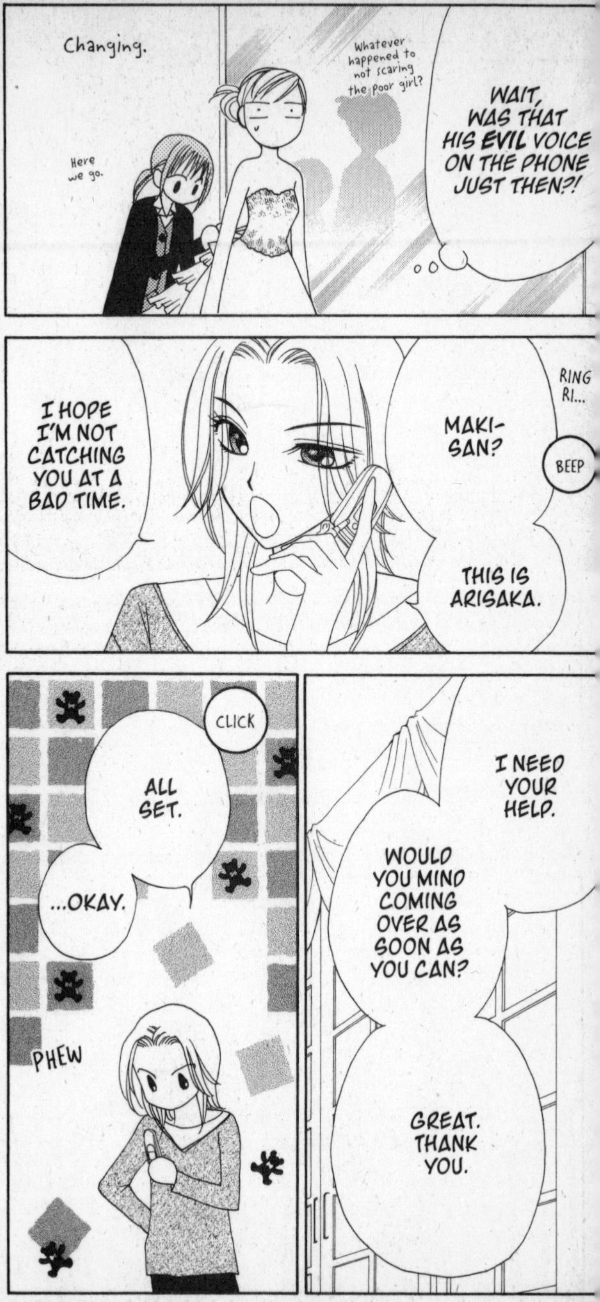
WAIT, WAS THAT HIS EVIL VOICE ON THE PHONE JUST THEN?!
Whatever happened to not scaring the poor girl?
Changing.
Here we go.
RING RI...
BEEP
MAKI-SAN?
THIS IS ARISAKA.
I HOPE I'M NOT CATCHING YOU AT A BAD TIME.
I NEED YOUR HELP.
WOULD YOU MIND COMING OVER AS SOON AS YOU CAN?
GREAT. THANK YOU.
CLICK
ALL SET.
...OKAY.
PHEW

Something happened to me recently that made me extremely happy.

I finally lost 1kg! It's a miracle!!

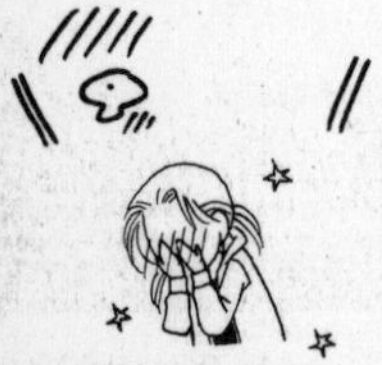

My secret? I stopped eating between meals and snacking (especially at night). It worked! ♥
I'm scared of weighing myself today. It might all just have been a wonderful dream. Ha ha. Anyway, gotta keep eating healthy 'coz there's a denim skirt that I'm dying to fit into.

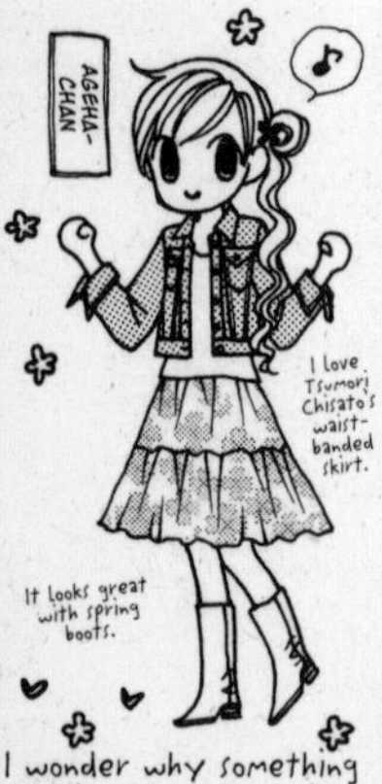
AGEHA-CHAN
I love Tsumori Chisato's waist-banded skirt.
It looks great with spring boots.

I wonder why something as unimportant as weight affects my self-image so much?

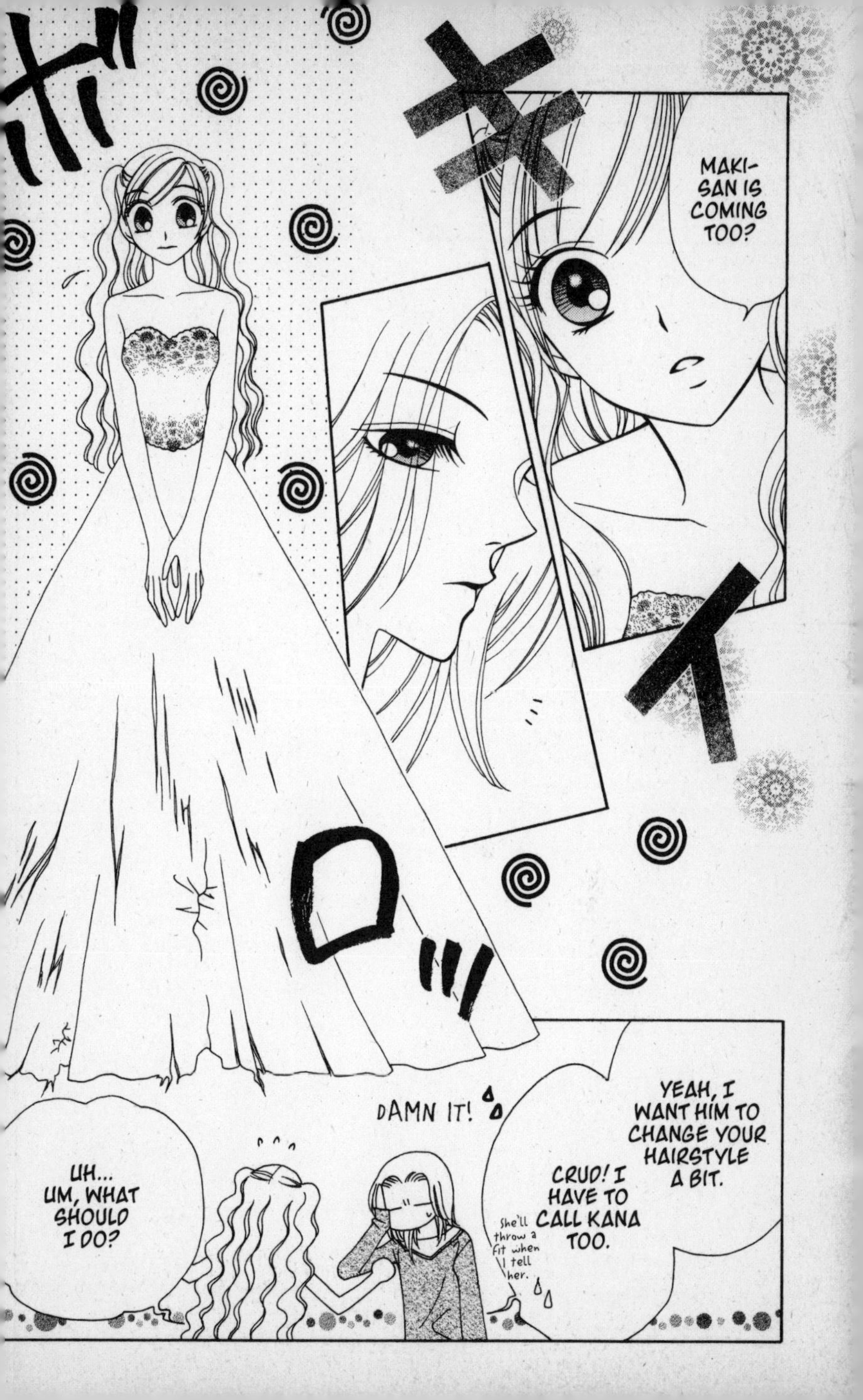
MAKI-SAN IS COMING TOO?
YEAH, I WANT HIM TO CHANGE YOUR HAIRSTYLE A BIT.
CRUD! I HAVE TO CALL KANA TOO.
She'll throw a fit when I tell her.
DAMN IT!
UH... UM, WHAT SHOULD I DO?

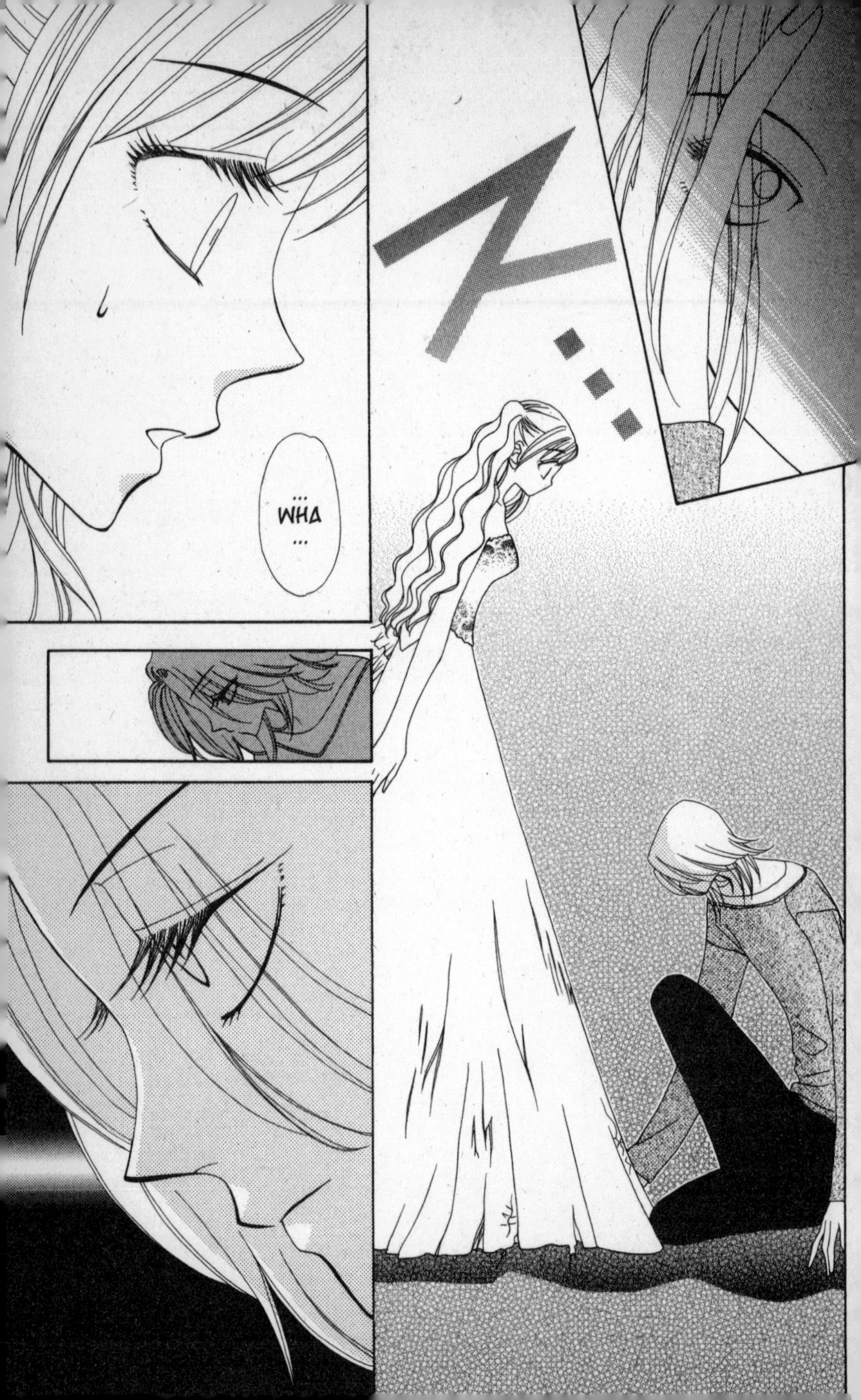
...WHA...

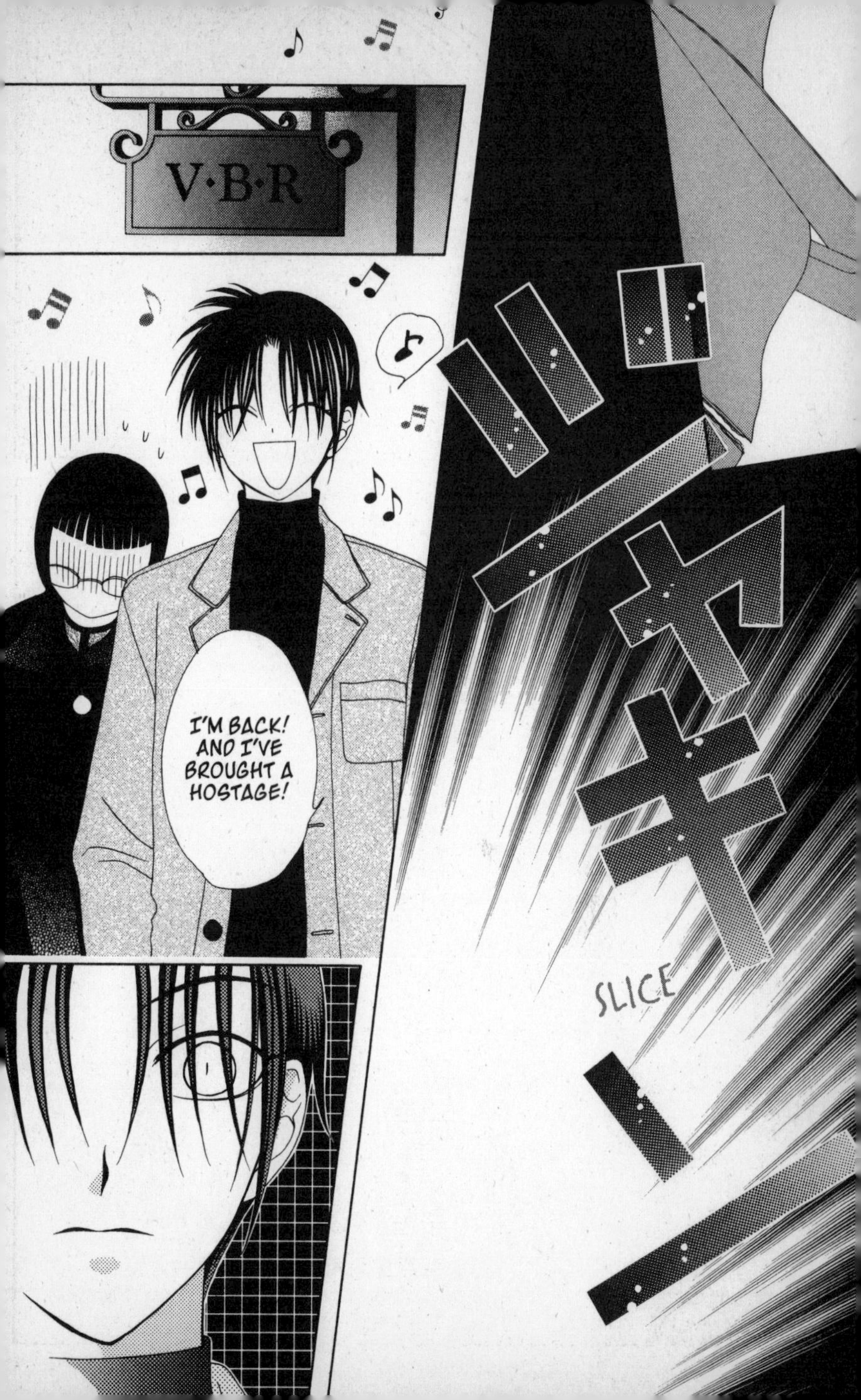
V·B·R
I'M BACK! AND I'VE BROUGHT A HOSTAGE!
SLICE

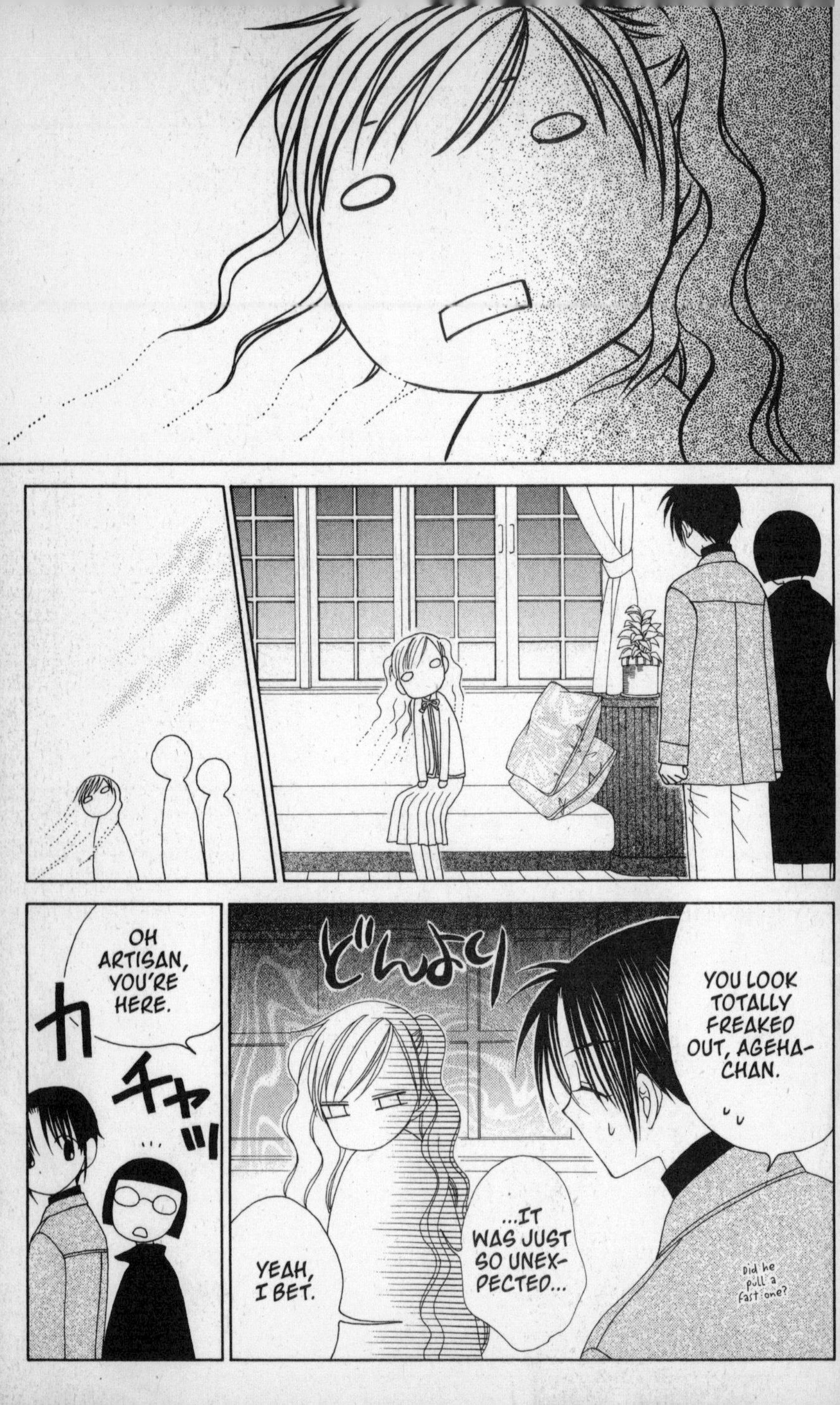
YOU LOOK TOTALLY FREAKED OUT, AGEHA-CHAN.
どんより
Did he pull a fast one?
...IT WAS JUST SO UNEX-PECTED...
YEAH, I BET.
OH ARTISAN, YOU'RE HERE.
カチャッ

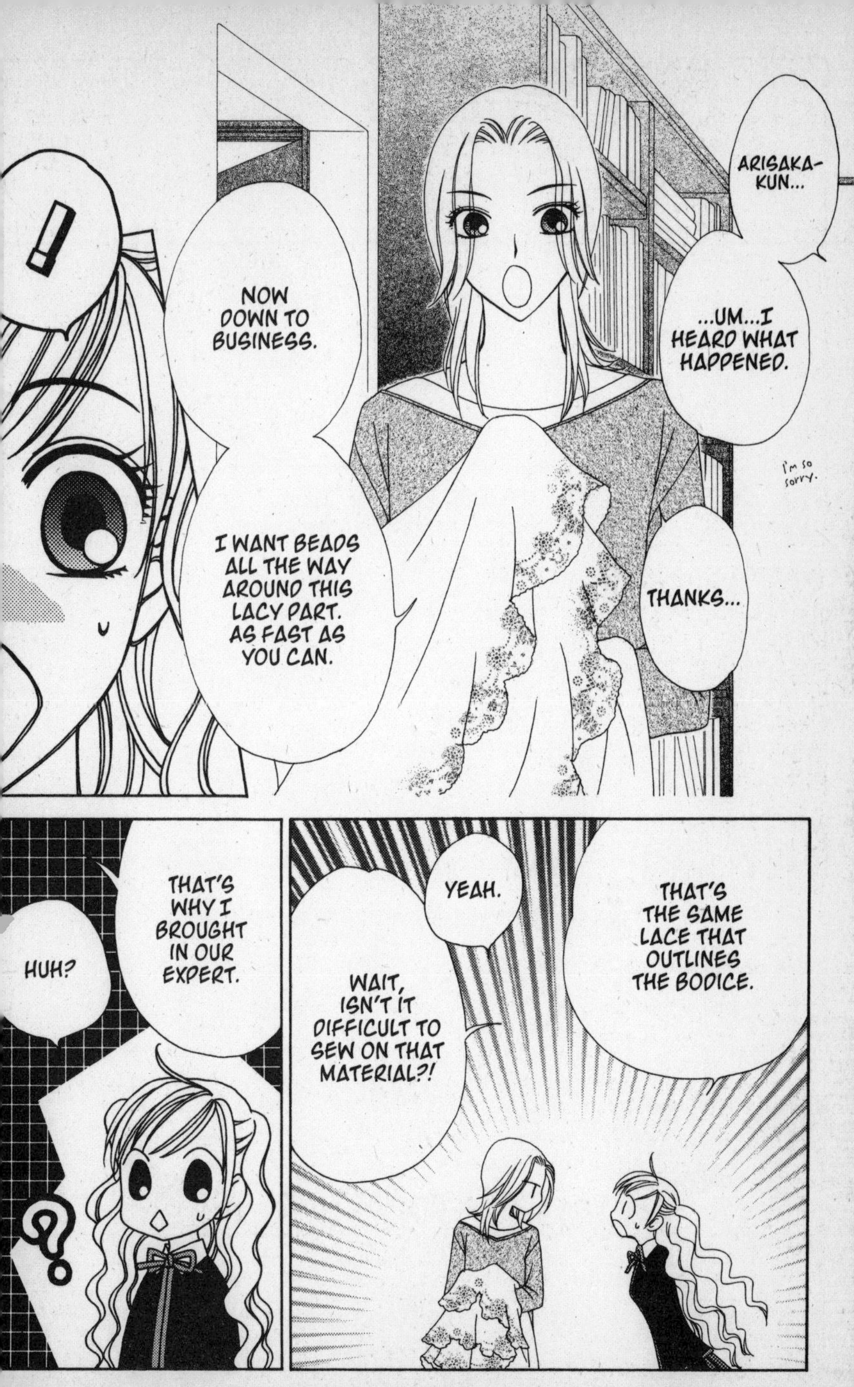
ARISAKA-KUN...
...UM...I HEARD WHAT HAPPENED.
I'm so sorry.
THANKS...
!
NOW DOWN TO BUSINESS.
I WANT BEADS ALL THE WAY AROUND THIS LACY PART. AS FAST AS YOU CAN.
THAT'S THE SAME LACE THAT OUTLINES THE BODICE.
YEAH.
WAIT, ISN'T IT DIFFICULT TO SEW ON THAT MATERIAL?!
THAT'S WHY I BROUGHT IN OUR EXPERT.
HUH?
?

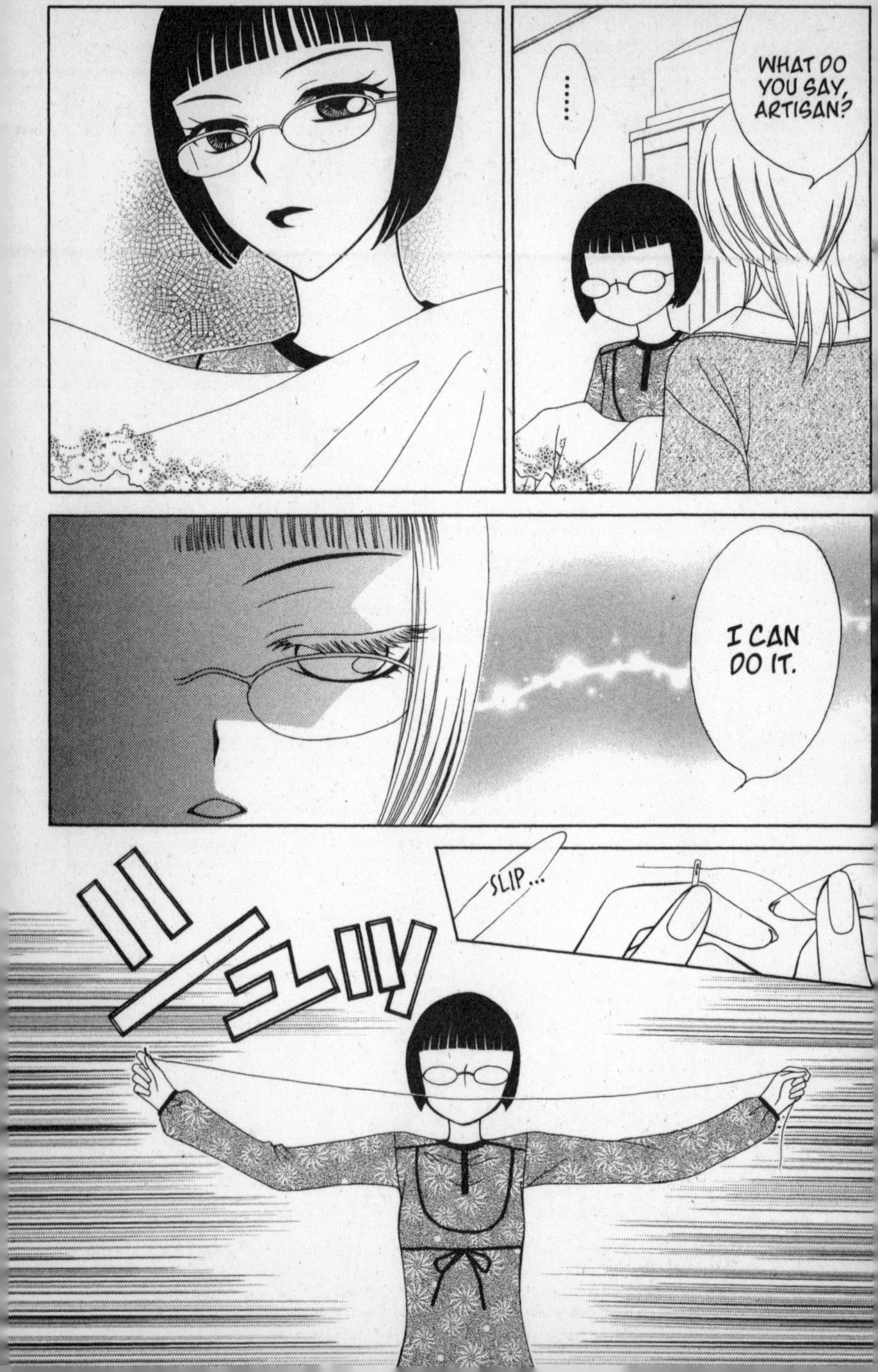
WHAT DO YOU SAY, ARTISAN?
......
I CAN DO IT.
SLIP...

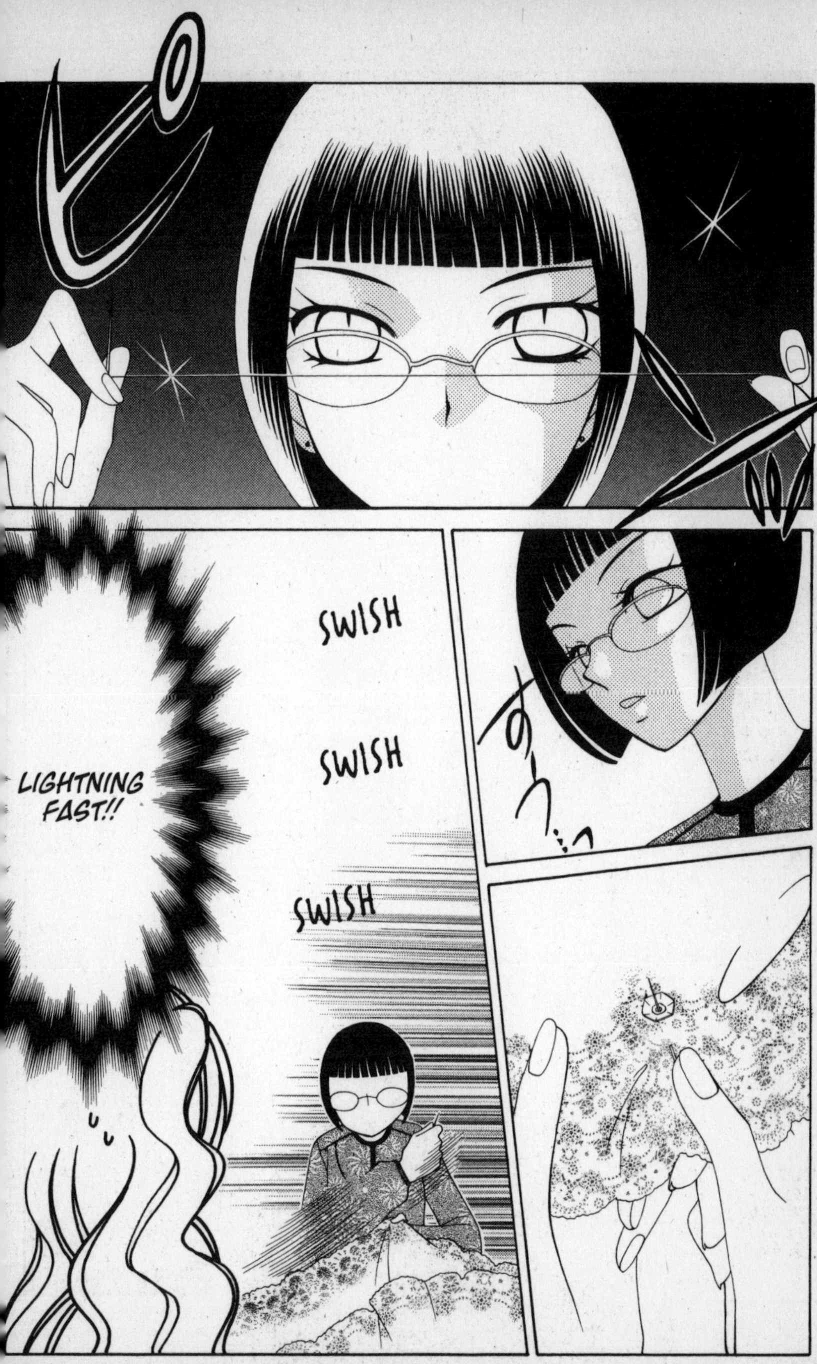
SWISH
SWISH
SWISH
LIGHTNING FAST!!

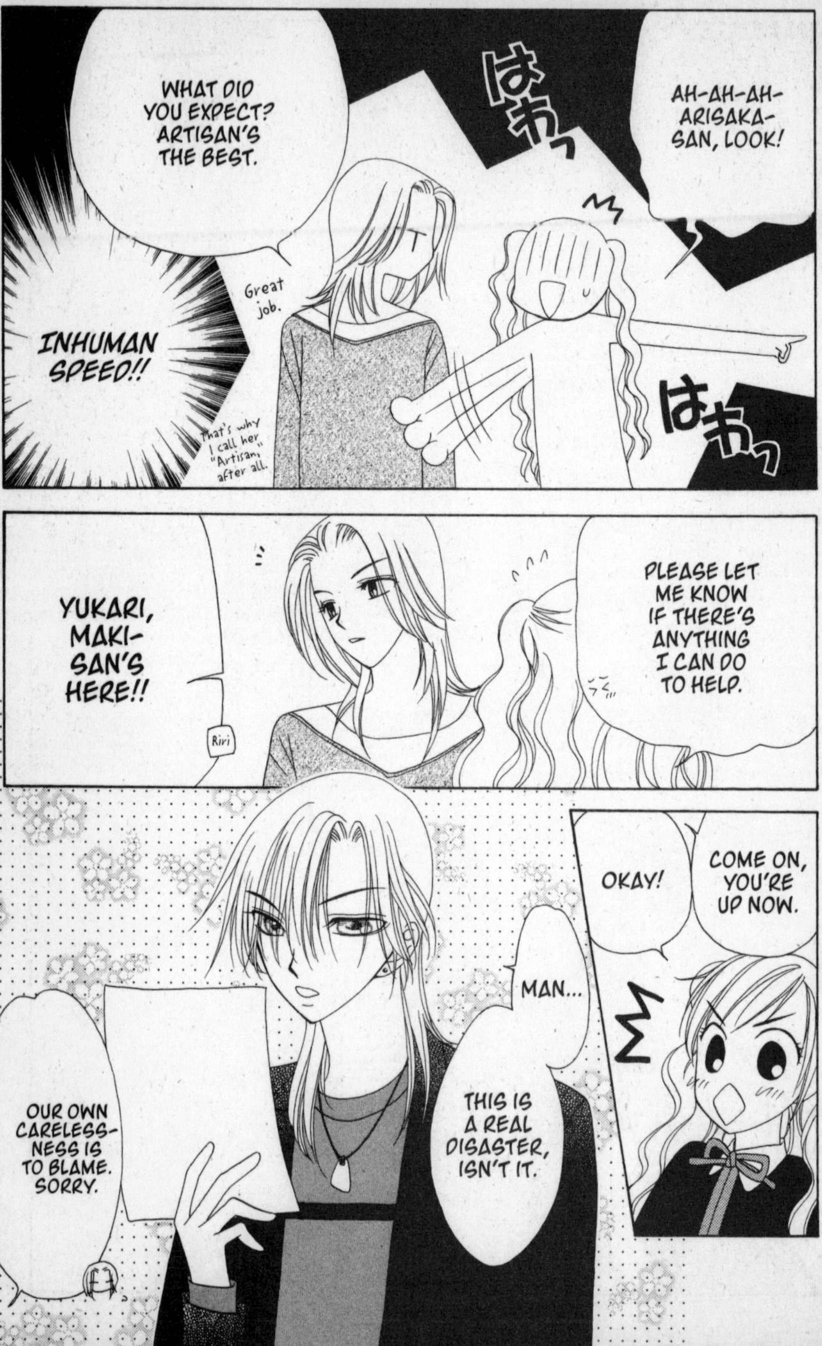

AH-AH-AH-ARISAKA-SAN, LOOK!
はわっ
はわっ
Great job.
WHAT DID YOU EXPECT? ARTISAN'S THE BEST.
INHUMAN SPEED!!
That's why I call her "Artisan," after all.
PLEASE LET ME KNOW IF THERE'S ANYTHING I CAN DO TO HELP.
YUKARI, MAKI-SAN'S HERE!!
Riri
COME ON, YOU'RE UP NOW.
OKAY!
MAN...
THIS IS A REAL DISASTER, ISN'T IT.
OUR OWN CARELESS-NESS IS TO BLAME. SORRY.

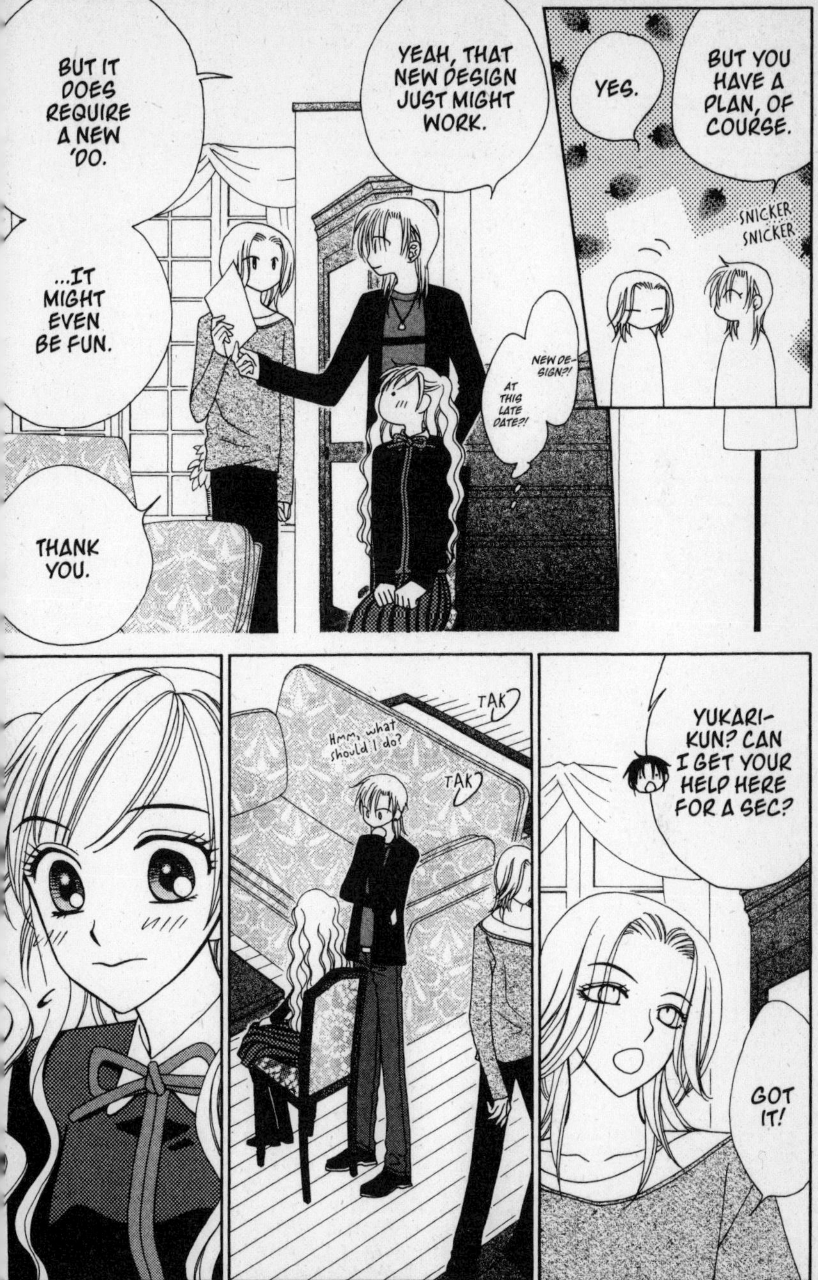
BUT YOU HAVE A PLAN, OF COURSE.
YES.
SNICKER SNICKER
YEAH, THAT NEW DESIGN JUST MIGHT WORK.
BUT IT DOES REQUIRE A NEW 'DO.
...IT MIGHT EVEN BE FUN.
NEW DESIGN?! AT THIS LATE DATE?!
THANK YOU.
YUKARI-KUN? CAN I GET YOUR HELP HERE FOR A SEC?
GOT IT!
TAK
TAK
Hmm, what should I do?

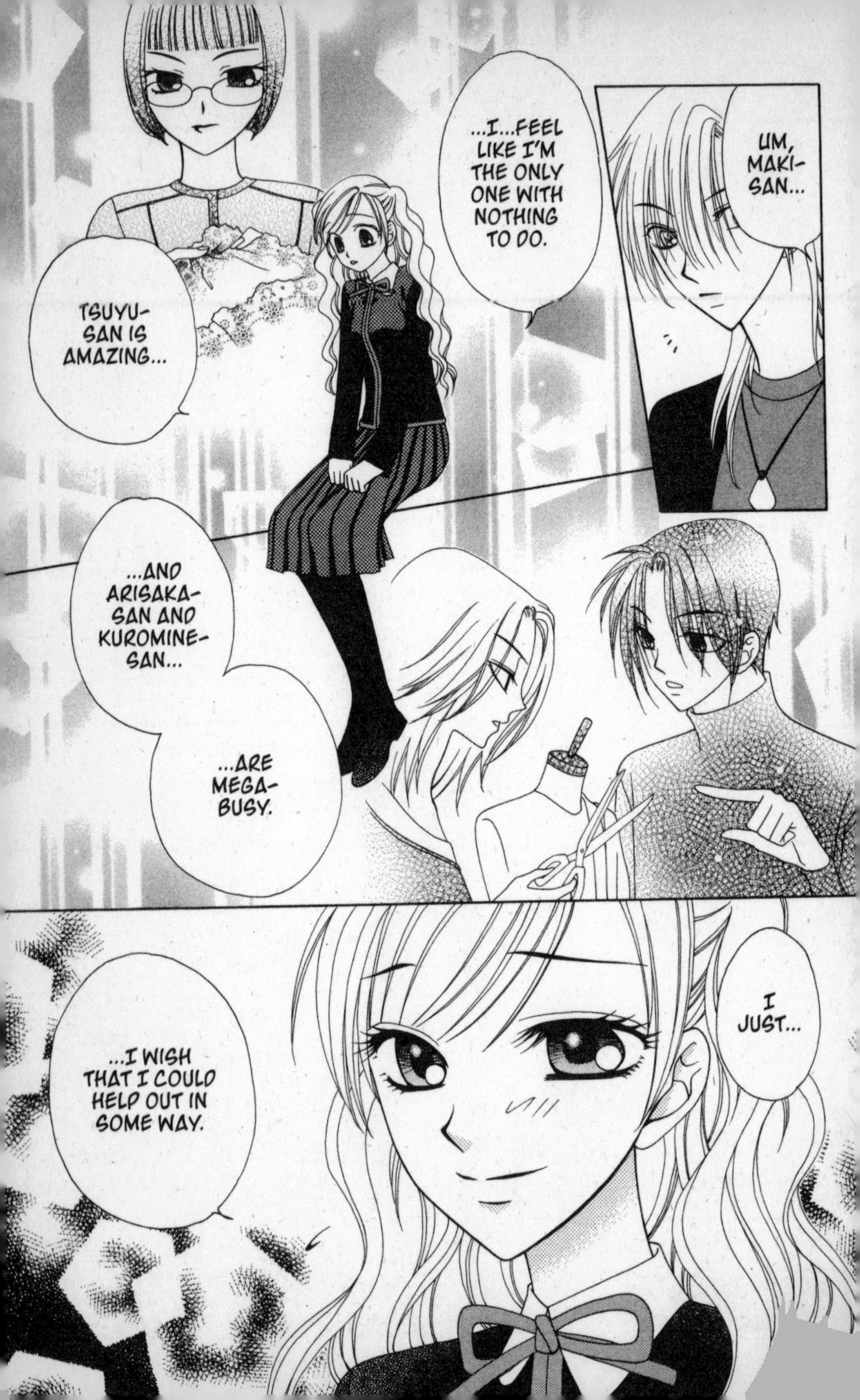
UM, MAKI-SAN...
...I...FEEL LIKE I'M THE ONLY ONE WITH NOTHING TO DO.
TSUYU-SAN IS AMAZING...
...AND ARISAKA-SAN AND KUROMINE-SAN...
...ARE MEGA-BUSY.
I JUST...
...I WISH THAT I COULD HELP OUT IN SOME WAY.

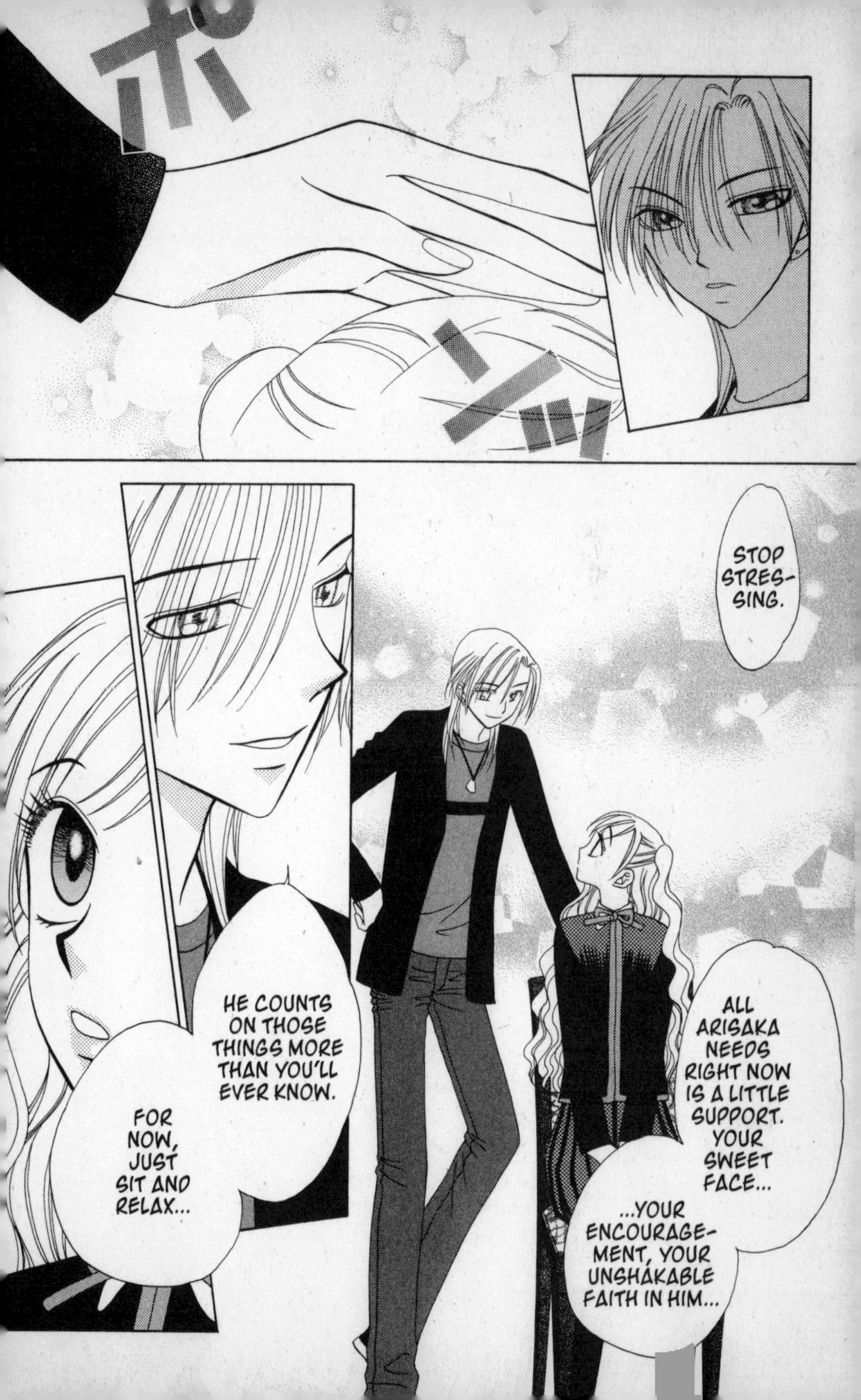
STOP STRES-SING.
ALL ARISAKA NEEDS RIGHT NOW IS A LITTLE SUPPORT. YOUR SWEET FACE...
...YOUR ENCOURAGE-MENT, YOUR UNSHAKABLE FAITH IN HIM...
HE COUNTS ON THOSE THINGS MORE THAN YOU'LL EVER KNOW.
FOR NOW, JUST SIT AND RELAX...

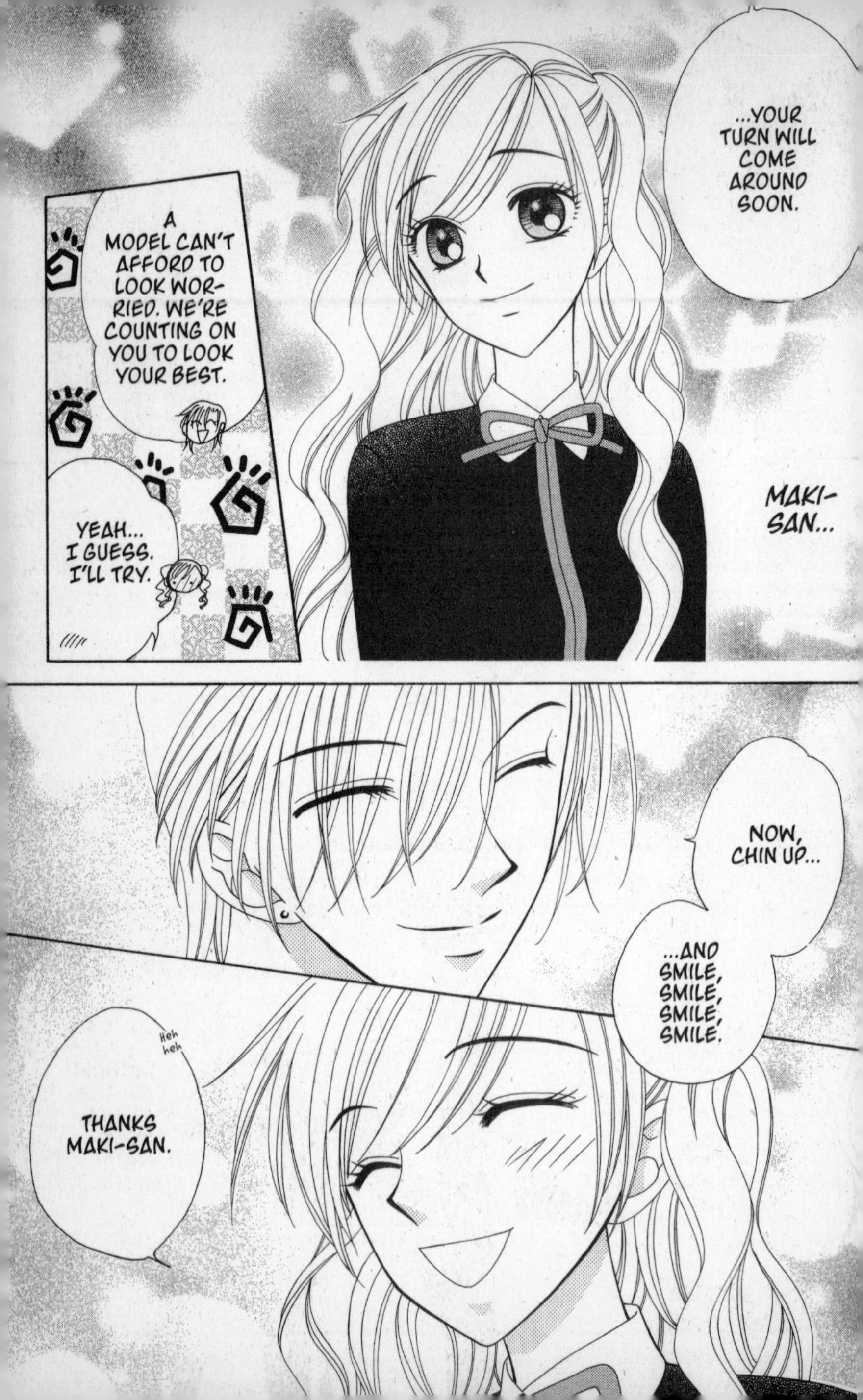
...YOUR TURN WILL COME AROUND SOON.
MAKI-SAN...
A MODEL CAN'T AFFORD TO LOOK WOR-RIED. WE'RE COUNTING ON YOU TO LOOK YOUR BEST.
YEAH... I GUESS. I'LL TRY.
NOW, CHIN UP...
...AND SMILE, SMILE, SMILE, SMILE.
Heh heh
THANKS MAKI-SAN.

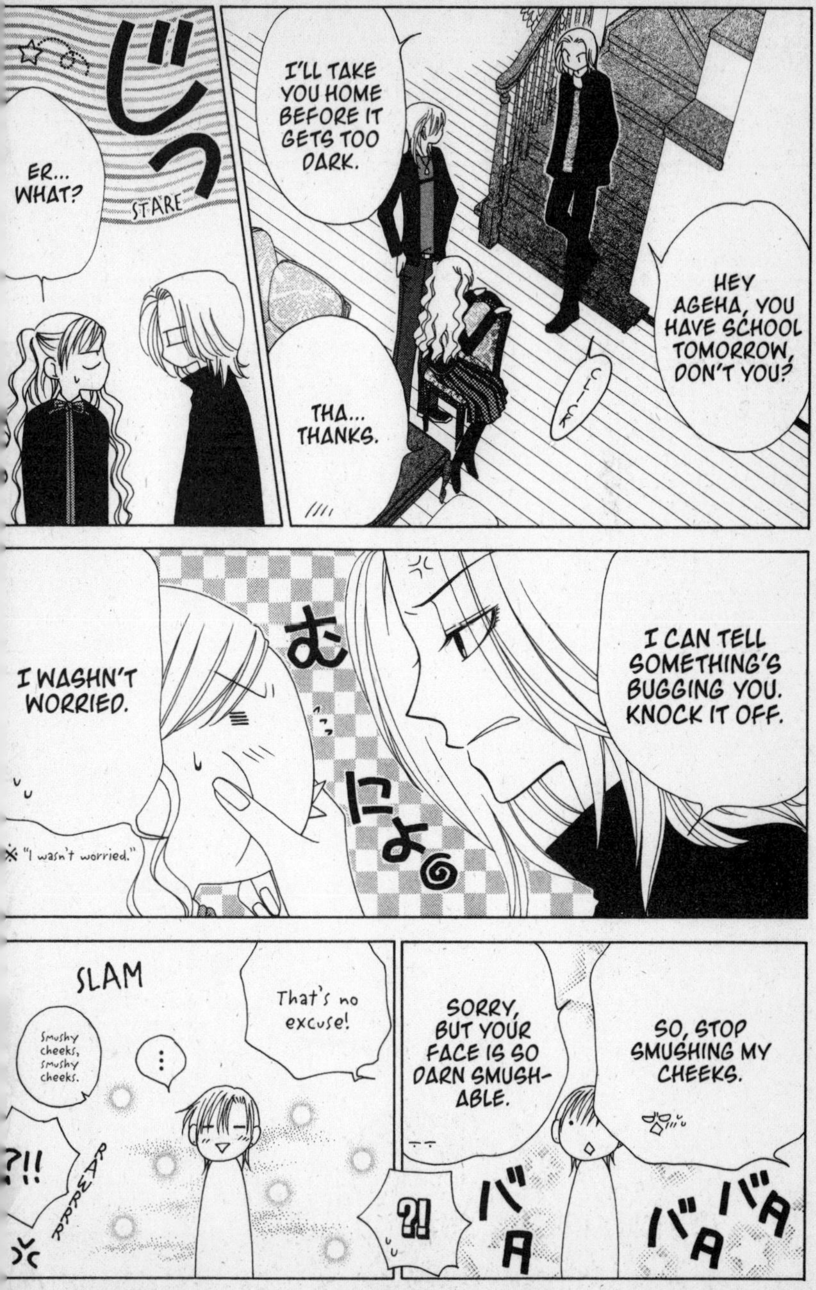
HEY AGEHA, YOU HAVE SCHOOL TOMORROW, DON'T YOU?
CLICK
I'LL TAKE YOU HOME BEFORE IT GETS TOO DARK.
THA... THANKS.
じっ
STARE
ER... WHAT?
I CAN TELL SOMETHING'S BUGGING YOU. KNOCK IT OFF.
むにょ
I WASHN'T WORRIED.
※ "I wasn't worried."
SO, STOP SMUSHING MY CHEEKS.
バババ
SORRY, BUT YOUR FACE IS SO DARN SMUSH-ABLE.
?!
That's no excuse!
...
Smushy cheeks, smushy cheeks.
SLAM
?!!
RAWRRRR

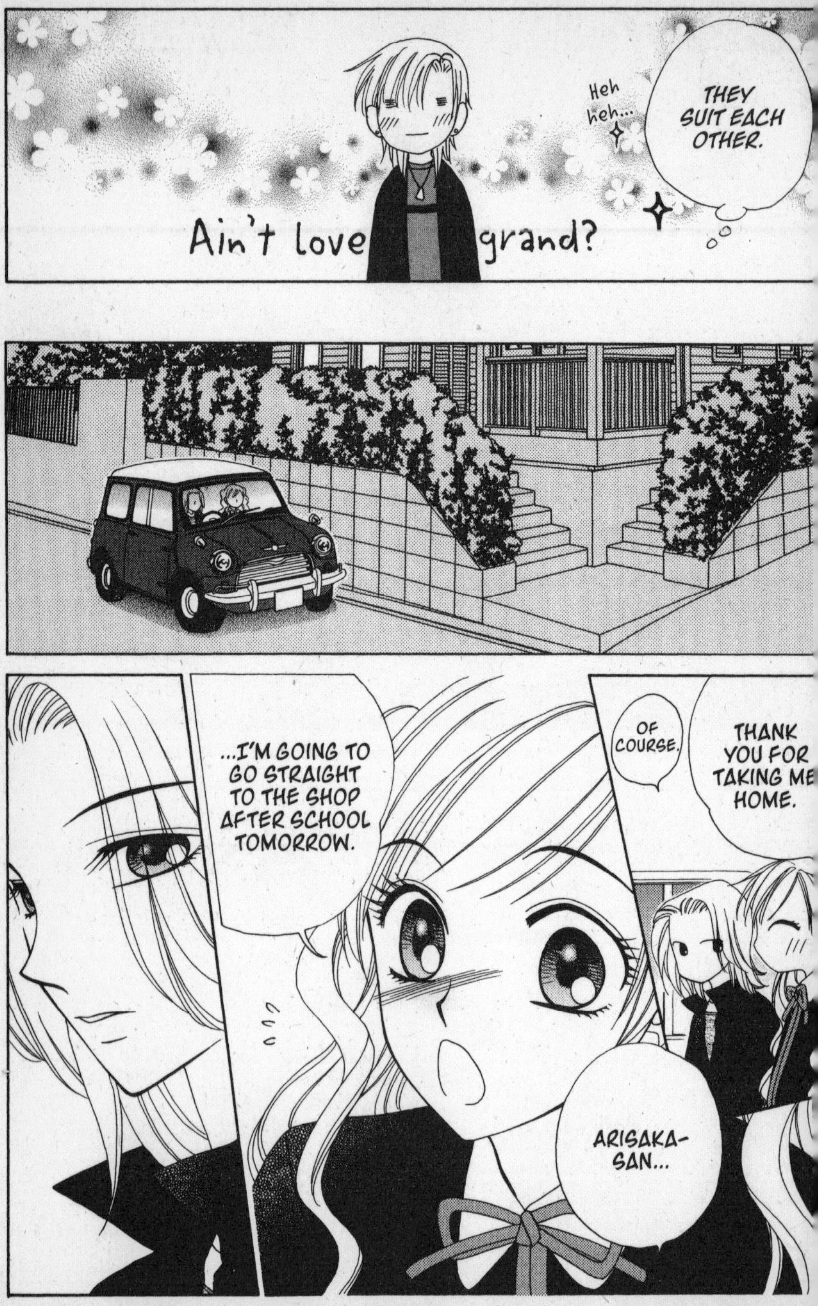
THEY SUIT EACH OTHER.
Heh heh...
Ain't love grand?
THANK YOU FOR TAKING ME HOME.
OF COURSE.
ARISAKA-SAN...
...I'M GOING TO GO STRAIGHT TO THE SHOP AFTER SCHOOL TOMORROW.

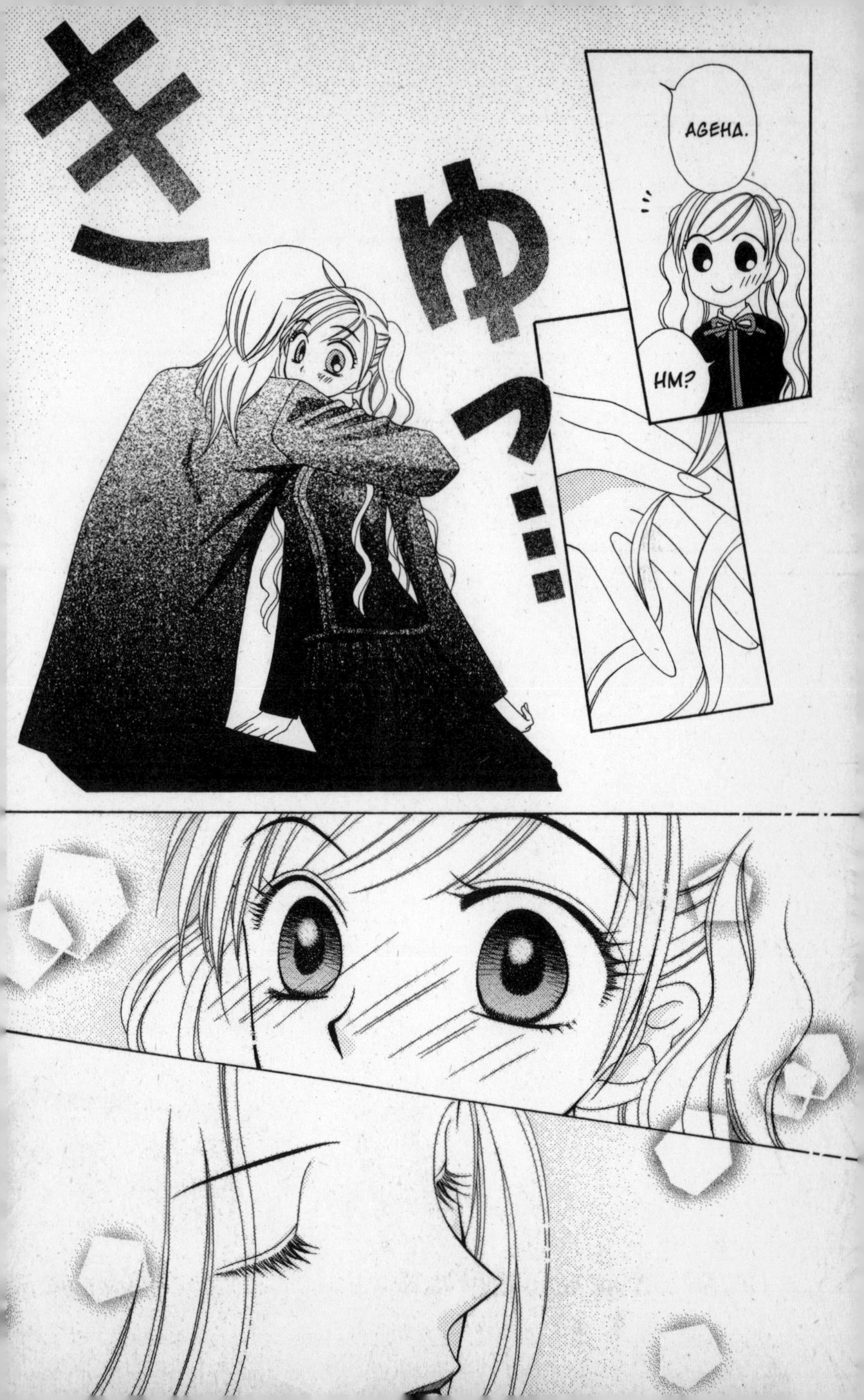
AGEHA.
HM?
きゅっ…

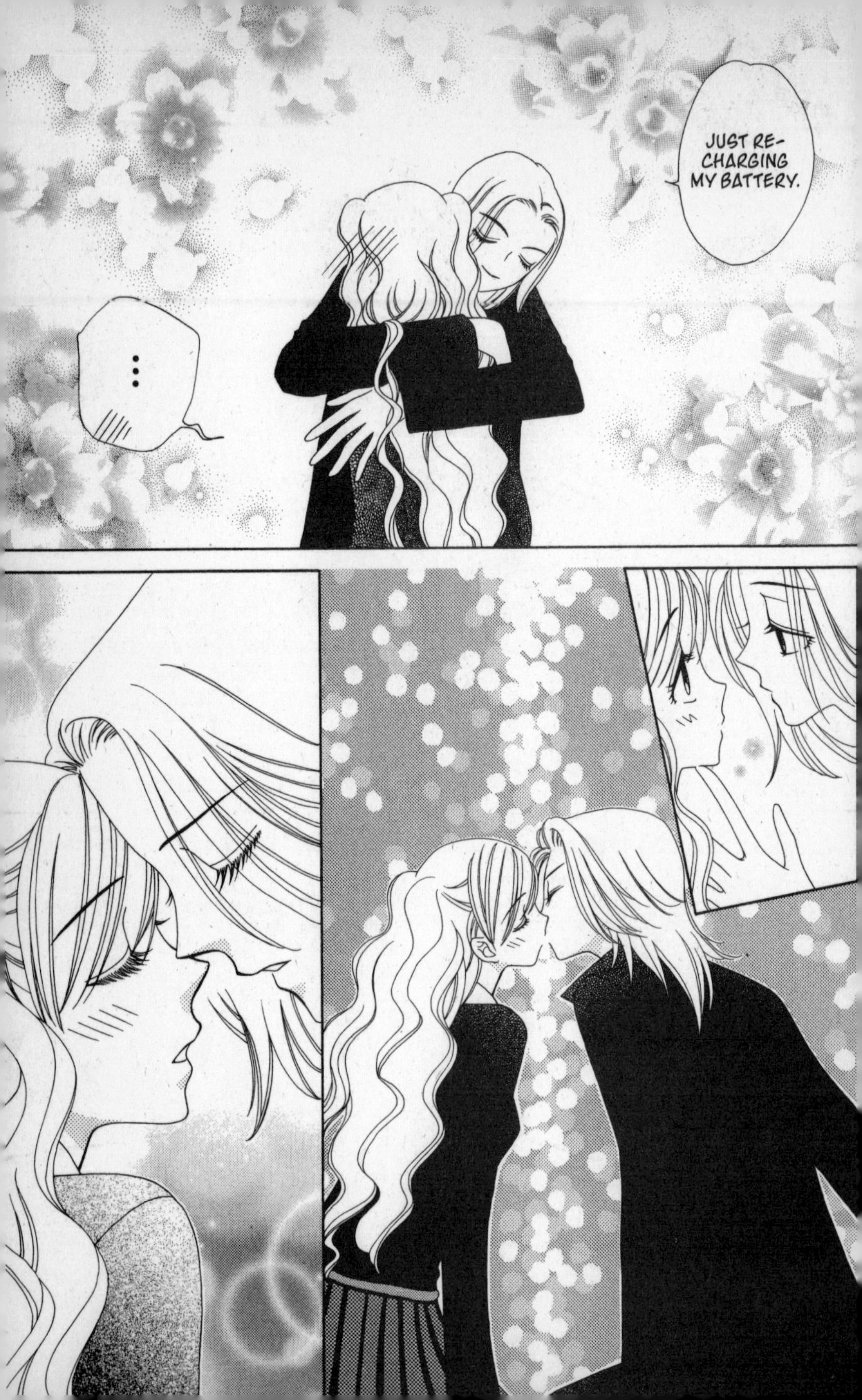
JUST RE-CHARGING MY BATTERY.
...

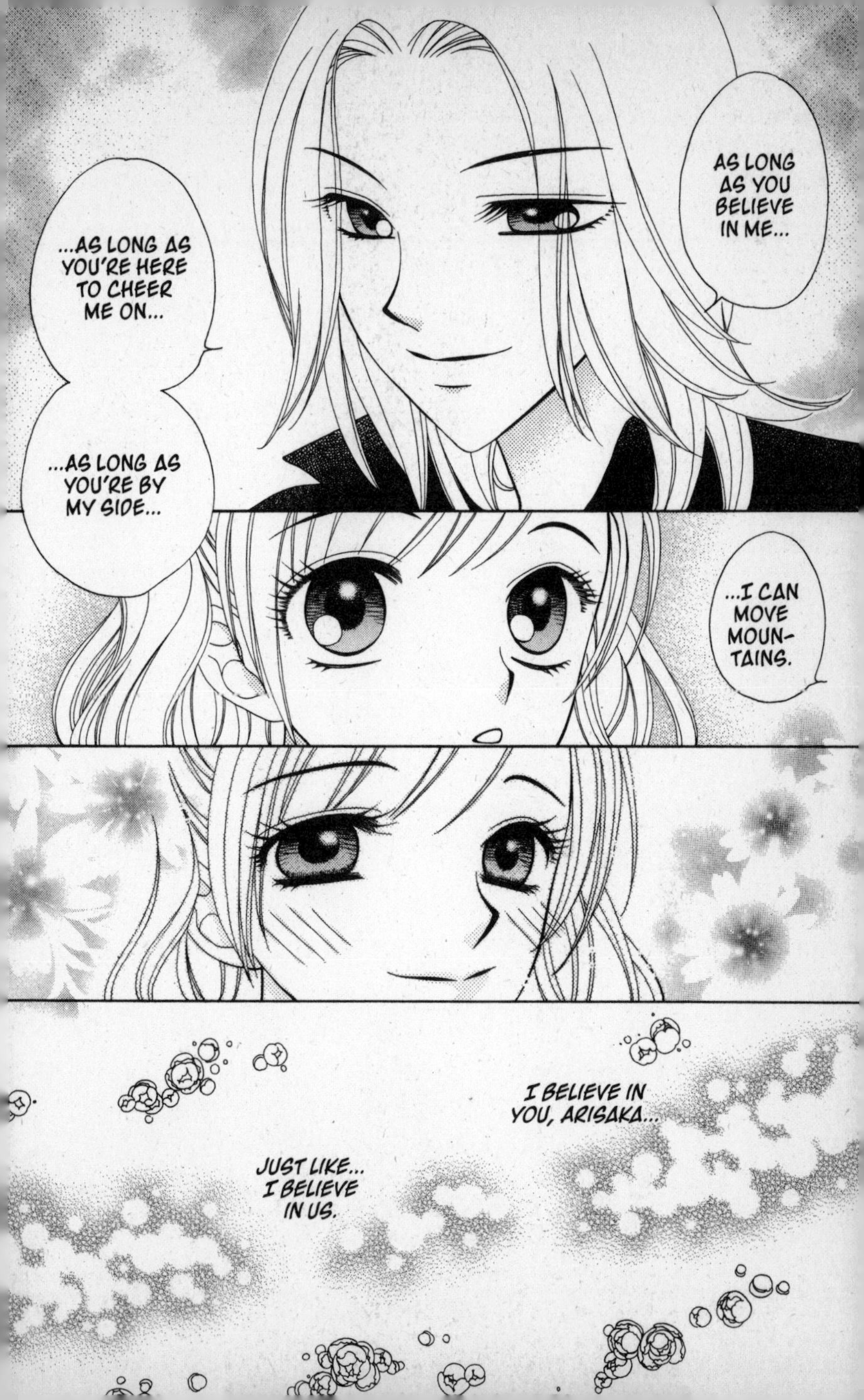
AS LONG AS YOU BELIEVE IN ME...
...AS LONG AS YOU'RE HERE TO CHEER ME ON...
...AS LONG AS YOU'RE BY MY SIDE...
...I CAN MOVE MOUN-TAINS.
I BELIEVE IN YOU, ARISAKA...
JUST LIKE... I BELIEVE IN US.

Episode 50

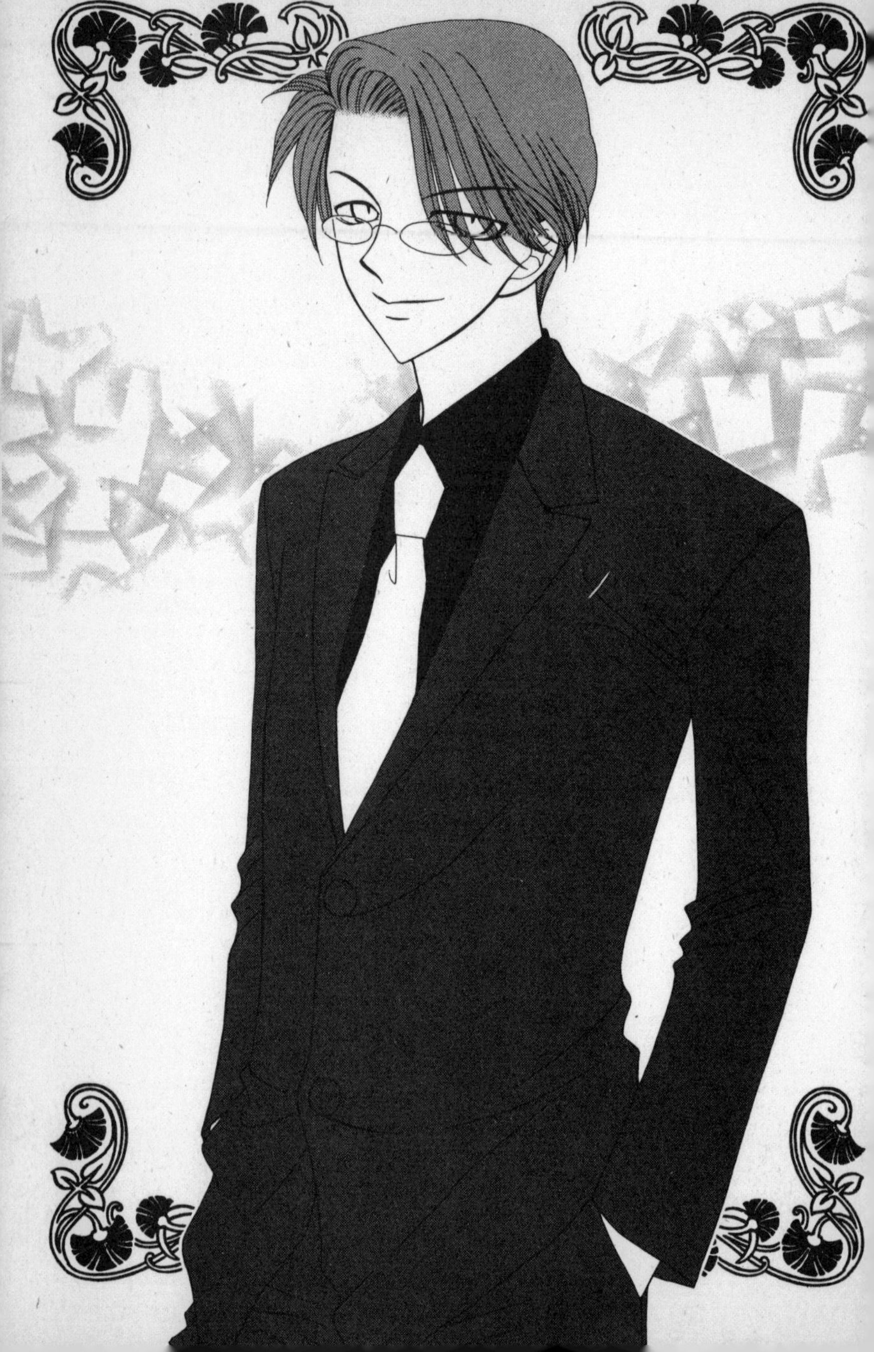

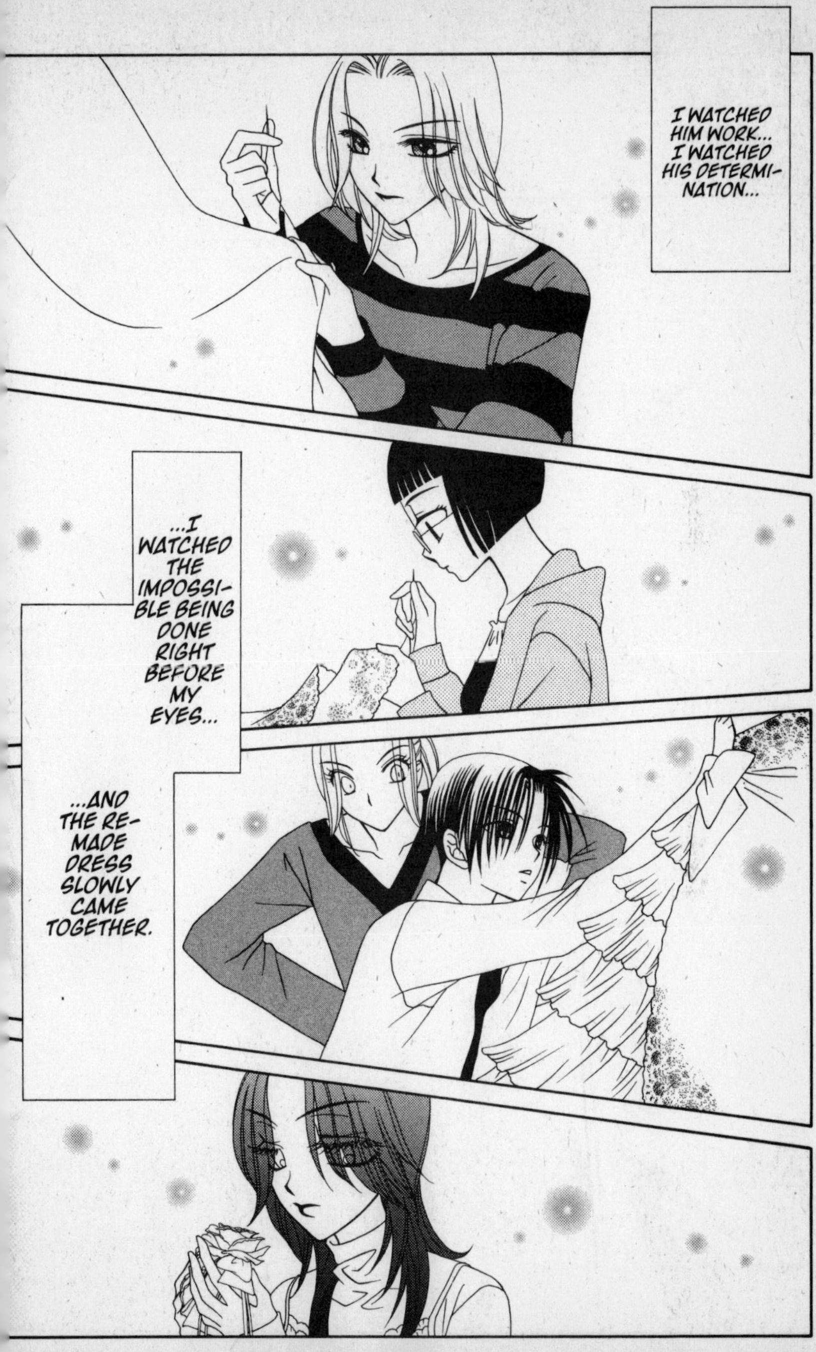
I WATCHED HIM WORK... I WATCHED HIS DETERMINATION...
...I WATCHED THE IMPOSSIBLE BEING DONE RIGHT BEFORE MY EYES...
...AND THE REMADE DRESS SLOWLY CAME TOGETHER.

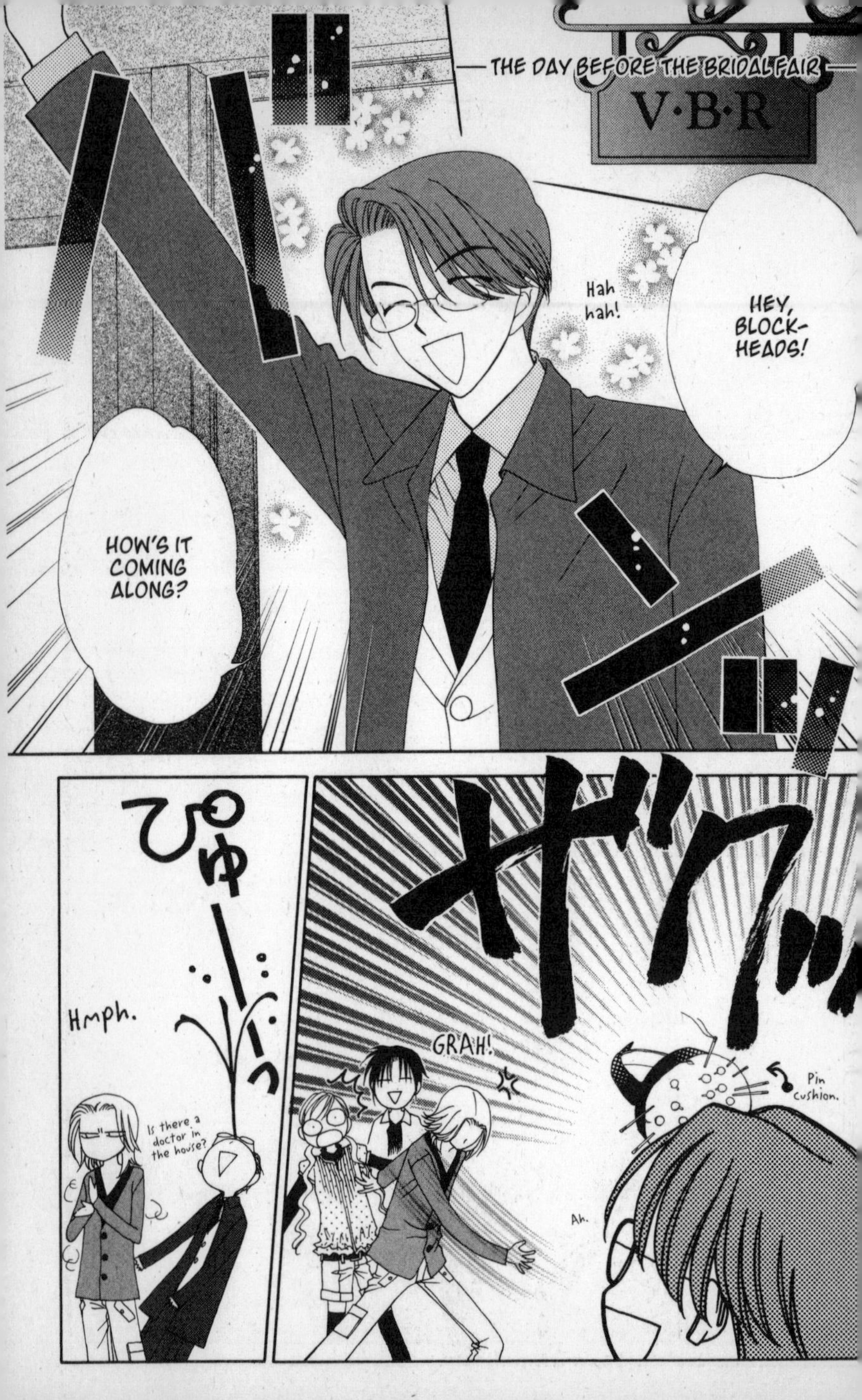
—THE DAY BEFORE THE BRIDAL FAIR—
V·B·R
HEY, BLOCK-HEADS!
Hah hah!
HOW'S IT COMING ALONG?
ザァ…
Pin cushion.
GRAH!
Ah.
ぴゅーーっ
Hmph.
Is there a doctor in the house?

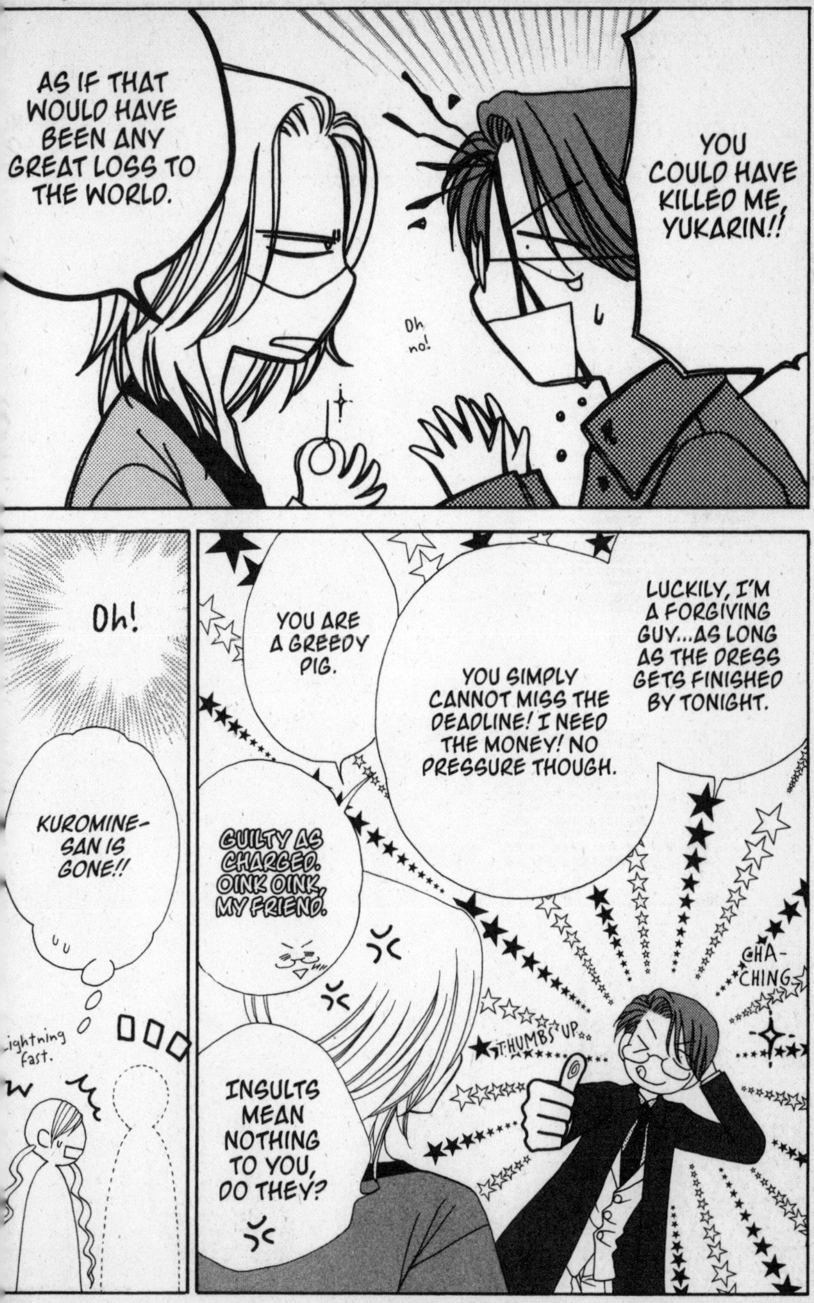
YOU COULD HAVE KILLED ME, YUKARIN!!
Oh no!
AS IF THAT WOULD HAVE BEEN ANY GREAT LOSS TO THE WORLD.
LUCKILY, I'M A FORGIVING GUY...AS LONG AS THE DRESS GETS FINISHED BY TONIGHT.
YOU SIMPLY CANNOT MISS THE DEADLINE! I NEED THE MONEY! NO PRESSURE THOUGH.
YOU ARE A GREEDY PIG.
GUILTY AS CHARGED. OINK OINK, MY FRIEND.
CHA-CHING
THUMBS UP
INSULTS MEAN NOTHING TO YOU, DO THEY?
Oh!
KUROMINE-SAN IS GONE!!
Lightning Fast.

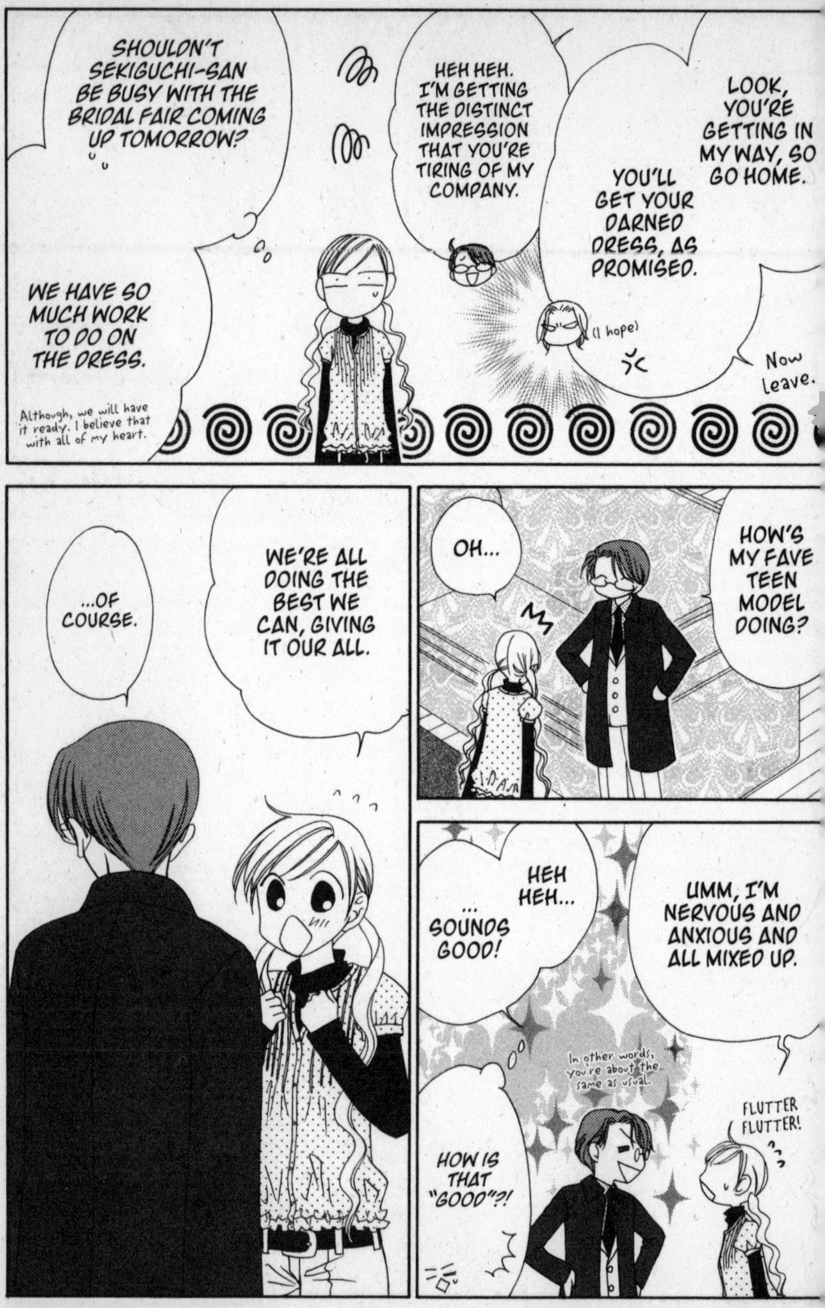
LOOK, YOU'RE GETTING IN MY WAY, SO GO HOME.
YOU'LL GET YOUR DARNED DRESS, AS PROMISED.
(I hope)
Now leave.
HEH HEH. I'M GETTING THE DISTINCT IMPRESSION THAT YOU'RE TIRING OF MY COMPANY.
SHOULDN'T SEKIGUCHI-SAN BE BUSY WITH THE BRIDAL FAIR COMING UP TOMORROW?
WE HAVE SO MUCH WORK TO DO ON THE DRESS.
Although, we will have it ready. I believe that with all of my heart.
HOW'S MY FAVE TEEN MODEL DOING?
OH...
UMM, I'M NERVOUS AND ANXIOUS AND ALL MIXED UP.
HEH HEH...
...SOUNDS GOOD!
In other words, you're about the same as usual.
FLUTTER FLUTTER!
HOW IS THAT "GOOD"?!
WE'RE ALL DOING THE BEST WE CAN, GIVING IT OUR ALL.
...OF COURSE.

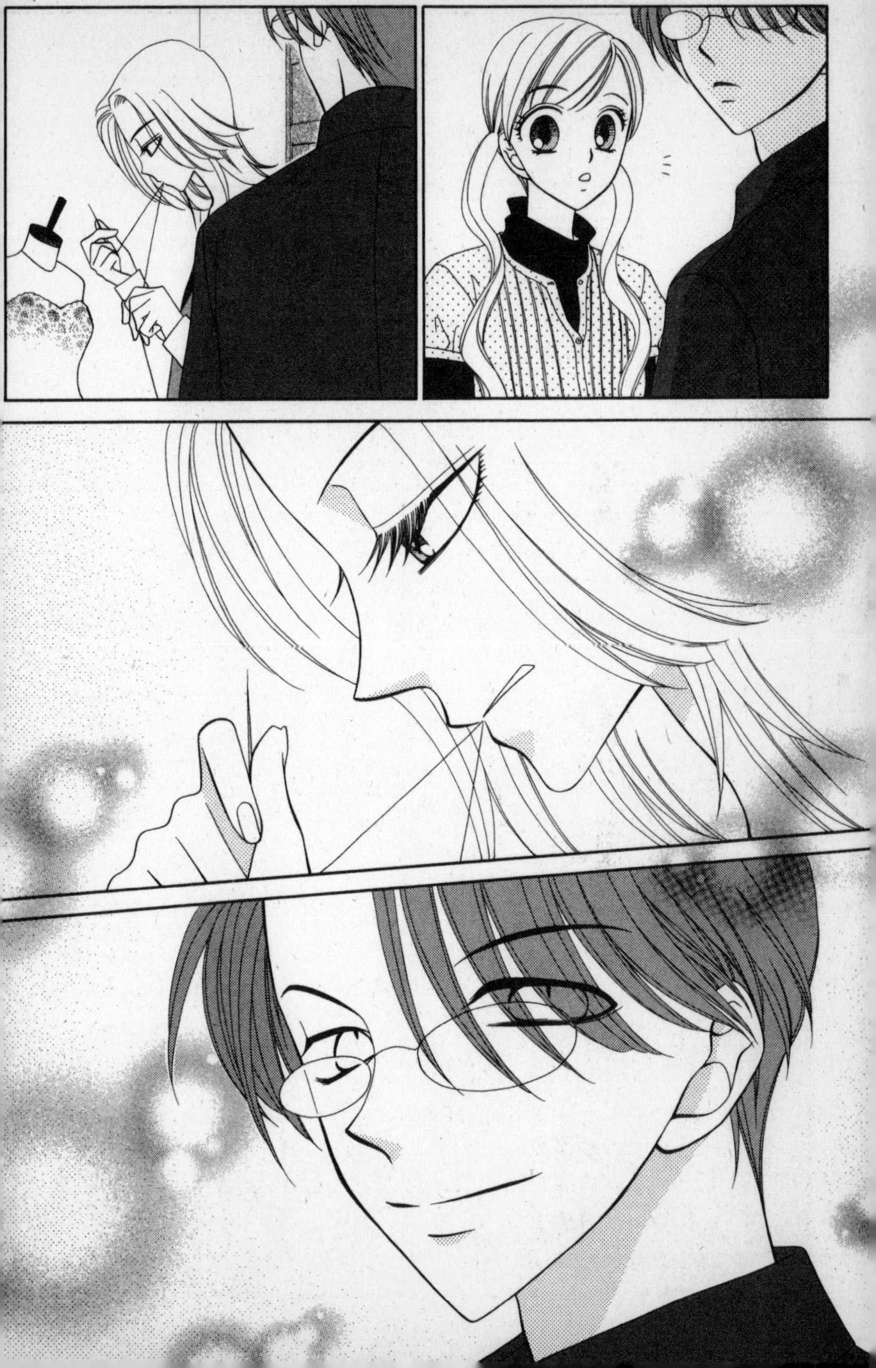

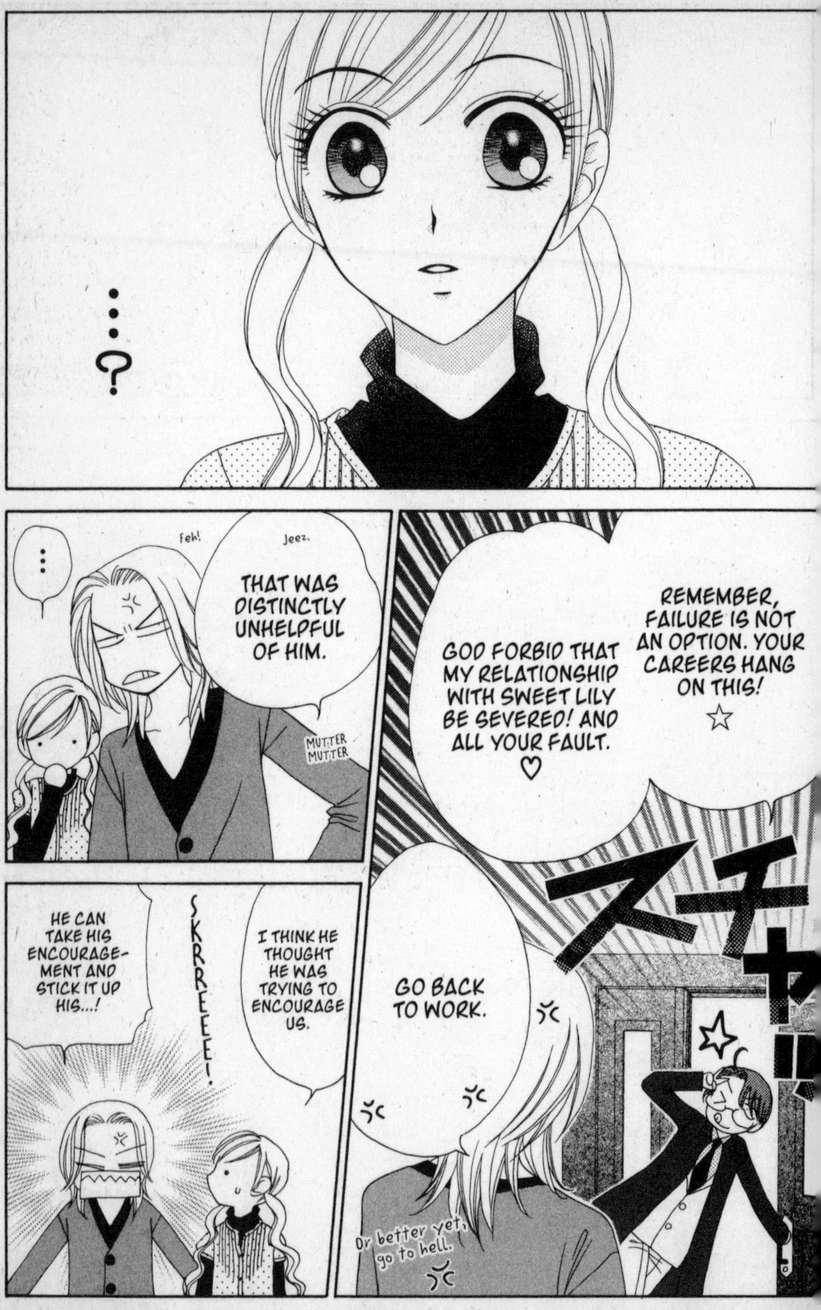
…?
REMEMBER, FAILURE IS NOT AN OPTION. YOUR CAREERS HANG ON THIS! ☆
GOD FORBID THAT MY RELATIONSHIP WITH SWEET LILY BE SEVERED! AND ALL YOUR FAULT. ♡
スチャ
GO BACK TO WORK.
Or better yet, go to hell.
Jeez.
THAT WAS DISTINCTLY UNHELPFUL OF HIM.
Feh!
…
MUTTER MUTTER
I THINK HE THOUGHT HE WAS TRYING TO ENCOURAGE US.
SKRREEEE!
HE CAN TAKE HIS ENCOURAGE-MENT AND STICK IT UP HIS...!

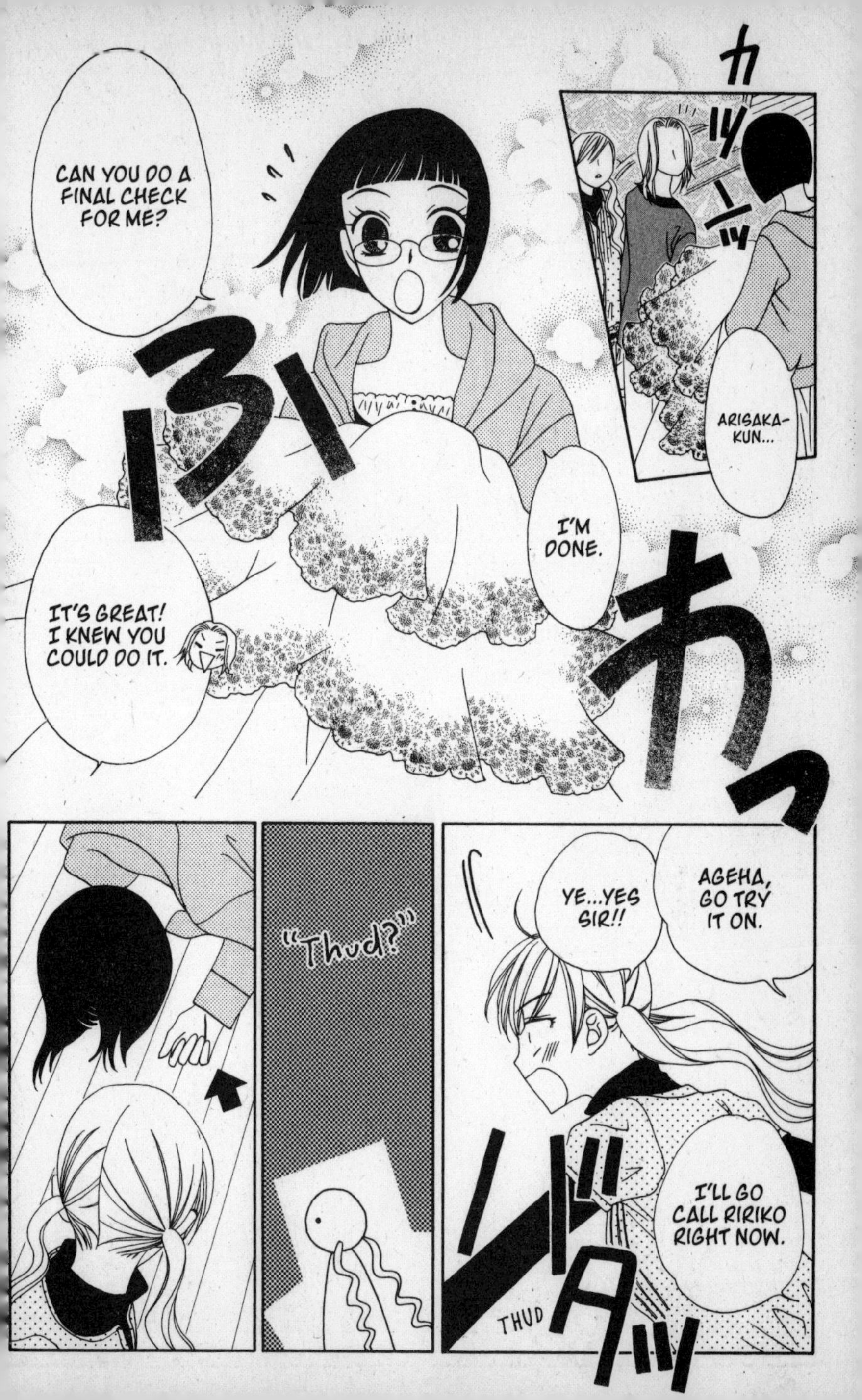
ARISAKA-KUN...
I'M DONE.
CAN YOU DO A FINAL CHECK FOR ME?
IT'S GREAT! I KNEW YOU COULD DO IT.
AGEHA, GO TRY IT ON.
YE...YES SIR!!
I'LL GO CALL RIRIKO RIGHT NOW.
THUD
"Thud?"

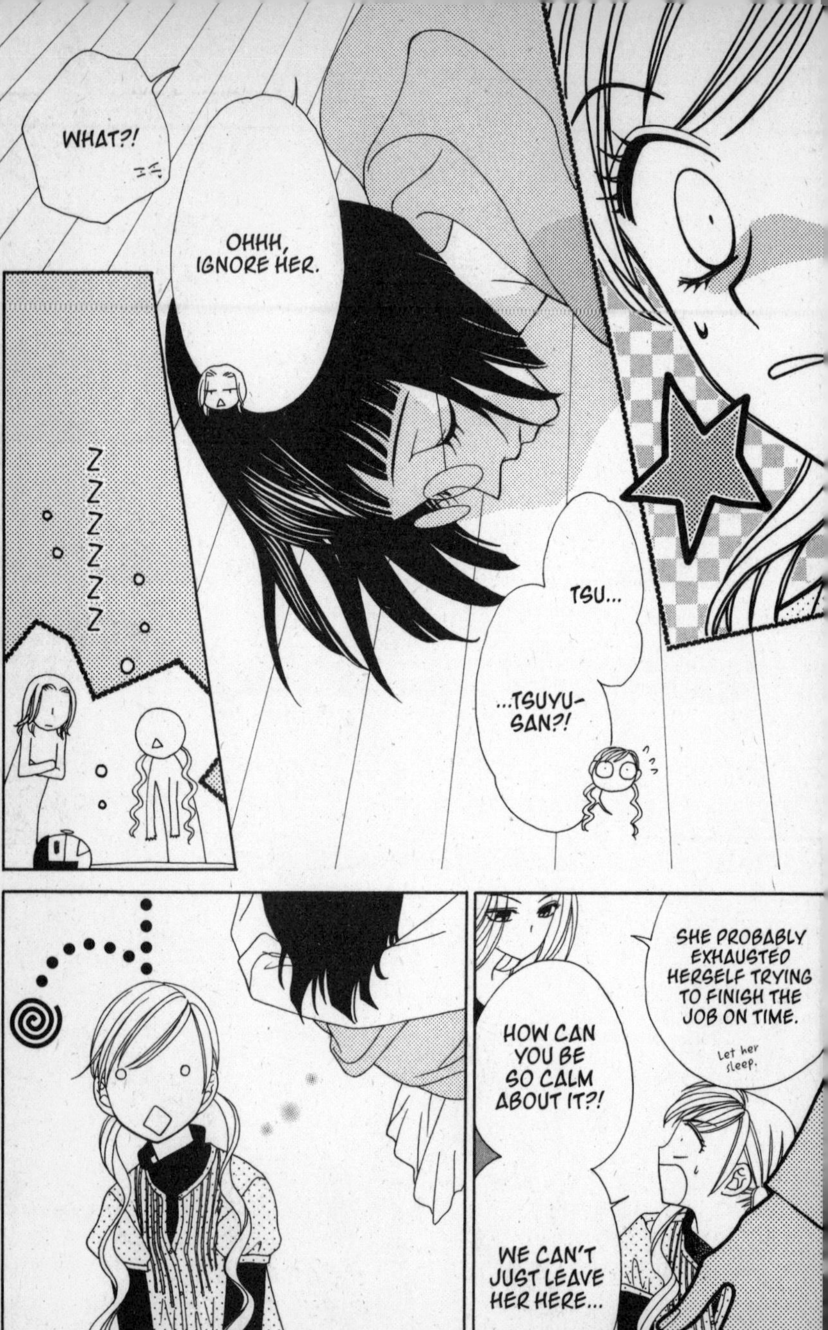
WHAT?!
OHHH, IGNORE HER.
TSU...
...TSUYU-SAN?!
ZZZZZZ
SHE PROBABLY EXHAUSTED HERSELF TRYING TO FINISH THE JOB ON TIME.
Let her sleep.
HOW CAN YOU BE SO CALM ABOUT IT?!
WE CAN'T JUST LEAVE HER HERE...

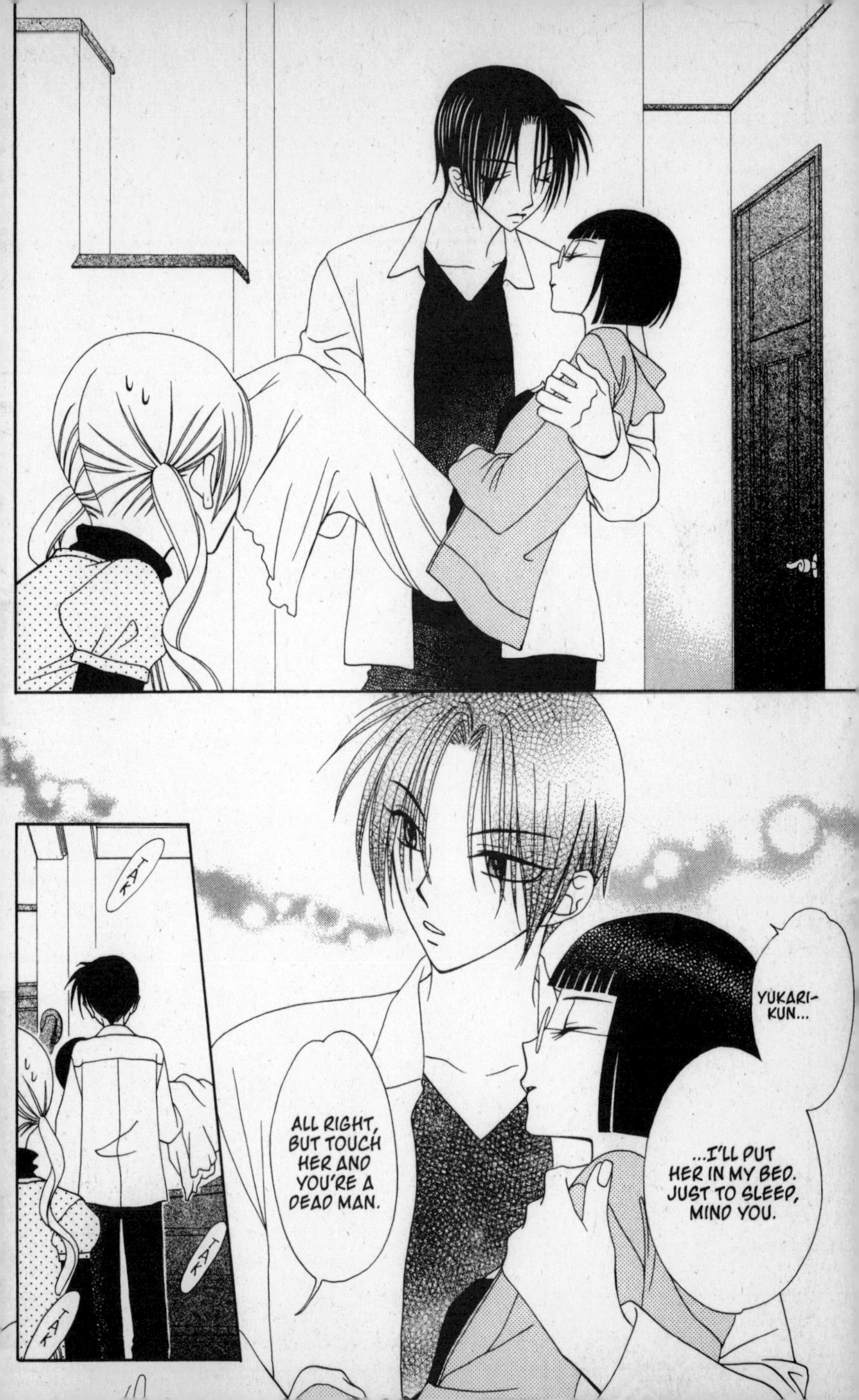
YUKARI-KUN...
...I'LL PUT HER IN MY BED. JUST TO SLEEP, MIND YOU.
ALL RIGHT, BUT TOUCH HER AND YOU'RE A DEAD MAN.
TAK
TAK
TAK

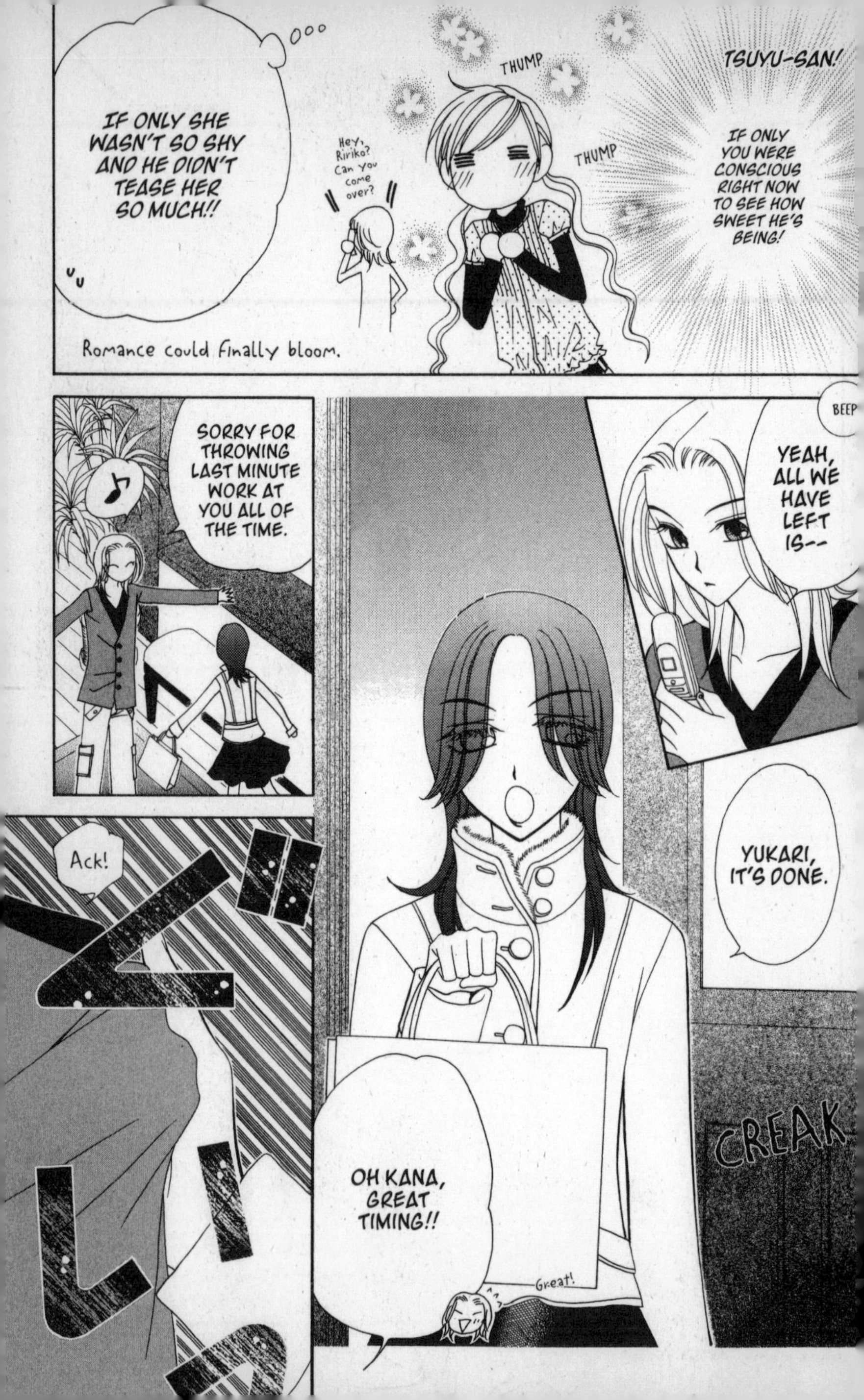
TSUYU-SAN!
IF ONLY YOU WERE CONSCIOUS RIGHT NOW TO SEE HOW SWEET HE'S BEING!
THUMP
THUMP
Hey, Ririko? Can you come over?
IF ONLY SHE WASN'T SO SHY AND HE DIDN'T TEASE HER SO MUCH!!
Romance could finally bloom.
BEEP
YEAH, ALL WE HAVE LEFT IS--
YUKARI, IT'S DONE.
CREAK
OH KANA, GREAT TIMING!!
Great!
SORRY FOR THROWING LAST MINUTE WORK AT YOU ALL OF THE TIME.
Ack!

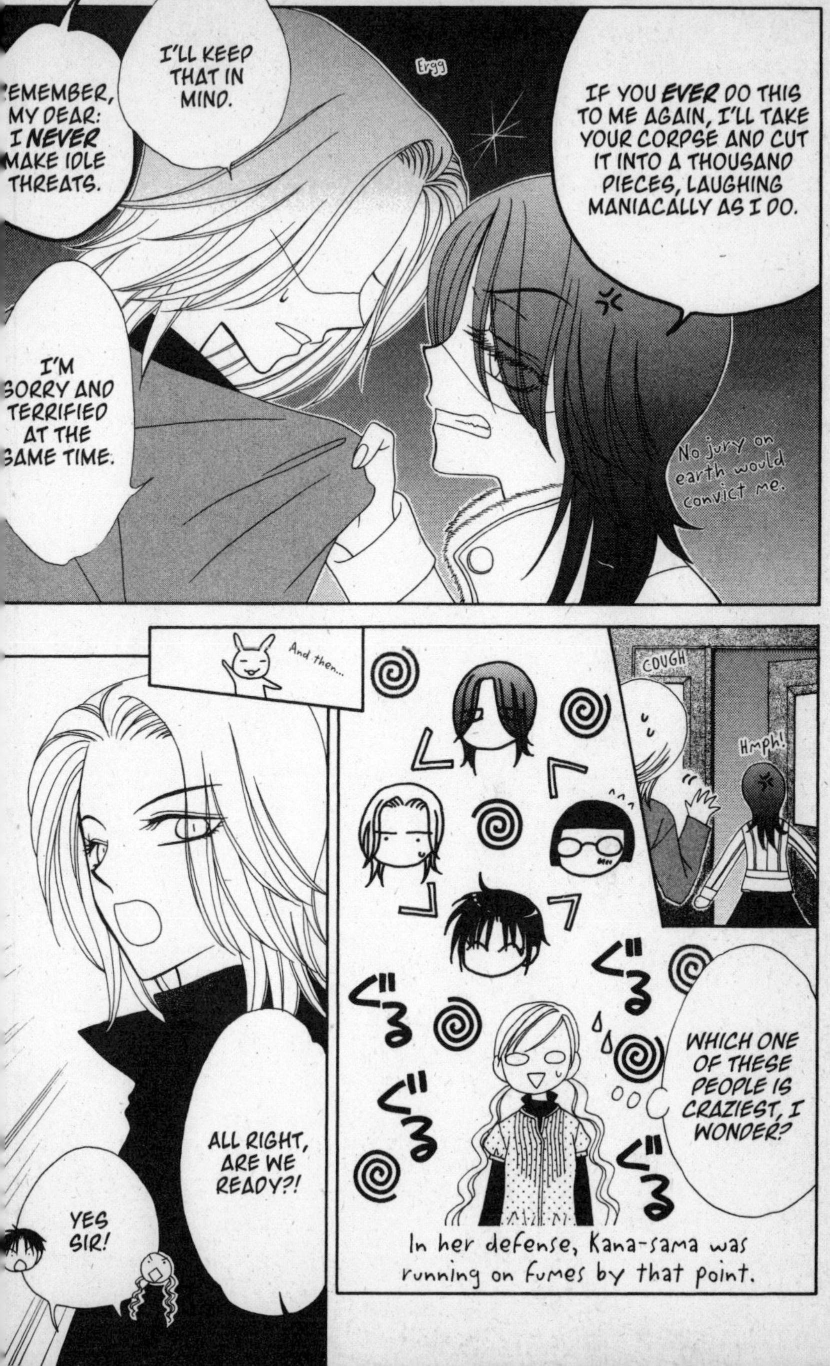
IF YOU EVER DO THIS TO ME AGAIN, I'LL TAKE YOUR CORPSE AND CUT IT INTO A THOUSAND PIECES, LAUGHING MANIACALLY AS I DO.
Ergg
I'LL KEEP THAT IN MIND.
REMEMBER, MY DEAR: I NEVER MAKE IDLE THREATS.
No jury on earth would convict me.
I'M SORRY AND TERRIFIED AT THE SAME TIME.
COUGH
Hmph!
ぐる
ぐる
ぐる
ぐる
ぐる
WHICH ONE OF THESE PEOPLE IS CRAZIEST, I WONDER?
In her defense, Kana-sama was running on fumes by that point.
And then...
ALL RIGHT, ARE WE READY?!
YES SIR!

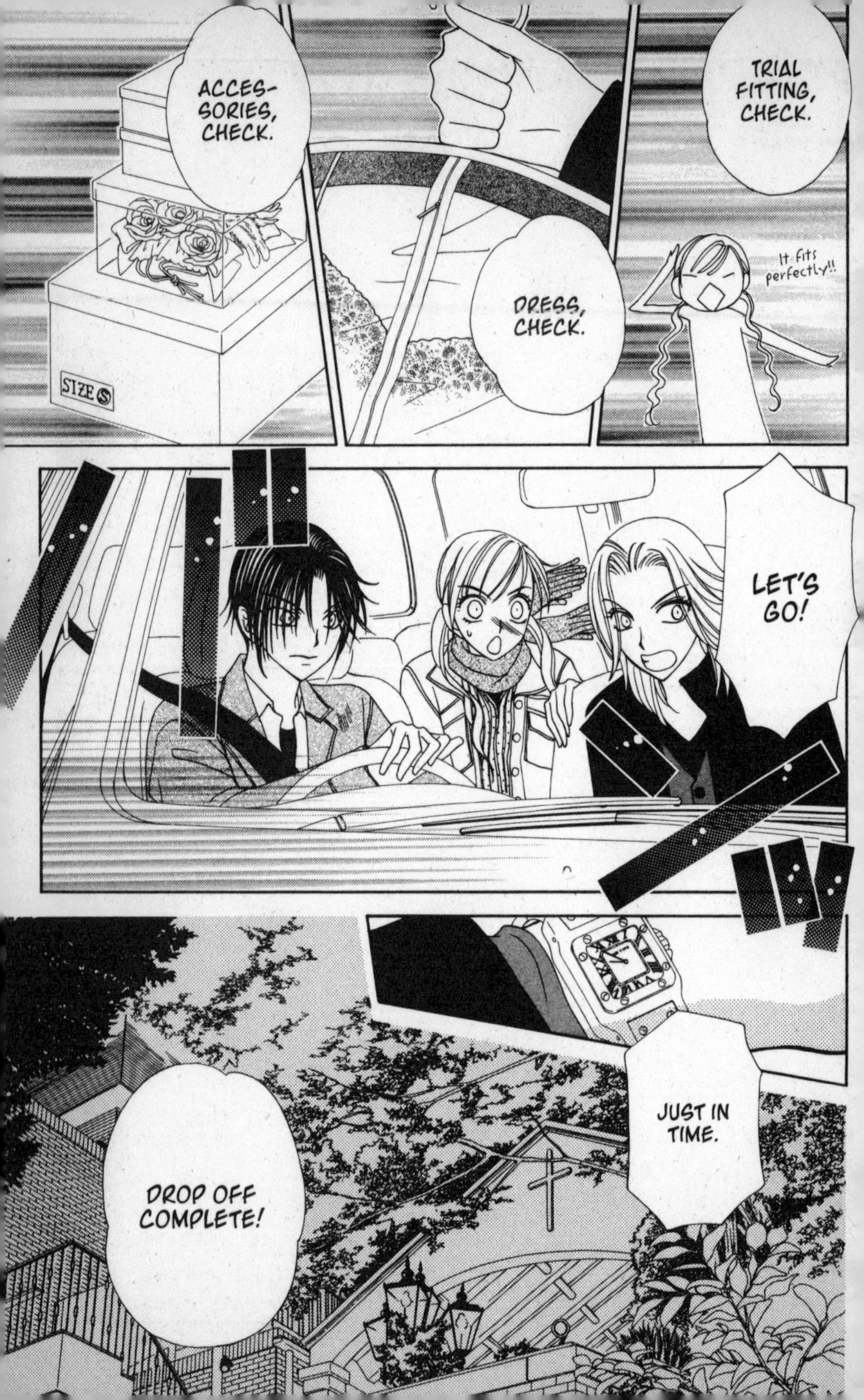
TRIAL FITTING, CHECK.
It fits perfectly!!
DRESS, CHECK.
ACCES-SORIES, CHECK.
SIZE S
LET'S GO!
JUST IN TIME.
DROP OFF COMPLETE!

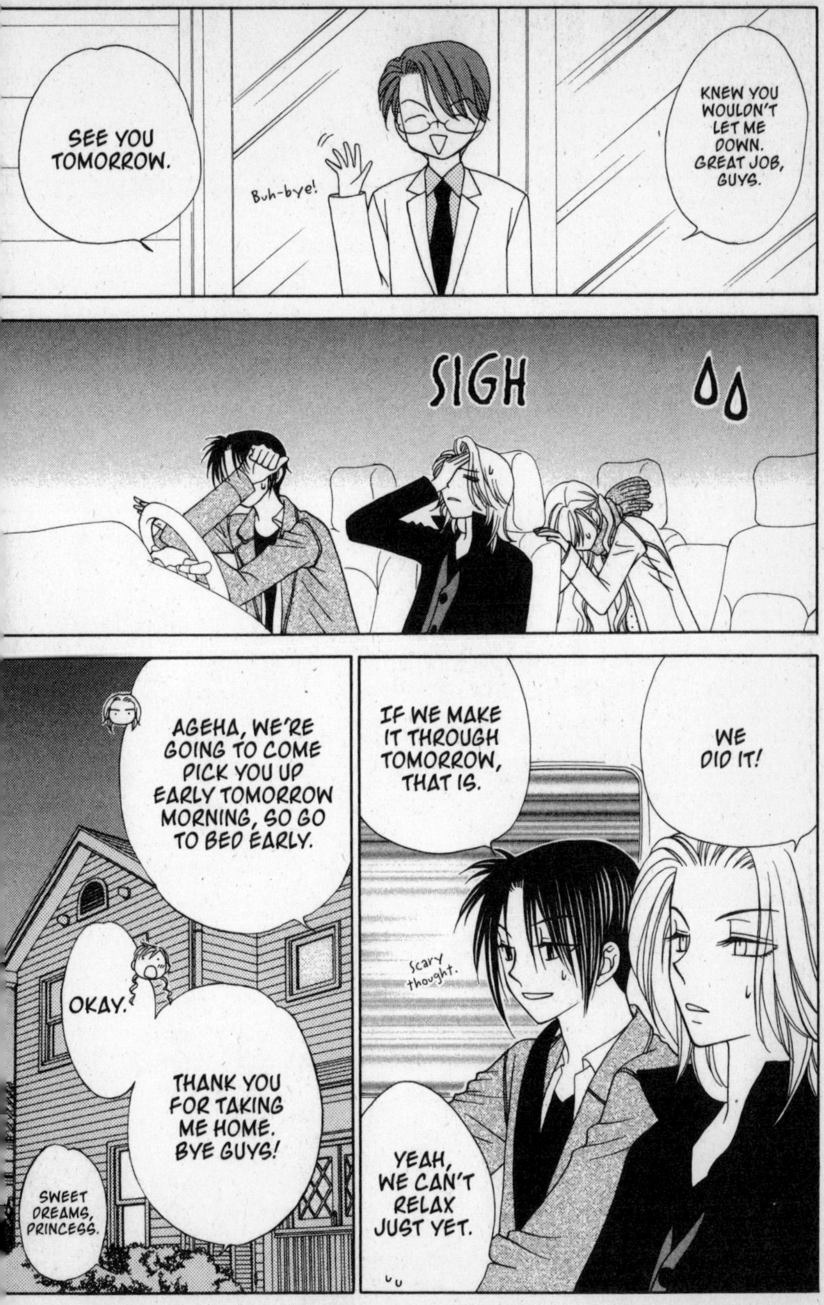
KNEW YOU WOULDN'T LET ME DOWN. GREAT JOB, GUYS.
Buh-bye!
SEE YOU TOMORROW.
SIGH
WE DID IT!
IF WE MAKE IT THROUGH TOMORROW, THAT IS.
Scary thought.
YEAH, WE CAN'T RELAX JUST YET.
AGEHA, WE'RE GOING TO COME PICK YOU UP EARLY TOMORROW MORNING, SO GO TO BED EARLY.
OKAY.
THANK YOU FOR TAKING ME HOME. BYE GUYS!
SWEET DREAMS, PRINCESS.

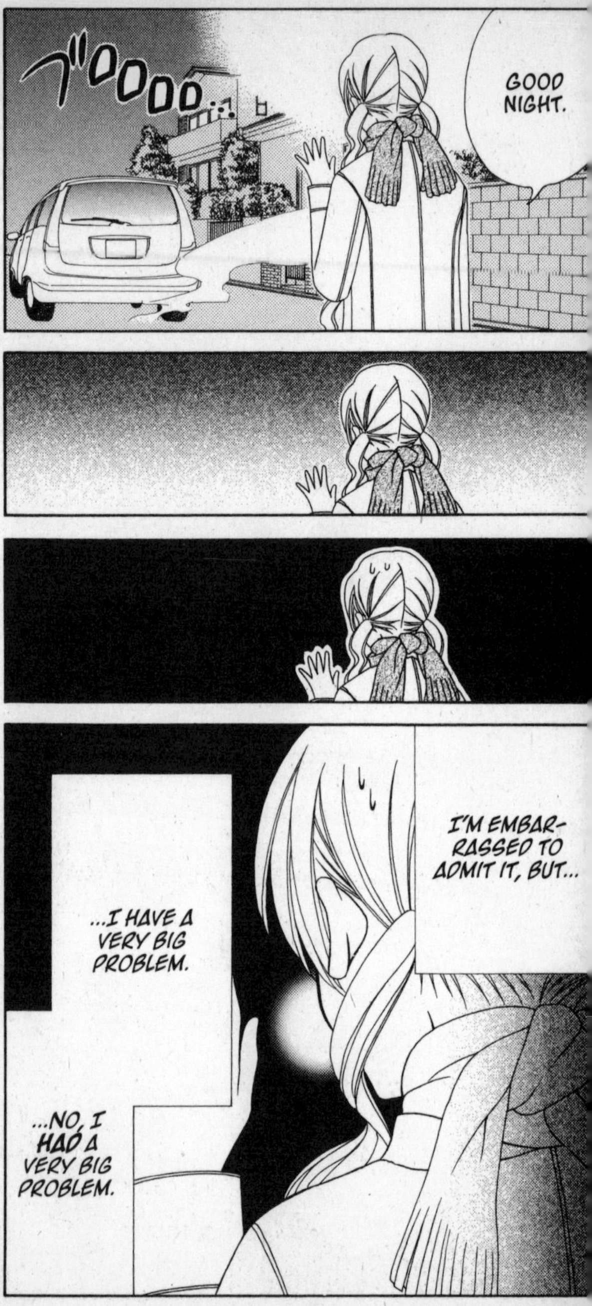
GOOD NIGHT.
I'M EMBAR-RASSED TO ADMIT IT, BUT...
...I HAVE A VERY BIG PROBLEM.
...NO, I HAD A VERY BIG PROBLEM.

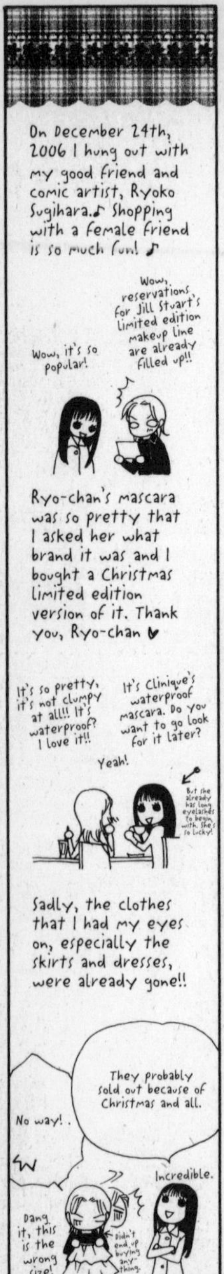
On December 24th, 2006 I hung out with my good friend and comic artist, Ryoko Sugihara.♪ Shopping with a female friend is so much fun! ♪
Wow, reservations for Jill Stuart's limited edition makeup line are already filled up!!
Wow, it's so popular!
Ryo-chan's mascara was so pretty that I asked her what brand it was and I bought a Christmas limited edition version of it. Thank you, Ryo-chan ♥
It's Clinique's waterproof mascara. Do you want to go look for it later?
It's so pretty, it's not clumpy at all!! It's waterproof? I love it!!
Yeah!
But she already has long eyelashes to begin with. She's so lucky!
Sadly, the clothes that I had my eyes on, especially the skirts and dresses, were already gone!!
They probably sold out because of Christmas and all.
No way!
Incredible.
Didn't end up buying anything.
Dang it, this is the wrong size!
The after-Christmas shoppers all seemed so happy, in spite of the crowds.

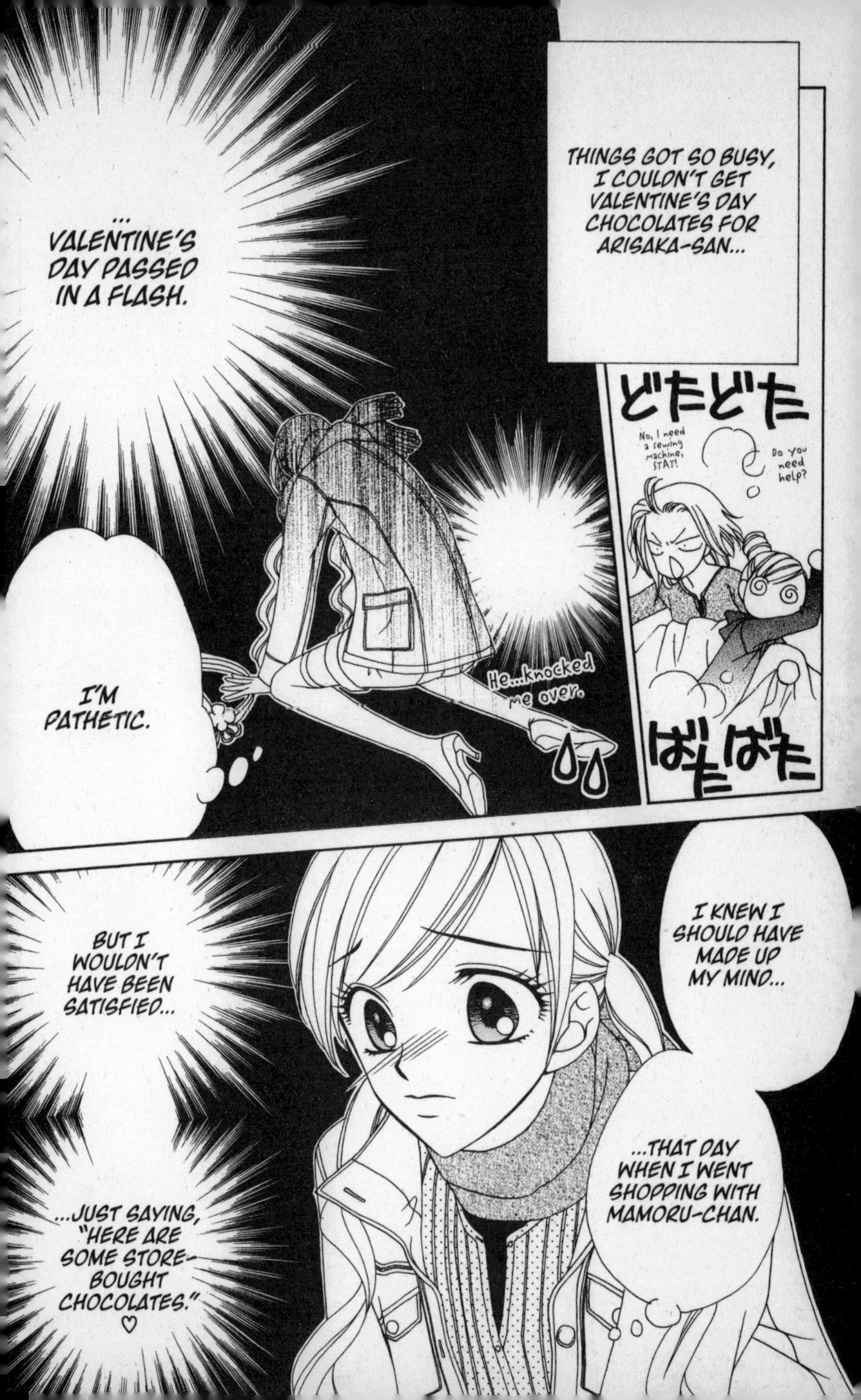
THINGS GOT SO BUSY, I COULDN'T GET VALENTINE'S DAY CHOCOLATES FOR ARISAKA-SAN...
どたどた
Do you need help?
No, I need a sewing machine, STAT!
ばたばた
...VALENTINE'S DAY PASSED IN A FLASH.
He...knocked me over.
I'M PATHETIC.
I KNEW I SHOULD HAVE MADE UP MY MIND...
...THAT DAY WHEN I WENT SHOPPING WITH MAMORU-CHAN.
BUT I WOULDN'T HAVE BEEN SATISFIED...
...JUST SAYING, "HERE ARE SOME STORE-BOUGHT CHOCOLATES." ♡

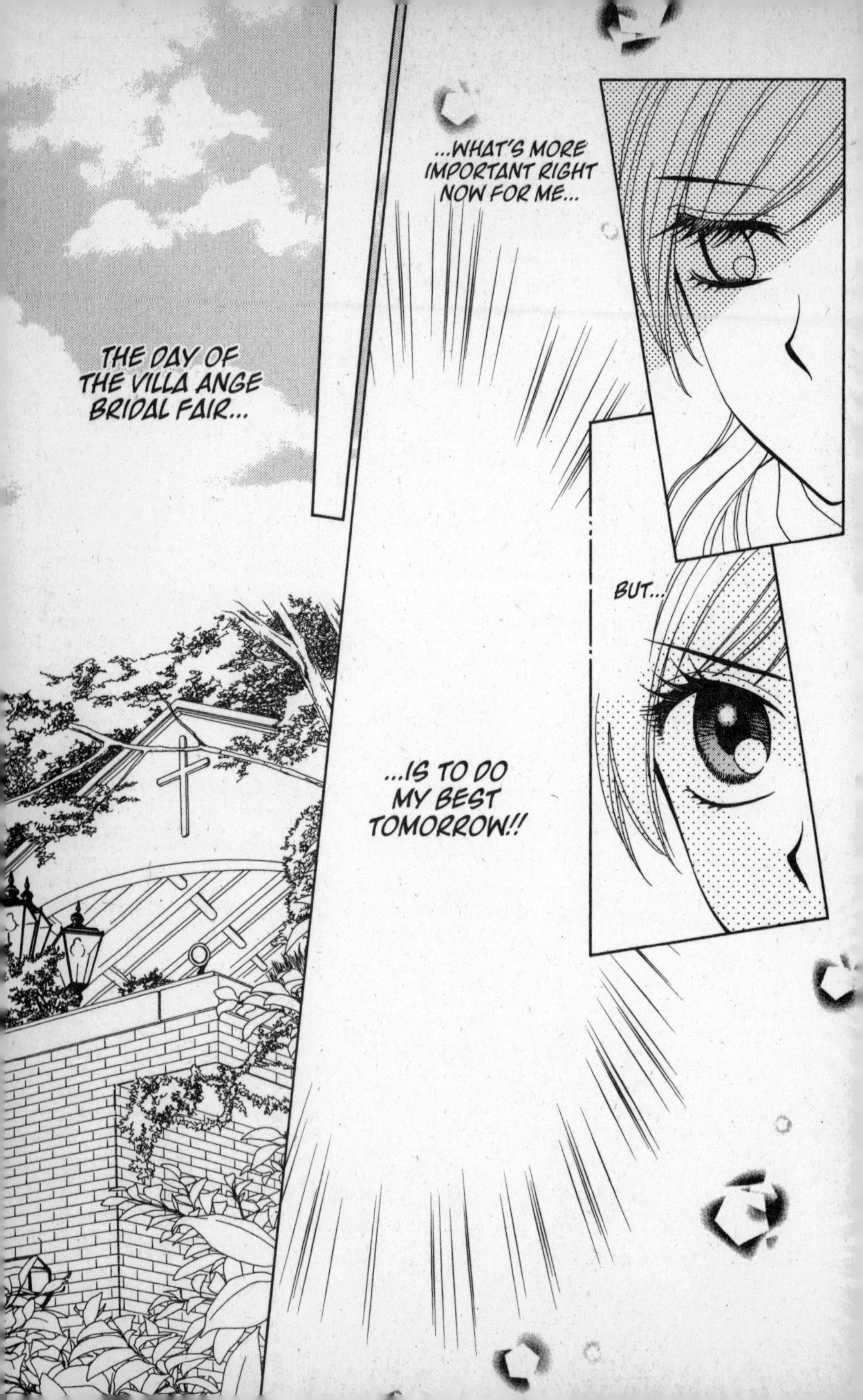
...WHAT'S MORE IMPORTANT RIGHT NOW FOR ME...
BUT...
...IS TO DO MY BEST TOMORROW!!
THE DAY OF THE VILLA ANGE BRIDAL FAIR...

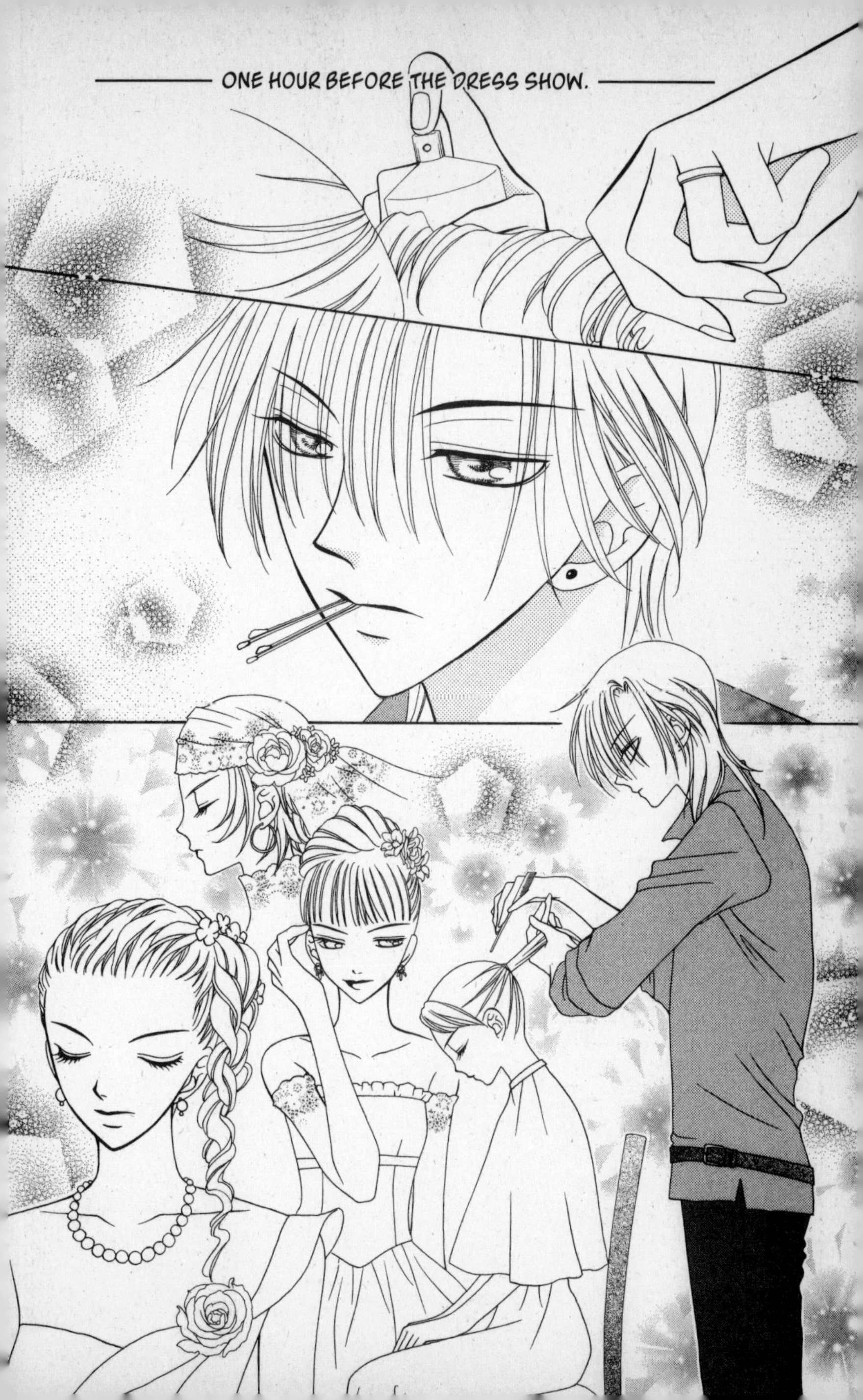
ONE HOUR BEFORE THE DRESS SHOW.

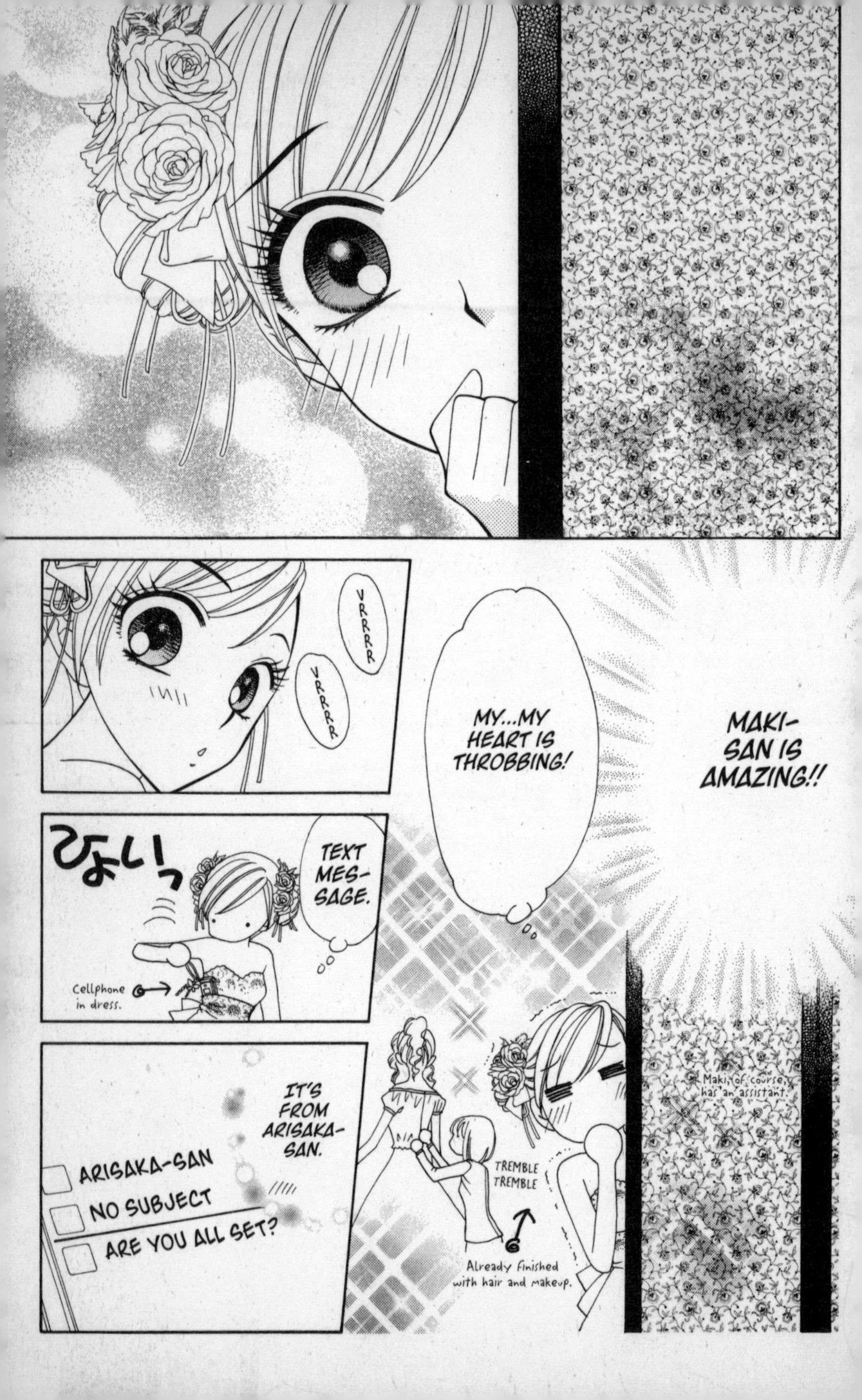
MAKI-SAN IS AMAZING!!
MY...MY HEART IS THROBBING!
Maki, of course, has an assistant.
TREMBLE TREMBLE
Already finished with hair and makeup.
VRRRR
VRRRR
ひょいっ
TEXT MES-SAGE.
Cellphone in dress.
IT'S FROM ARISAKA-SAN.
ARISAKA-SAN
NO SUBJECT
ARE YOU ALL SET?

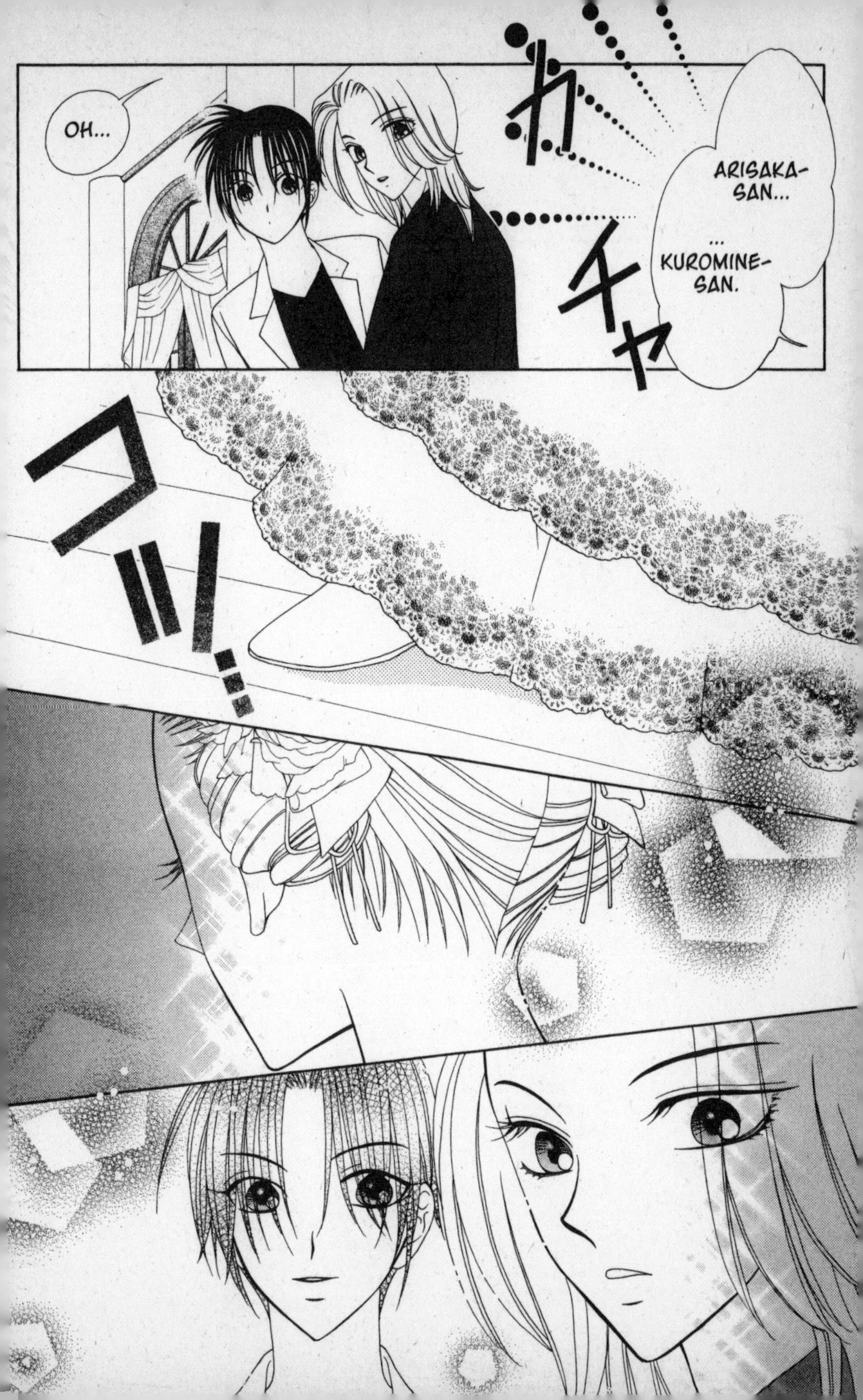

ガチャ
ARISAKA-SAN... ...KUROMINE-SAN.
OH...
ワッ!!

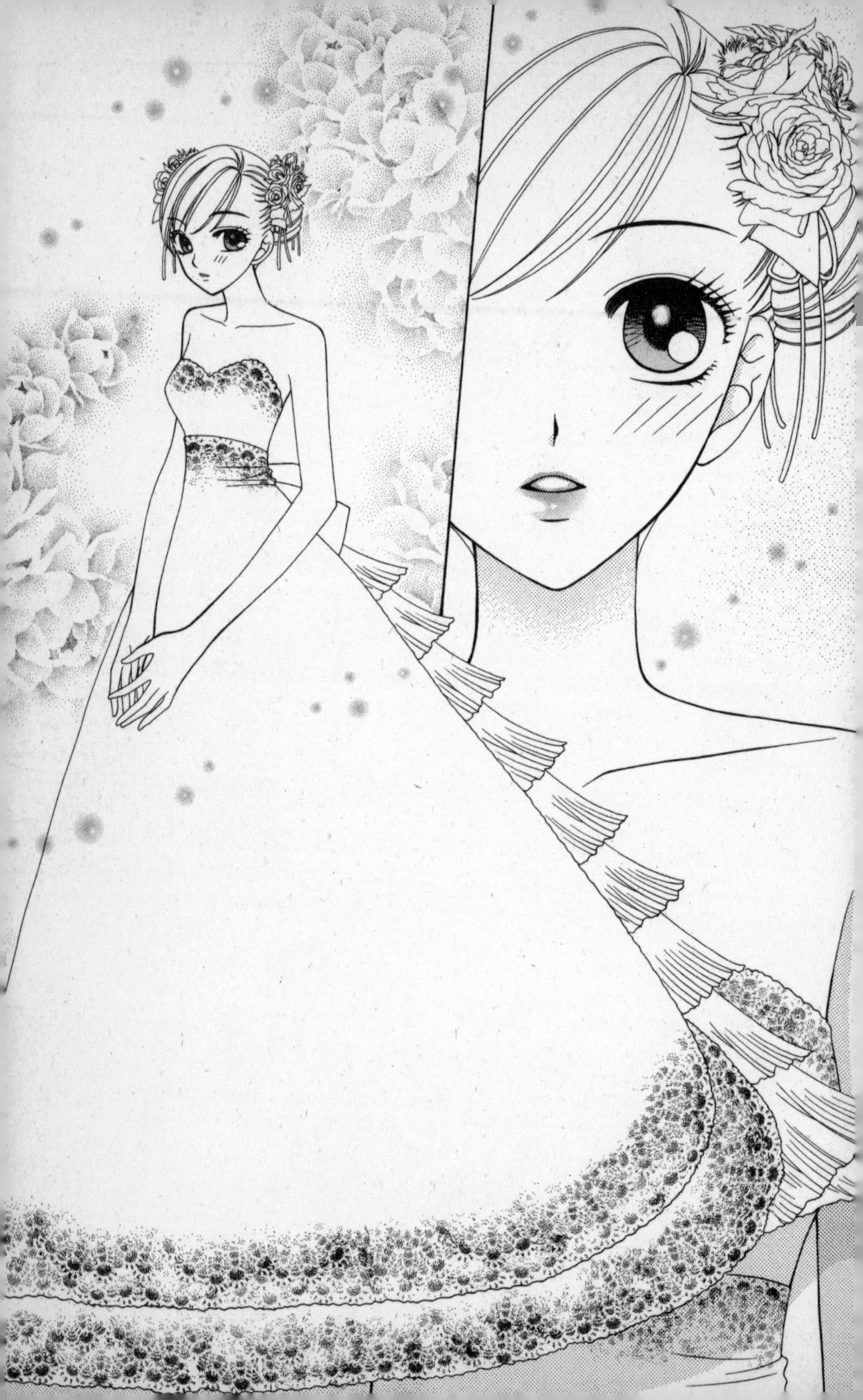

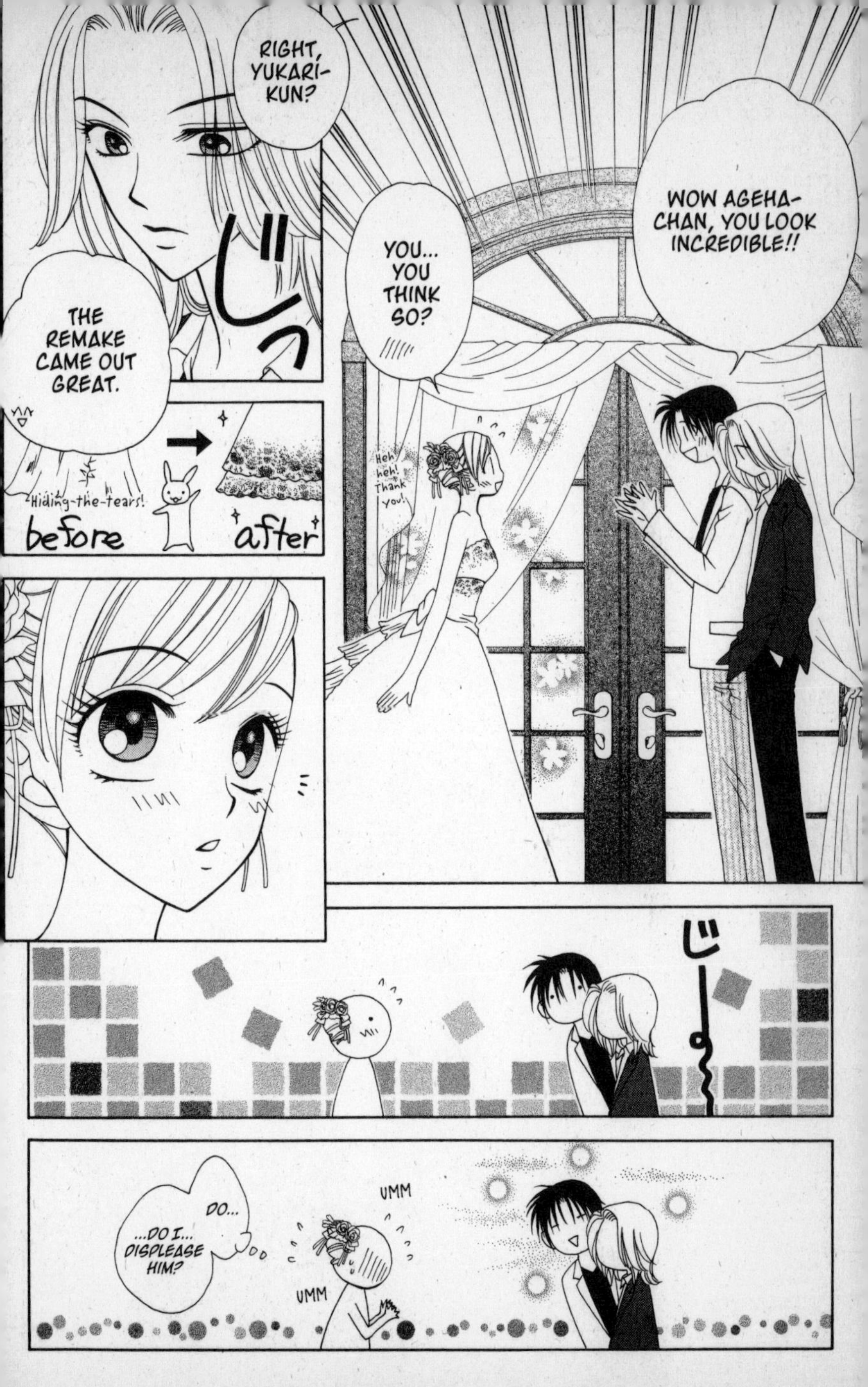
WOW AGEHA-CHAN, YOU LOOK INCREDIBLE!!
YOU... YOU THINK SO?
Heh heh! Thank you!
RIGHT, YUKARI-KUN?
じっ
THE REMAKE CAME OUT GREAT.
after
before
Hiding-the-tears!
じーっ
UMM
DO... ...DO I... DISPLEASE HIM?
UMM

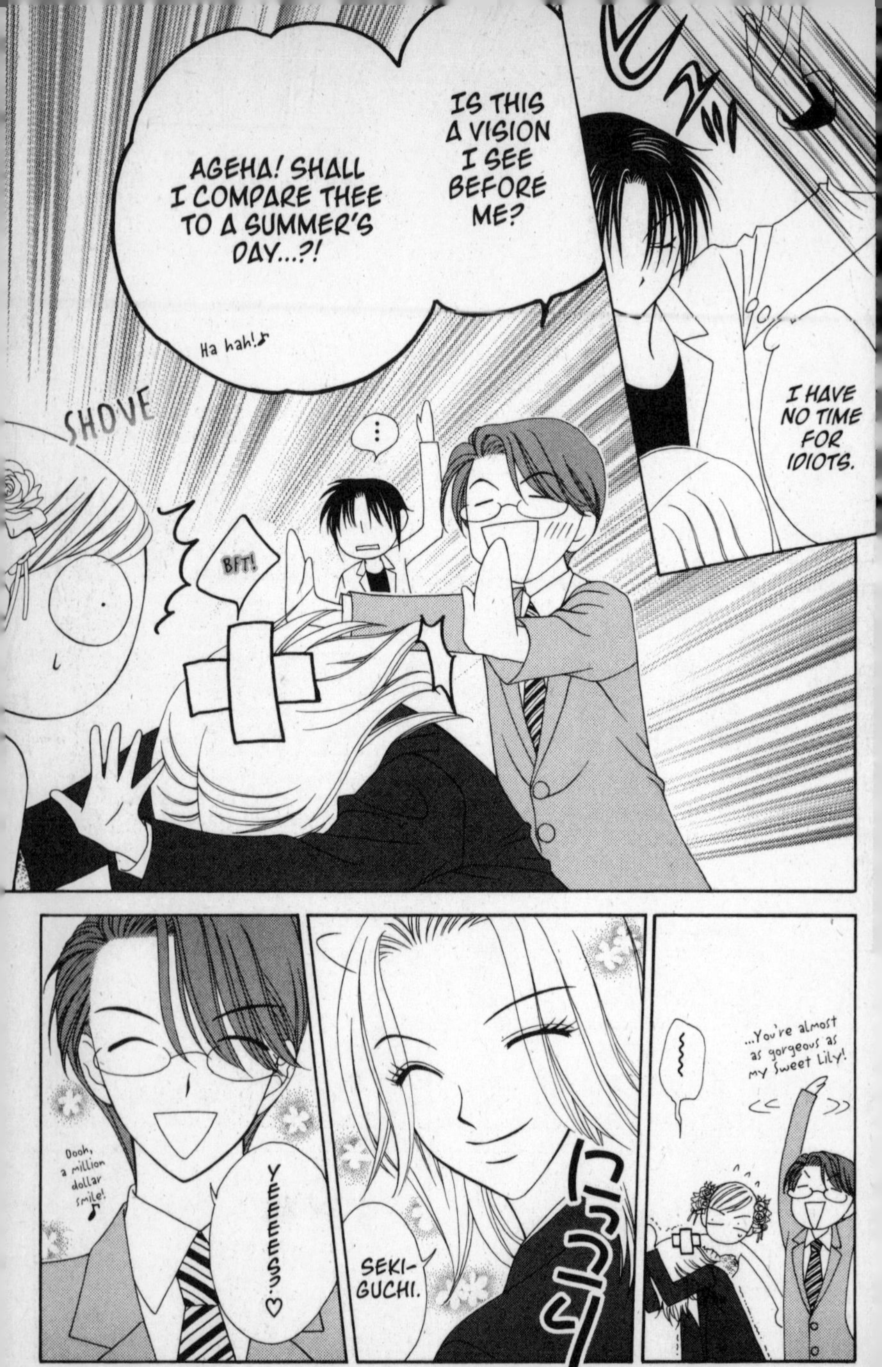
IS THIS A VISION I SEE BEFORE ME?
AGEHA! SHALL I COMPARE THEE TO A SUMMER'S DAY...?!
Ha hah!♪
I HAVE NO TIME FOR IDIOTS.
...
SHOVE
BFT!
...You're almost as gorgeous as my Sweet Lily!
SEKI-GUCHI.
YEEESS.♡
Oooh, a million dollar smile!♪

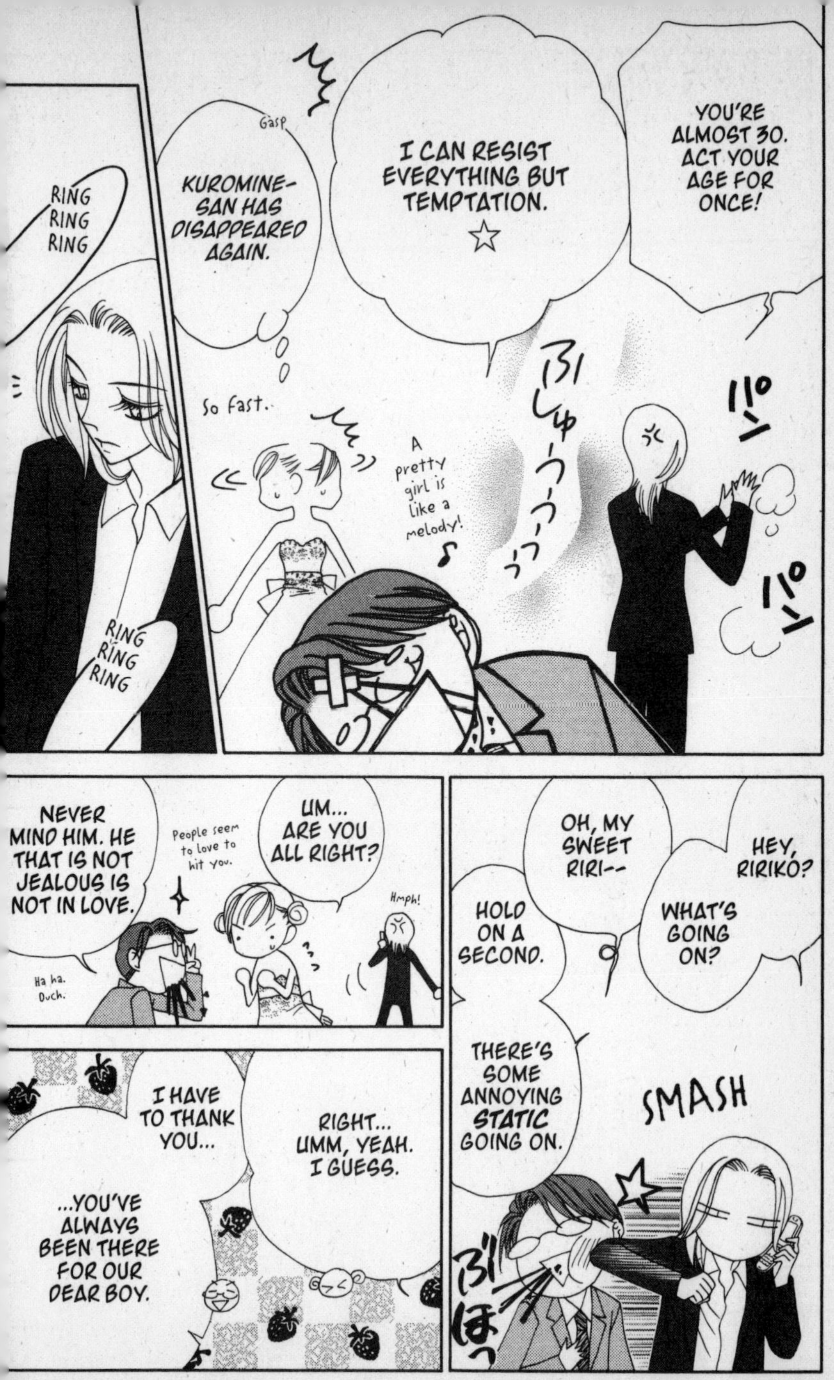
YOU'RE ALMOST 30. ACT YOUR AGE FOR ONCE!
パン
パン
I CAN RESIST EVERYTHING BUT TEMPTATION. ☆
A pretty girl is like a melody! ♪
ぶしゅうううう
Gasp
KUROMINE-SAN HAS DISAPPEARED AGAIN.
So fast..
RING RING RING
RING RING RING
HEY, RIRIKO?
WHAT'S GOING ON?
OH, MY SWEET RIRI--
HOLD ON A SECOND.
THERE'S SOME ANNOYING STATIC GOING ON.
SMASH
ぶほっ
UM... ARE YOU ALL RIGHT?
Hmph!
People seem to love to hit you.
NEVER MIND HIM. HE THAT IS NOT JEALOUS IS NOT IN LOVE.
Ha ha. Ouch.
I HAVE TO THANK YOU...
...YOU'VE ALWAYS BEEN THERE FOR OUR DEAR BOY.
RIGHT... UMM, YEAH. I GUESS.

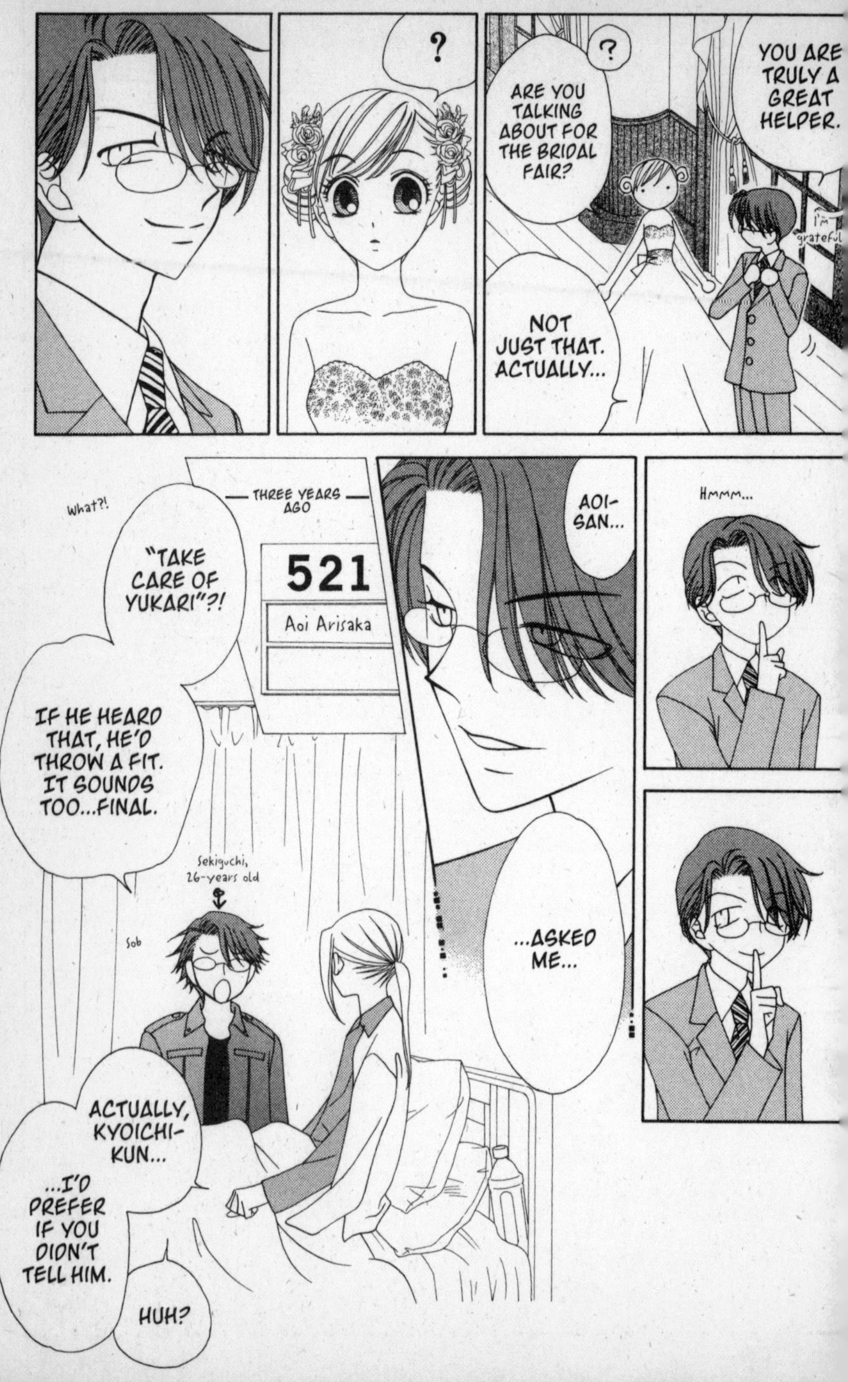
YOU ARE TRULY A GREAT HELPER.
I'm grateful
?
ARE YOU TALKING ABOUT FOR THE BRIDAL FAIR?
NOT JUST THAT. ACTUALLY...
?
Hmmm...
AOI-SAN...
...ASKED ME...
— THREE YEARS AGO —
521
Aoi Arisaka
"TAKE CARE OF YUKARI"?!
What?!
IF HE HEARD THAT, HE'D THROW A FIT. IT SOUNDS TOO...FINAL.
Sekiguchi, 26-years old
Sob
ACTUALLY, KYOICHI-KUN...
...I'D PREFER IF YOU DIDN'T TELL HIM.
HUH?

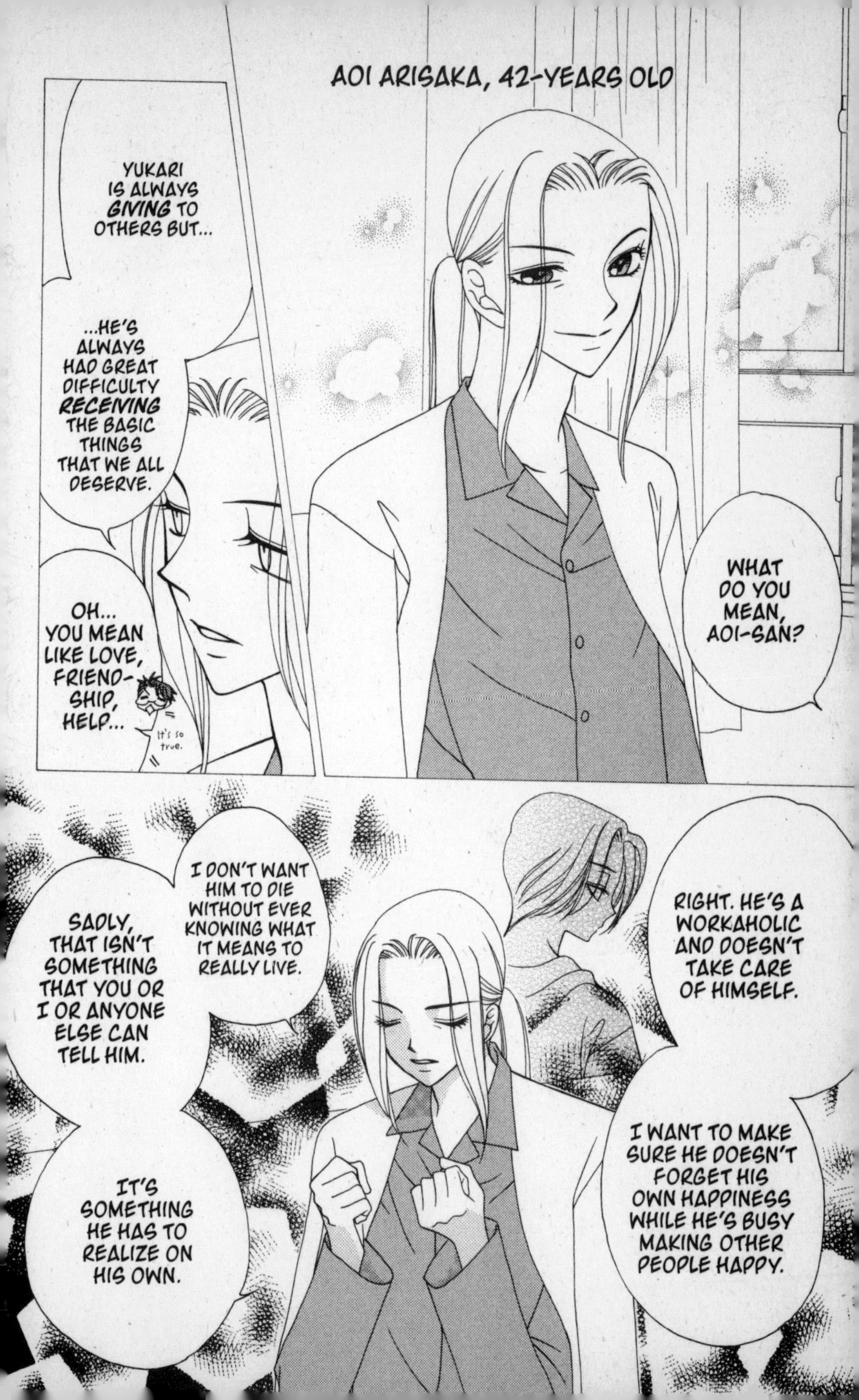
AOI ARISAKA, 42-YEARS OLD
YUKARI IS ALWAYS GIVING TO OTHERS BUT...
...HE'S ALWAYS HAD GREAT DIFFICULTY RECEIVING THE BASIC THINGS THAT WE ALL DESERVE.
WHAT DO YOU MEAN, AOI-SAN?
OH... YOU MEAN LIKE LOVE, FRIEND-SHIP, HELP...
It's so true.
RIGHT. HE'S A WORKAHOLIC AND DOESN'T TAKE CARE OF HIMSELF.
I WANT TO MAKE SURE HE DOESN'T FORGET HIS OWN HAPPINESS WHILE HE'S BUSY MAKING OTHER PEOPLE HAPPY.
I DON'T WANT HIM TO DIE WITHOUT EVER KNOWING WHAT IT MEANS TO REALLY LIVE.
SADLY, THAT ISN'T SOMETHING THAT YOU OR I OR ANYONE ELSE CAN TELL HIM.
IT'S SOMETHING HE HAS TO REALIZE ON HIS OWN.

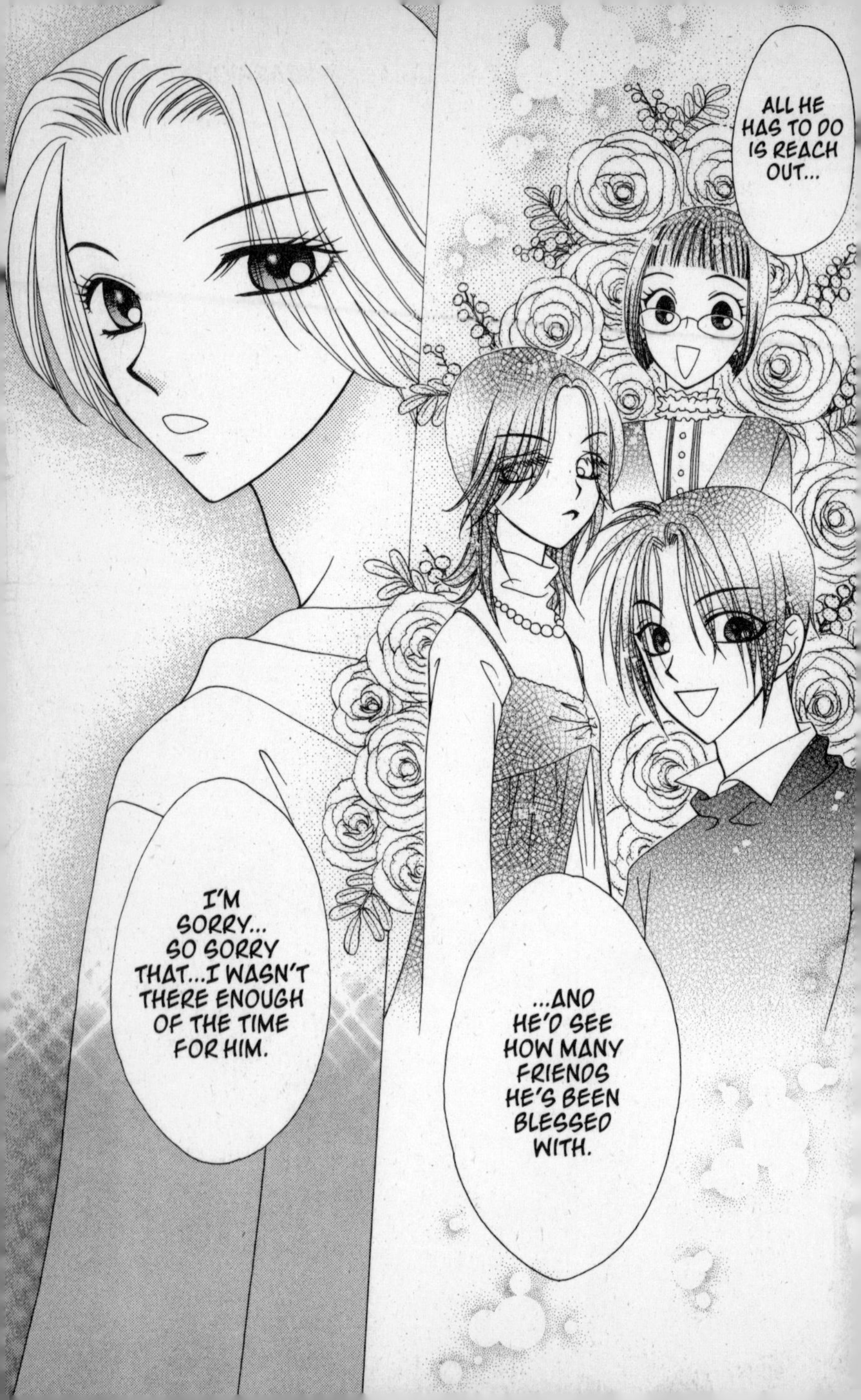
ALL HE HAS TO DO IS REACH OUT...
...AND HE'D SEE HOW MANY FRIENDS HE'S BEEN BLESSED WITH.
I'M SORRY... SO SORRY THAT...I WASN'T THERE ENOUGH OF THE TIME FOR HIM.

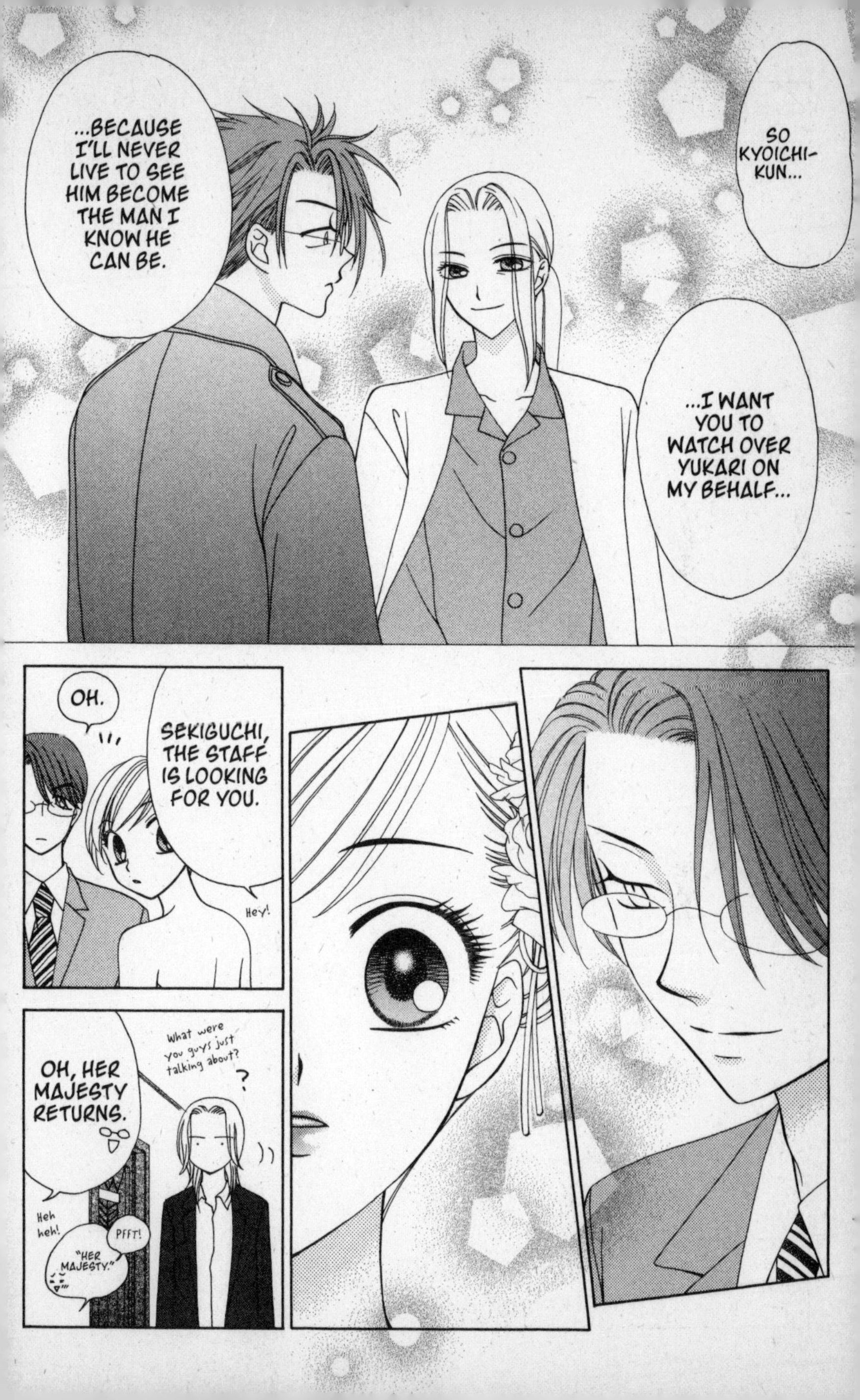
...BECAUSE I'LL NEVER LIVE TO SEE HIM BECOME THE MAN I KNOW HE CAN BE.
SO KYOICHI-KUN...
...I WANT YOU TO WATCH OVER YUKARI ON MY BEHALF...
SEKIGUCHI, THE STAFF IS LOOKING FOR YOU.
Hey!
OH.
What were you guys just talking about?
?
OH, HER MAJESTY RETURNS.
PFFT!
Heh heh!
"HER MAJESTY."

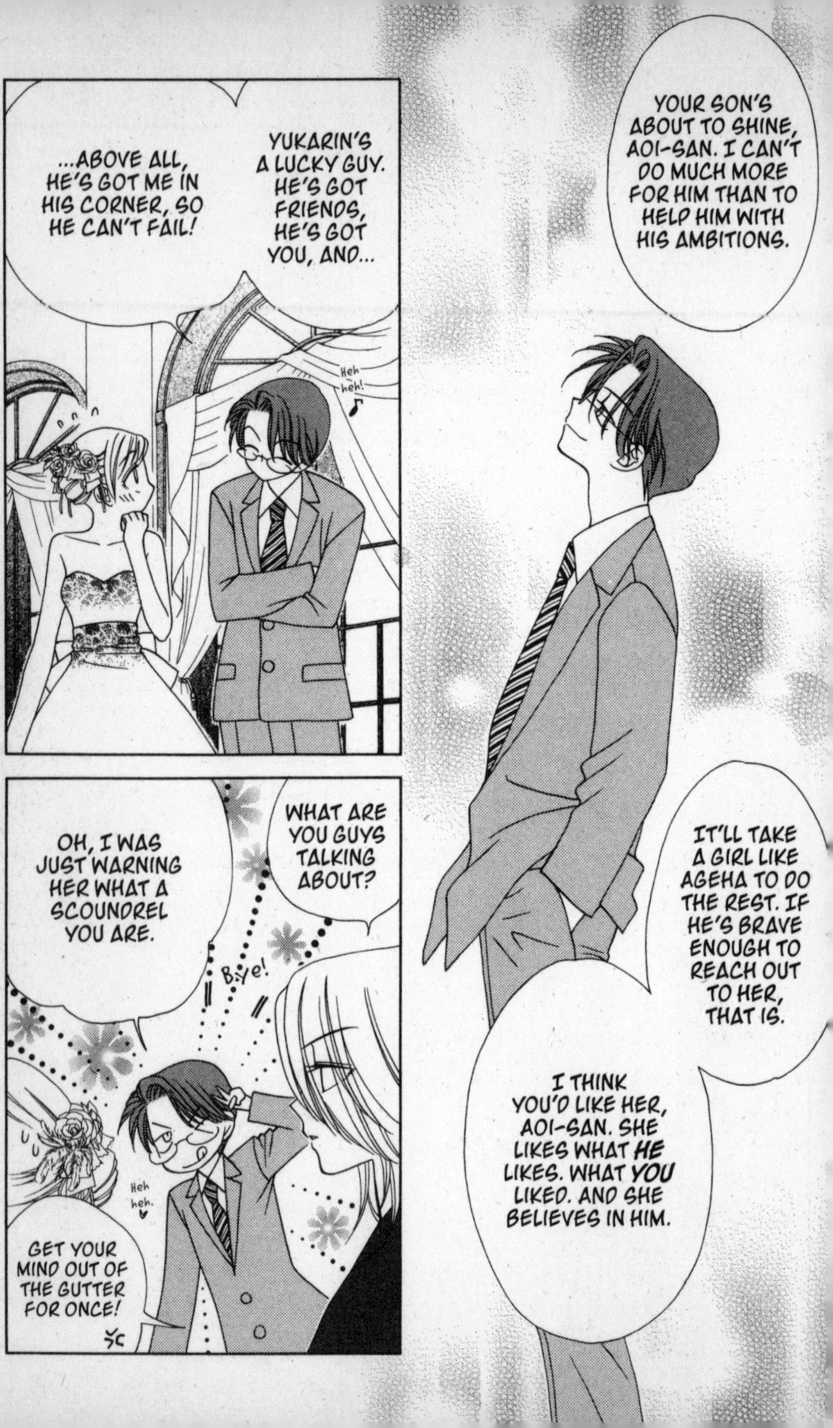
YOUR SON'S ABOUT TO SHINE, AOI-SAN. I CAN'T DO MUCH MORE FOR HIM THAN TO HELP HIM WITH HIS AMBITIONS.
IT'LL TAKE A GIRL LIKE AGEHA TO DO THE REST. IF HE'S BRAVE ENOUGH TO REACH OUT TO HER, THAT IS.
I THINK YOU'D LIKE HER, AOI-SAN. SHE LIKES WHAT *HE* LIKES. WHAT *YOU* LIKED. AND SHE BELIEVES IN HIM.
YUKARIN'S A LUCKY GUY. HE'S GOT FRIENDS, HE'S GOT YOU, AND...
...ABOVE ALL, HE'S GOT ME IN HIS CORNER, SO HE CAN'T FAIL!
Heh heh!
WHAT ARE YOU GUYS TALKING ABOUT?
OH, I WAS JUST WARNING HER WHAT A SCOUNDREL YOU ARE.
B-ye!
Heh heh.
GET YOUR MIND OUT OF THE GUTTER FOR ONCE!

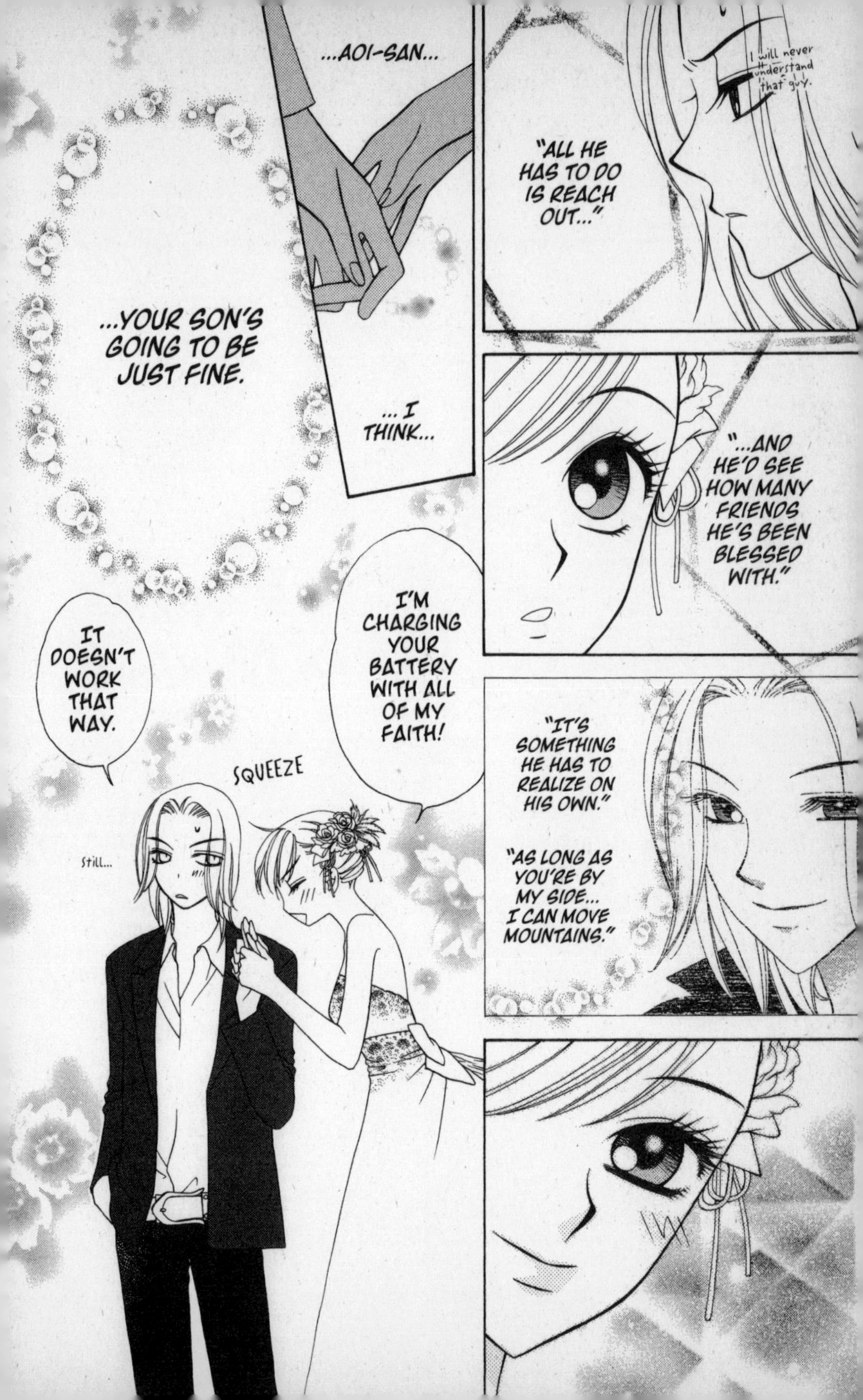
I will never understand that guy.
"ALL HE HAS TO DO IS REACH OUT..."
"...AND HE'D SEE HOW MANY FRIENDS HE'S BEEN BLESSED WITH."
"IT'S SOMETHING HE HAS TO REALIZE ON HIS OWN."
"AS LONG AS YOU'RE BY MY SIDE... I CAN MOVE MOUNTAINS."
...AOI-SAN...
...YOUR SON'S GOING TO BE JUST FINE.
... I THINK...
I'M CHARGING YOUR BATTERY WITH ALL OF MY FAITH!
IT DOESN'T WORK THAT WAY.
SQUEEZE
Still...

Episode 51

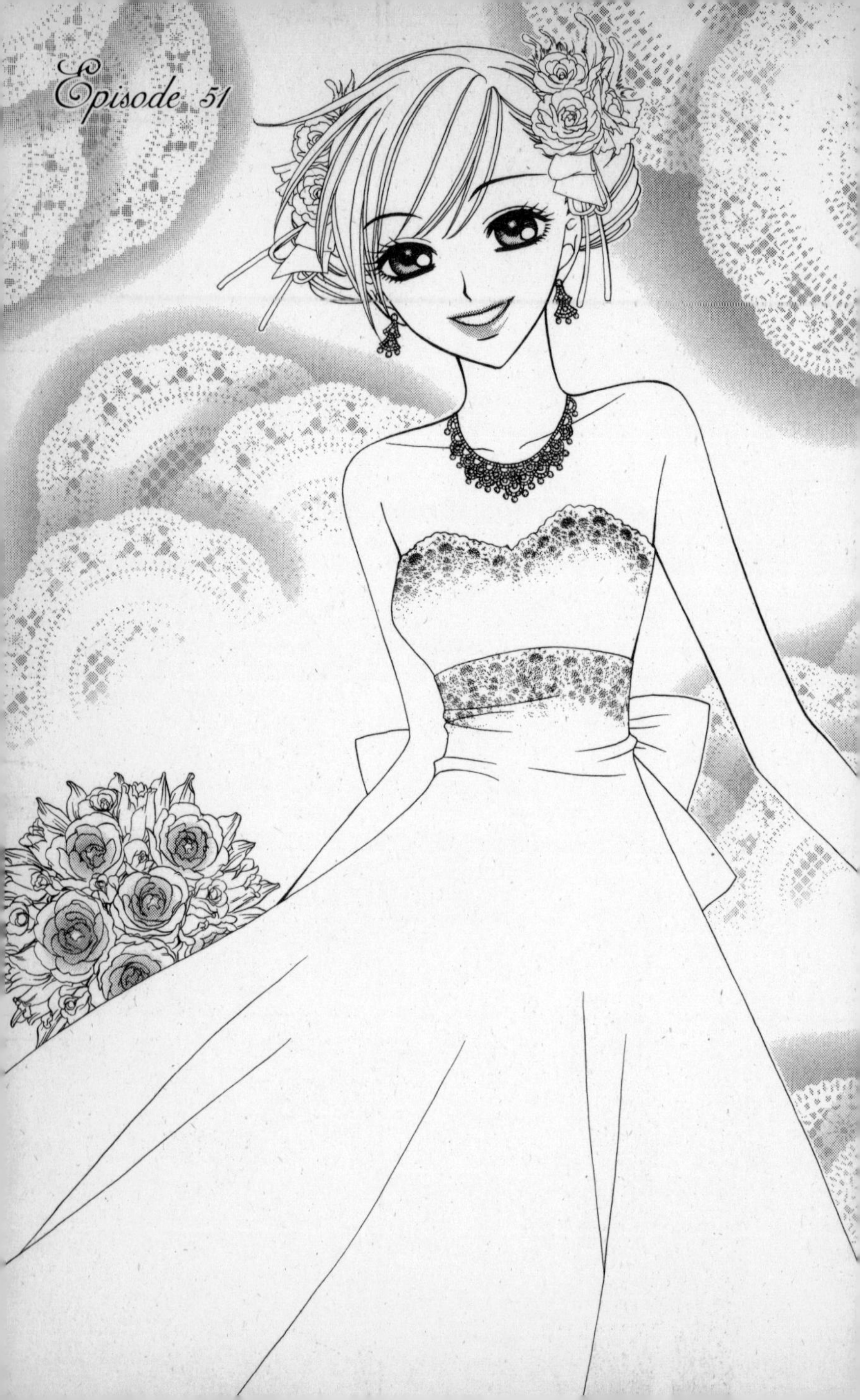

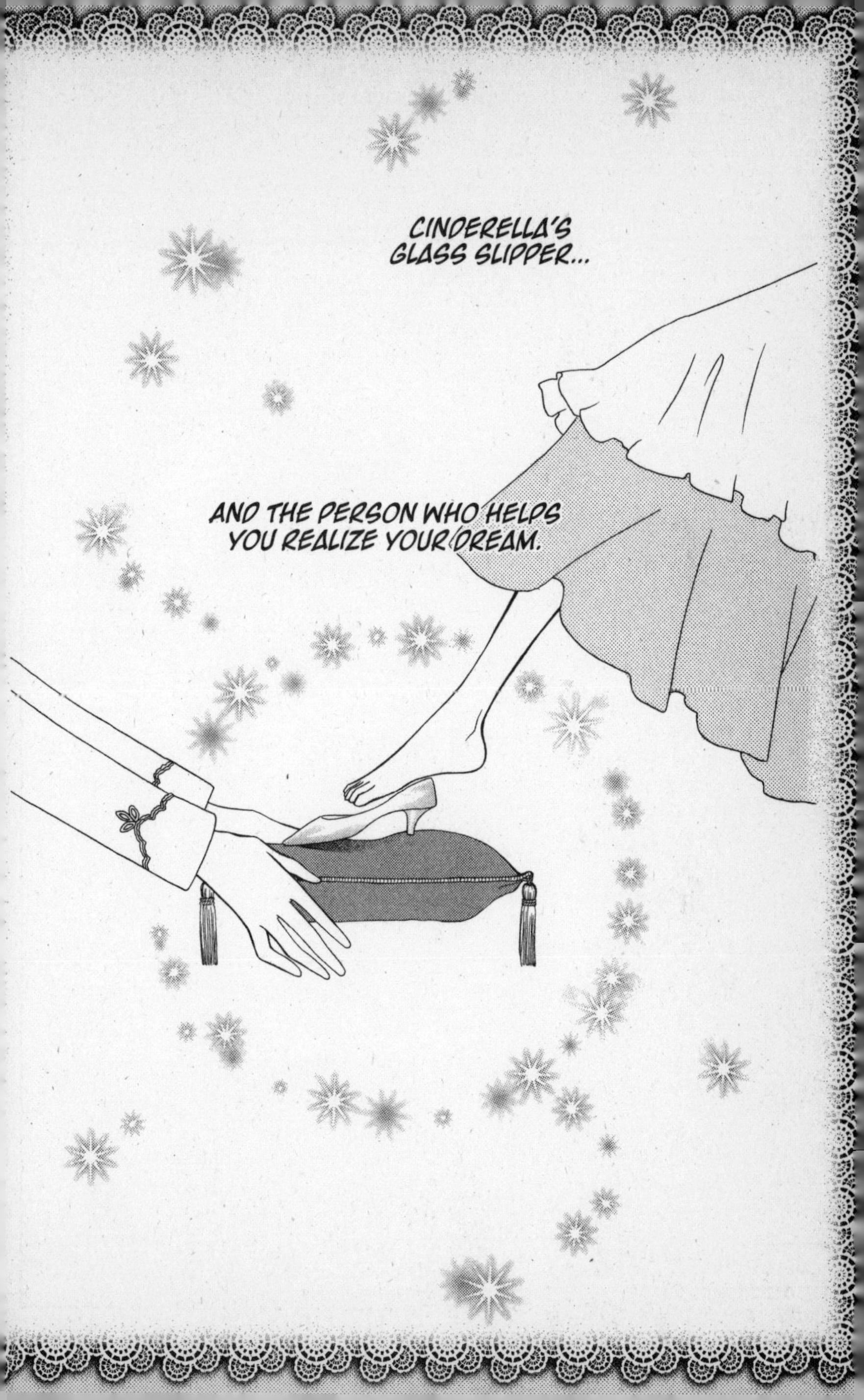
CINDERELLA'S GLASS SLIPPER...
AND THE PERSON WHO HELPS YOU REALIZE YOUR DREAM.

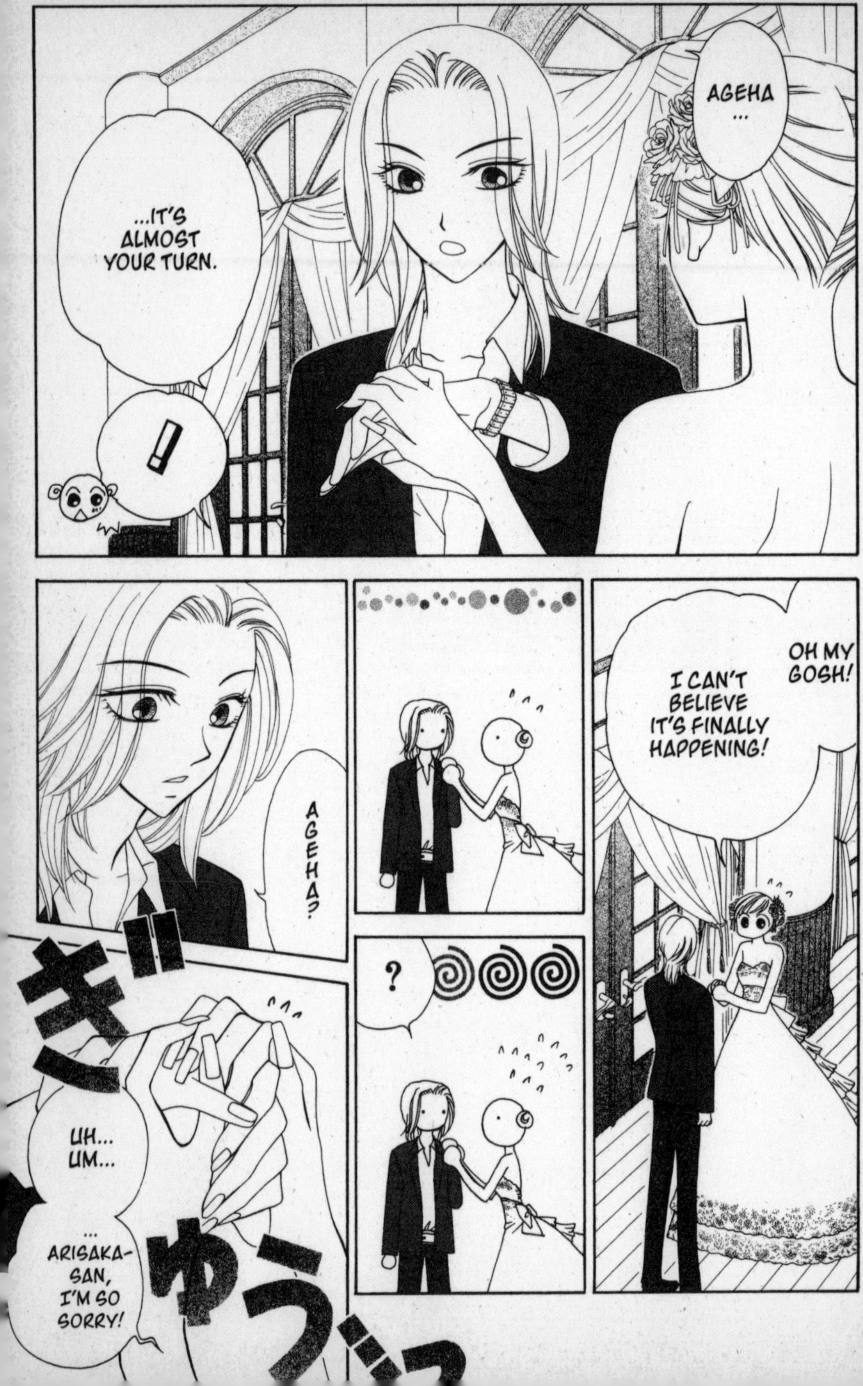
AGEHA ...
...IT'S ALMOST YOUR TURN.
!
OH MY GOSH!
I CAN'T BELIEVE IT'S FINALLY HAPPENING!
?
AGEHA?
UH... UM...
... ARISAKA-SAN, I'M SO SORRY!

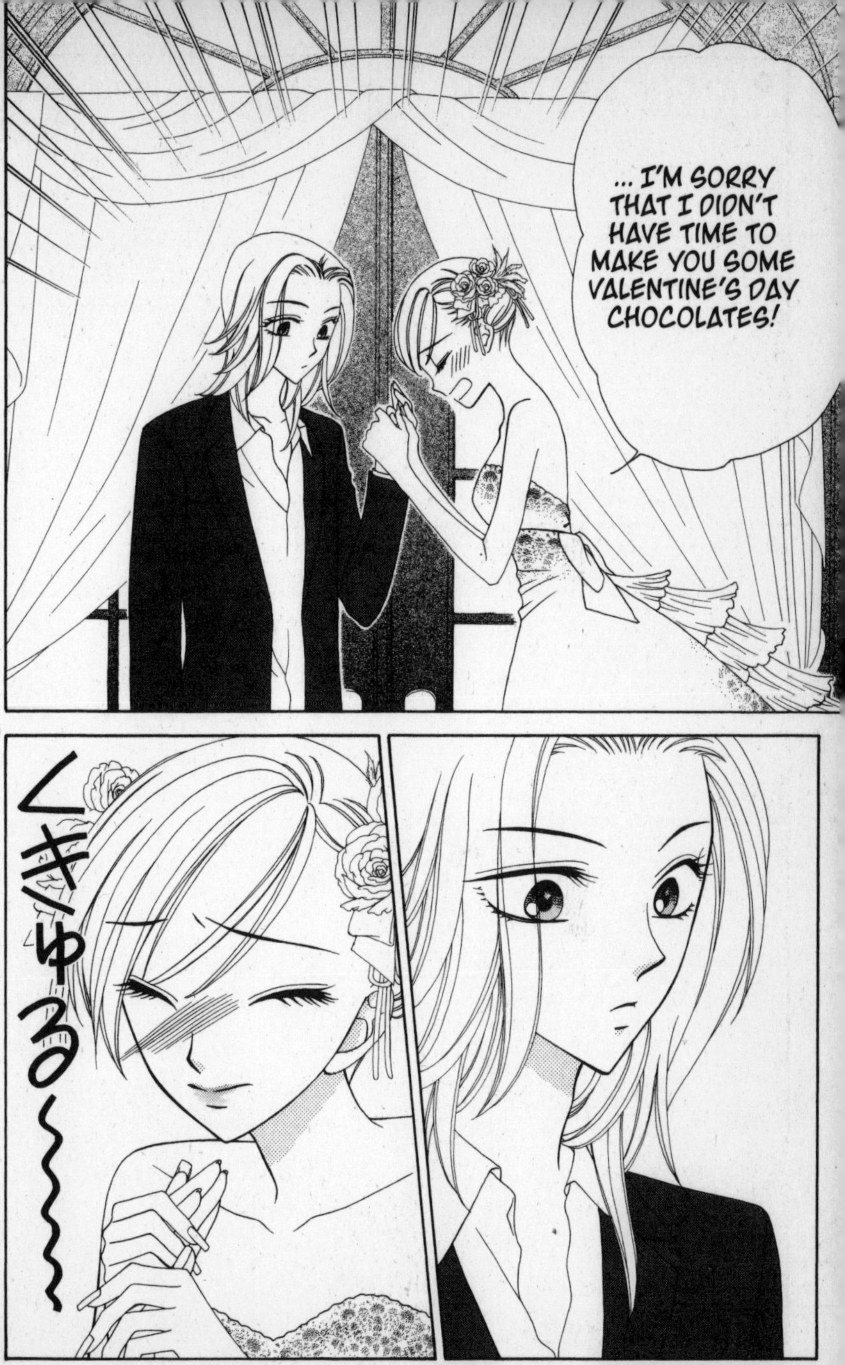
... I'M SORRY THAT I DIDN'T HAVE TIME TO MAKE YOU SOME VALENTINE'S DAY CHOCOLATES!
くきゅる〜〜〜

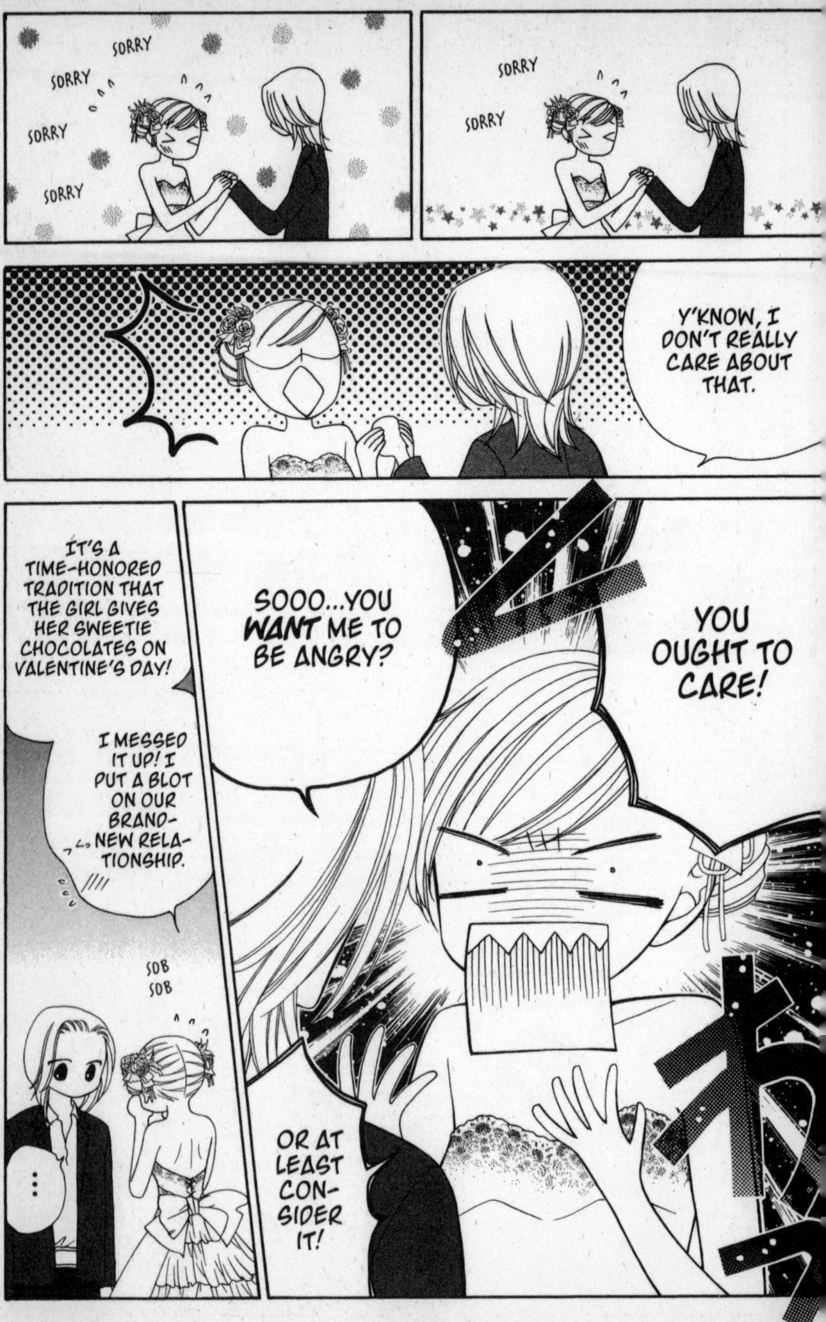
SORRY
SORRY
SORRY
SORRY
SORRY
SORRY
Y'KNOW, I DON'T REALLY CARE ABOUT THAT.
YOU OUGHT TO CARE!
SOOO...YOU *WANT* ME TO BE ANGRY?
OR AT LEAST CONSIDER IT!
IT'S A TIME-HONORED TRADITION THAT THE GIRL GIVES HER SWEETIE CHOCOLATES ON VALENTINE'S DAY!
I MESSED IT UP! I PUT A BLOT ON OUR BRAND-NEW RELATIONSHIP.
SOB SOB
...

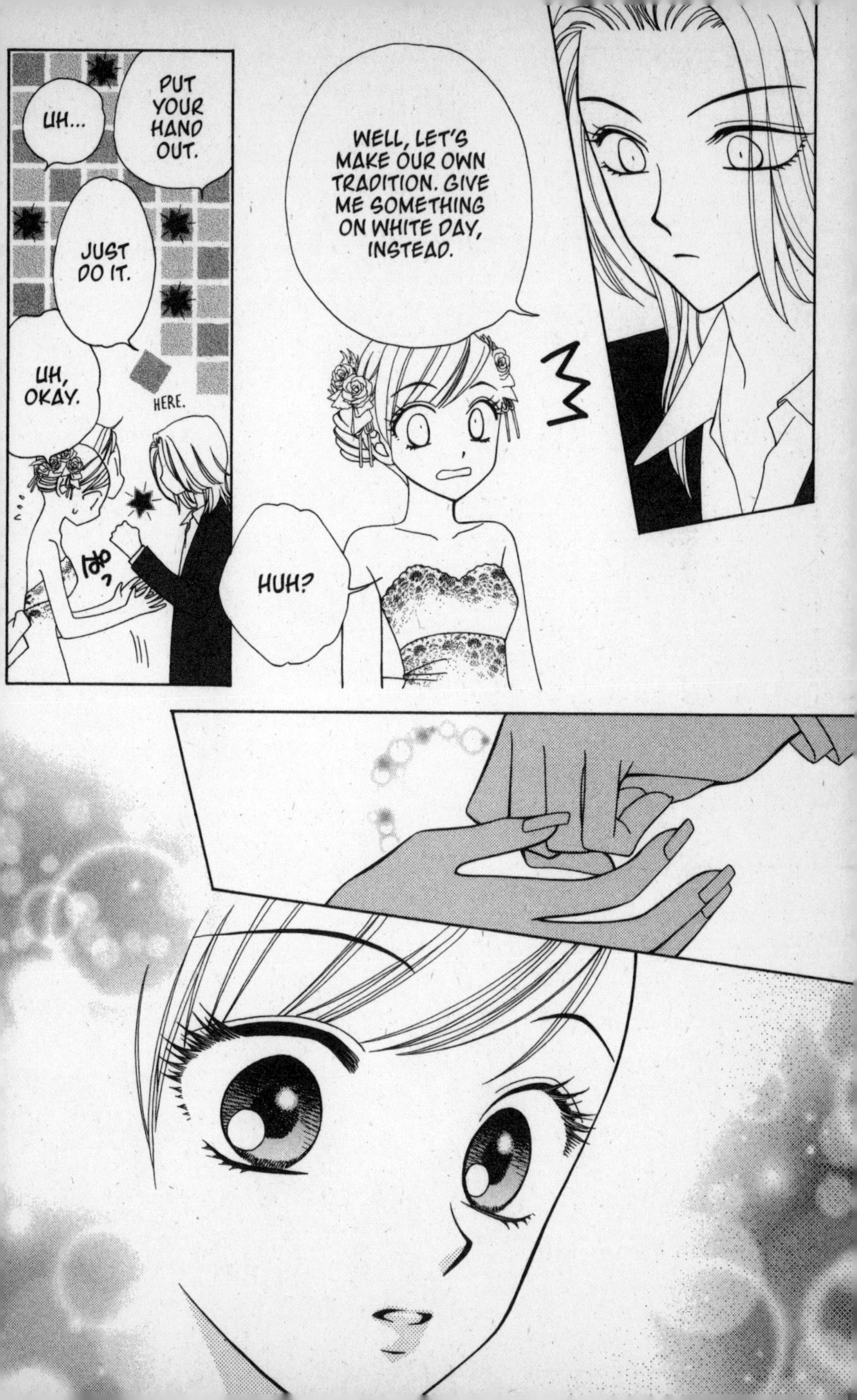
WELL, LET'S MAKE OUR OWN TRADITION. GIVE ME SOMETHING ON WHITE DAY, INSTEAD.
HUH?
PUT YOUR HAND OUT.
UH...
JUST DO IT.
UH, OKAY.
HERE.
ぱっ

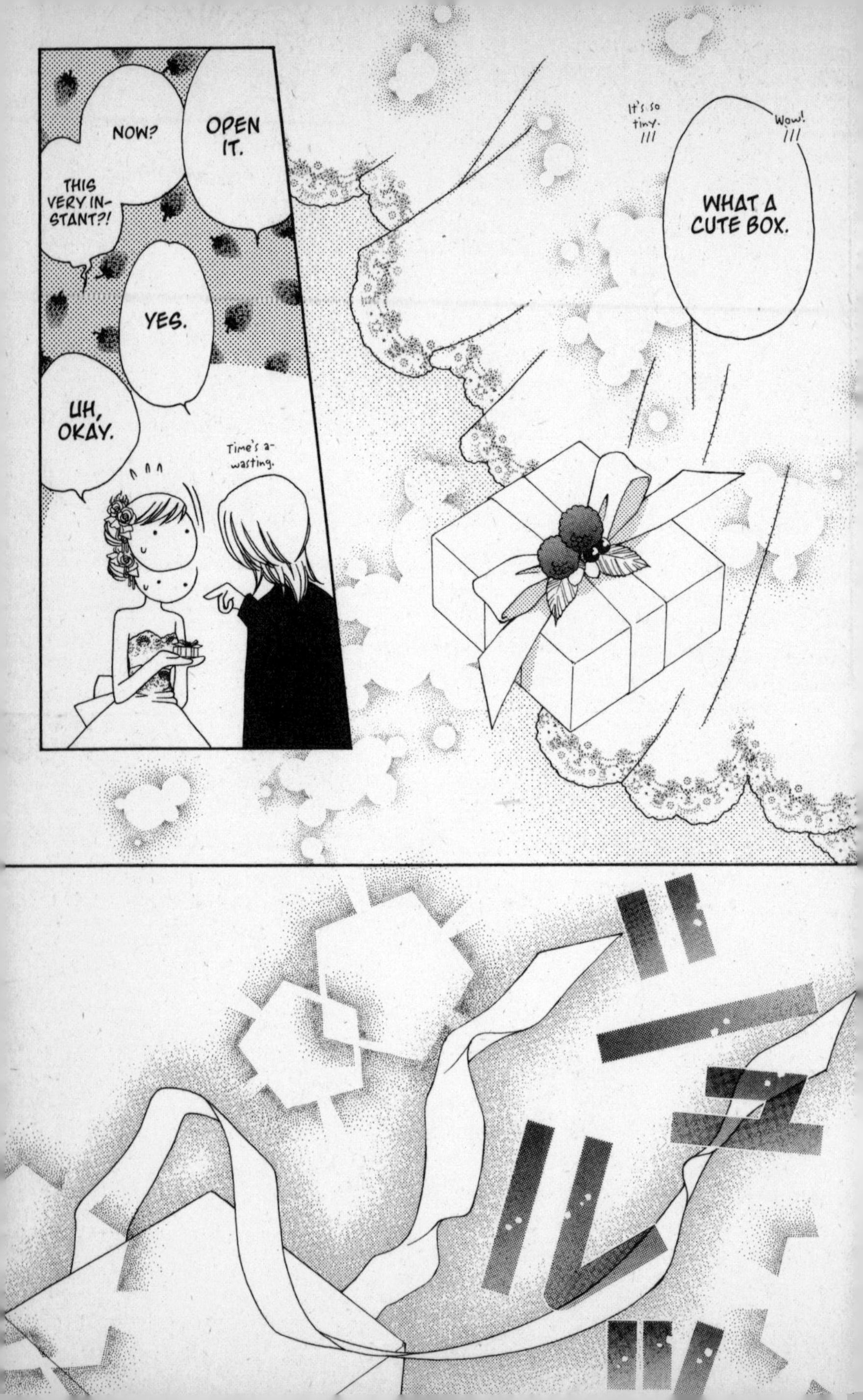
Wow!
It's so tiny.
WHAT A CUTE BOX.
OPEN IT.
NOW? THIS VERY IN-STANT?!
YES.
UH, OKAY.
Time's a-wasting.

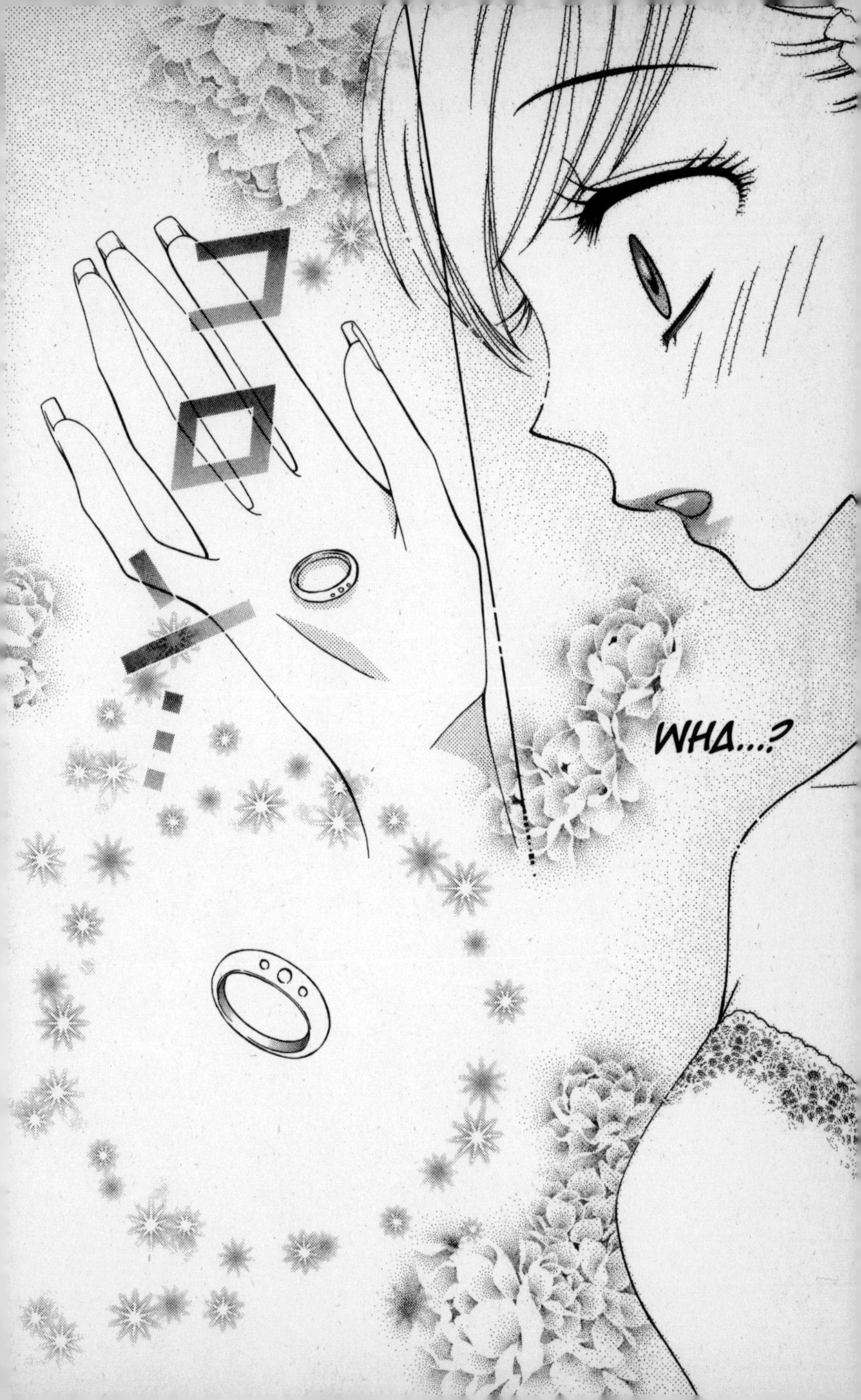
WHA...?

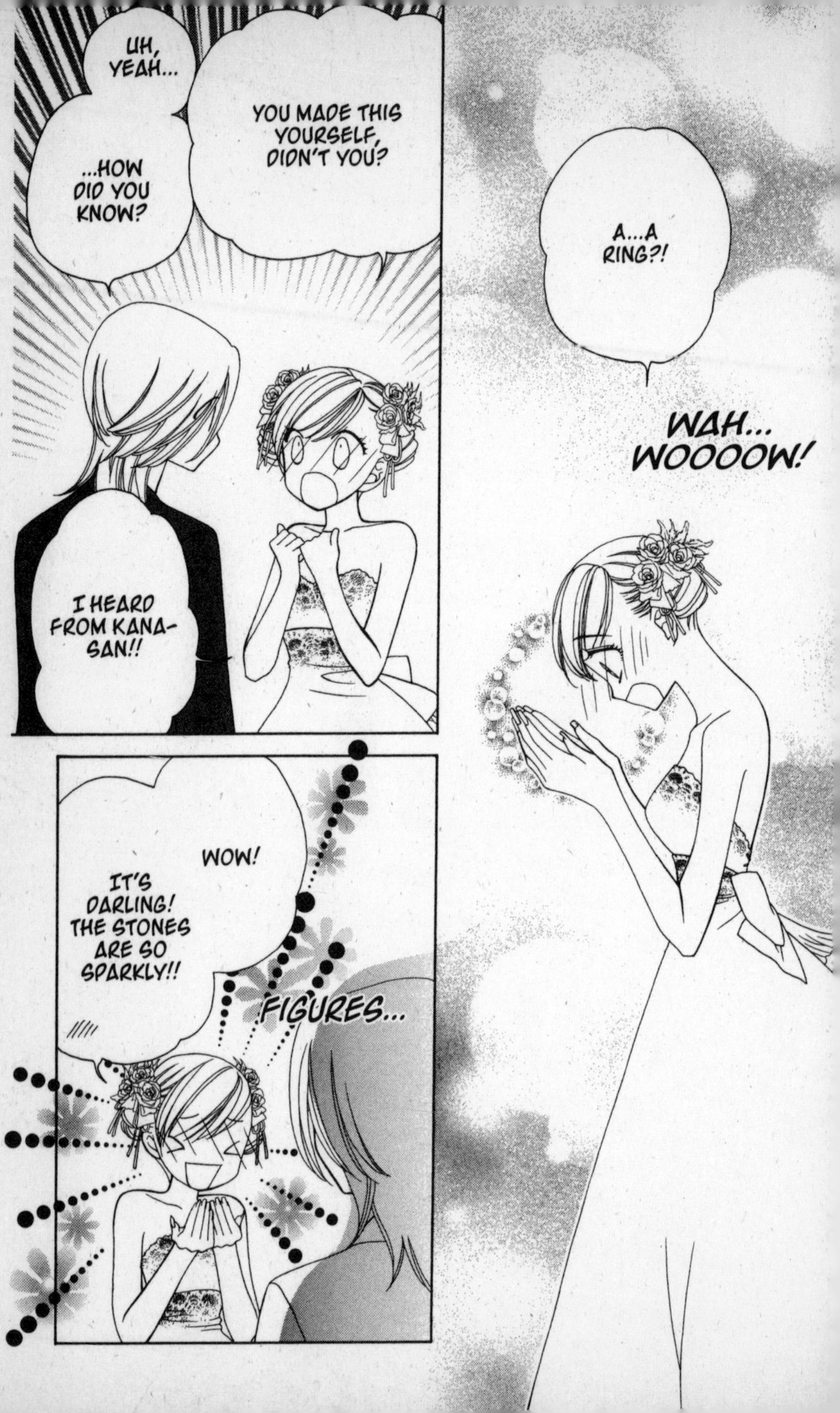
A...A RING?!
WAH... WOOOOW!
YOU MADE THIS YOURSELF, DIDN'T YOU?
UH, YEAH...
...HOW DID YOU KNOW?
I HEARD FROM KANA-SAN!!
WOW!
IT'S DARLING! THE STONES ARE SO SPARKLY!!
FIGURES...

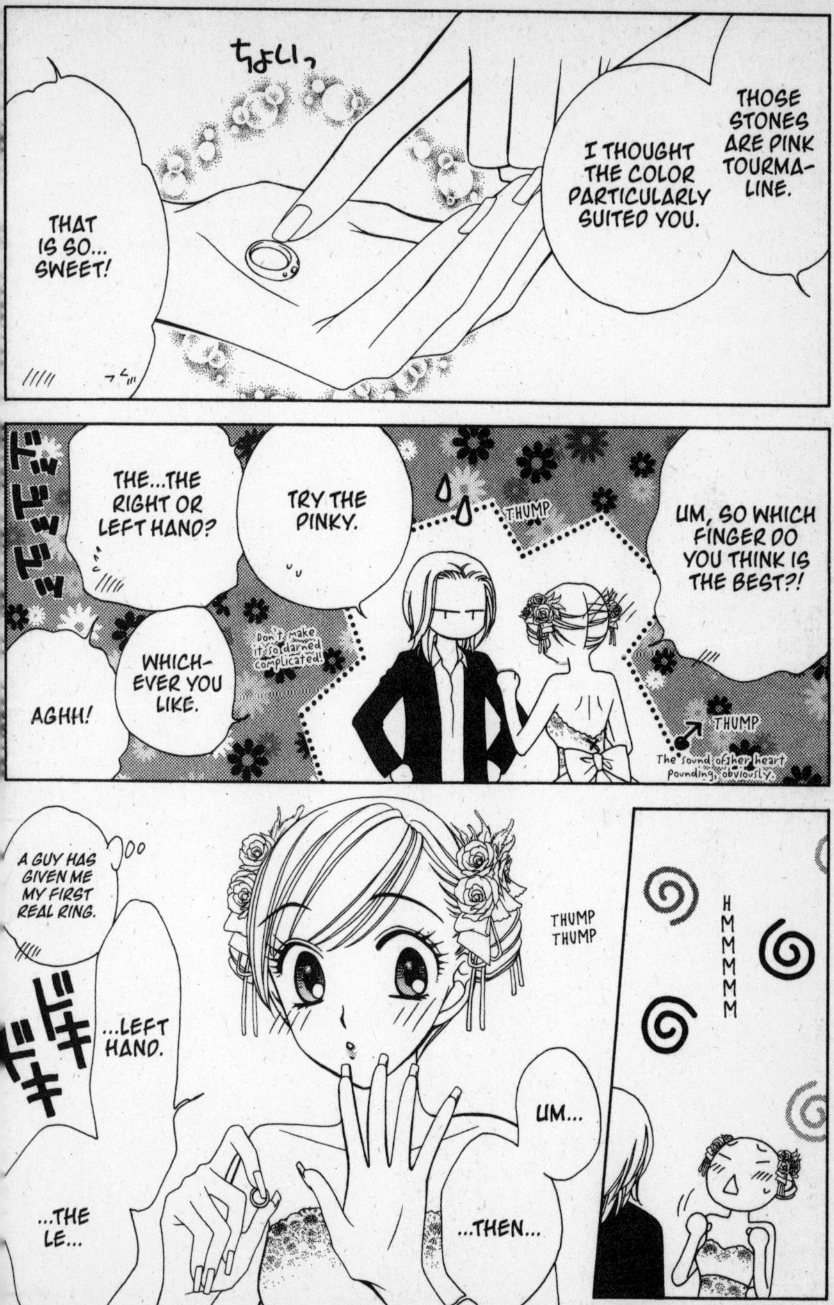
ちょいっ
THOSE STONES ARE PINK TOURMA-LINE.
I THOUGHT THE COLOR PARTICULARLY SUITED YOU.
THAT IS SO... SWEET!
UM, SO WHICH FINGER DO YOU THINK IS THE BEST?!
THUMP
THUMP
The sound of her heart pounding, obviously.
TRY THE PINKY.
Don't make it so darned complicated!
THE...THE RIGHT OR LEFT HAND?
WHICH-EVER YOU LIKE.
AGHH!
HMMMMM
THUMP THUMP
UM...
...THEN...
A GUY HAS GIVEN ME MY FIRST REAL RING.
...LEFT HAND.
...THE LE...

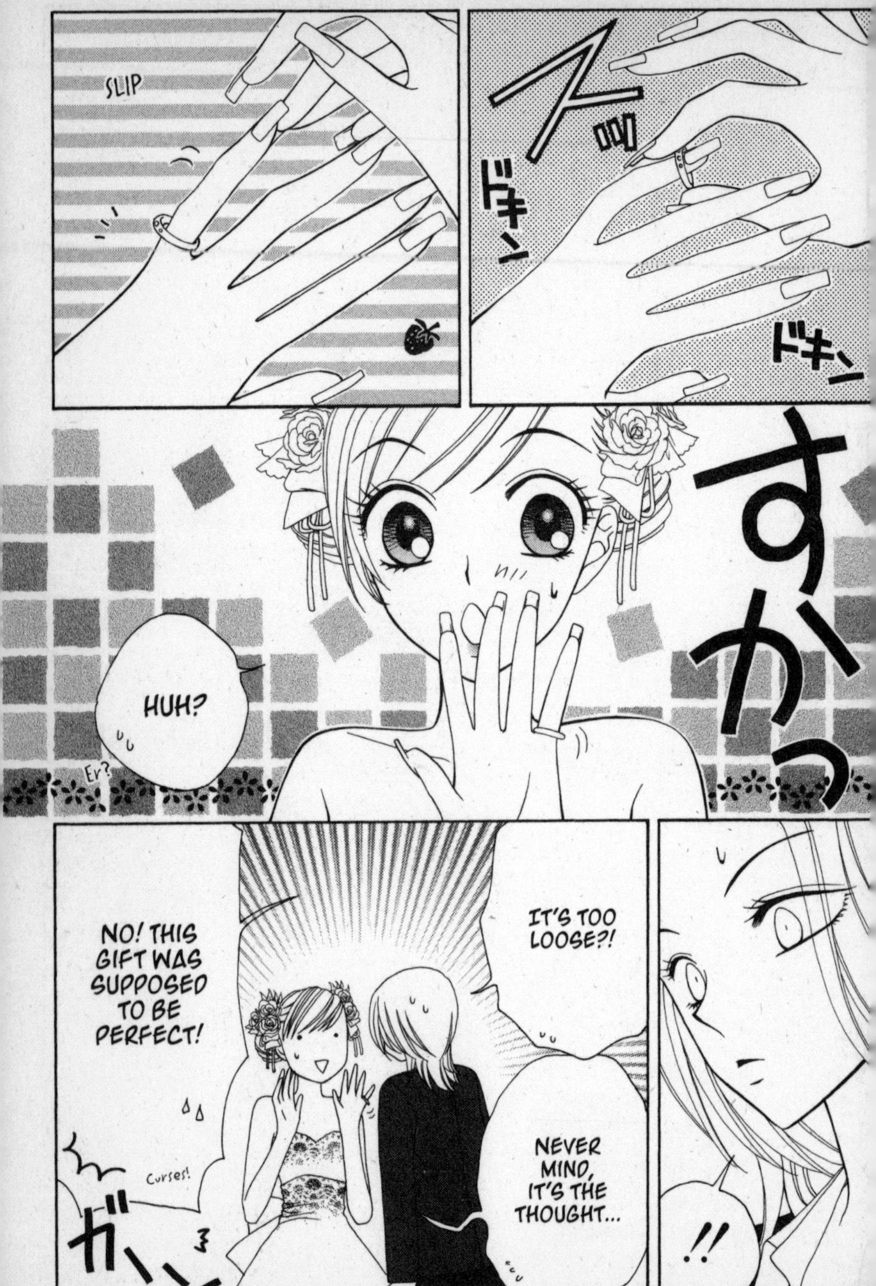

スッ
ドキン
ドキン
SLIP
すかっ
HUH?
Er?
!!
IT'S TOO LOOSE?!
NEVER MIND, IT'S THE THOUGHT...
NO! THIS GIFT WAS SUPPOSED TO BE PERFECT!
Curses!
ガーンッ

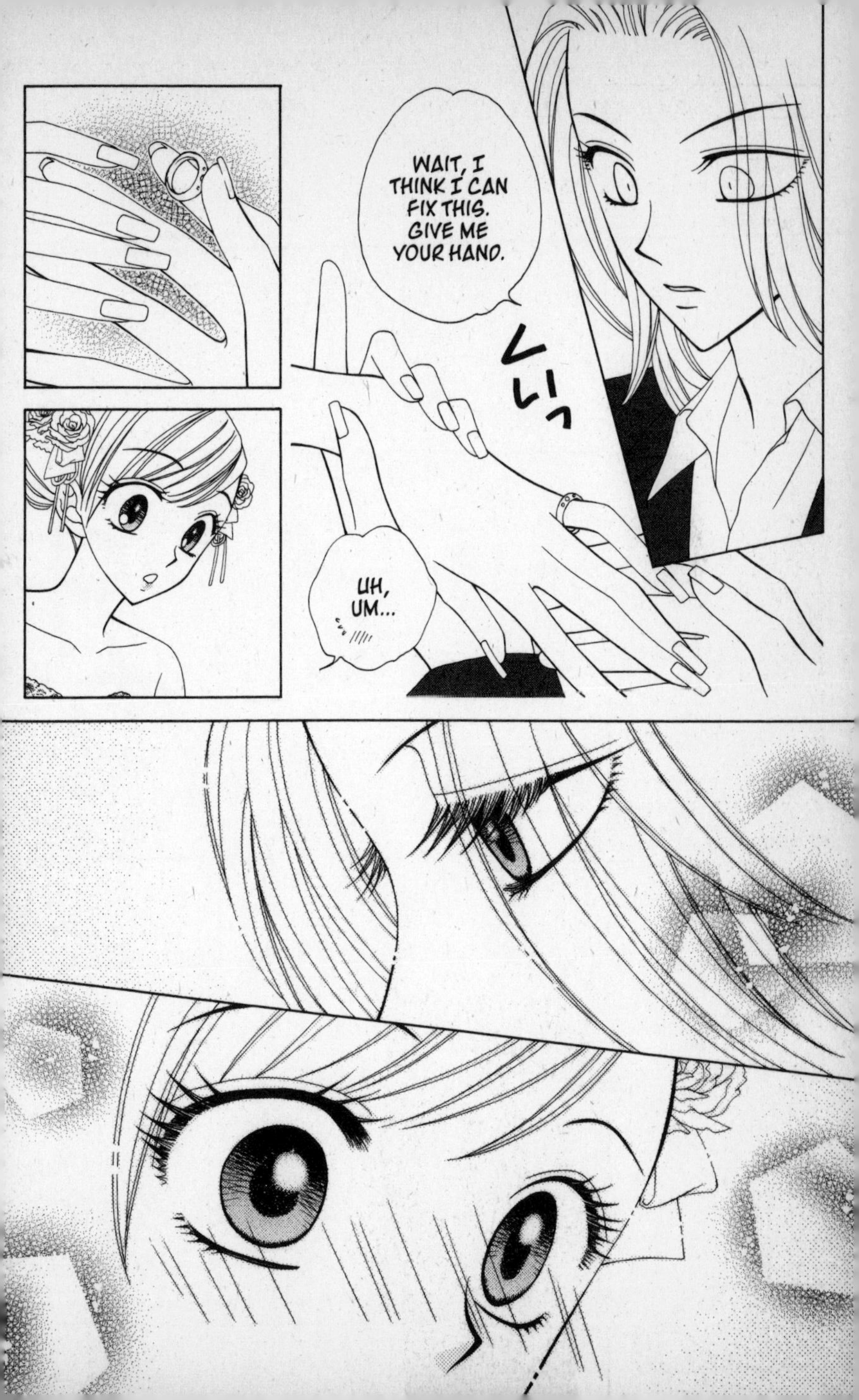
WAIT, I THINK I CAN FIX THIS. GIVE ME YOUR HAND.
くいっ
UH, UM...

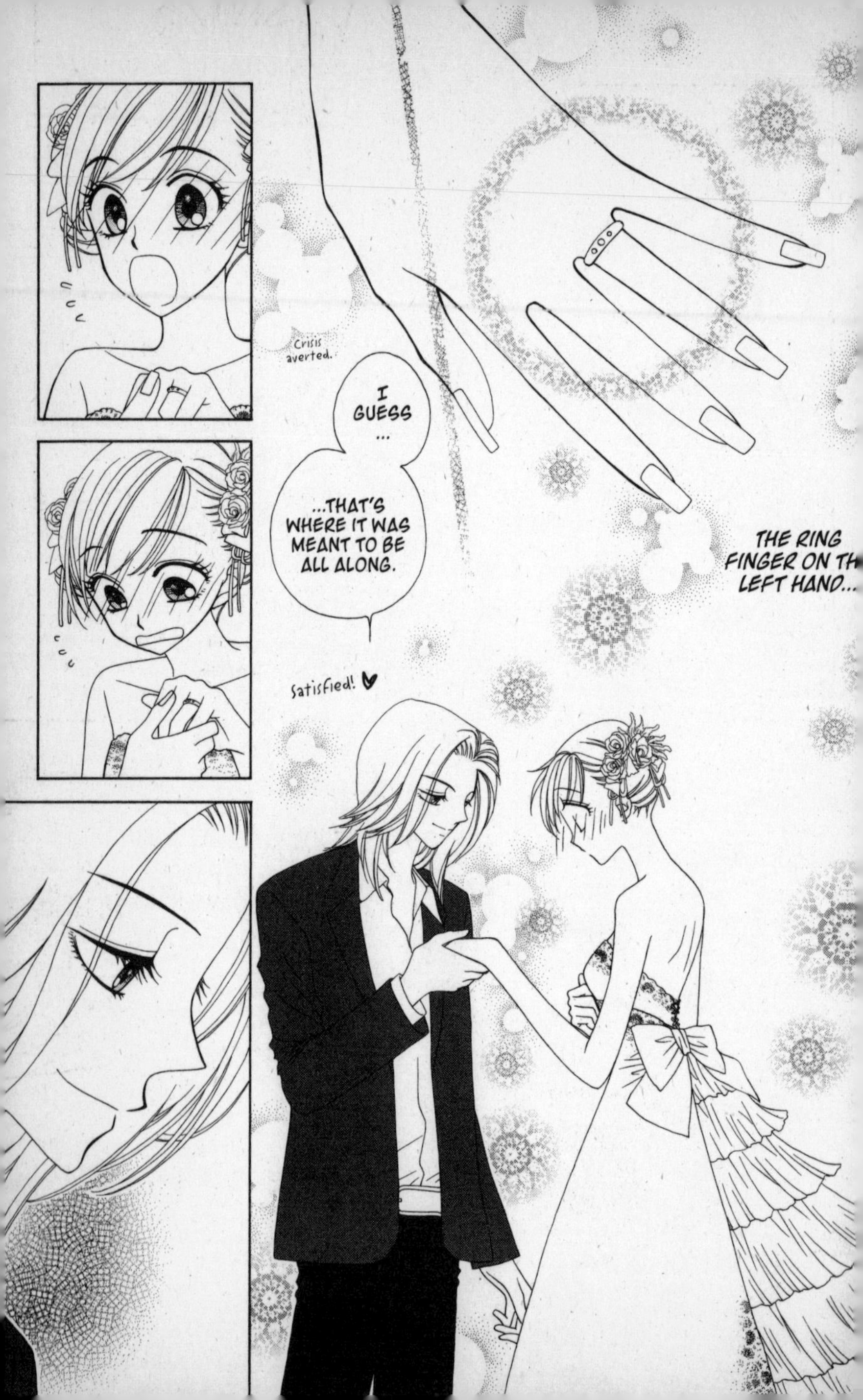
THE RING FINGER ON TH LEFT HAND...
I GUESS ...
...THAT'S WHERE IT WAS MEANT TO BE ALL ALONG.
Crisis averted.
Satisfied!

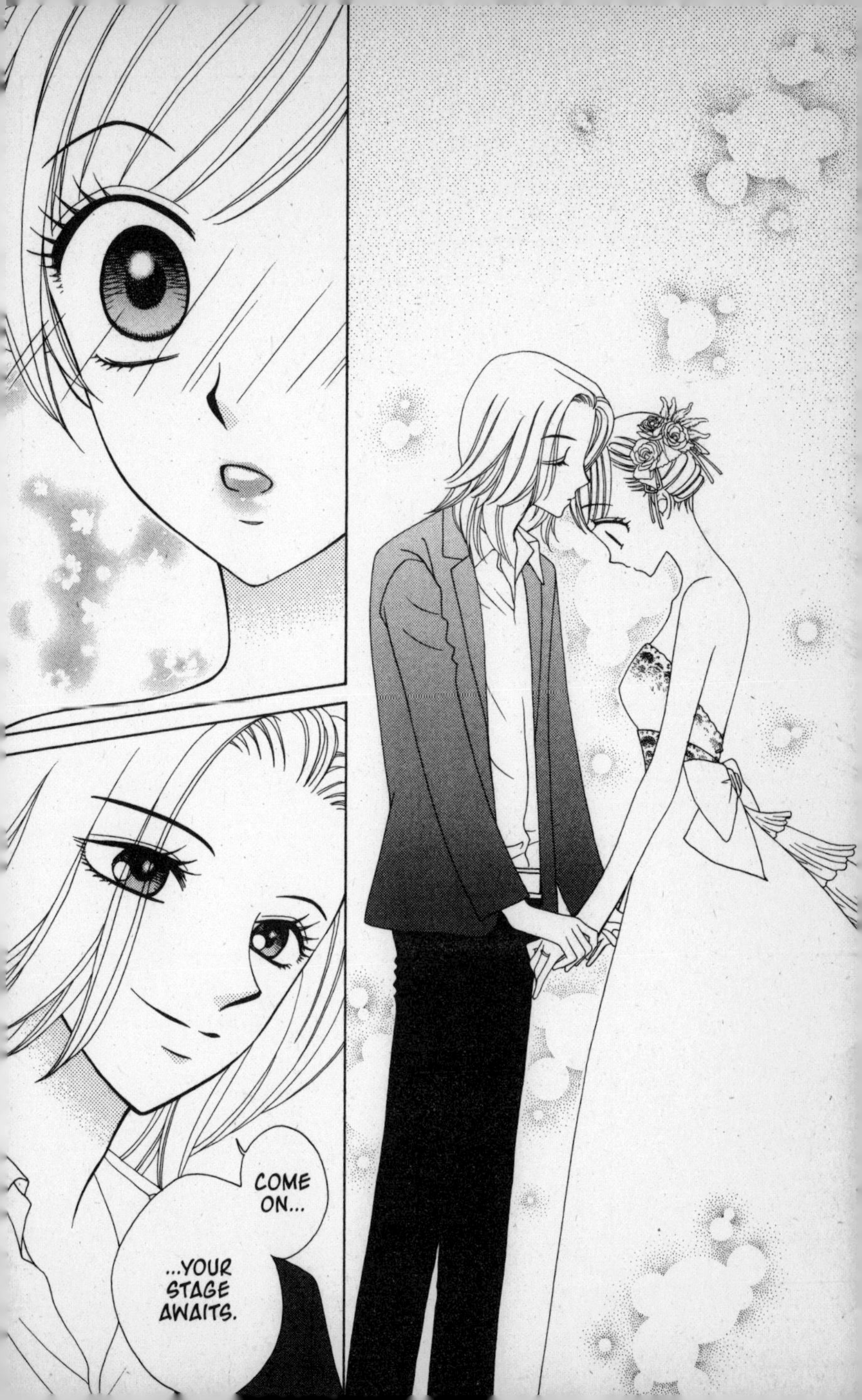
COME ON...
...YOUR STAGE AWAITS.

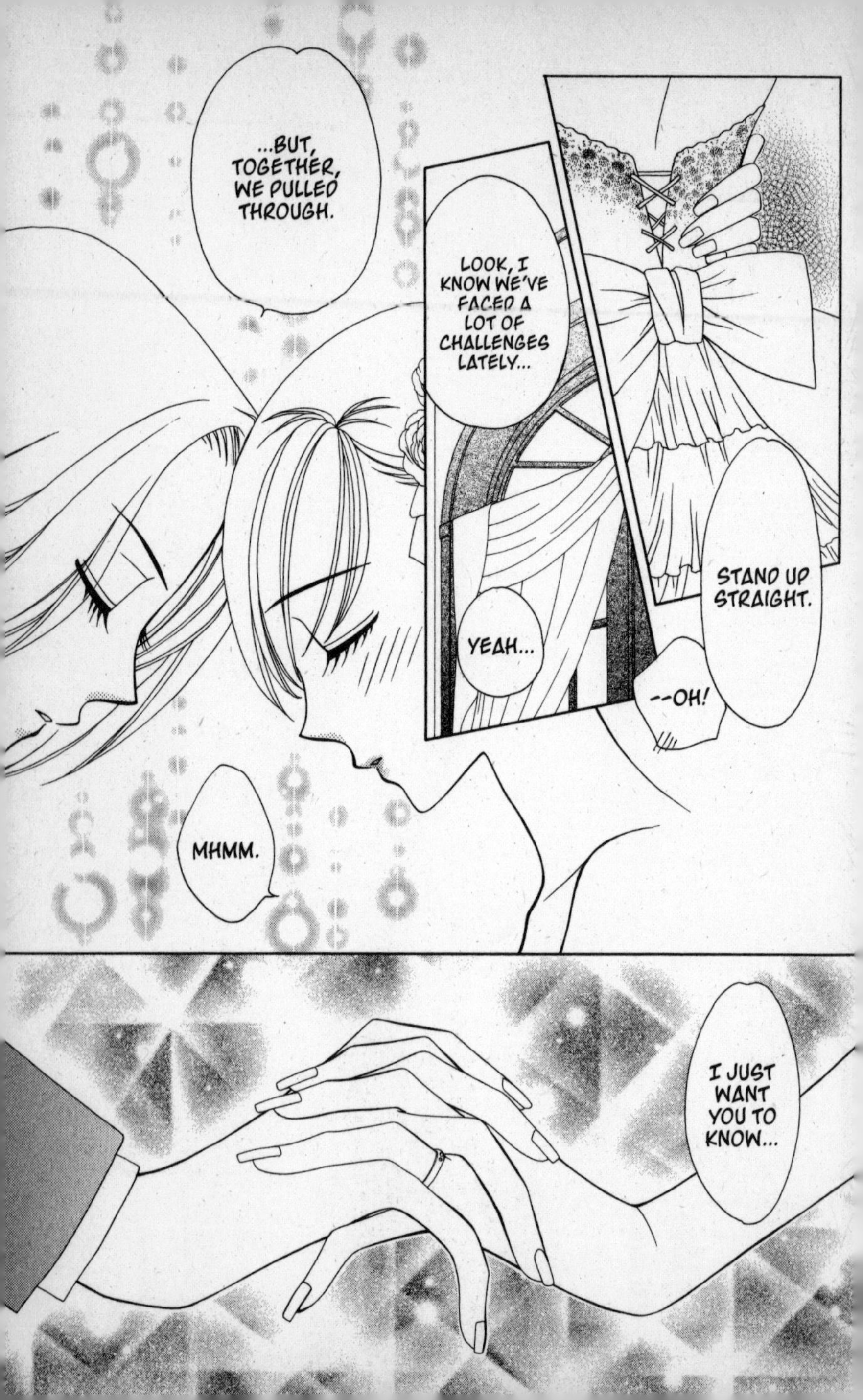
STAND UP STRAIGHT.
--OH!
LOOK, I KNOW WE'VE FACED A LOT OF CHALLENGES LATELY...
YEAH...
...BUT, TOGETHER, WE PULLED THROUGH.
MHMM.
I JUST WANT YOU TO KNOW...

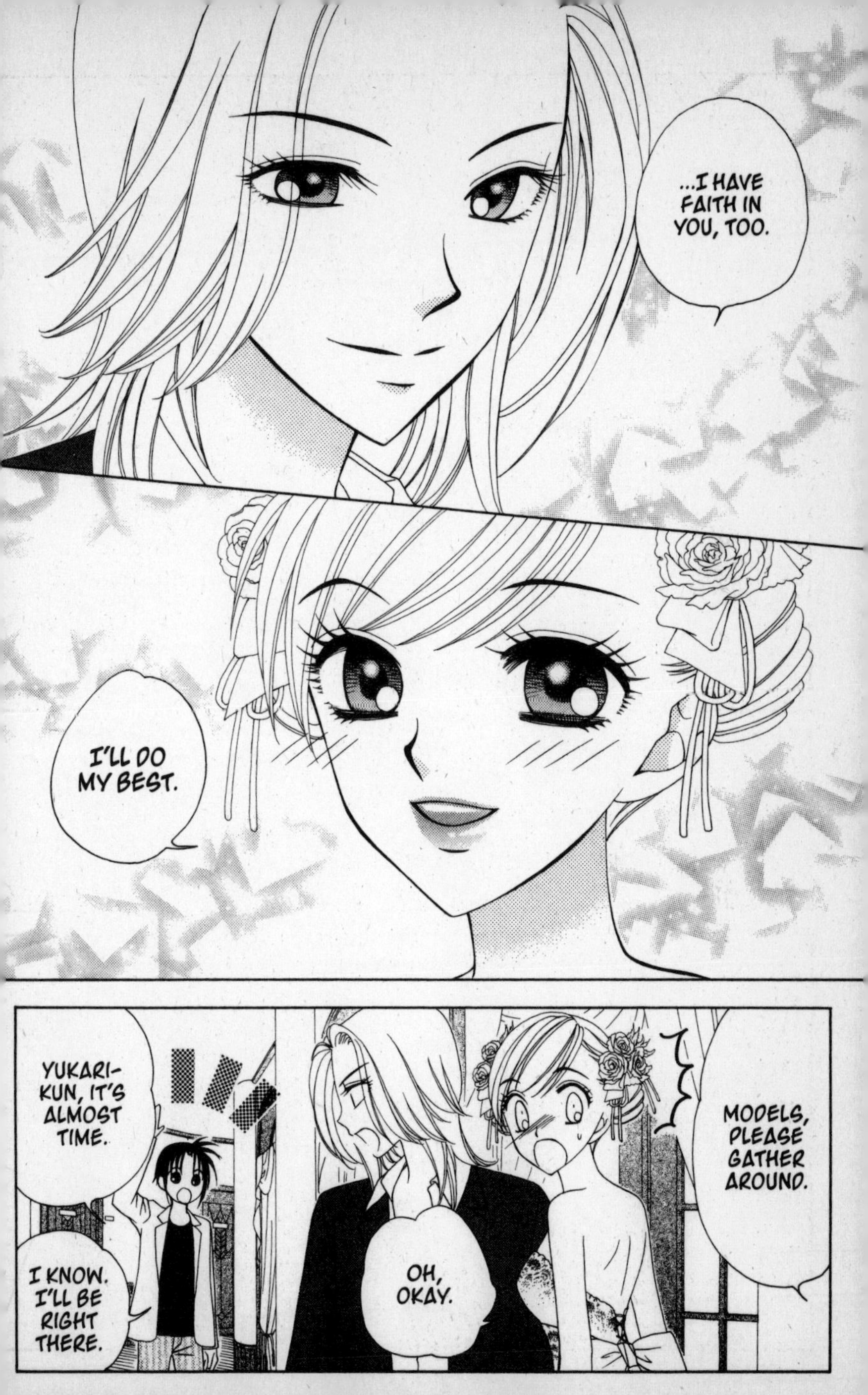
...I HAVE FAITH IN YOU, TOO.
I'LL DO MY BEST.
MODELS, PLEASE GATHER AROUND.
OH, OKAY.
YUKARI-KUN, IT'S ALMOST TIME.
I KNOW. I'LL BE RIGHT THERE.

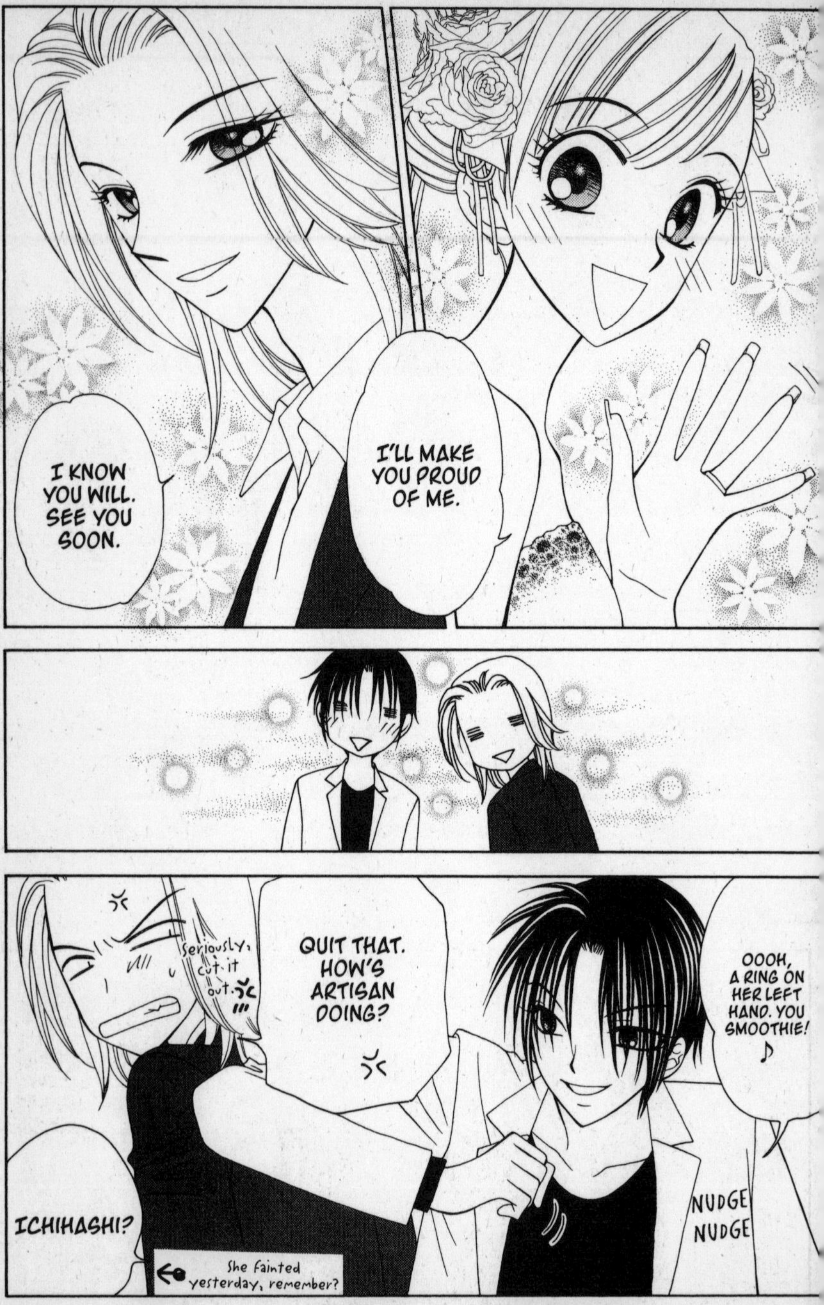
I'LL MAKE YOU PROUD OF ME.
I KNOW YOU WILL. SEE YOU SOON.
OOOH, A RING ON HER LEFT HAND. YOU SMOOTHIE! ♪
NUDGE NUDGE
QUIT THAT. HOW'S ARTISAN DOING?
Seriously, cut it out.
ICHIHASHI?
She fainted yesterday, remember?

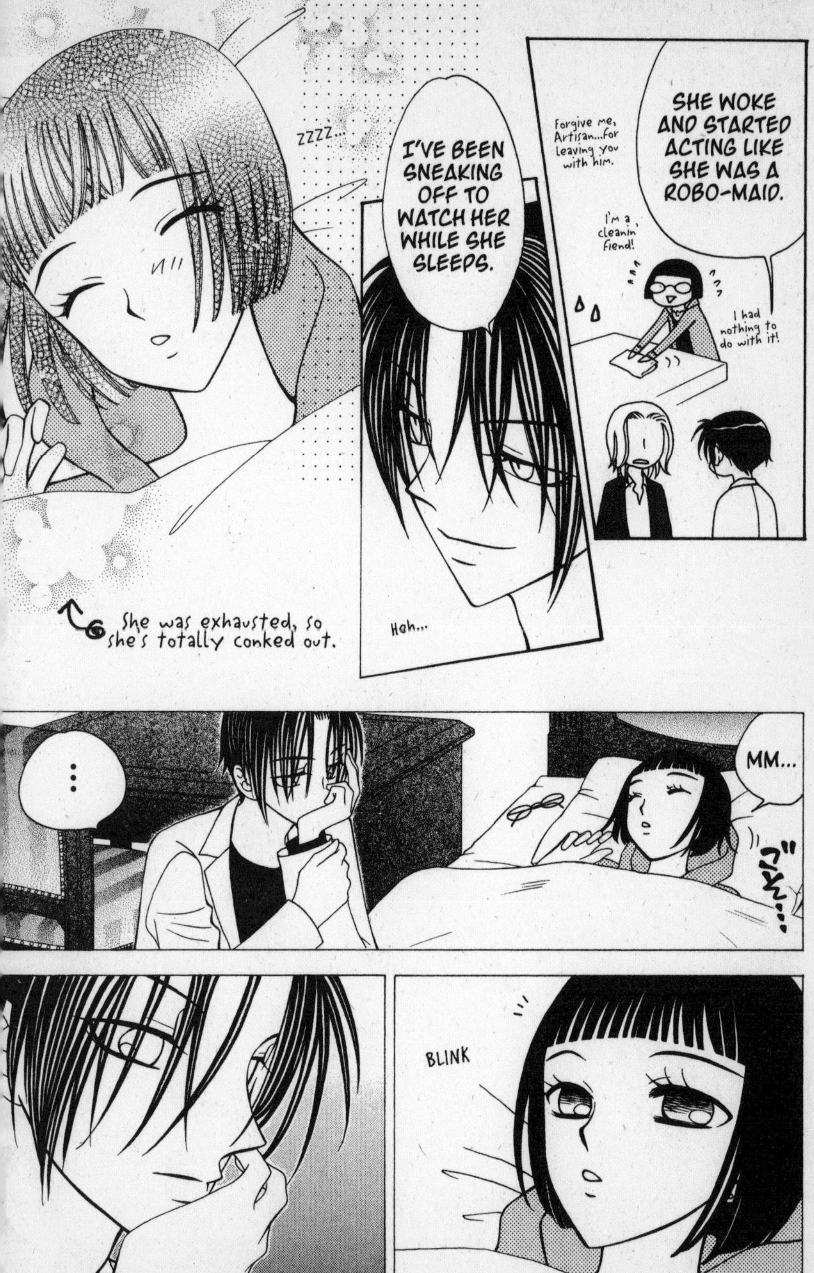
SHE WOKE AND STARTED ACTING LIKE SHE WAS A ROBO-MAID.
Forgive me, Artisan...for leaving you with him.
I'm a cleanin' fiend!
I had nothing to do with it!
I'VE BEEN SNEAKING OFF TO WATCH HER WHILE SHE SLEEPS.
Heh...
ZZZZ...
She was exhausted, so she's totally conked out.
MM...
...
BLINK

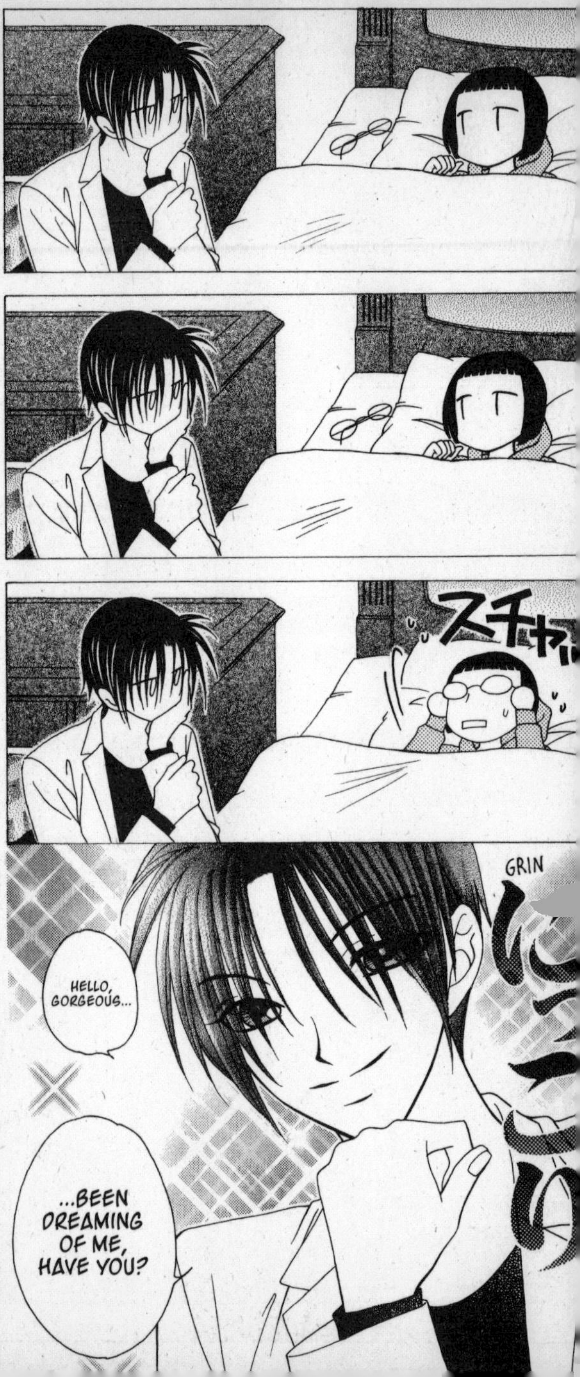
スチャ
GRIN
HELLO, GORGEOUS...
...BEEN DREAMING OF ME, HAVE YOU?

Story continued: That night, we walked around the bustling city, admiring all of the decorations.

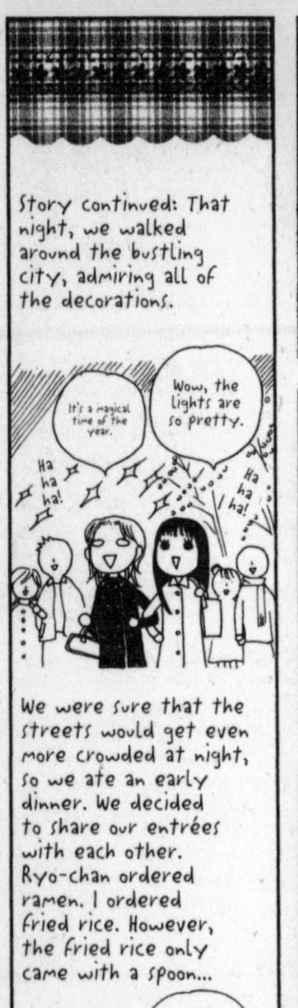
Wow, the lights are so pretty.
It's a magical time of the year.
Ha ha ha!
Ha ha ha!

We were sure that the streets would get even more crowded at night, so we ate an early dinner. We decided to share our entrées with each other. Ryo-chan ordered ramen. I ordered fried rice. However, the fried rice only came with a spoon...

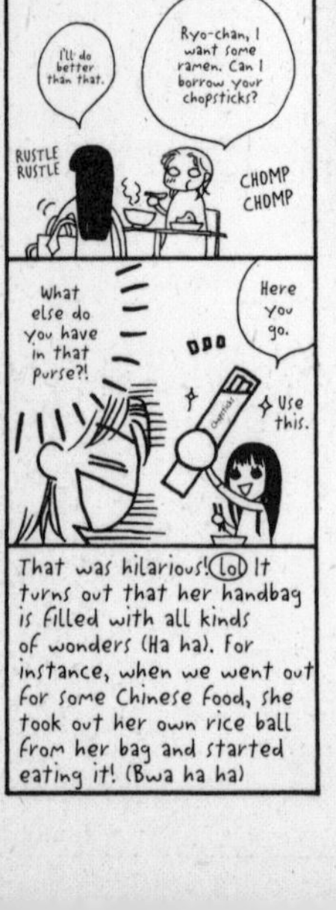
Ryo-chan, I want some ramen. Can I borrow your chopsticks?
I'll do better than that.
RUSTLE RUSTLE
CHOMP CHOMP
Here you go.
What else do you have in that purse?!
Use this.

That was hilarious! (lol) It turns out that her handbag is filled with all kinds of wonders (Ha ha). For instance, when we went out for some Chinese food, she took out her own rice ball from her bag and started eating it! (Bwa ha ha)

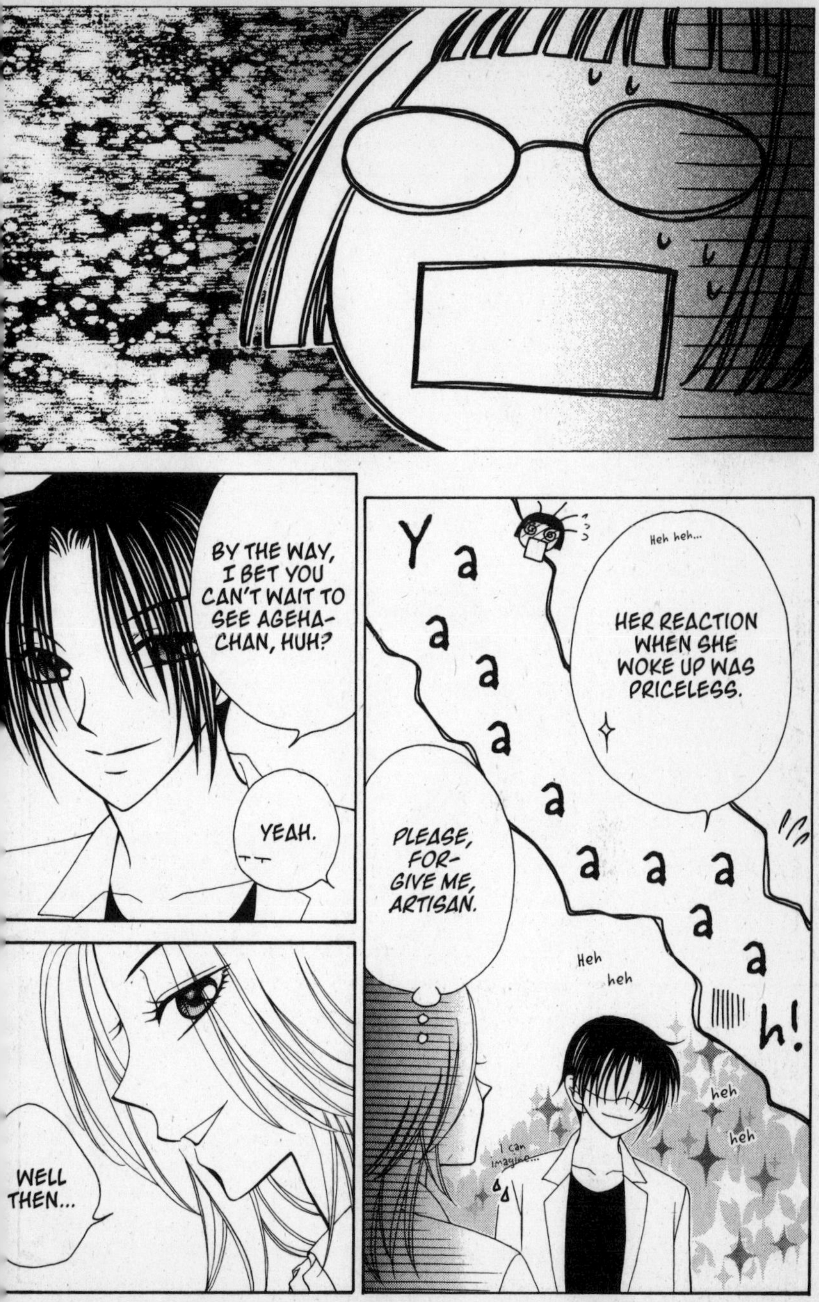
Heh heh...
HER REACTION WHEN SHE WOKE UP WAS PRICELESS.
Yaaaaaaaaaaaah!
Heh heh
PLEASE, FOR-GIVE ME, ARTISAN.
heh heh
I can imagine...
BY THE WAY, I BET YOU CAN'T WAIT TO SEE AGEHA-CHAN, HUH?
YEAH.
WELL THEN...

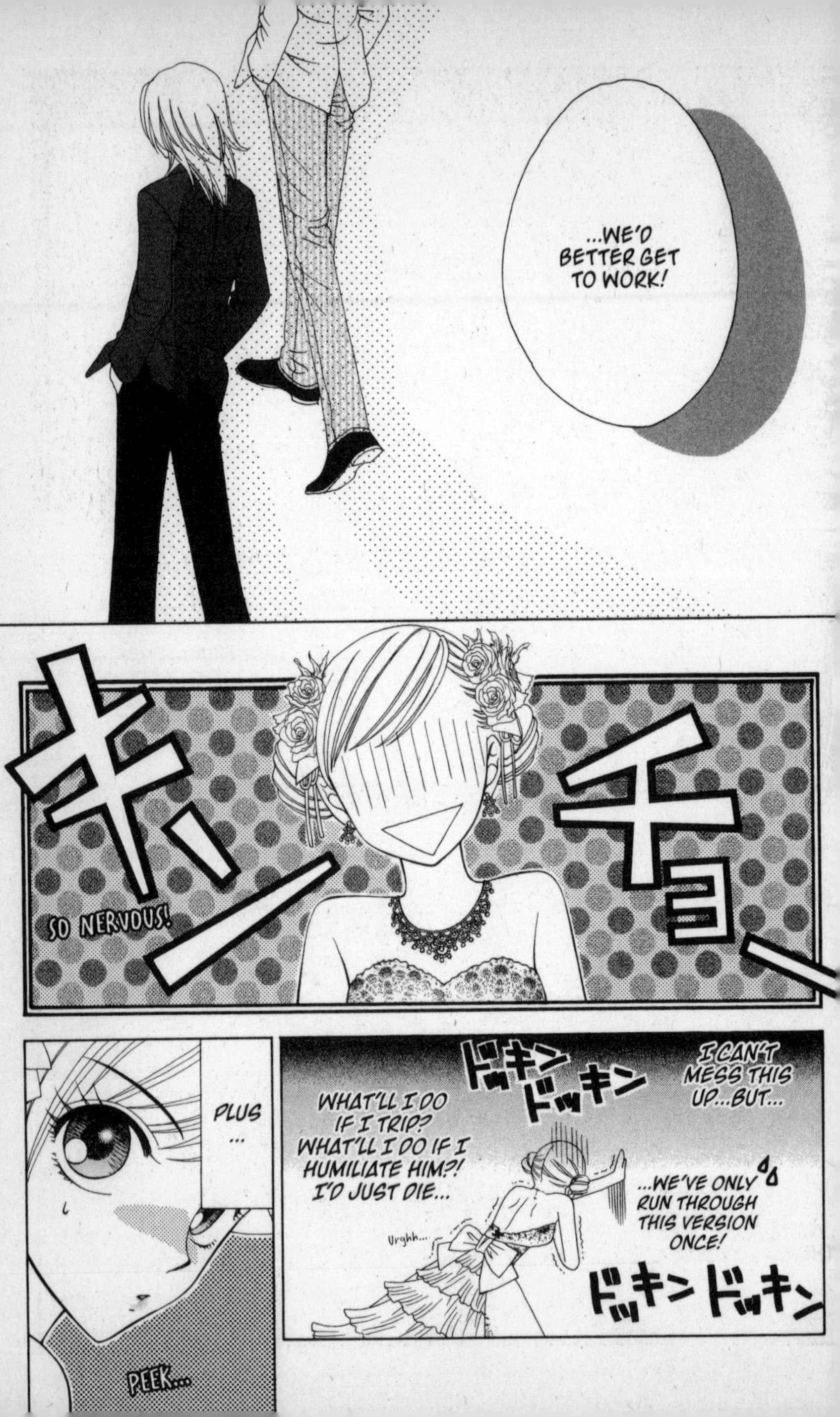
...WE'D BETTER GET TO WORK!
キンチョー
SO NERVOUS!
I CAN'T MESS THIS UP...BUT...
ドッキンドッキン
WHAT'LL I DO IF I TRIP? WHAT'LL I DO IF I HUMILIATE HIM?! I'D JUST DIE...
...WE'VE ONLY RUN THROUGH THIS VERSION ONCE!
Urghh...
ドッキンドッキン
PLUS ...
PEEK...

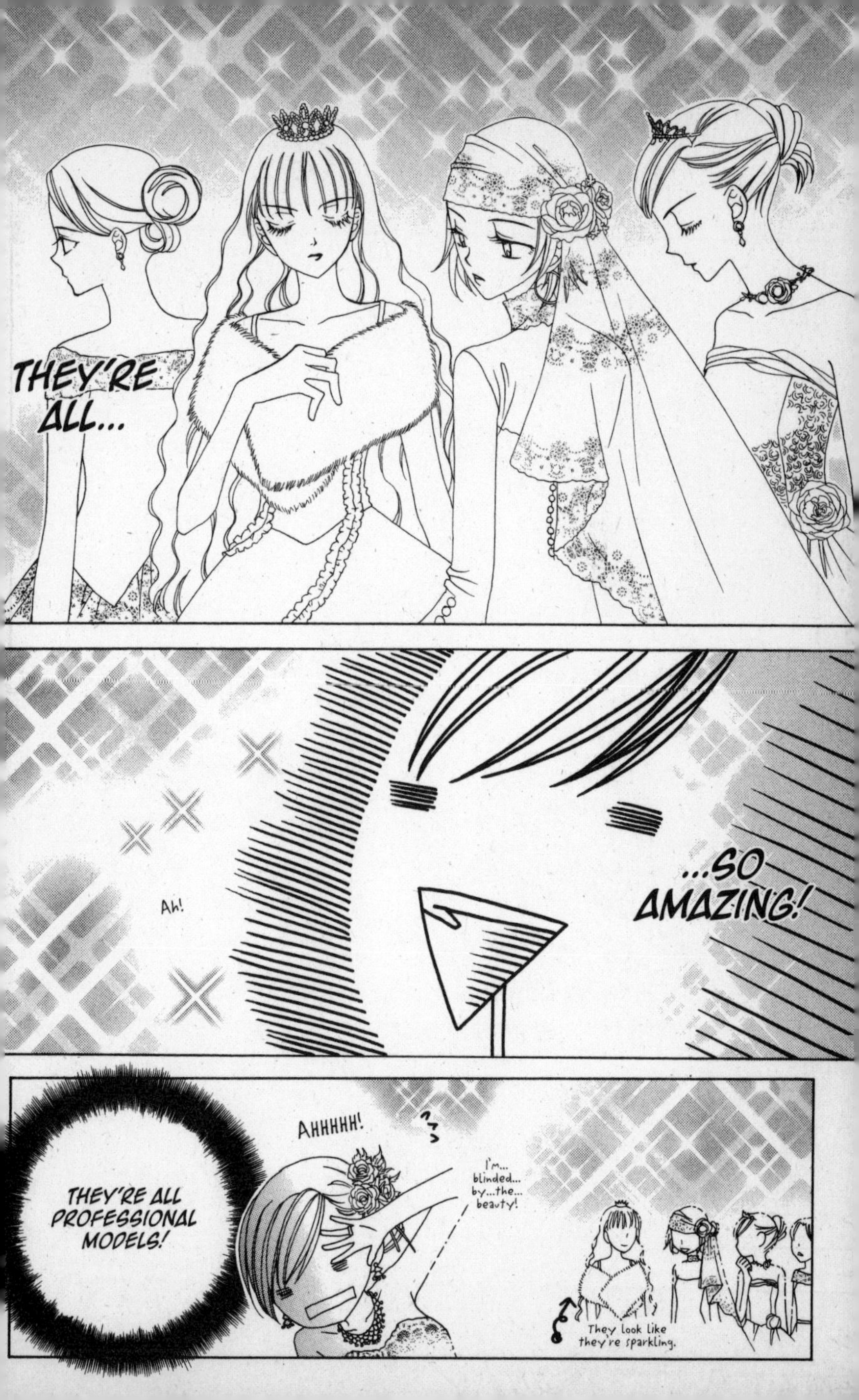
THEY'RE ALL...
...SO AMAZING!
Ah!
AHHHHH!
I'm... blinded... by...the... beauty!
They look like they're sparkling.
THEY'RE ALL PROFESSIONAL MODELS!

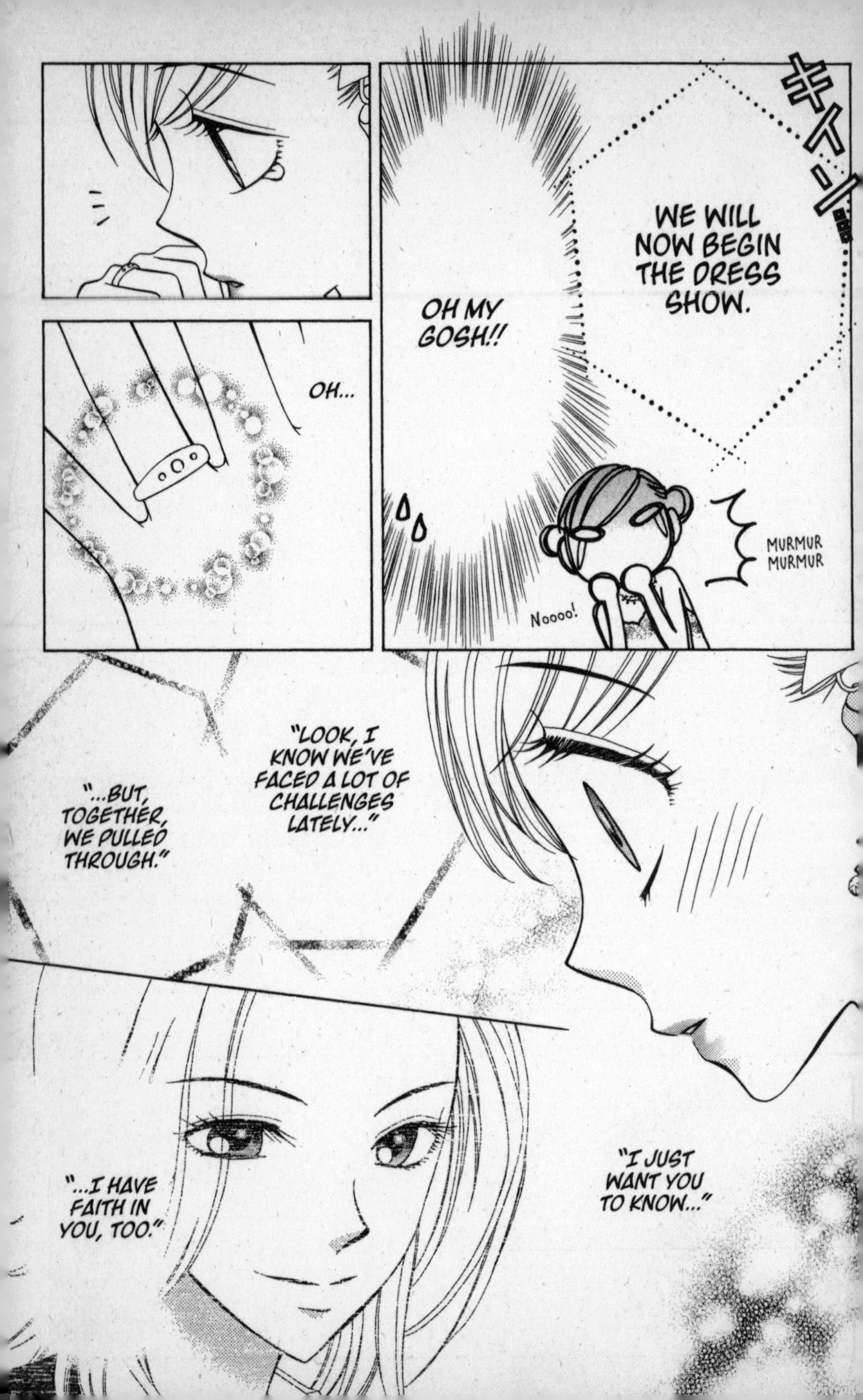
WE WILL NOW BEGIN THE DRESS SHOW.
OH MY GOSH!!
MURMUR MURMUR
Noooo!
OH...
"LOOK, I KNOW WE'VE FACED A LOT OF CHALLENGES LATELY..."
"...BUT, TOGETHER, WE PULLED THROUGH."
"I JUST WANT YOU TO KNOW..."
"...I HAVE FAITH IN YOU, TOO."

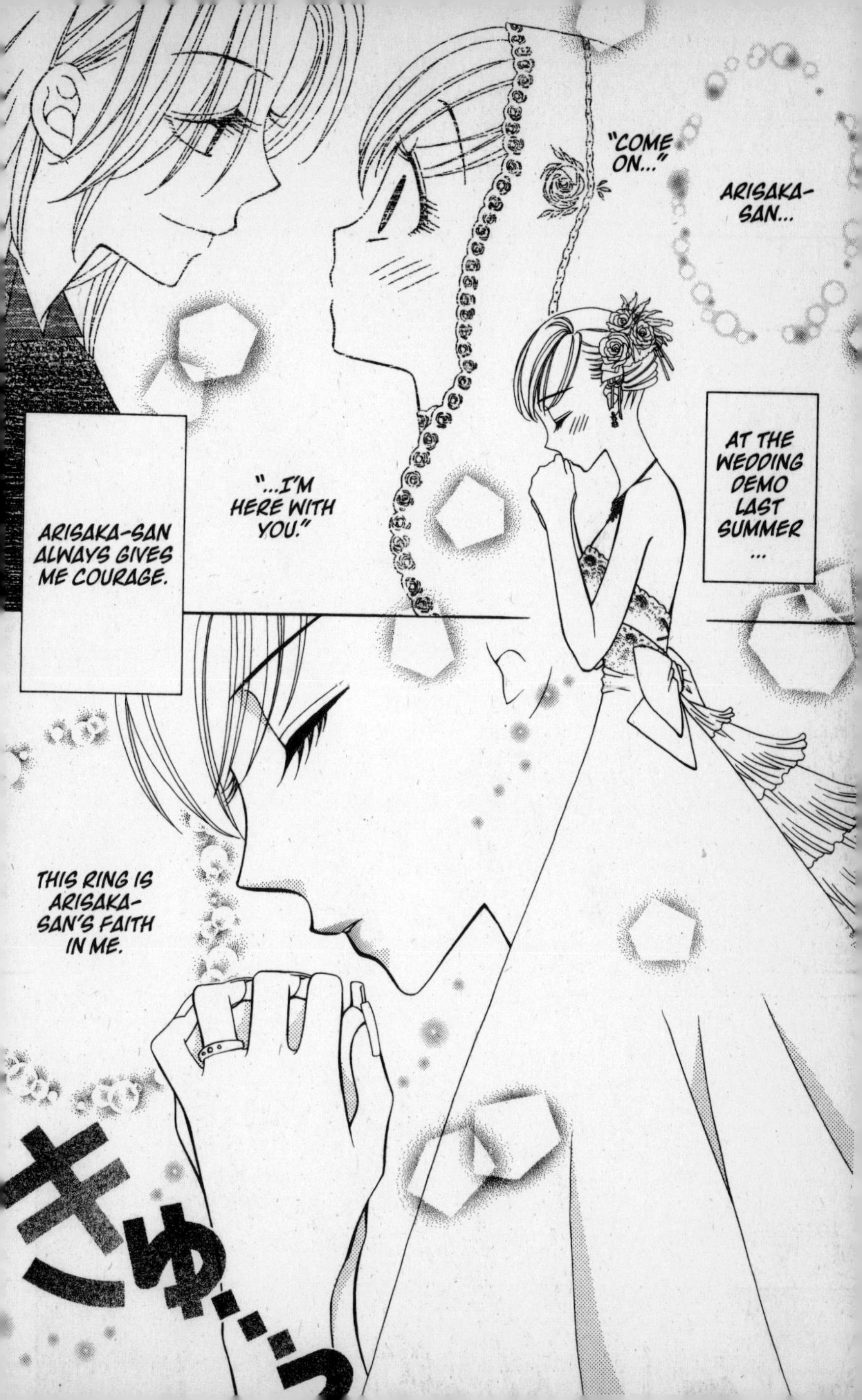
ARISAKA-SAN...
"COME ON..."
AT THE WEDDING DEMO LAST SUMMER...
"...I'M HERE WITH YOU."
ARISAKA-SAN ALWAYS GIVES ME COURAGE.
THIS RING IS ARISAKA-SAN'S FAITH IN ME.
きゅ…っ

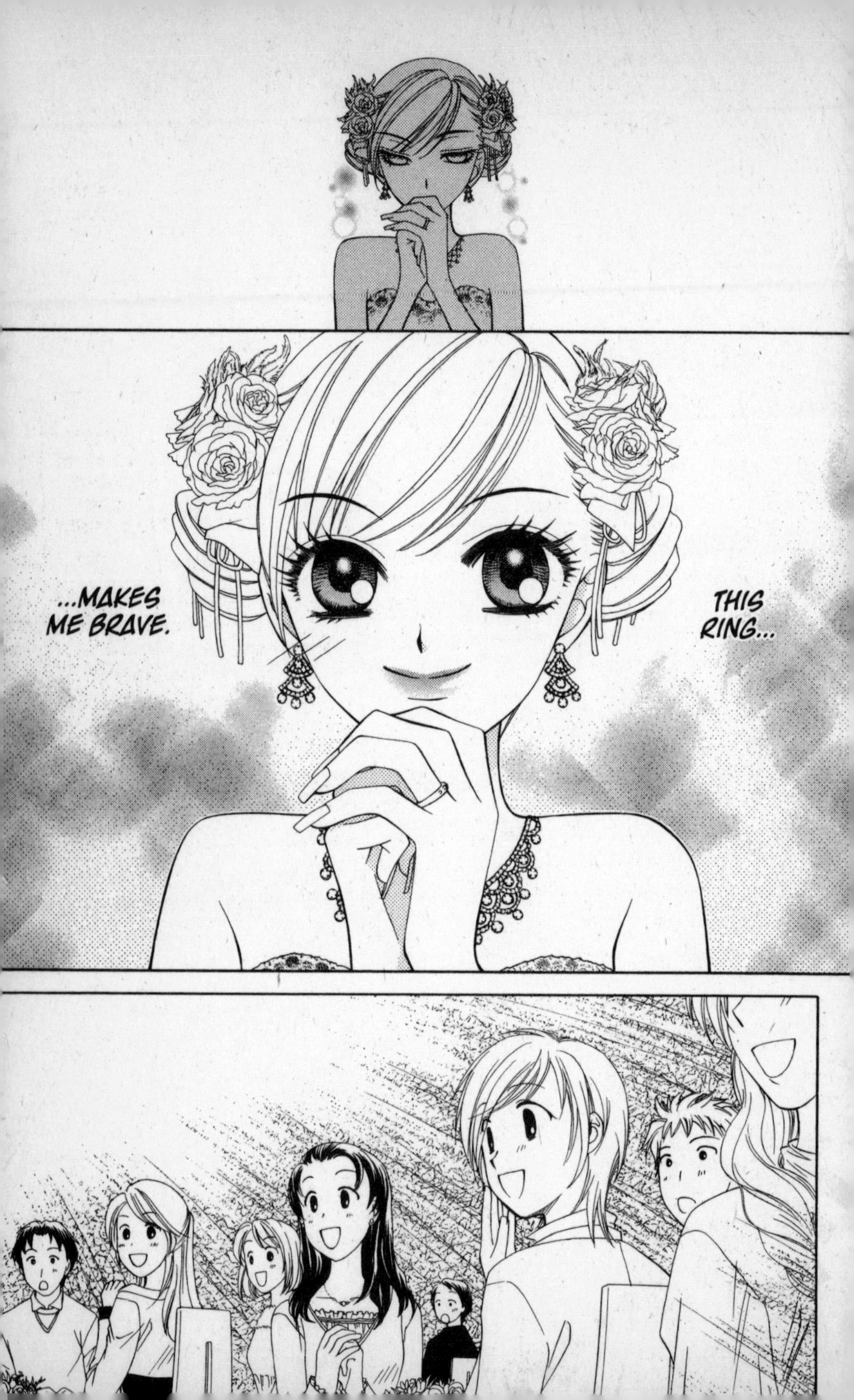
THIS RING...
...MAKES ME BRAVE.

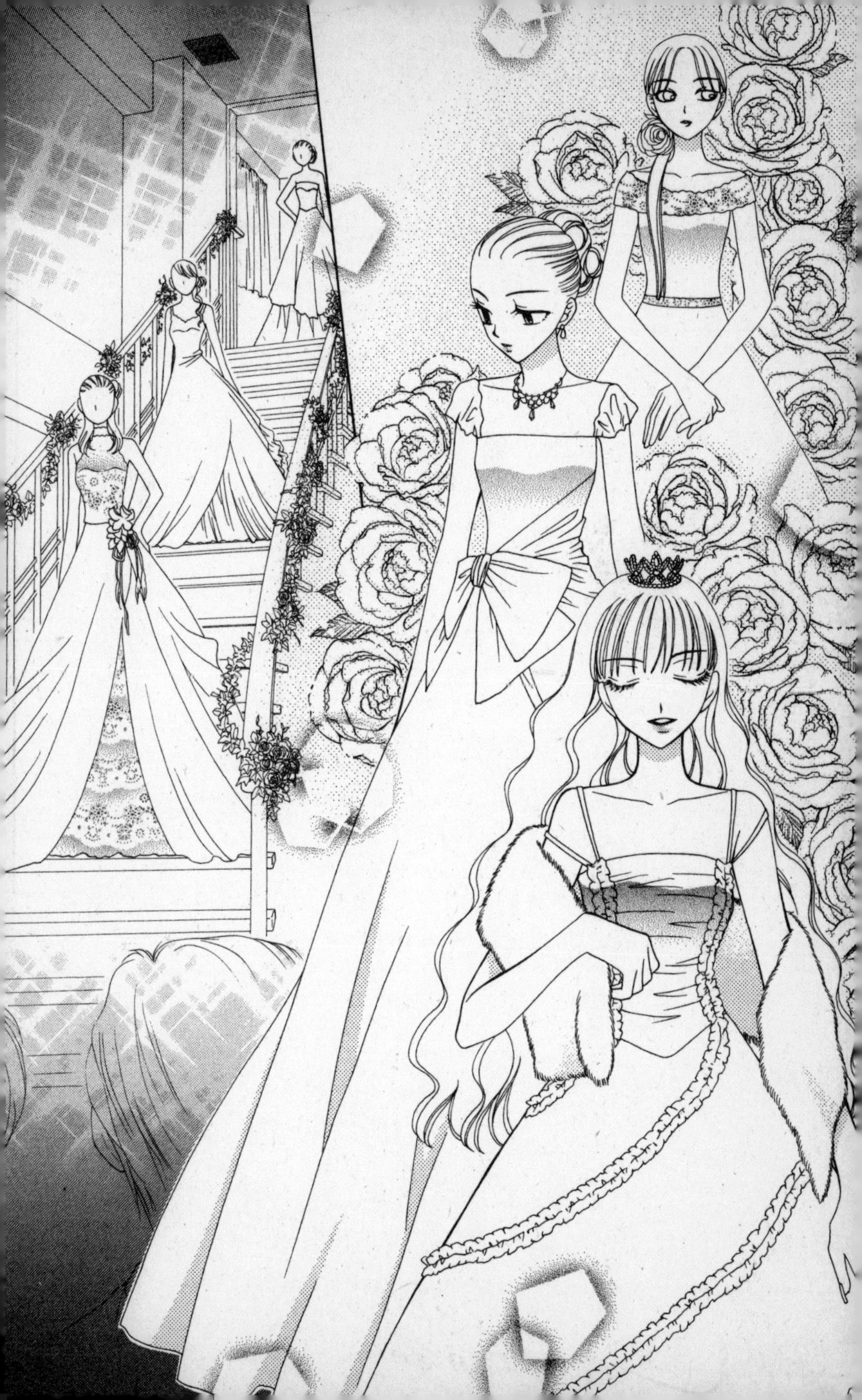

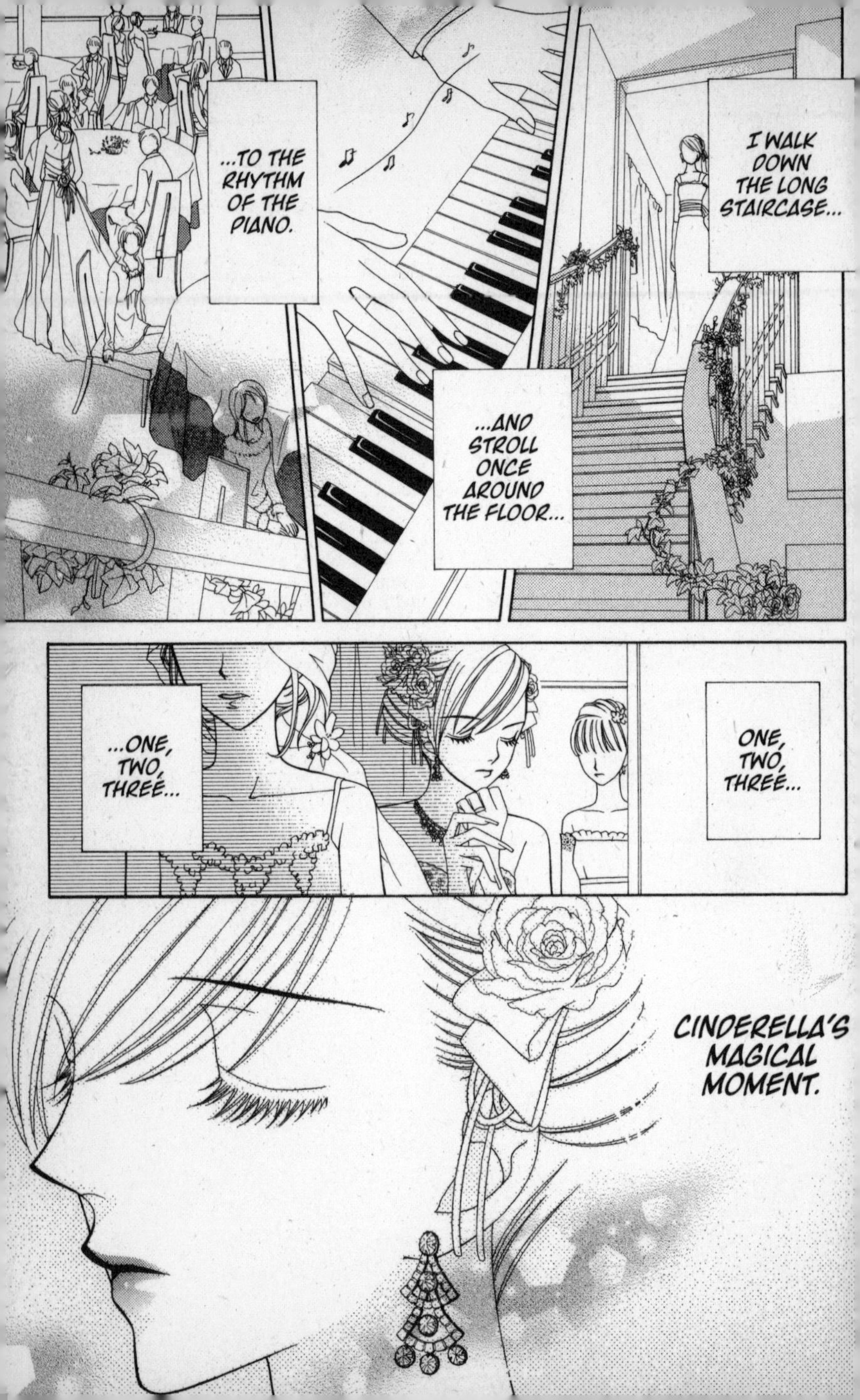
I WALK DOWN THE LONG STAIRCASE...
...AND STROLL ONCE AROUND THE FLOOR...
...TO THE RHYTHM OF THE PIANO.
ONE, TWO, THREE...
...ONE, TWO, THREE...
CINDERELLA'S MAGICAL MOMENT.

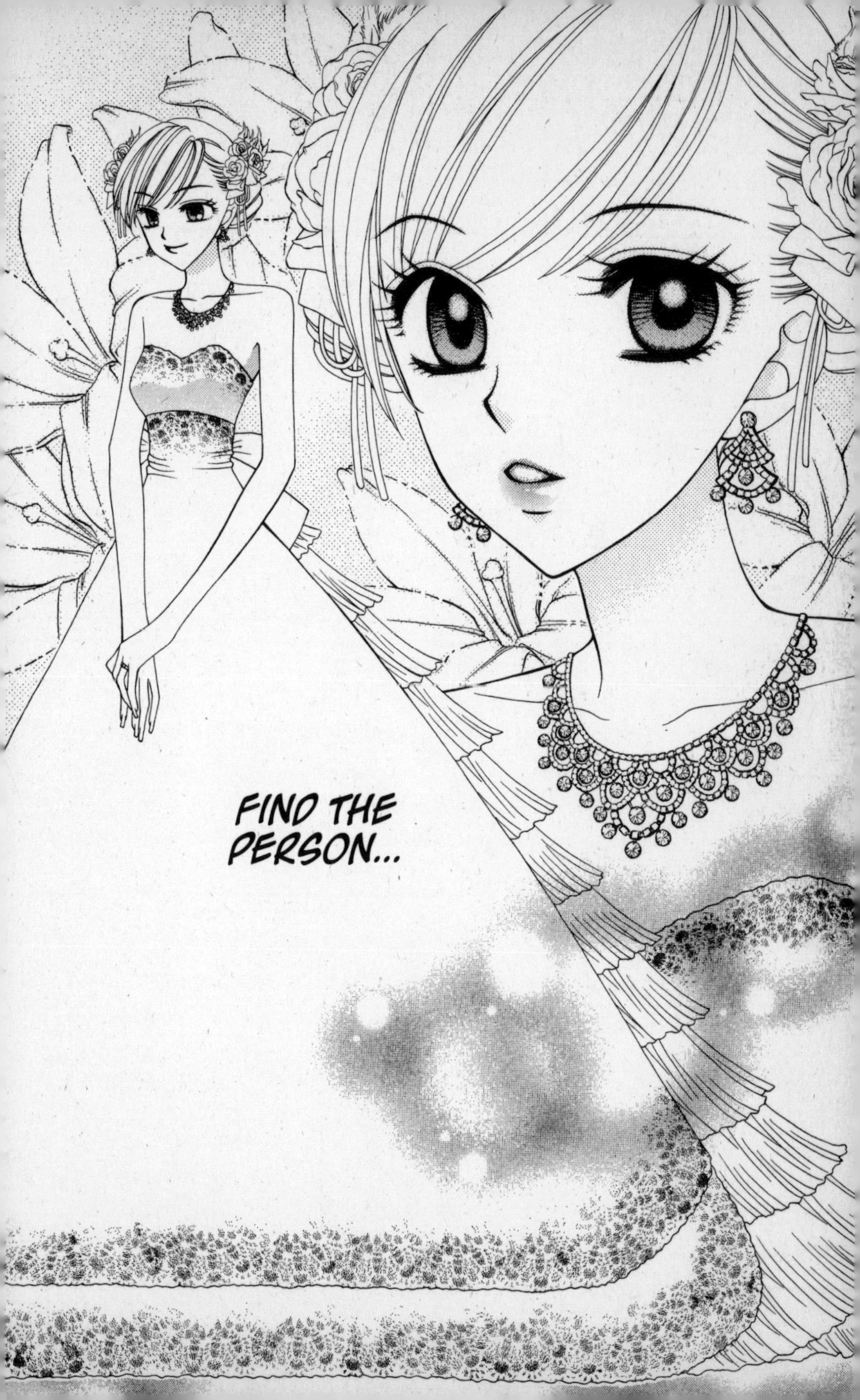
FIND THE PERSON...

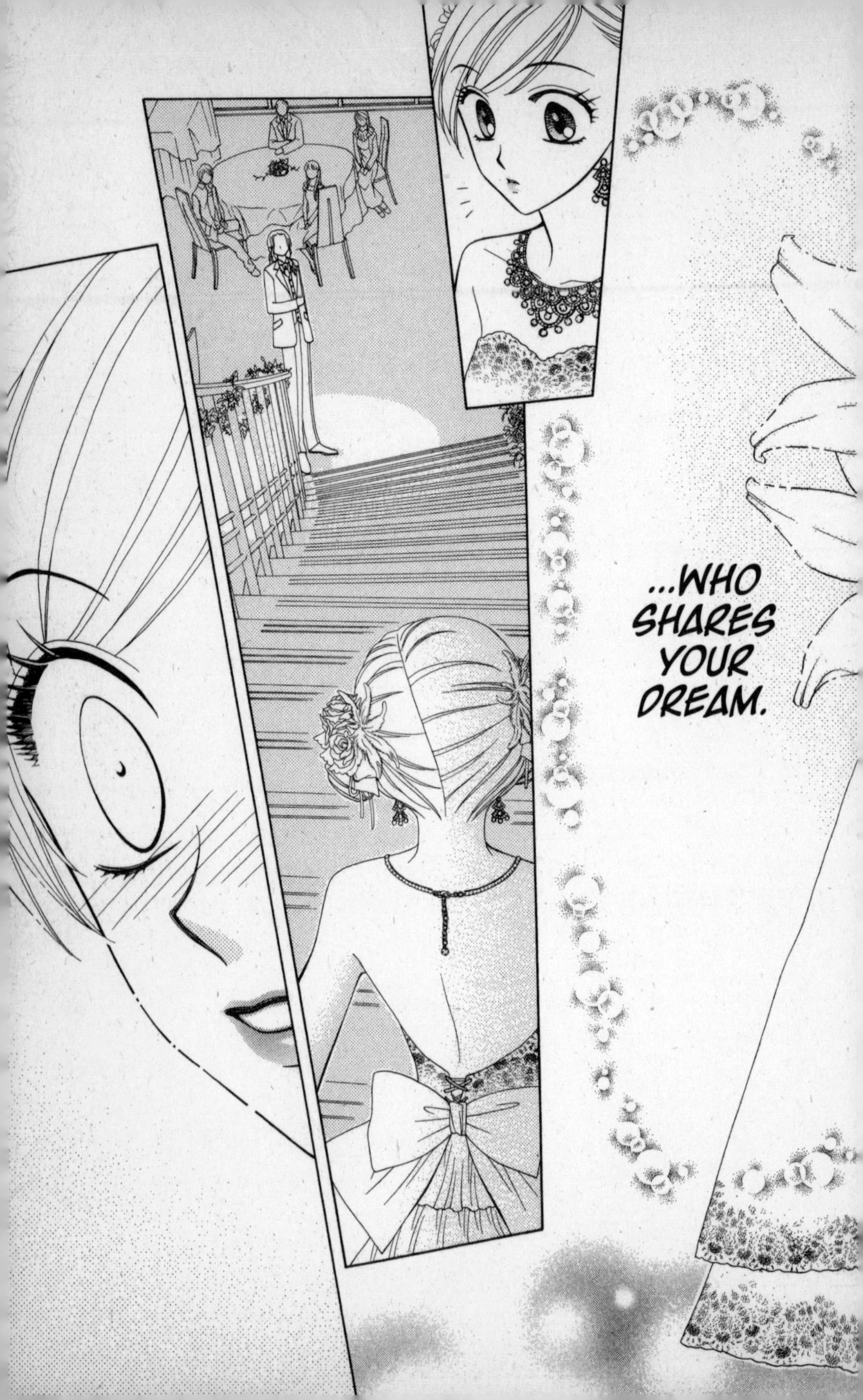
...WHO SHARES YOUR DREAM.

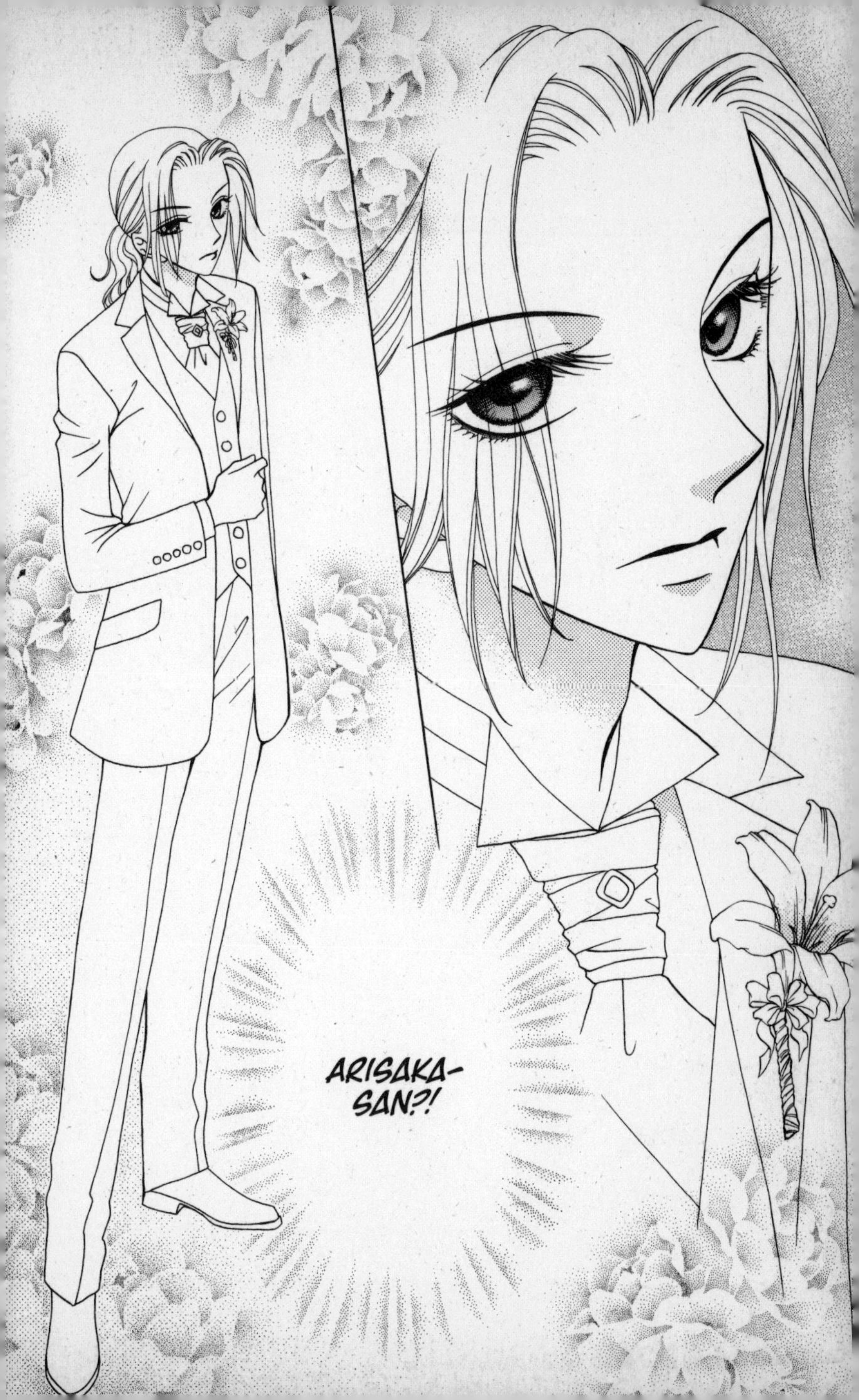
ARISAKA-
SAN?!

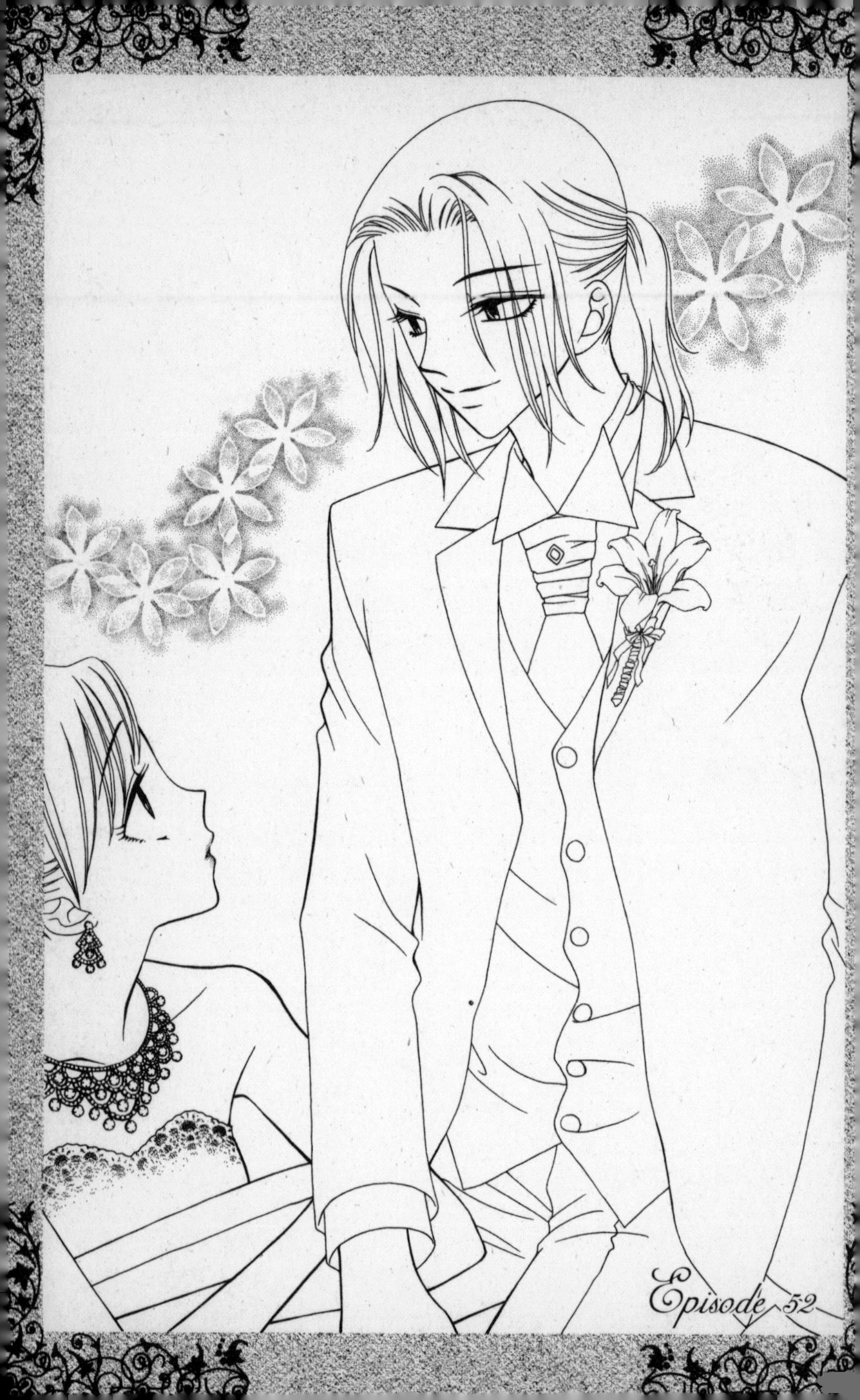
Episode 52

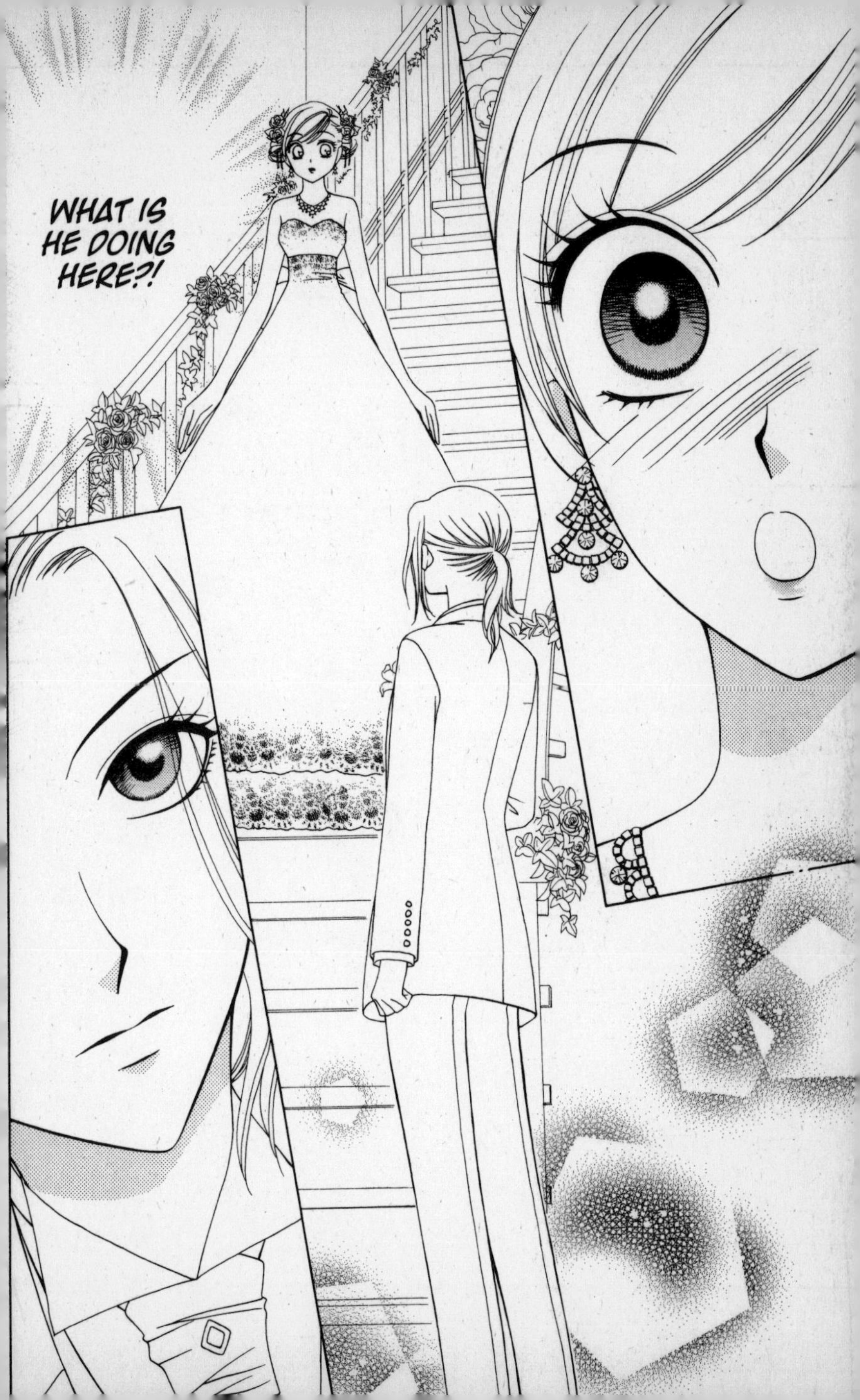
WHAT IS HE DOING HERE?!

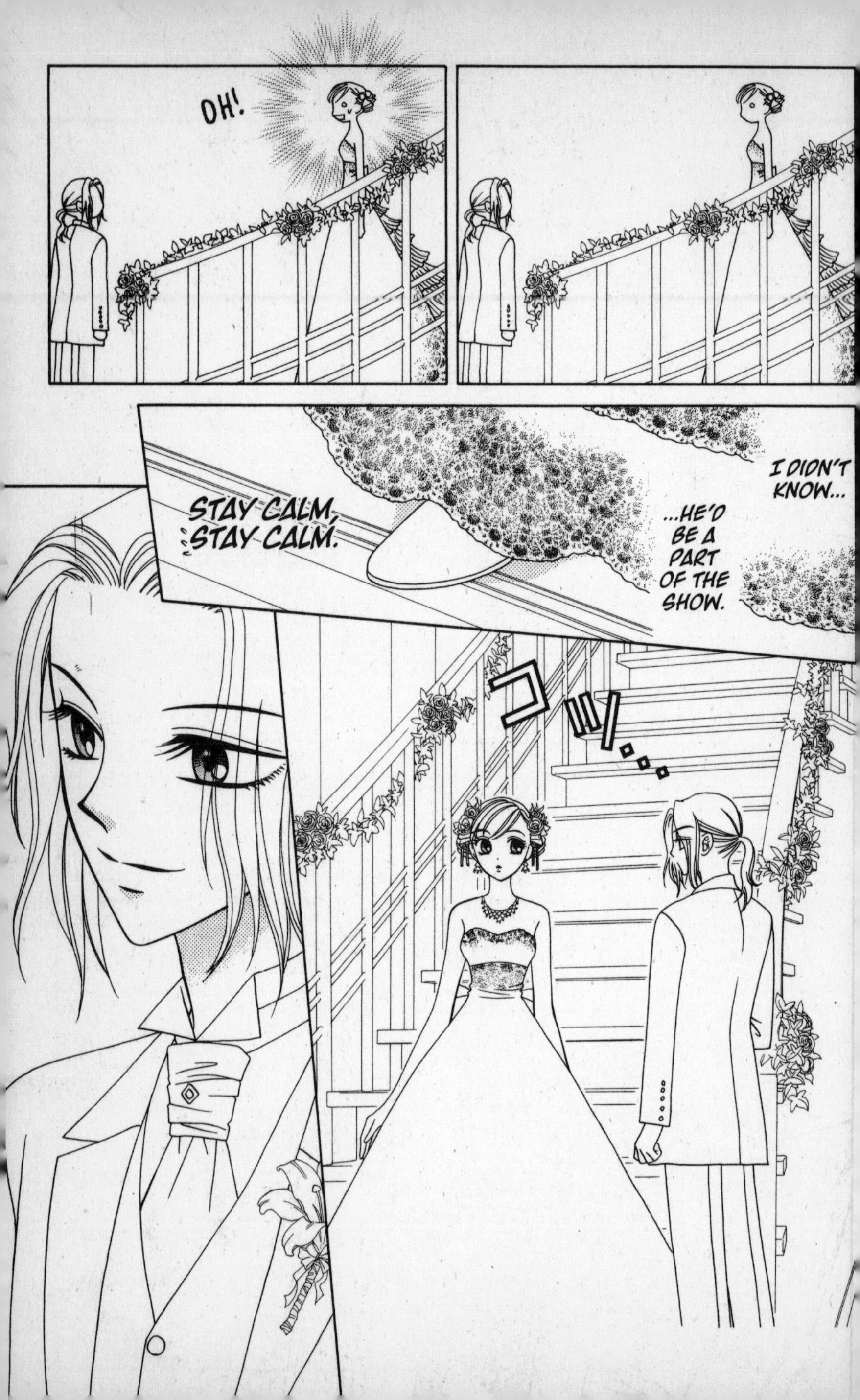
OH!
I DIDN'T KNOW...
...HE'D BE A PART OF THE SHOW.
STAY CALM, STAY CALM.
コツ...

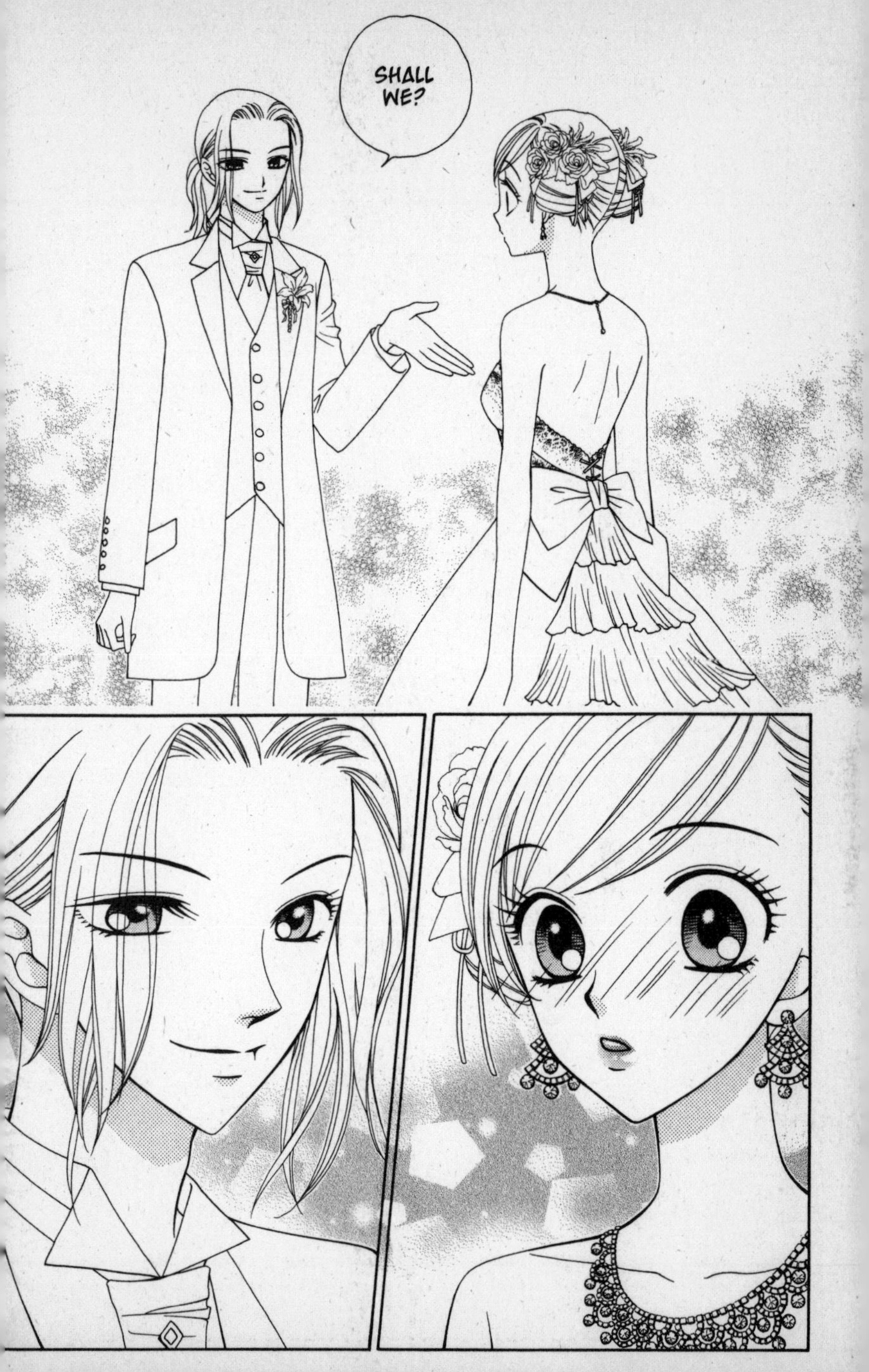
SHALL WE?

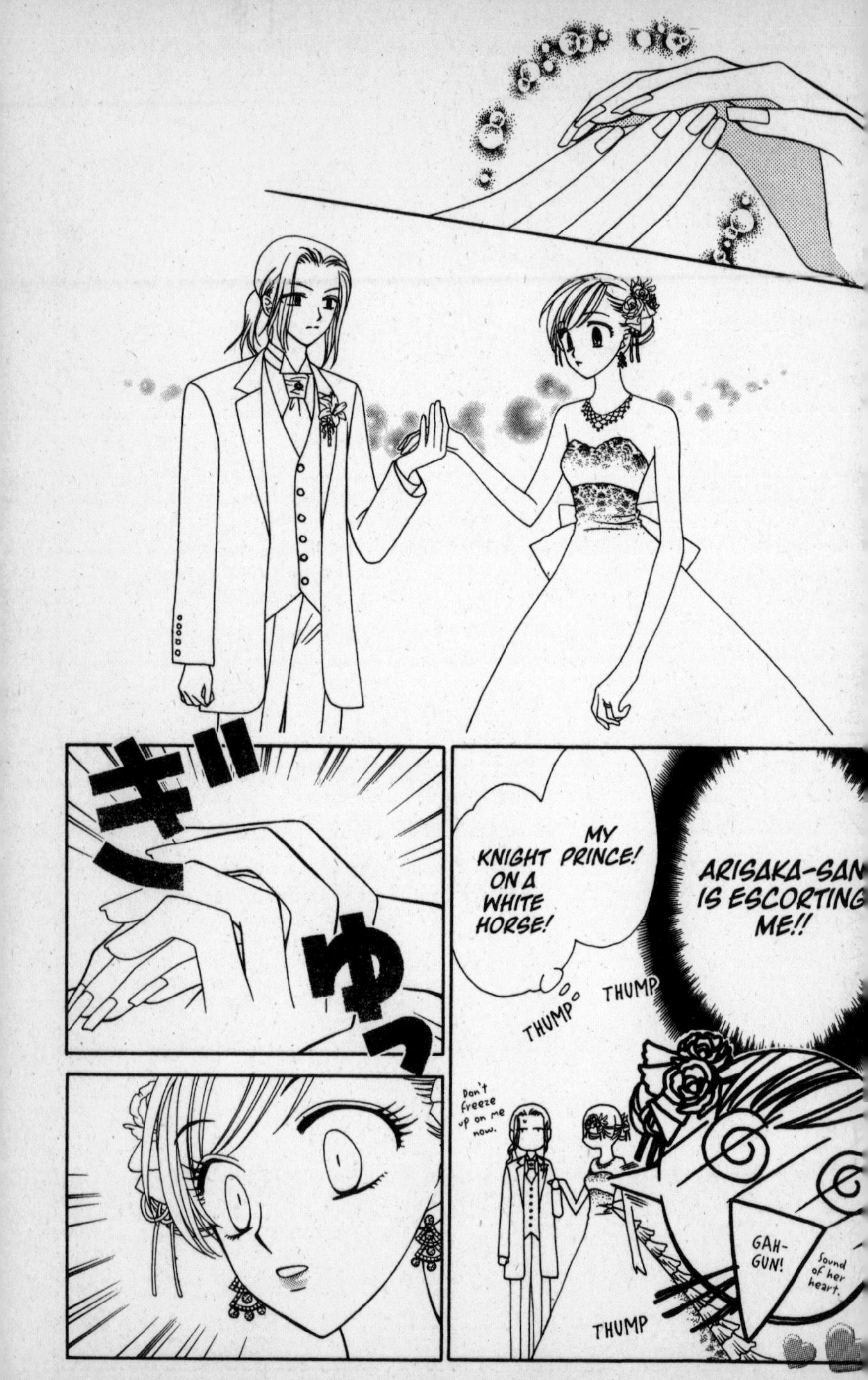
ARISAKA-SAN IS ESCORTING ME!!
MY PRINCE! KNIGHT ON A WHITE HORSE!
THUMP THUMP
Sound of her heart.
GAH-GUN!
Don't freeze up on me now.
THUMP
ぎゅっ

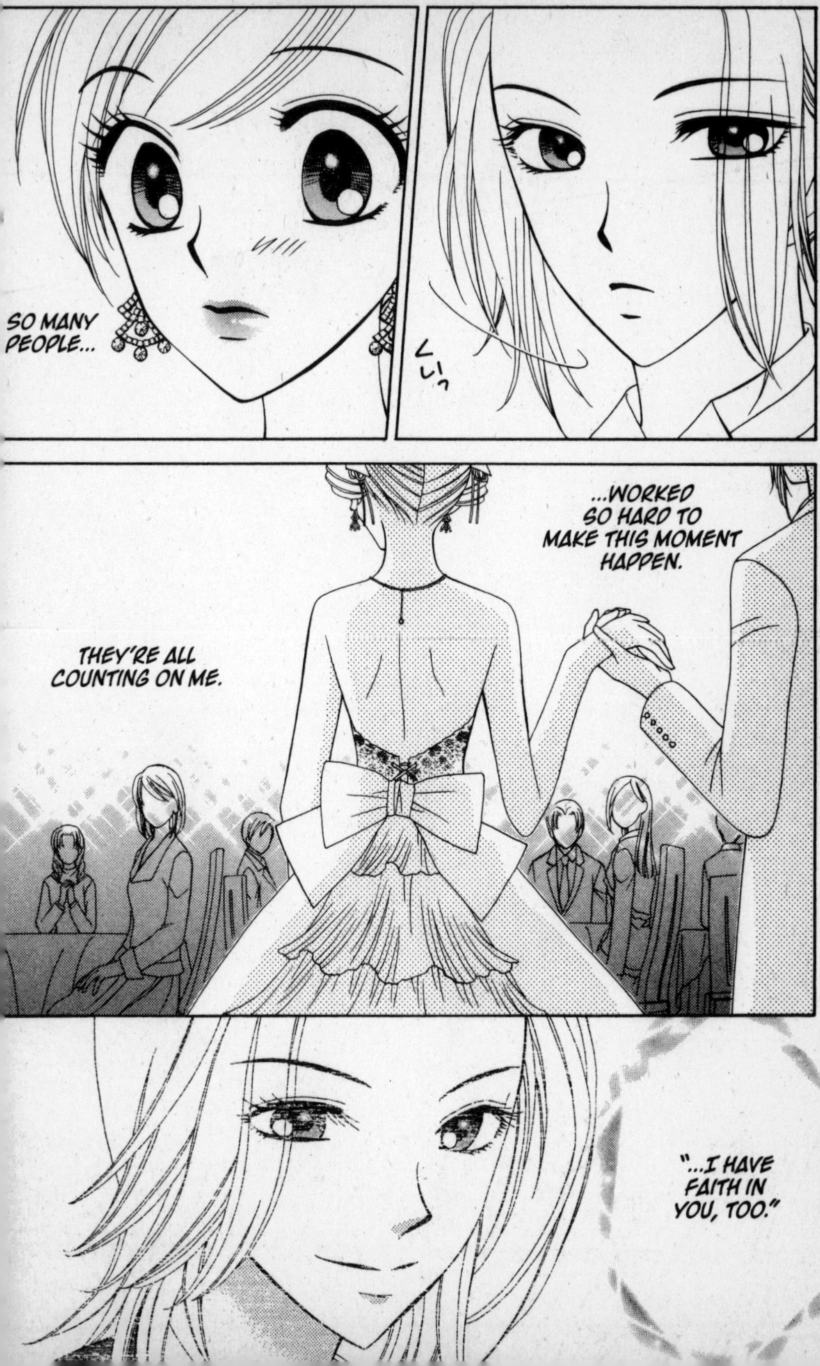
くいっ
SO MANY PEOPLE...
...WORKED SO HARD TO MAKE THIS MOMENT HAPPEN.
THEY'RE ALL COUNTING ON ME.
"...I HAVE FAITH IN YOU, TOO."

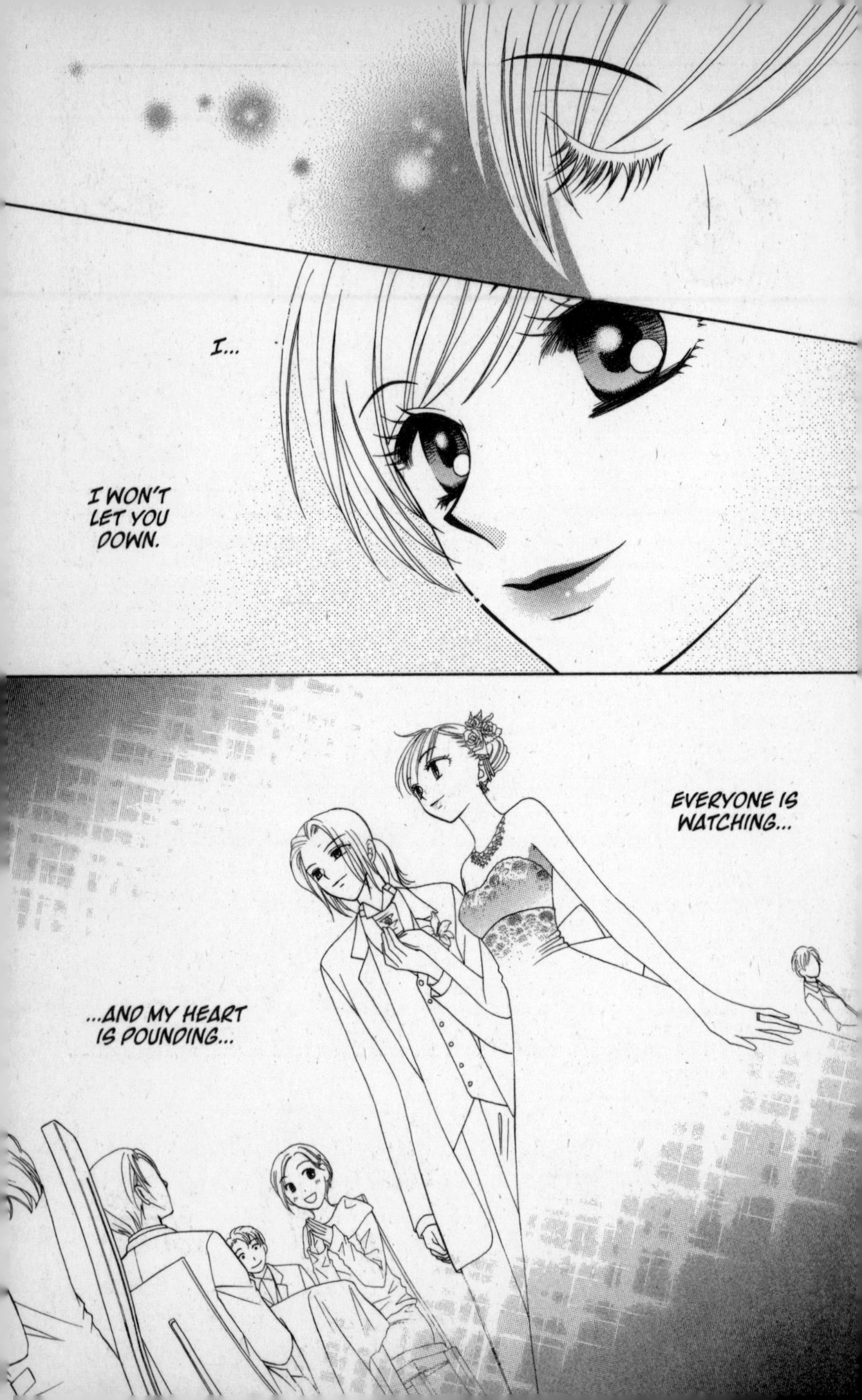
I...
I WON'T LET YOU DOWN.
EVERYONE IS WATCHING...
...AND MY HEART IS POUNDING...

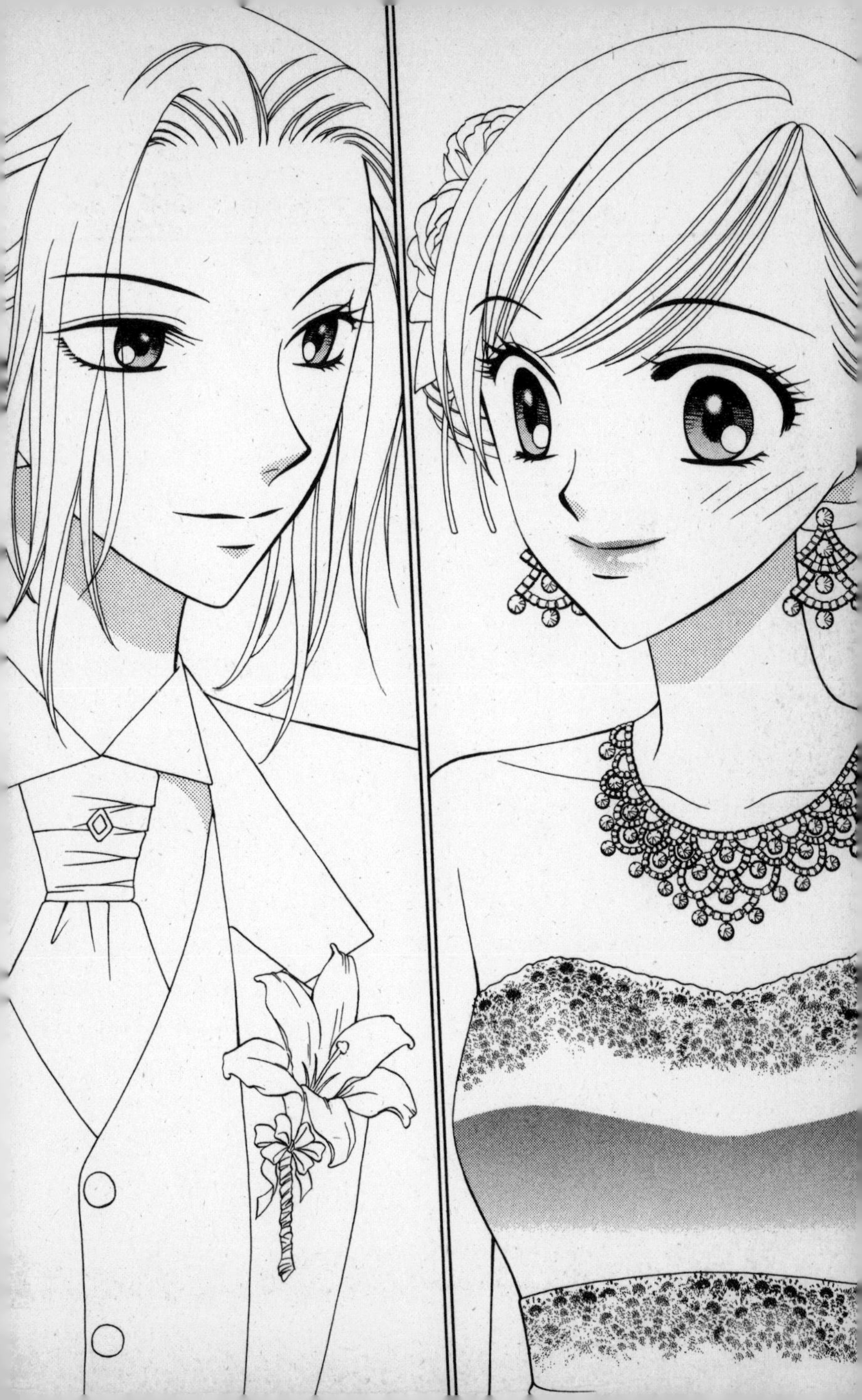

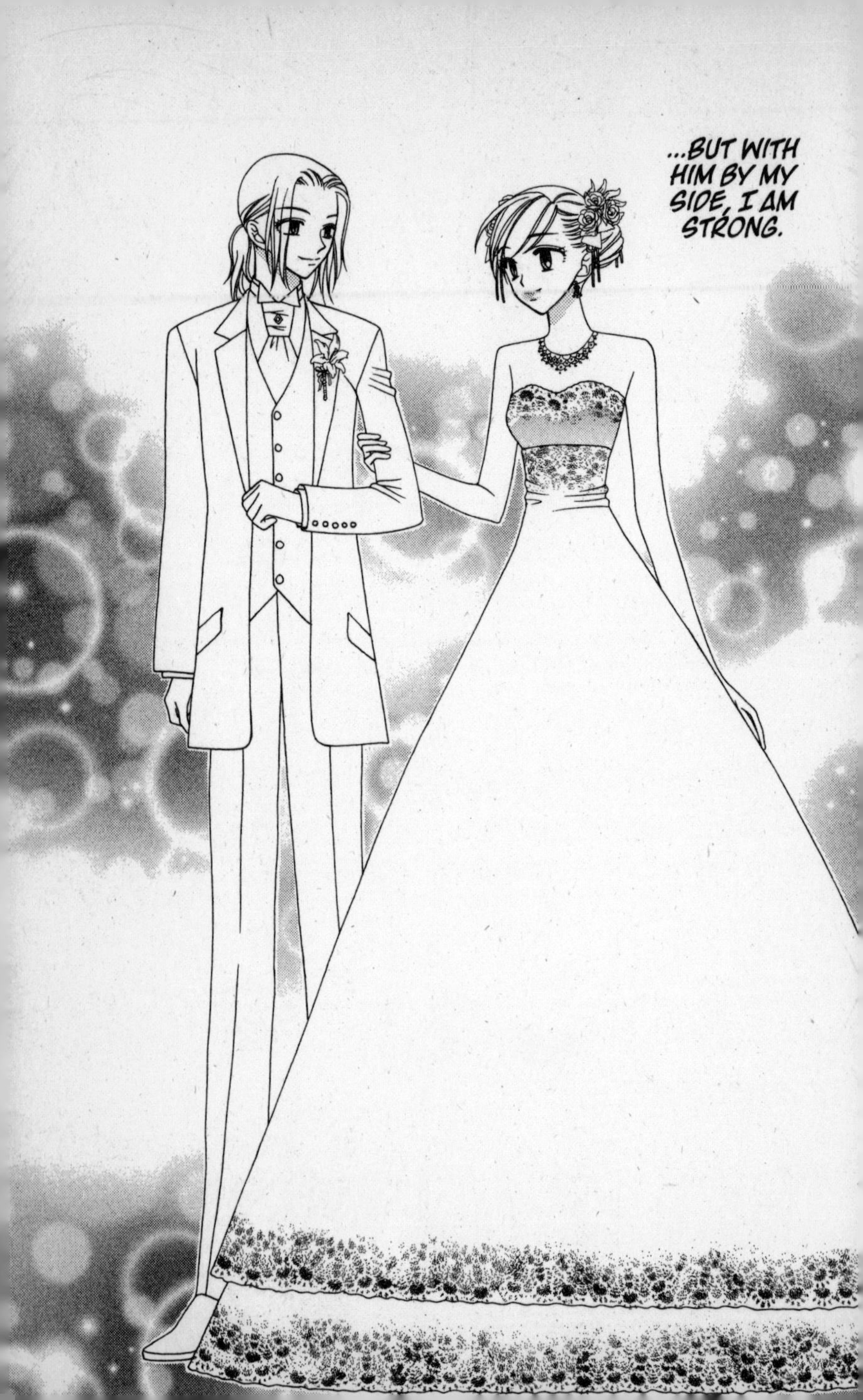
...BUT WITH HIM BY MY SIDE, I AM STRONG.

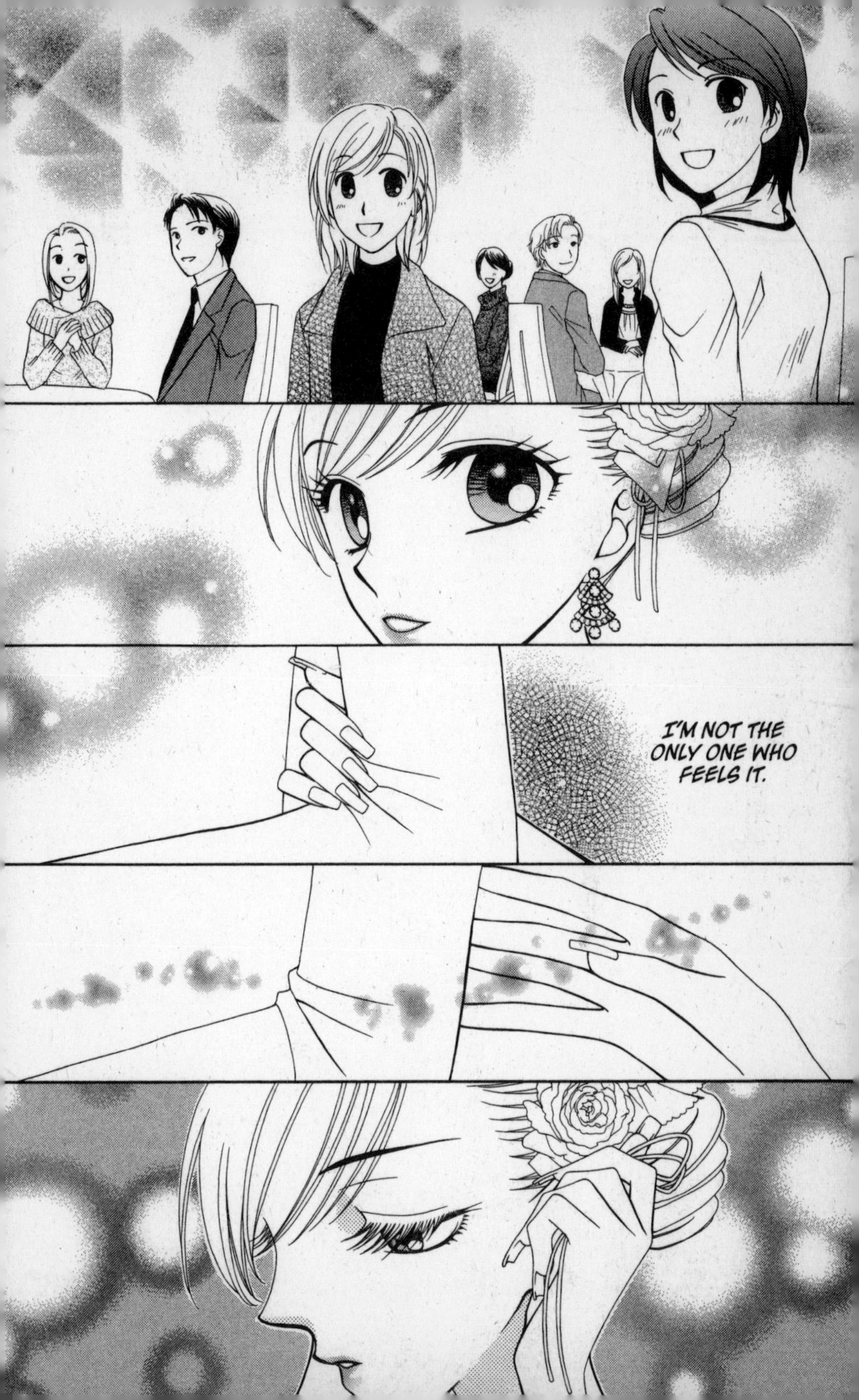
I'M NOT THE ONLY ONE WHO FEELS IT.

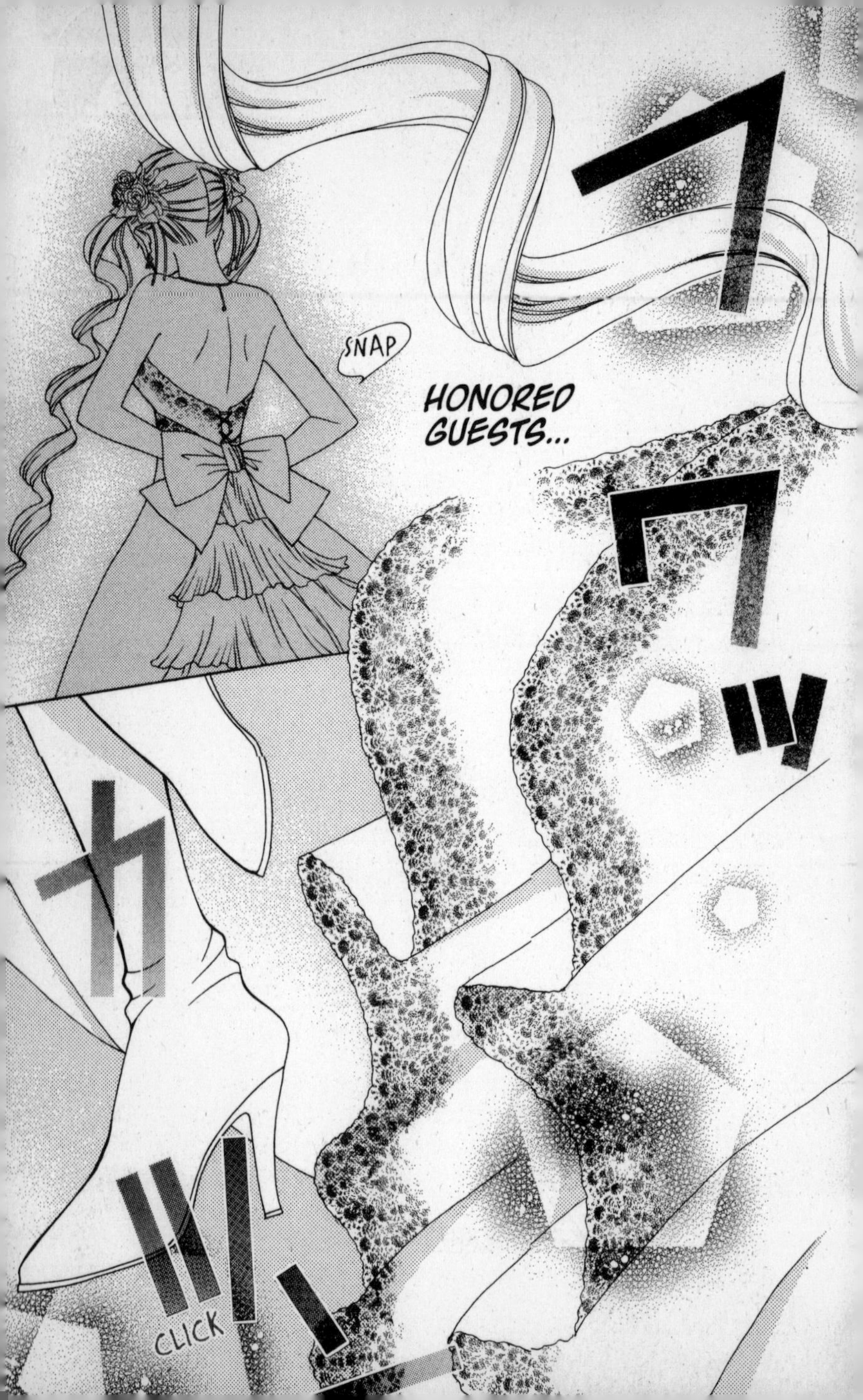
フワッ
HONORED GUESTS...
SNAP
CLICK

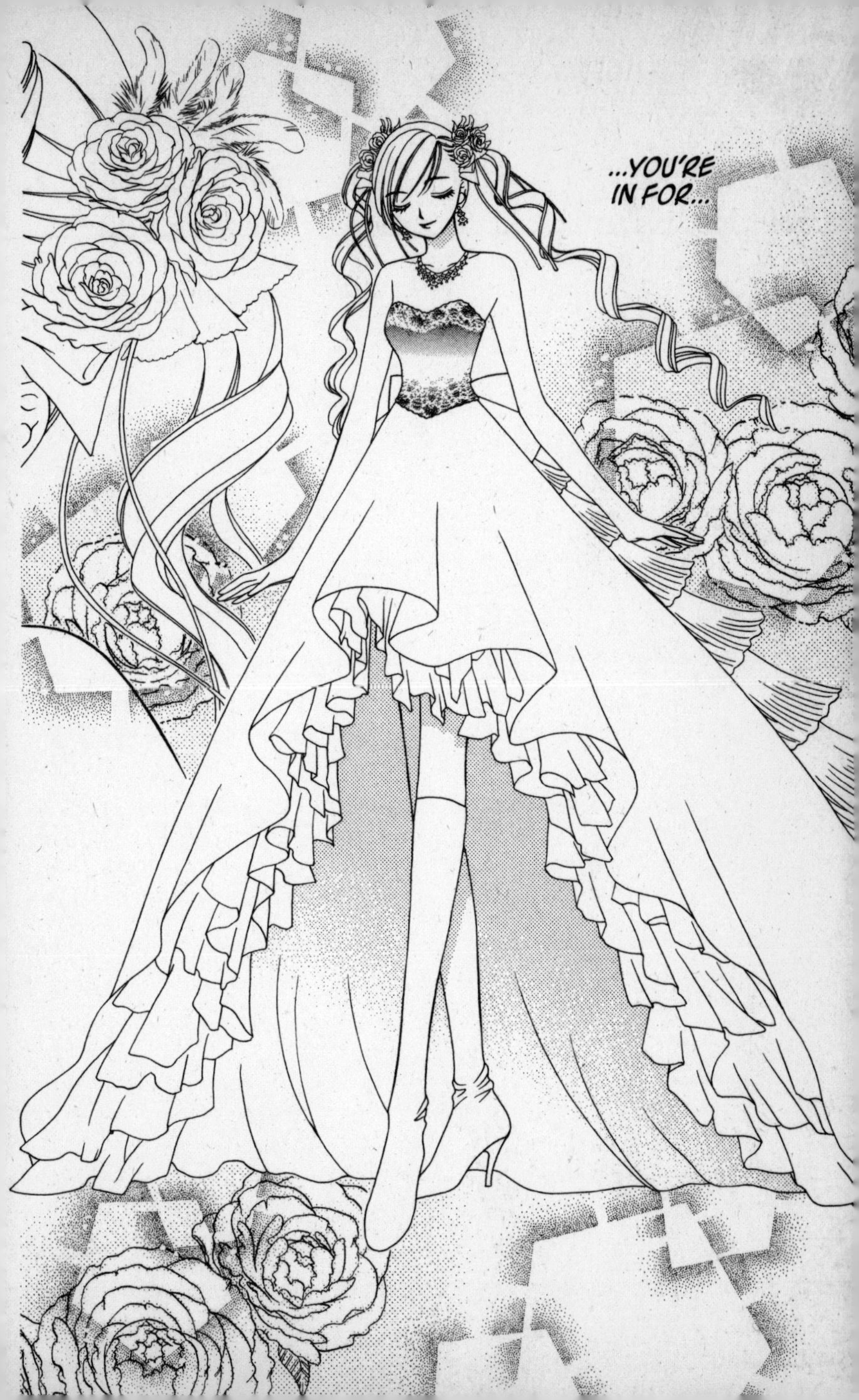
...YOU'RE IN FOR...

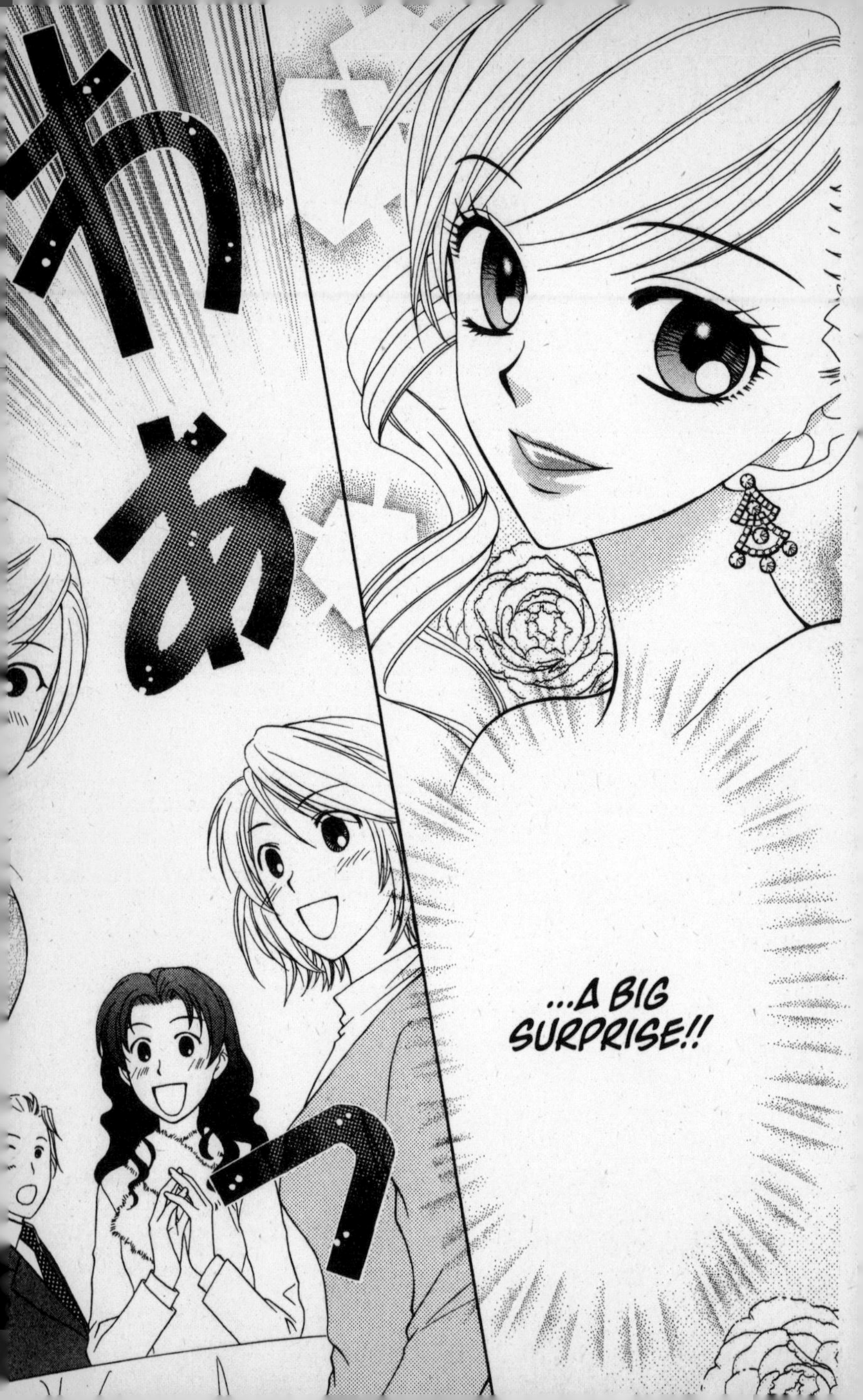
...A BIG SURPRISE!!

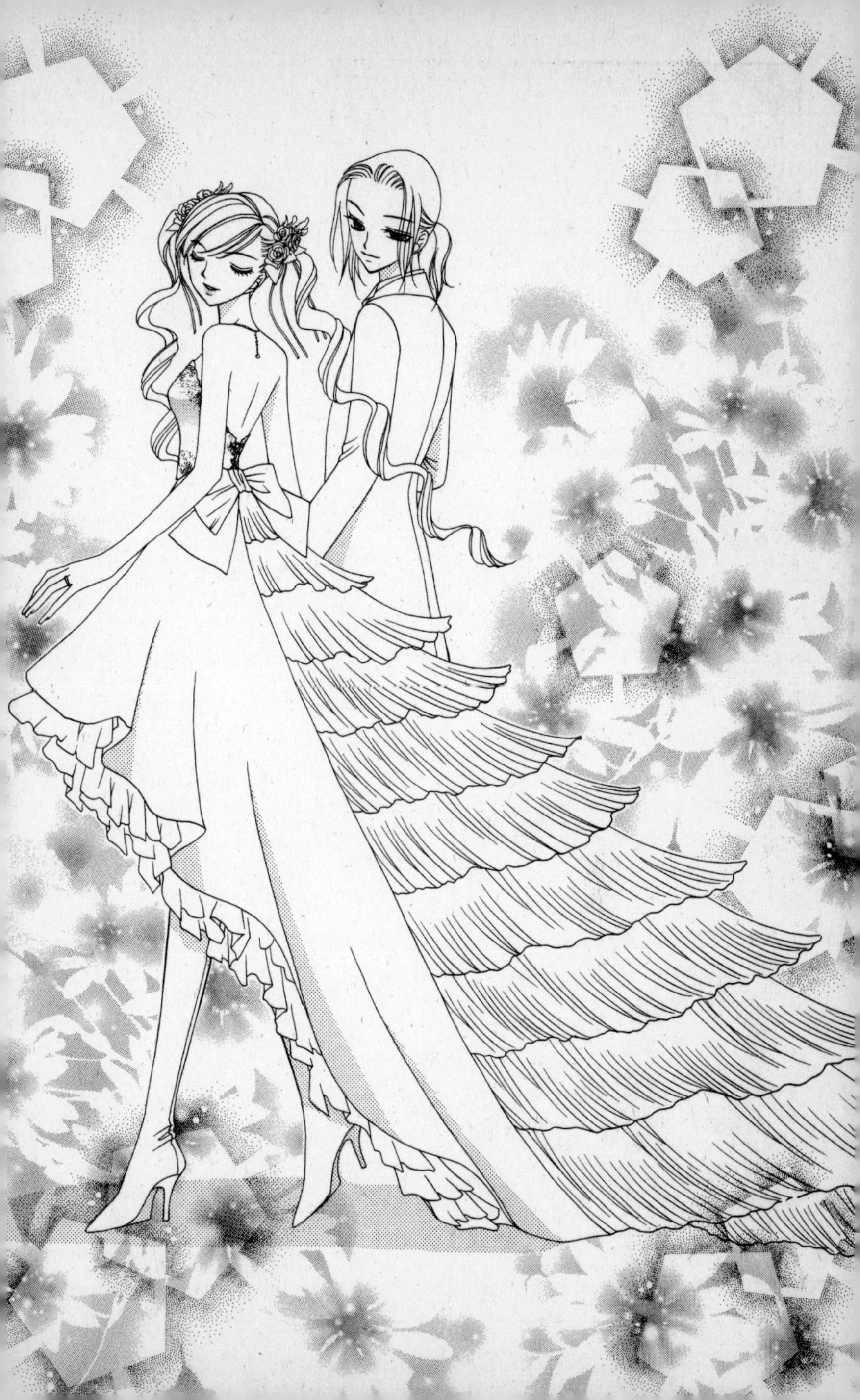

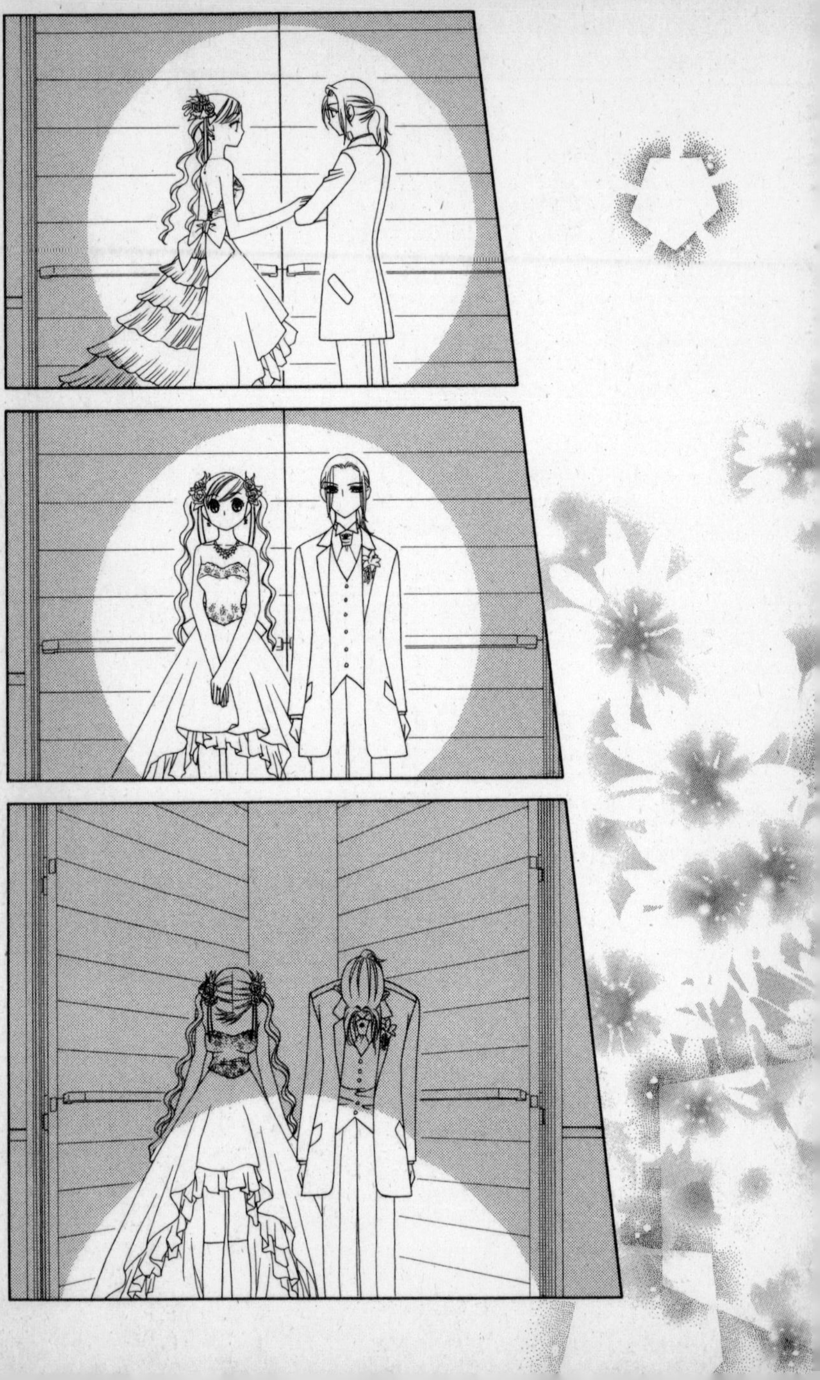

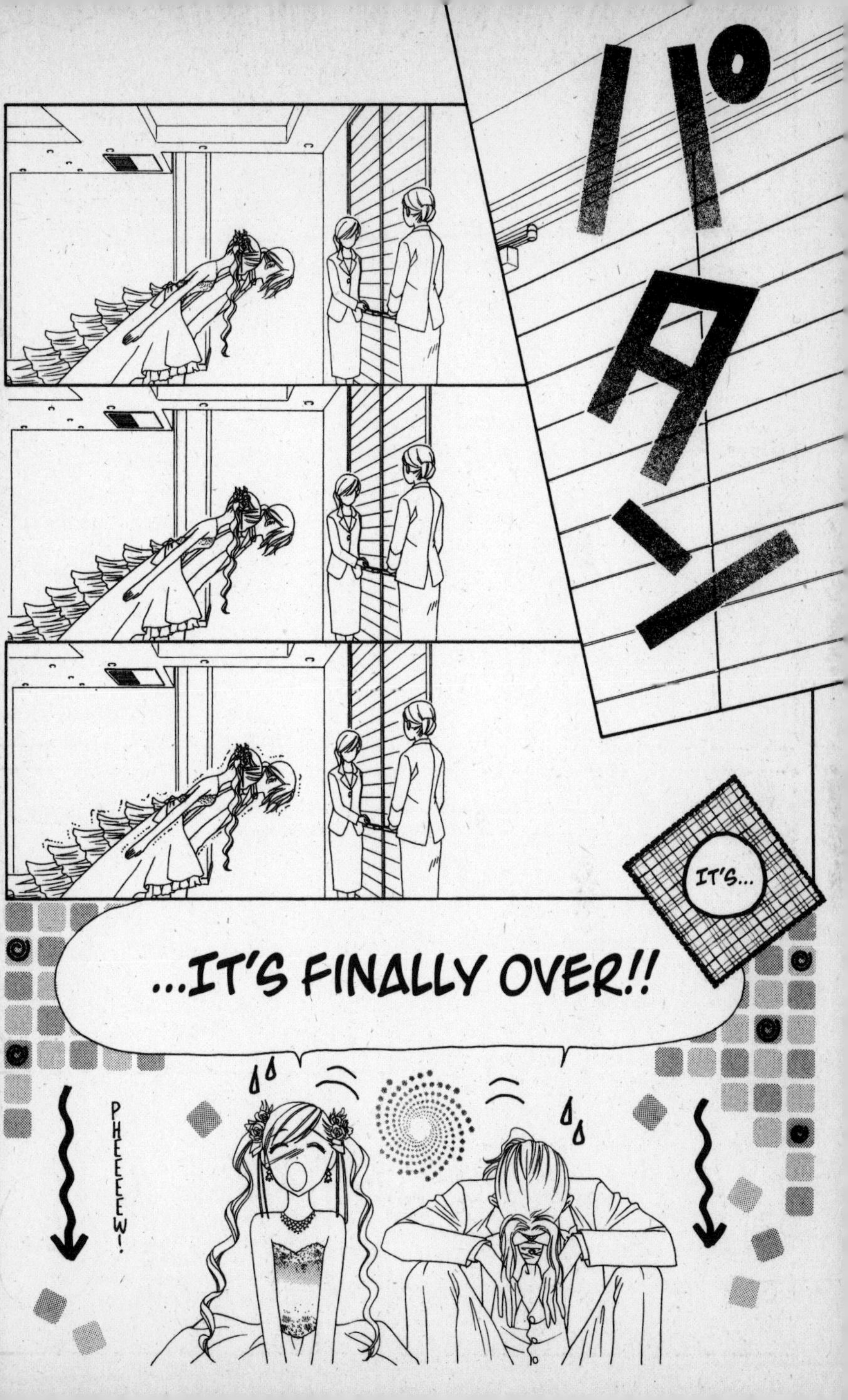
パタン
IT'S...
...IT'S FINALLY OVER!!
PHEEEEEW!

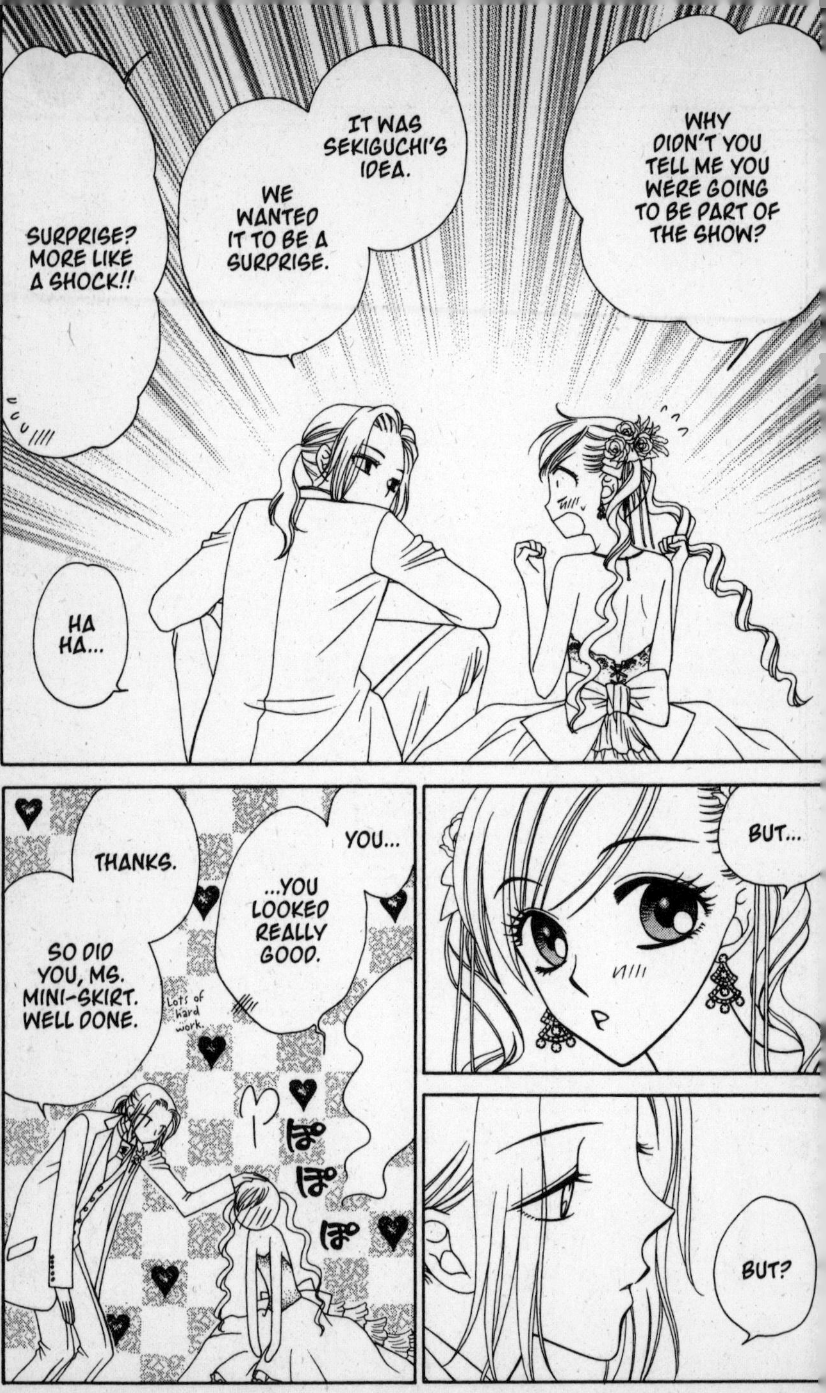
WHY DIDN'T YOU TELL ME YOU WERE GOING TO BE PART OF THE SHOW?
IT WAS SEKIGUCHI'S IDEA.
WE WANTED IT TO BE A SURPRISE.
SURPRISE? MORE LIKE A SHOCK!!
HA HA...
BUT...
BUT?
YOU...
...YOU LOOKED REALLY GOOD.
THANKS.
SO DID YOU, MS. MINI-SKIRT. WELL DONE.
Lots of hard work.
ぽぽぽ

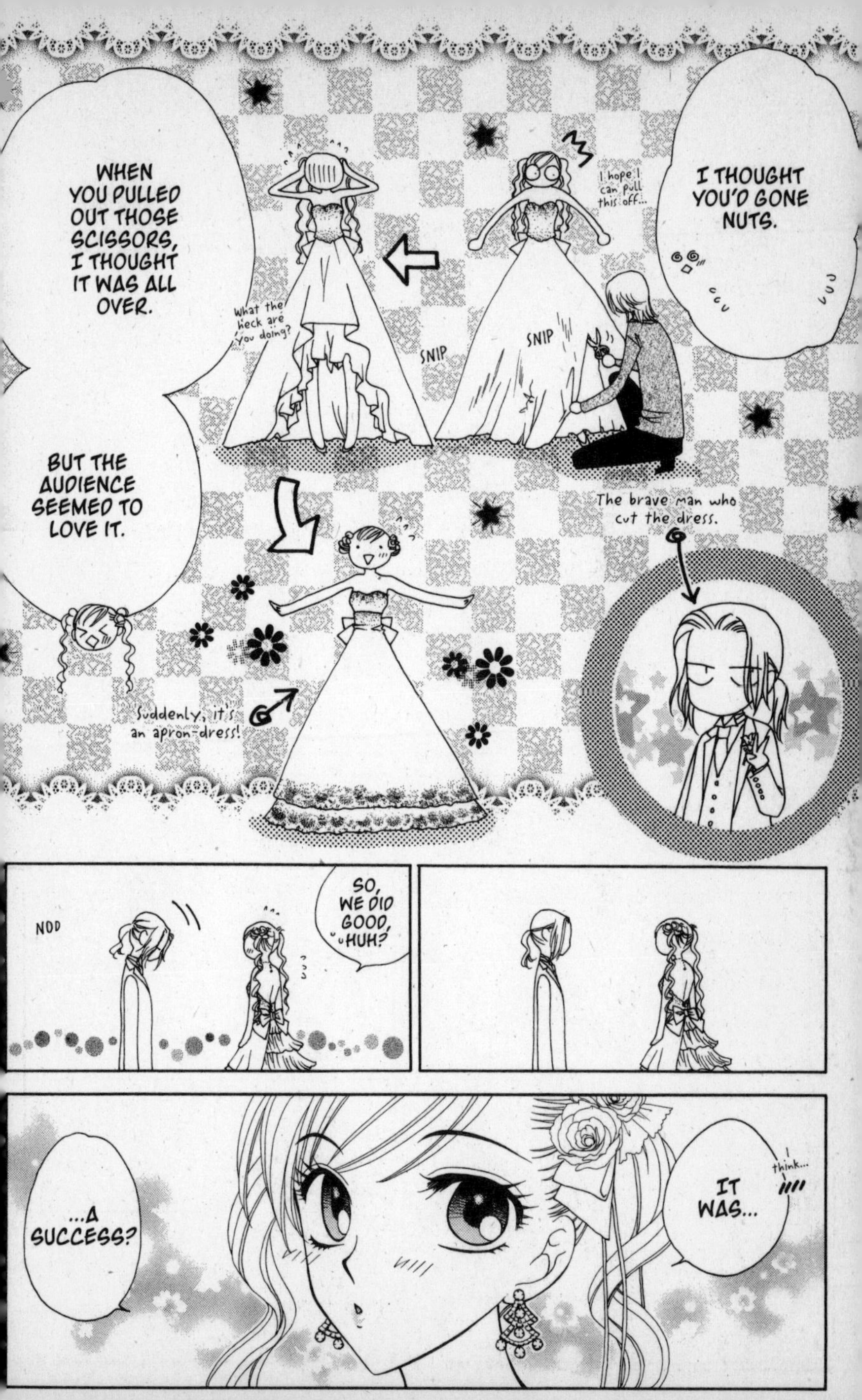
I THOUGHT YOU'D GONE NUTS.
I hope I can pull this off...
SNIP
SNIP
What the heck are you doing?
WHEN YOU PULLED OUT THOSE SCISSORS, I THOUGHT IT WAS ALL OVER.
The brave man who cut the dress.
BUT THE AUDIENCE SEEMED TO LOVE IT.
Suddenly, it's an apron-dress!
SO, WE DID GOOD, HUH?
NOD
IT WAS...
I think...
...A SUCCESS?

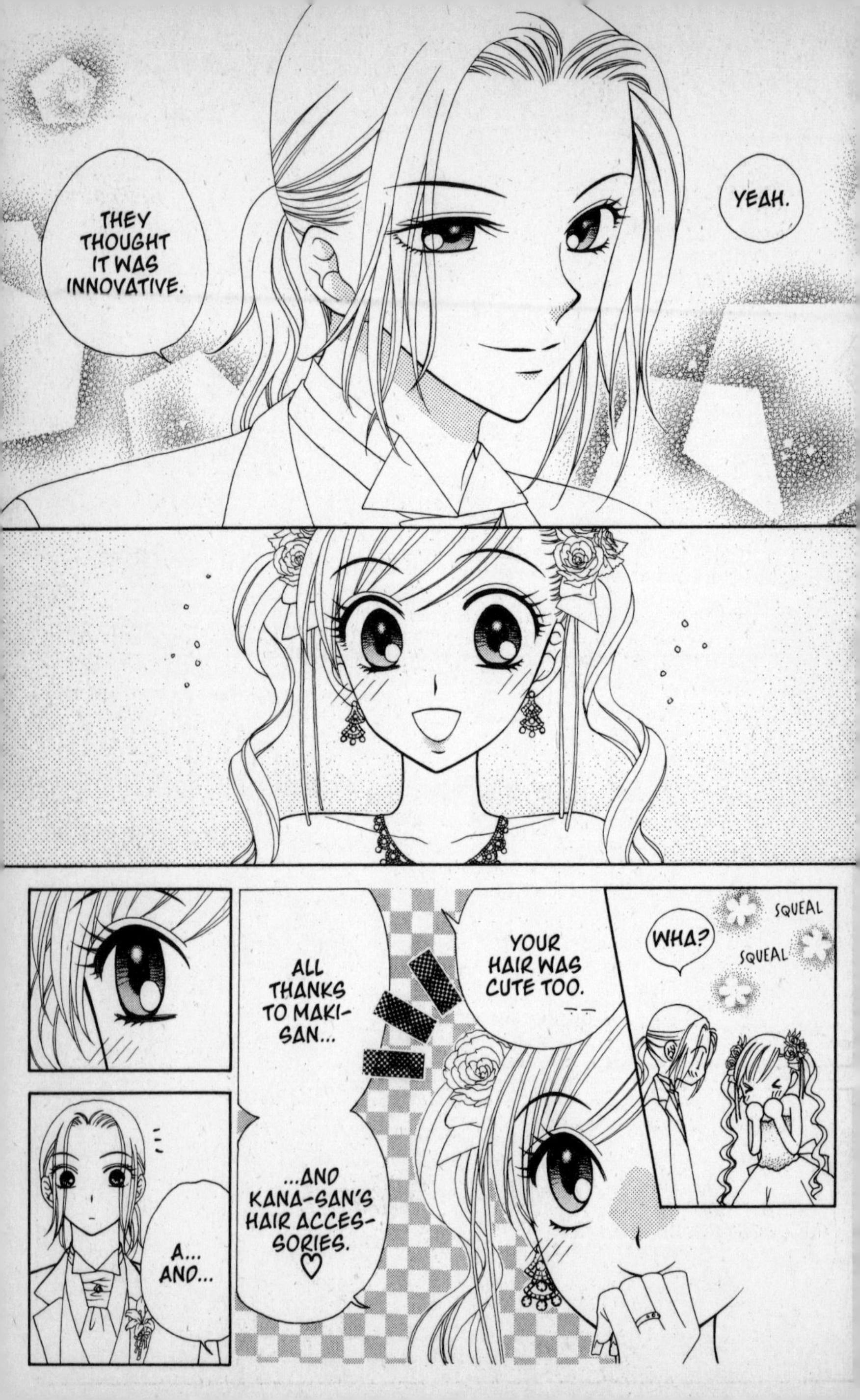
YEAH.
THEY THOUGHT IT WAS INNOVATIVE.
WHA?
SQUEAL
SQUEAL
YOUR HAIR WAS CUTE TOO.
ALL THANKS TO MAKI-SAN...
...AND KANA-SAN'S HAIR ACCES-SORIES. ♥
A... AND...

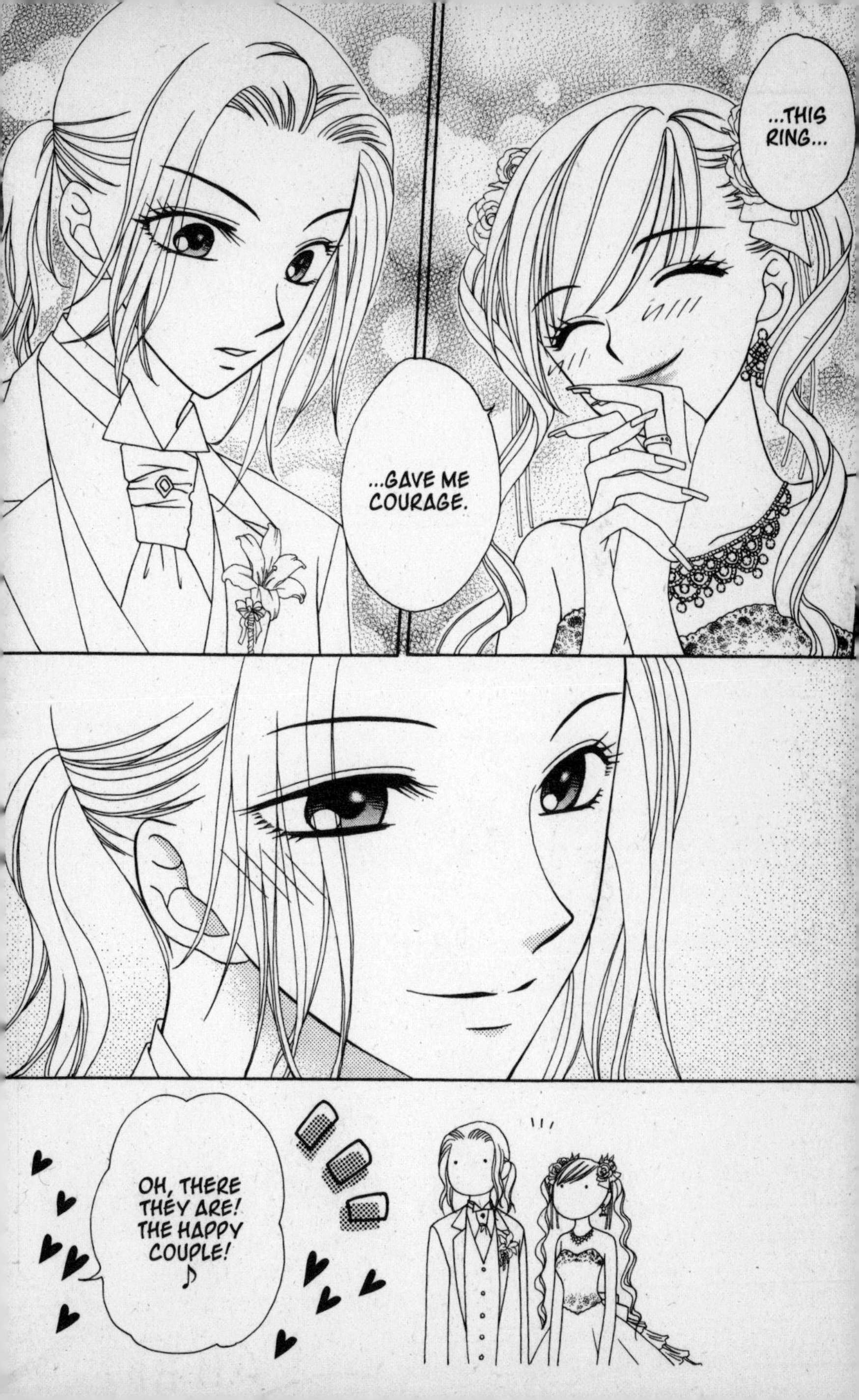
...THIS RING...
...GAVE ME COURAGE.
OH, THERE THEY ARE! THE HAPPY COUPLE! ♪

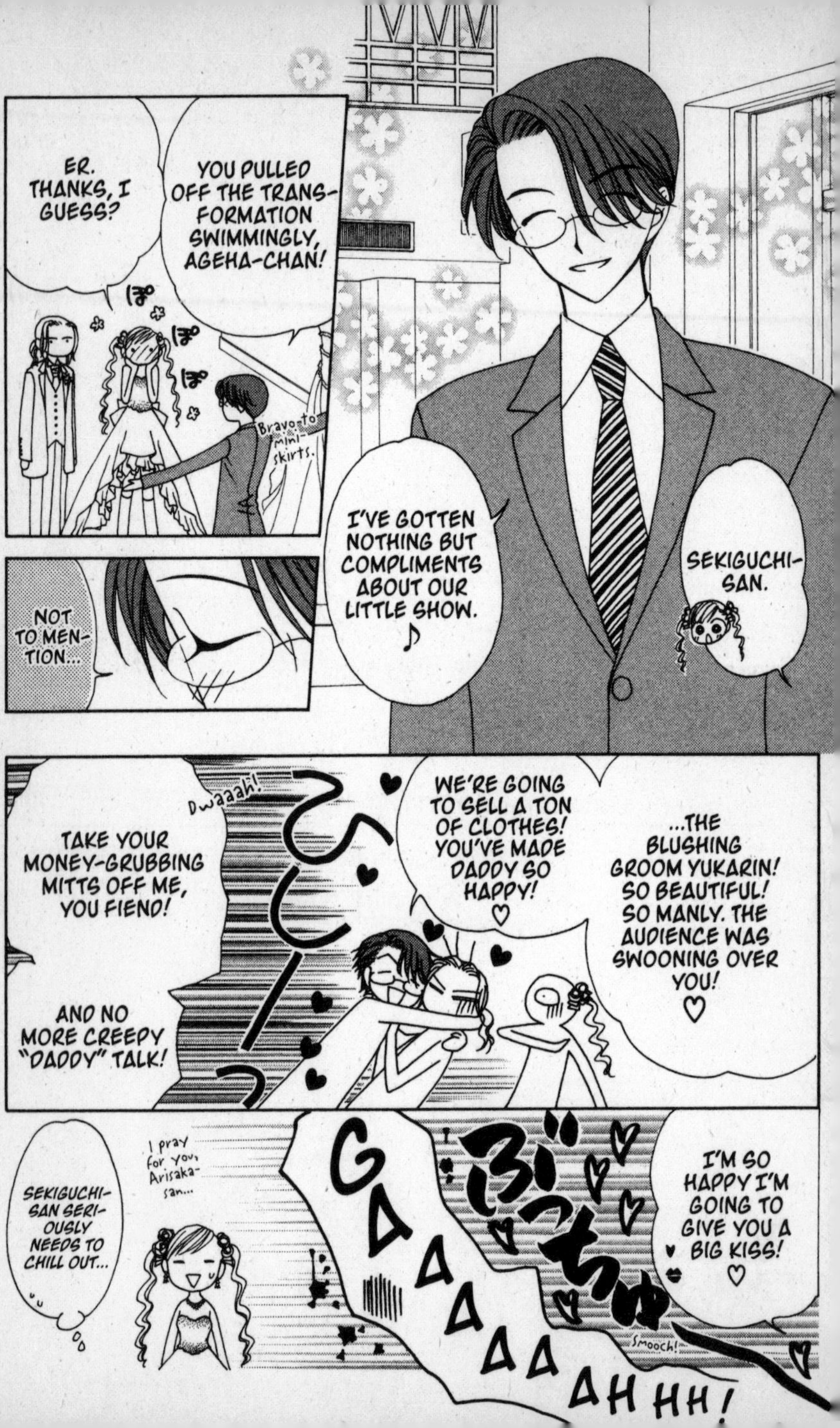
SEKIGUCHI-SAN.
I'VE GOTTEN NOTHING BUT COMPLIMENTS ABOUT OUR LITTLE SHOW. ♪
YOU PULLED OFF THE TRANSFORMATION SWIMMINGLY, AGEHA-CHAN!
ER. THANKS, I GUESS?
ぽ ぽ ぽ
Bravo to mini-skirts.
NOT TO MENTION...
...THE BLUSHING GROOM YUKARIN! SO BEAUTIFUL! SO MANLY. THE AUDIENCE WAS SWOONING OVER YOU! ♡
WE'RE GOING TO SELL A TON OF CLOTHES! YOU'VE MADE DADDY SO HAPPY! ♡
Dwaaah!
TAKE YOUR MONEY-GRUBBING MITTS OFF ME, YOU FIEND!
AND NO MORE CREEPY "DADDY" TALK!
I'M SO HAPPY I'M GOING TO GIVE YOU A BIG KISS! ♡
ぶっちゅ
Smooch!
GAAAAAAAAHHH!
I pray for you, Arisaka-san...
SEKIGUCHI-SAN SERIOUSLY NEEDS TO CHILL OUT...

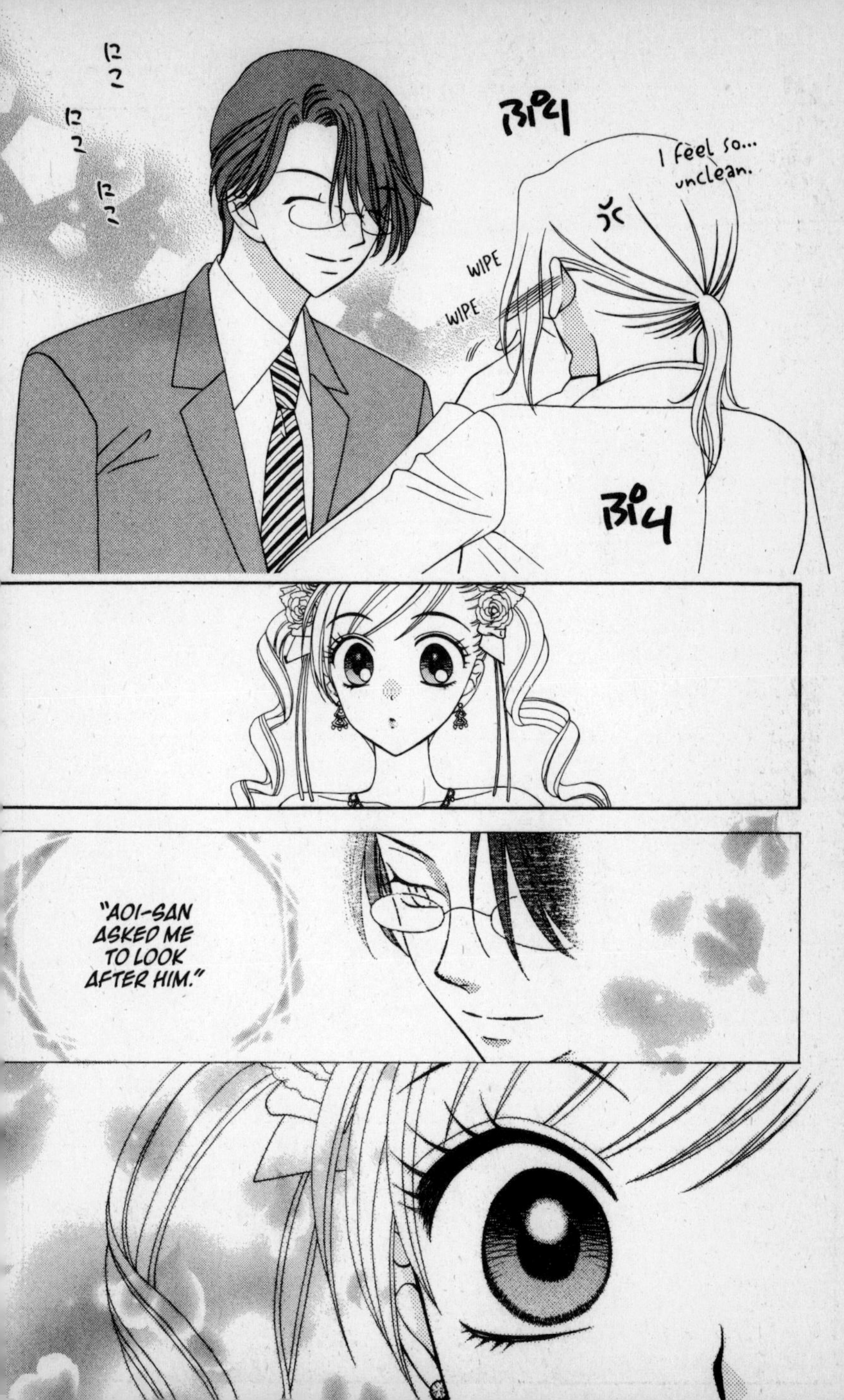
I feel so... unclean.
WIPE
WIPE
"AOI-SAN ASKED ME TO LOOK AFTER HIM."

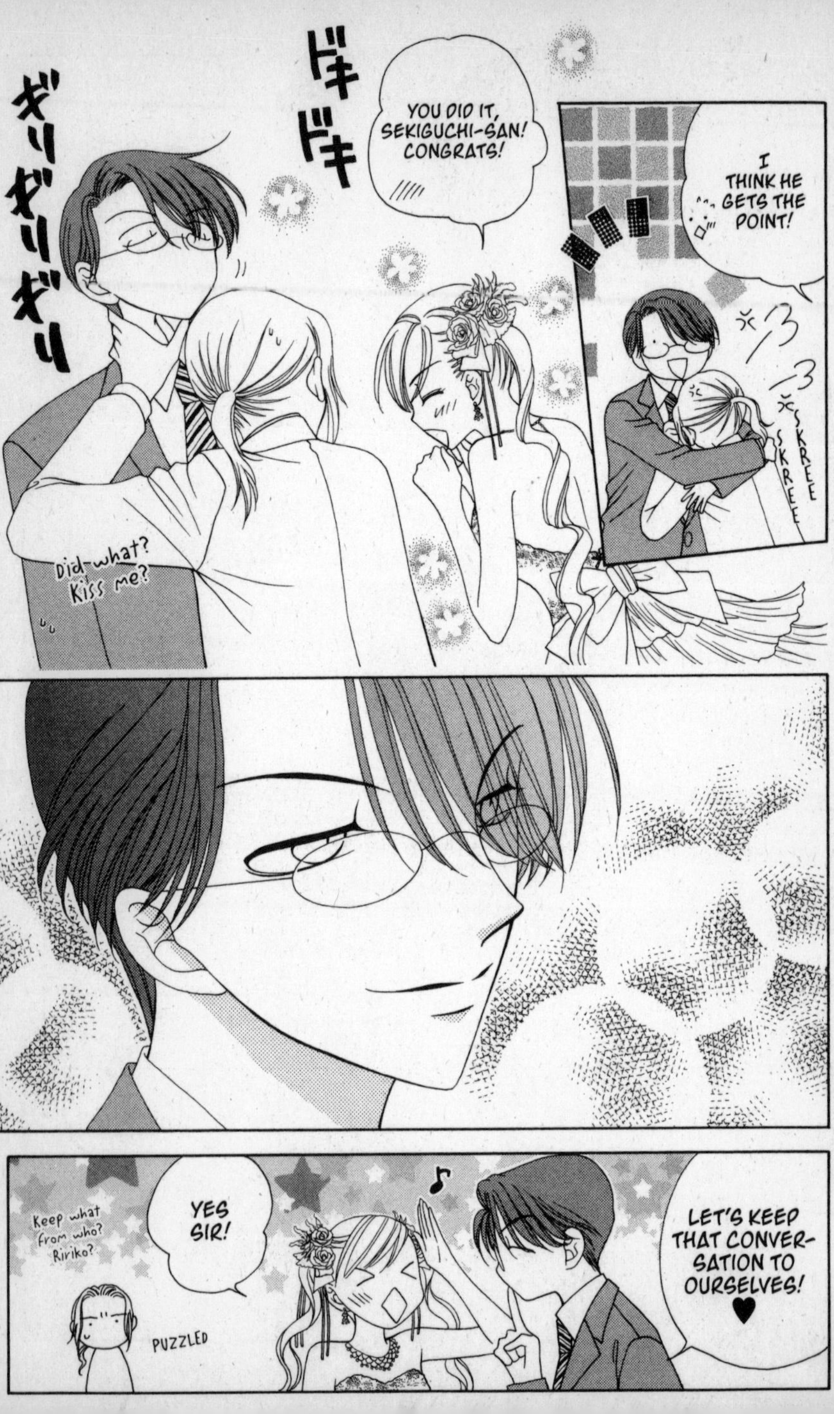
I THINK HE GETS THE POINT!
SKREE
SKREE
ドキドキ
YOU DID IT, SEKIGUCHI-SAN! CONGRATS!
ぎりぎりぎり
Did-what? Kiss me?
LET'S KEEP THAT CONVERSATION TO OURSELVES! ♥
YES SIR!
Keep what from who? Ririko?
PUZZLED

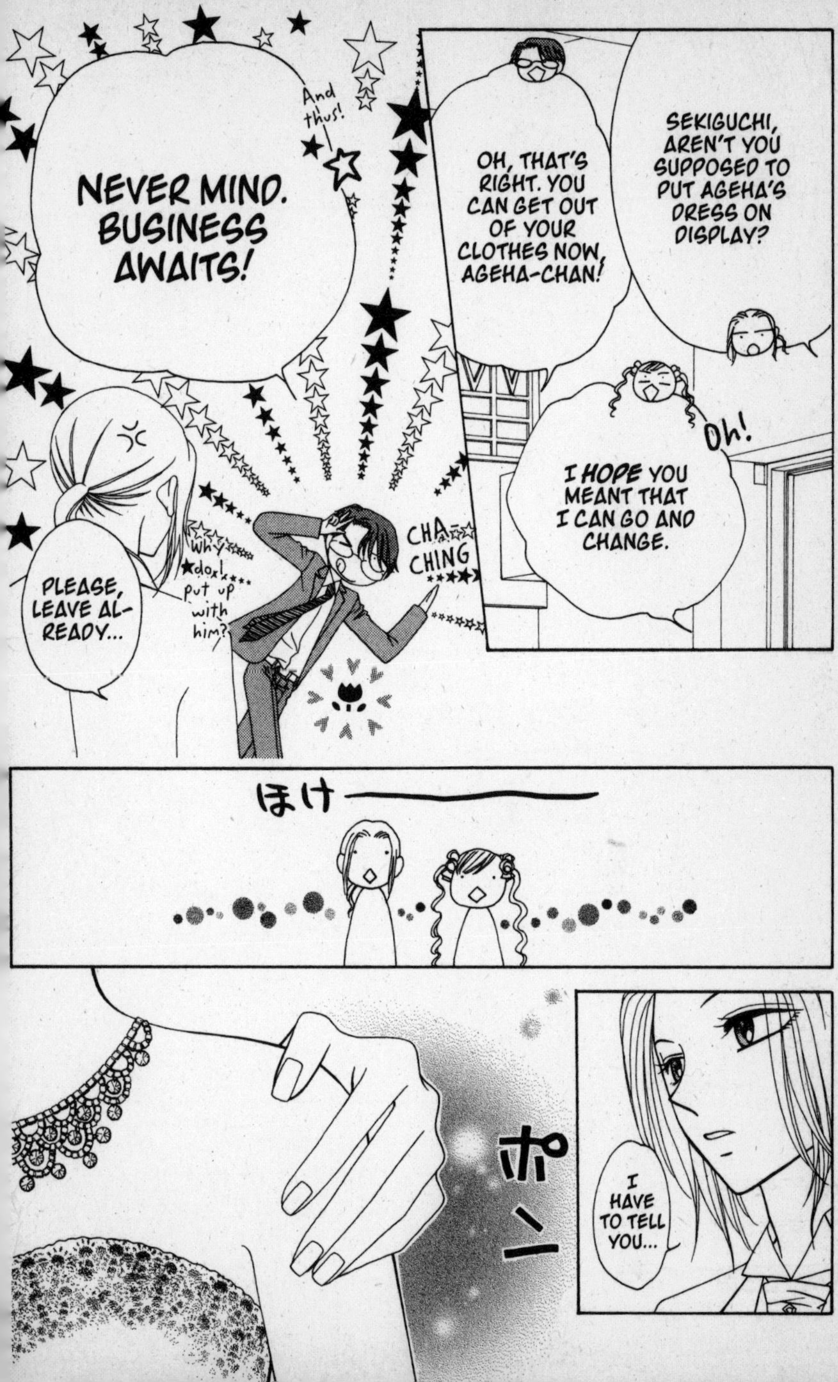
SEKIGUCHI, AREN'T YOU SUPPOSED TO PUT AGEHA'S DRESS ON DISPLAY?
OH, THAT'S RIGHT. YOU CAN GET OUT OF YOUR CLOTHES NOW, AGEHA-CHAN!
Oh!
I *HOPE* YOU MEANT THAT I CAN GO AND CHANGE.
NEVER MIND. BUSINESS AWAITS!
And thus!
CHA-CHING
Why do I put up with him?
PLEASE, LEAVE AL-READY...
ほけ――――
I HAVE TO TELL YOU...
ポン

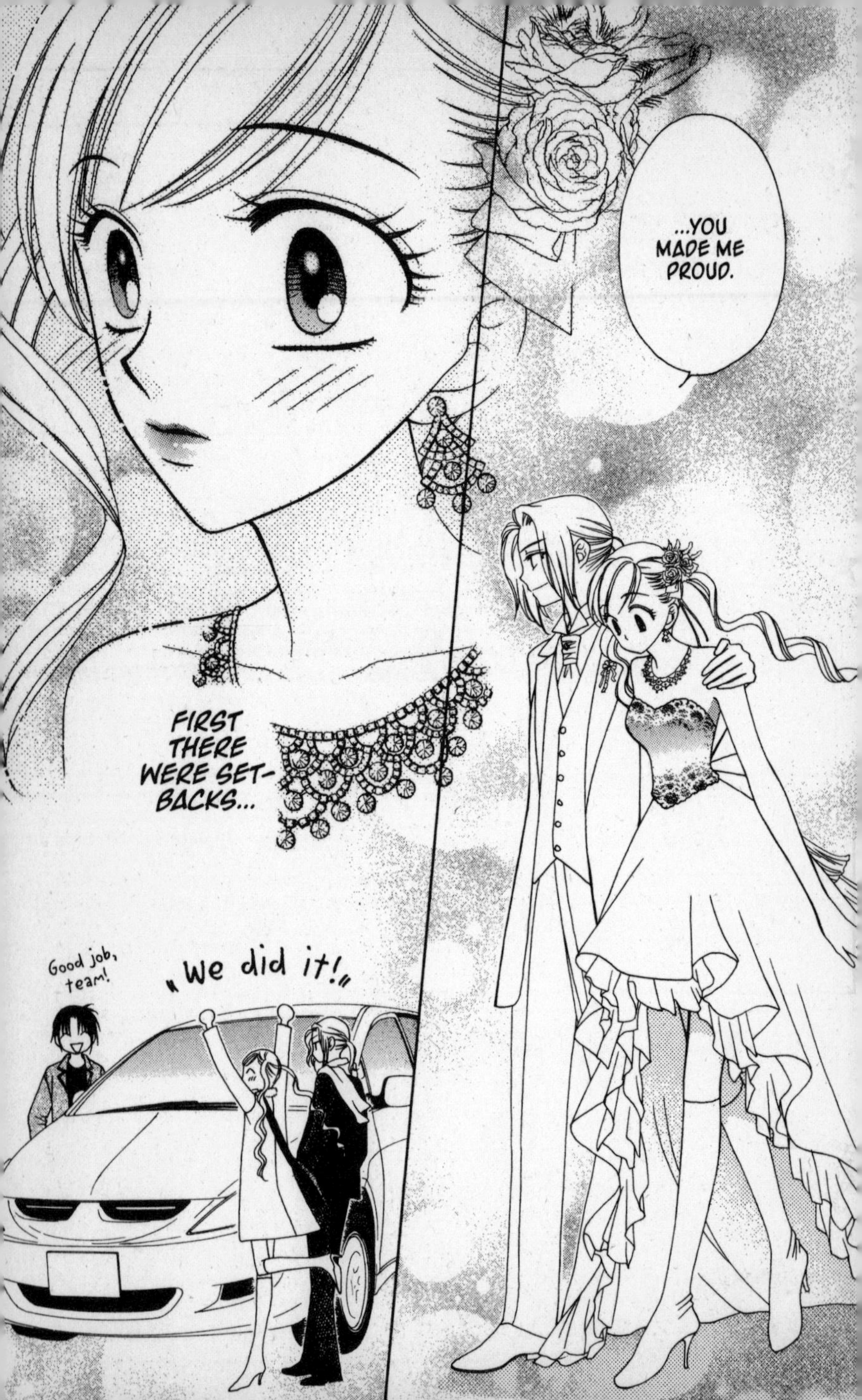
...YOU MADE ME PROUD.
FIRST THERE WERE SET-BACKS...
"We did it!"
Good job, team!

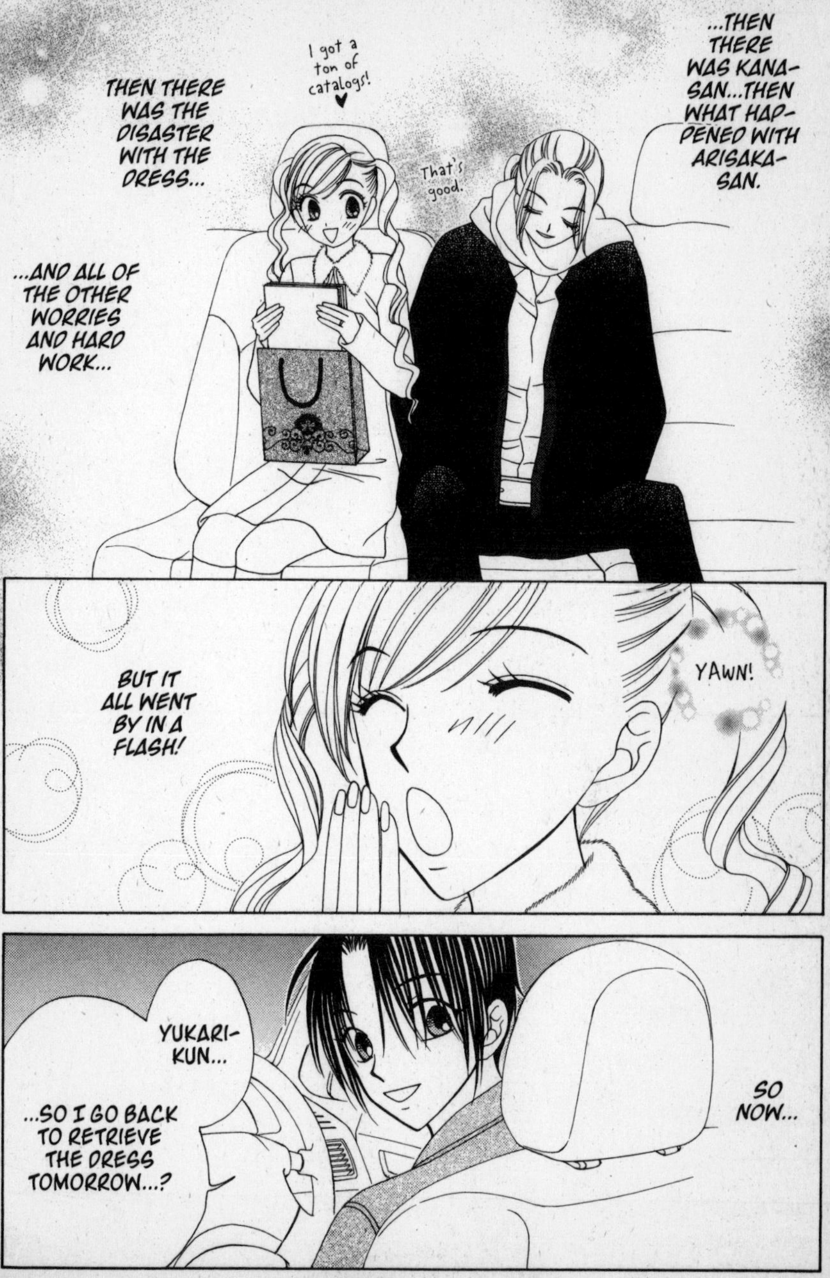
...THEN THERE WAS KANA-SAN...THEN WHAT HAPPENED WITH ARISAKA-SAN.
I got a ton of catalogs! ♥
That's good.
THEN THERE WAS THE DISASTER WITH THE DRESS...
...AND ALL OF THE OTHER WORRIES AND HARD WORK...
YAWN!
BUT IT ALL WENT BY IN A FLASH!
SO NOW...
YUKARI-KUN...
...SO I GO BACK TO RETRIEVE THE DRESS TOMORROW...?

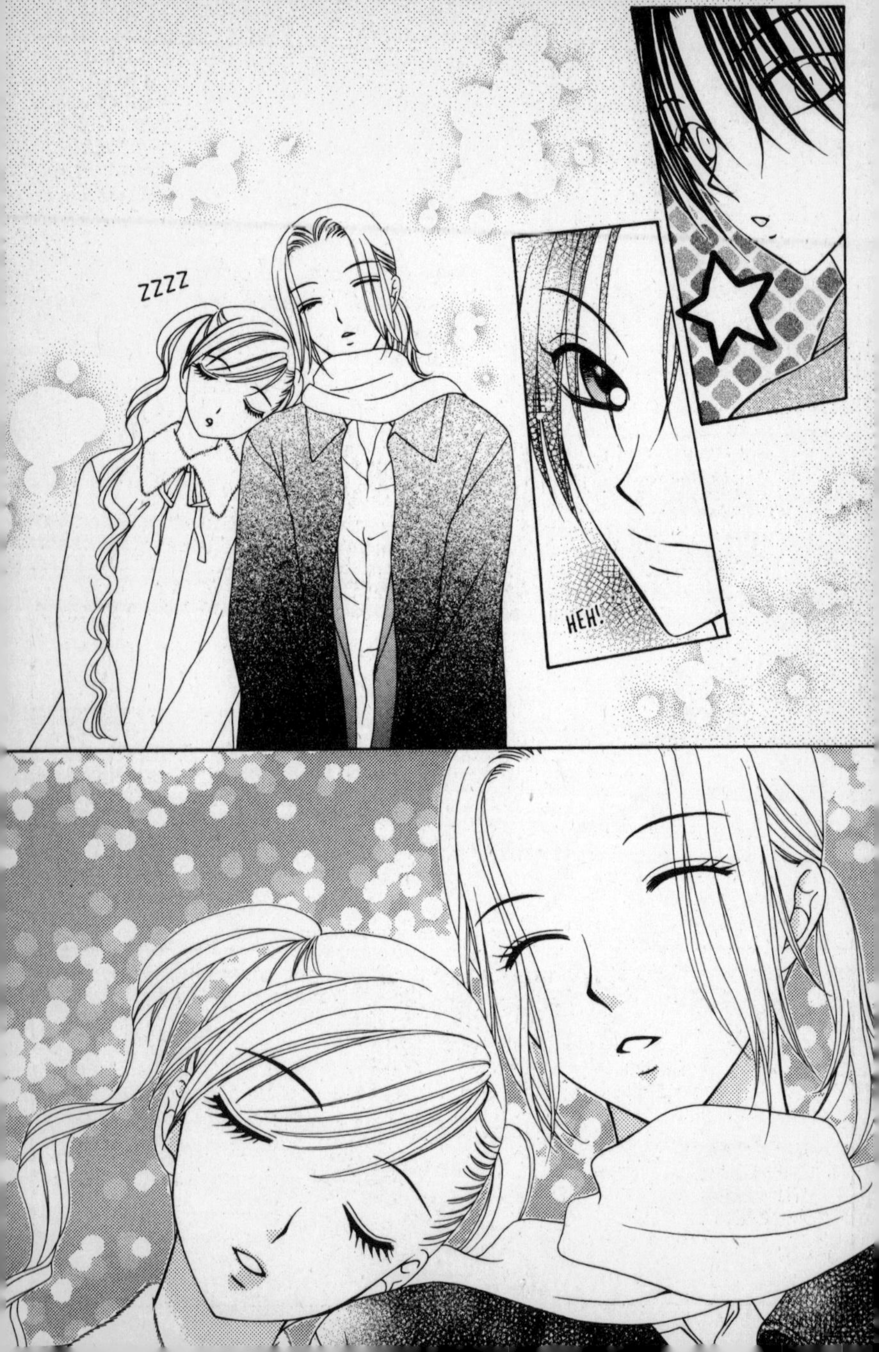
HEH!
ZZZZ

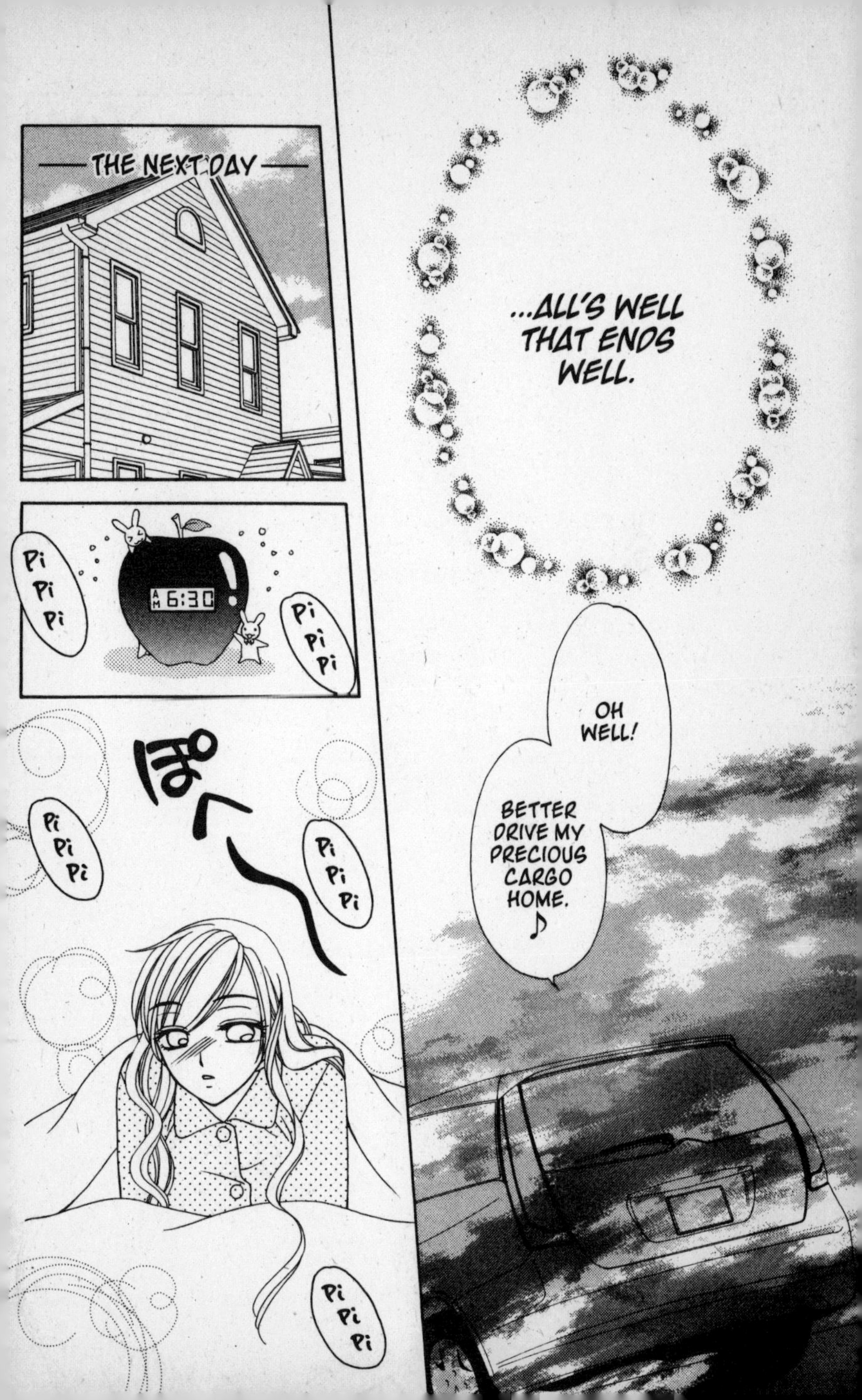
...ALL'S WELL THAT ENDS WELL.
OH WELL!
BETTER DRIVE MY PRECIOUS CARGO HOME. ♪
THE NEXT DAY
AM 6:30
Pi Pi Pi
Pi Pi Pi
ぽへ〜
Pi Pi Pi
Pi Pi Pi
Pi Pi Pi

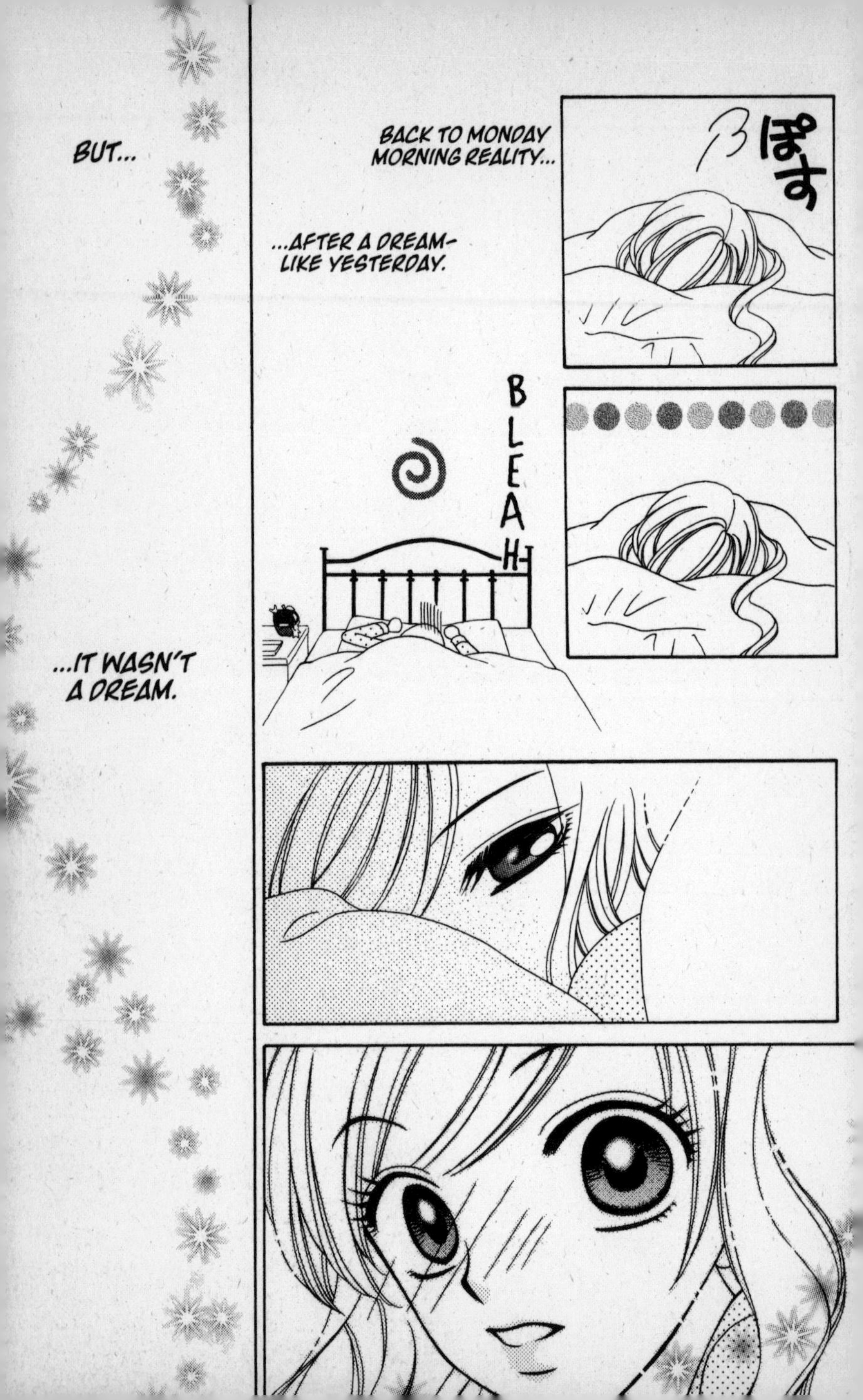
ぽす
BACK TO MONDAY MORNING REALITY...
...AFTER A DREAM-LIKE YESTERDAY.
BLEAH-
BUT...
...IT WASN'T A DREAM.

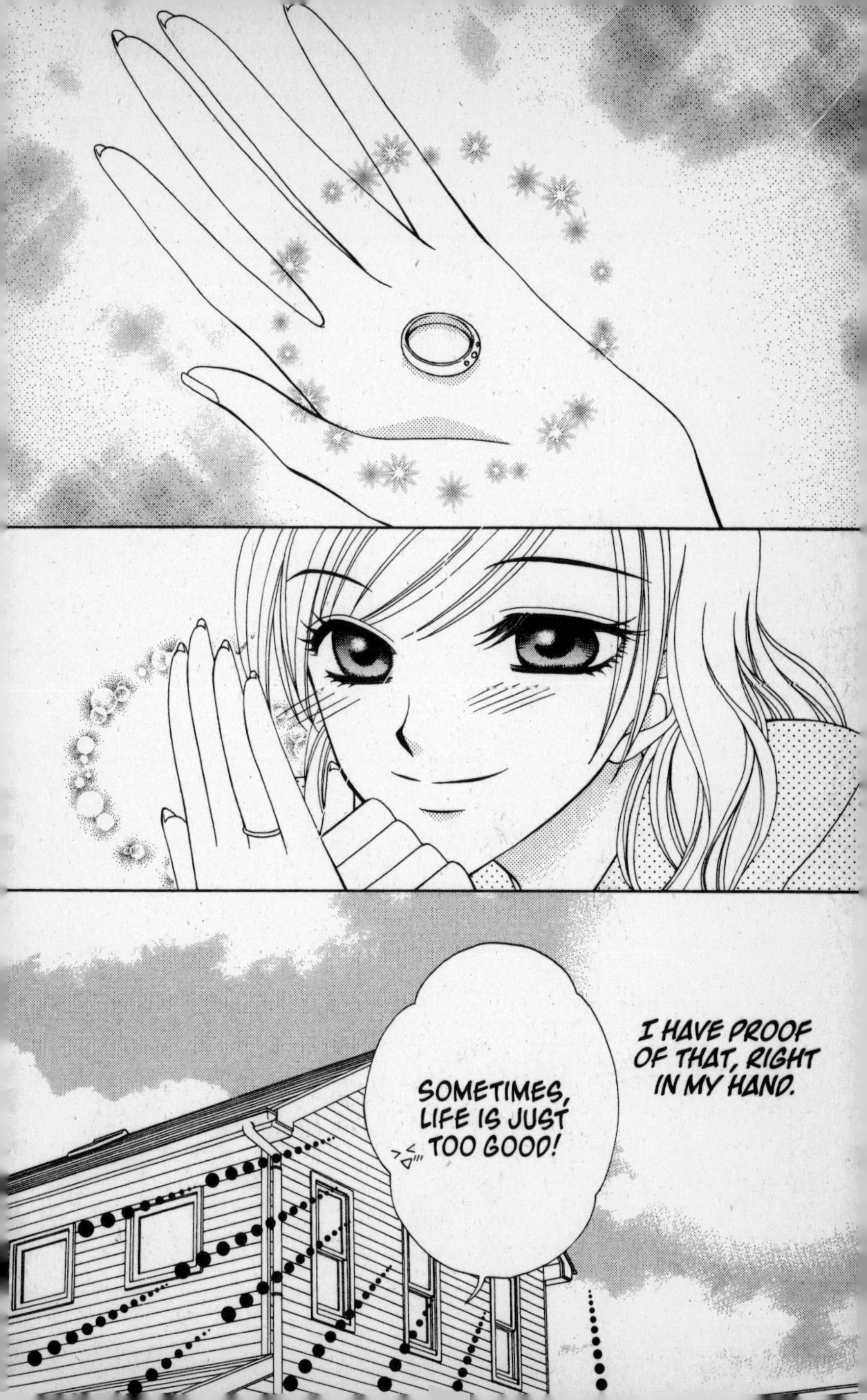
I HAVE PROOF OF THAT, RIGHT IN MY HAND.
SOMETIMES, LIFE IS JUST TOO GOOD!

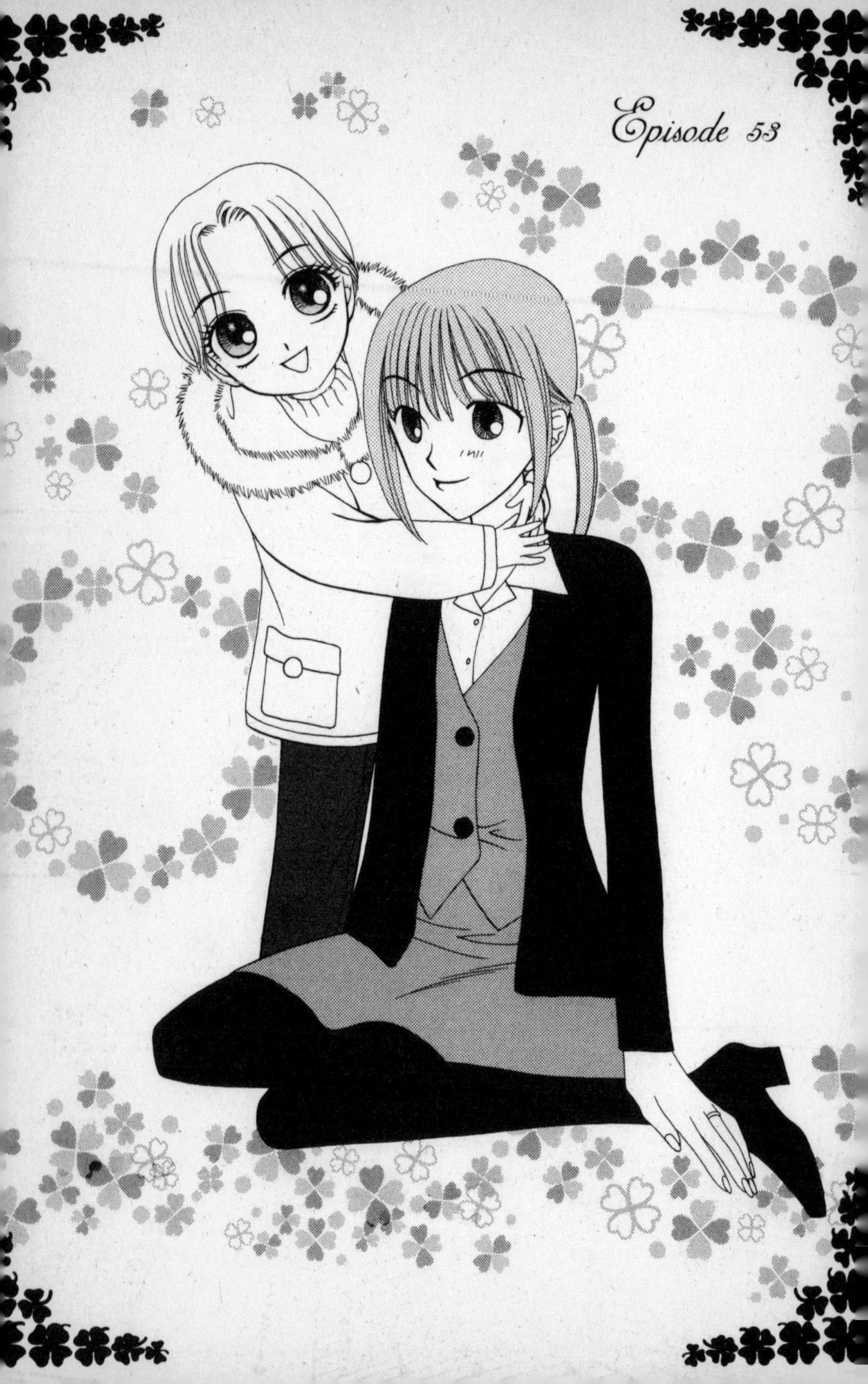
Episode 53

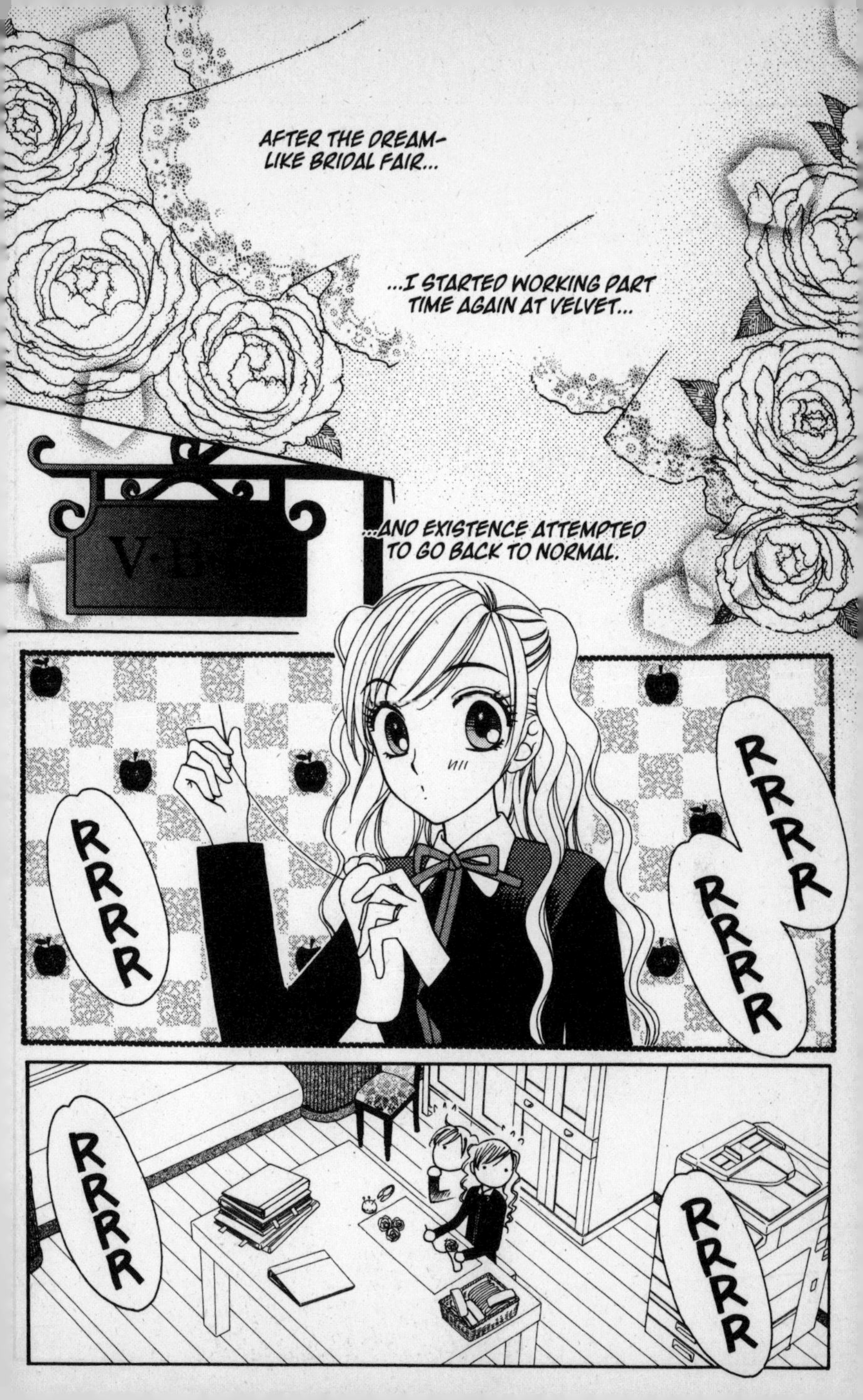
AFTER THE DREAM-LIKE BRIDAL FAIR...
...I STARTED WORKING PART TIME AGAIN AT VELVET...
...AND EXISTENCE ATTEMPTED TO GO BACK TO NORMAL.
RRRR RRRR
RRRR
RRRR
RRRR

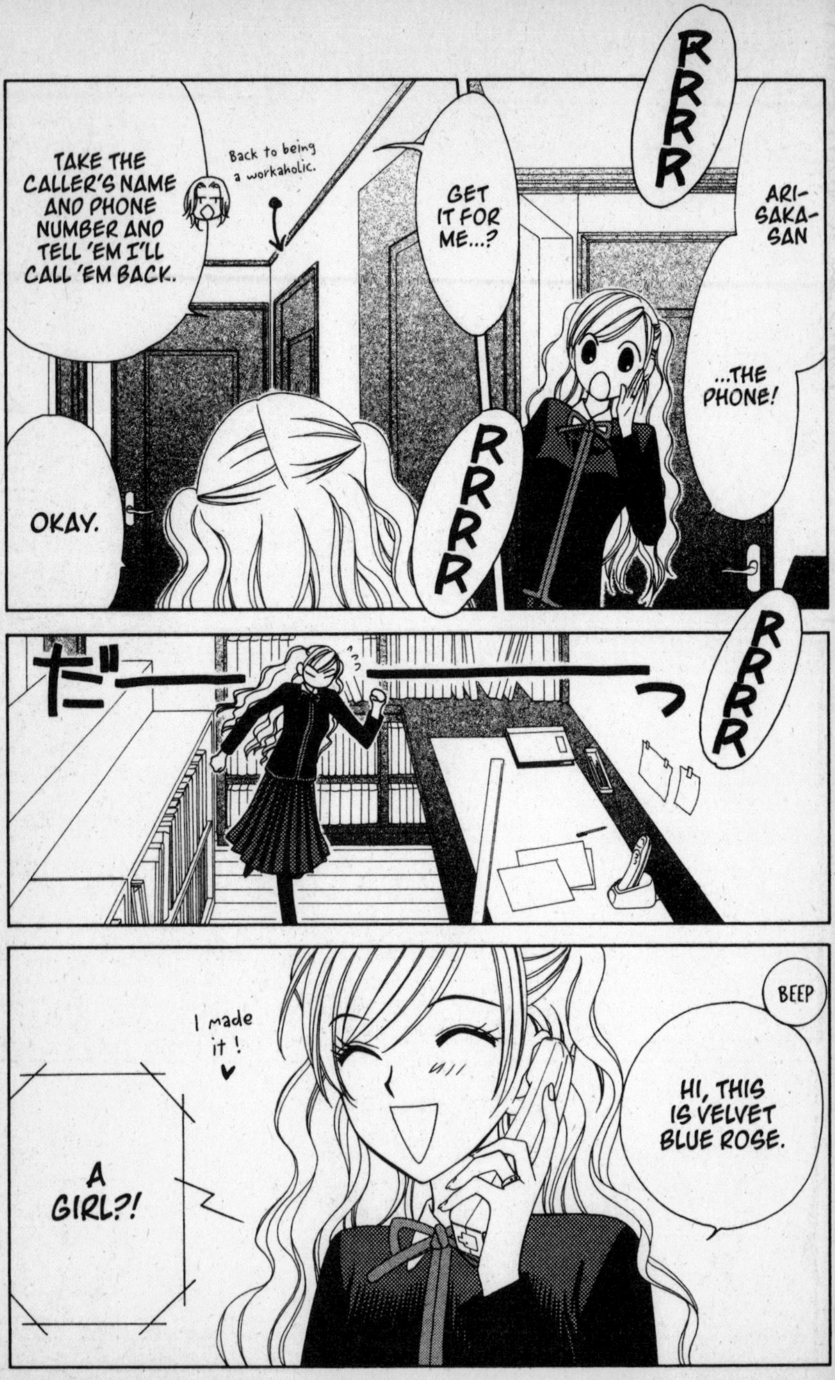
RRRR
ARI-SAKA-SAN
...THE PHONE!
GET IT FOR ME...?
RRRR
Back to being a workaholic.
TAKE THE CALLER'S NAME AND PHONE NUMBER AND TELL 'EM I'LL CALL 'EM BACK.
OKAY.
RRRR
だーーーっ
BEEP
HI, THIS IS VELVET BLUE ROSE.
I made it!
A GIRL?!

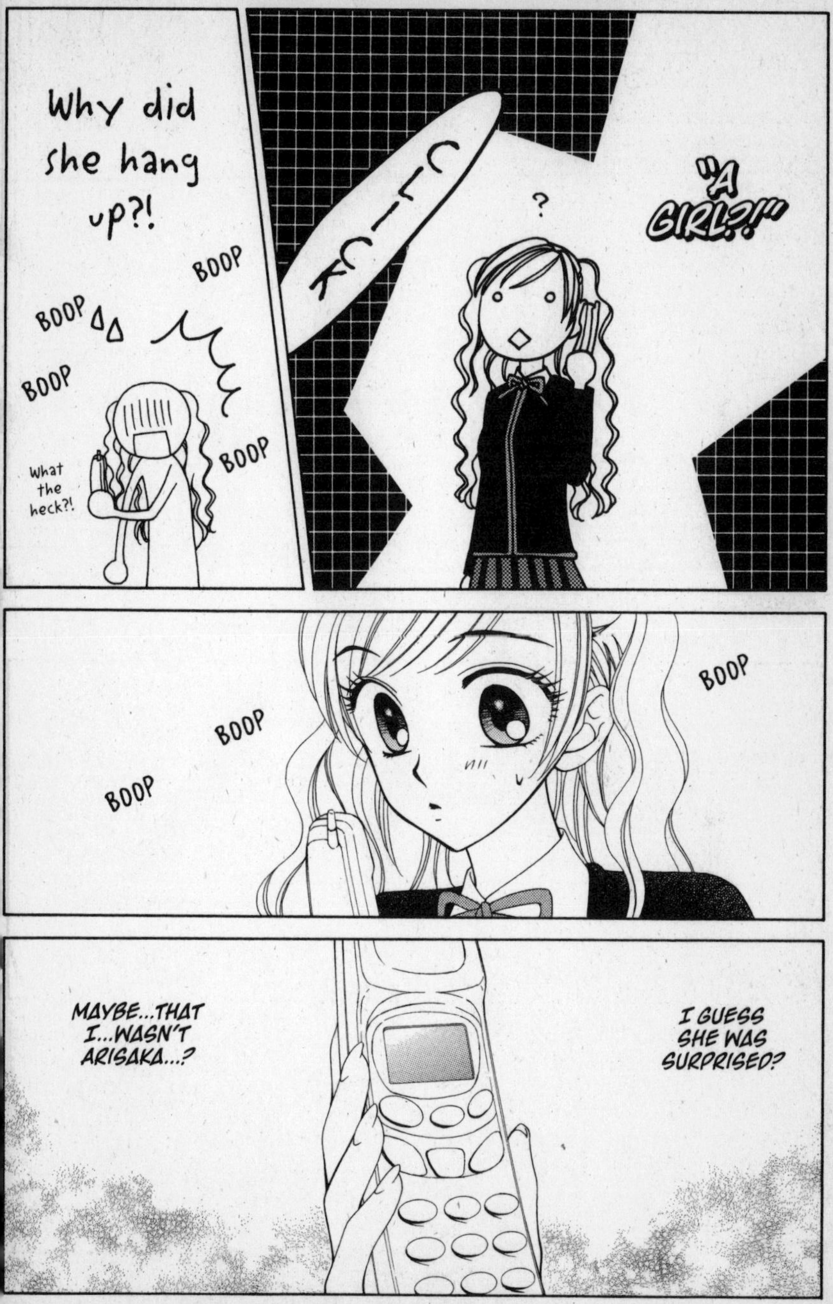
"A GIRL?!"
CLICK
?
Why did she hang up?!
BOOP
BOOP
BOOP
BOOP
What the heck?!
BOOP
BOOP
BOOP
I GUESS SHE WAS SURPRISED?
MAYBE...THAT I...WASN'T ARISAKA...?

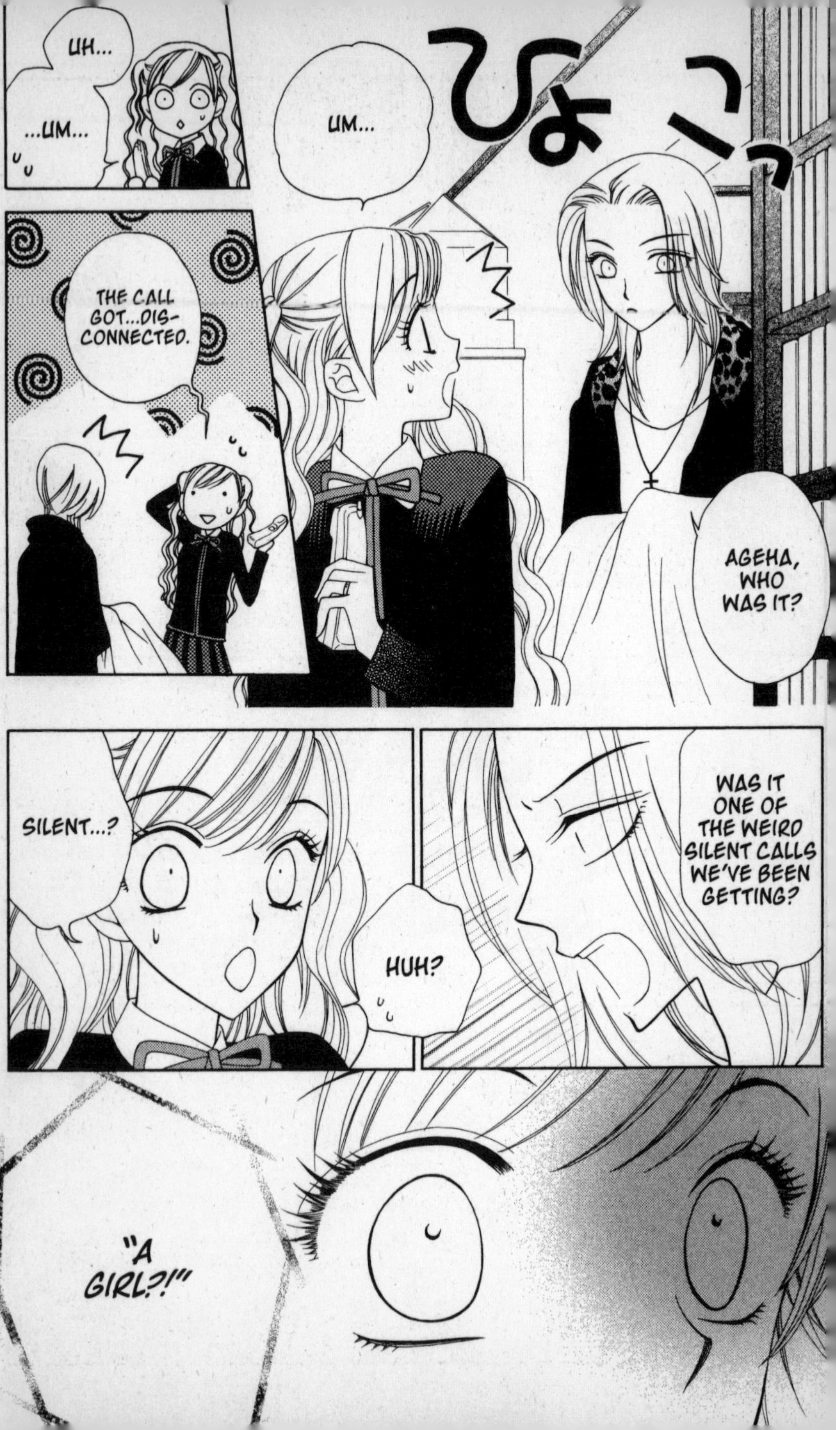
ひょこっ
UM...
AGEHA, WHO WAS IT?
UH...
...UM...
THE CALL GOT...DIS-CONNECTED.
WAS IT ONE OF THE WEIRD SILENT CALLS WE'VE BEEN GETTING?
HUH?
SILENT...?
"A GIRL?!"

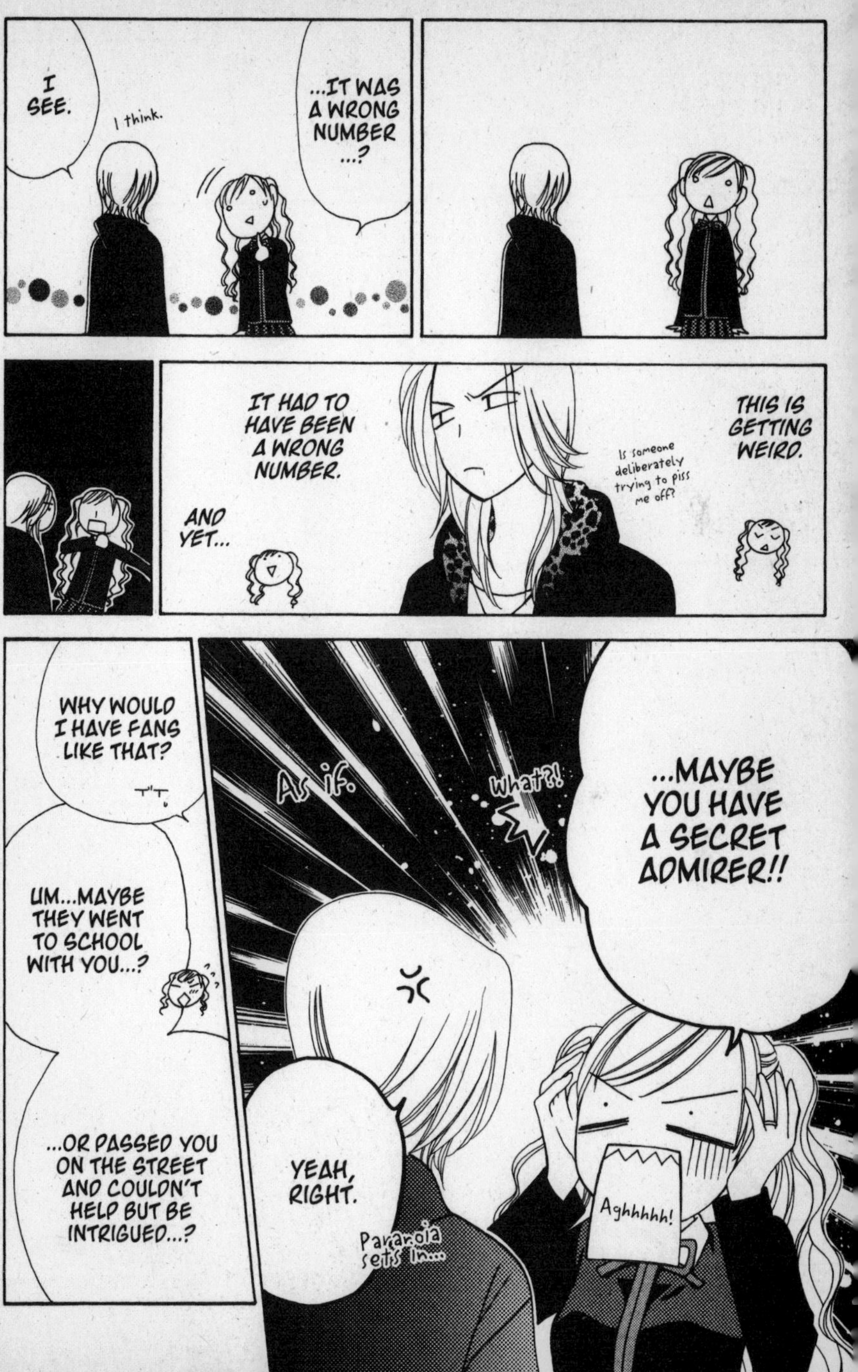
...IT WAS A WRONG NUMBER ...?
I SEE.
I think.
THIS IS GETTING WEIRD.
Is someone deliberately trying to piss me off?
IT HAD TO HAVE BEEN A WRONG NUMBER.
AND YET...
...MAYBE YOU HAVE A SECRET ADMIRER!!
what?!
As if.
Aghhhhh!
YEAH, RIGHT.
Paranoia sets in...
WHY WOULD I HAVE FANS LIKE THAT?
UM...MAYBE THEY WENT TO SCHOOL WITH YOU...?
...OR PASSED YOU ON THE STREET AND COULDN'T HELP BUT BE INTRIGUED...?

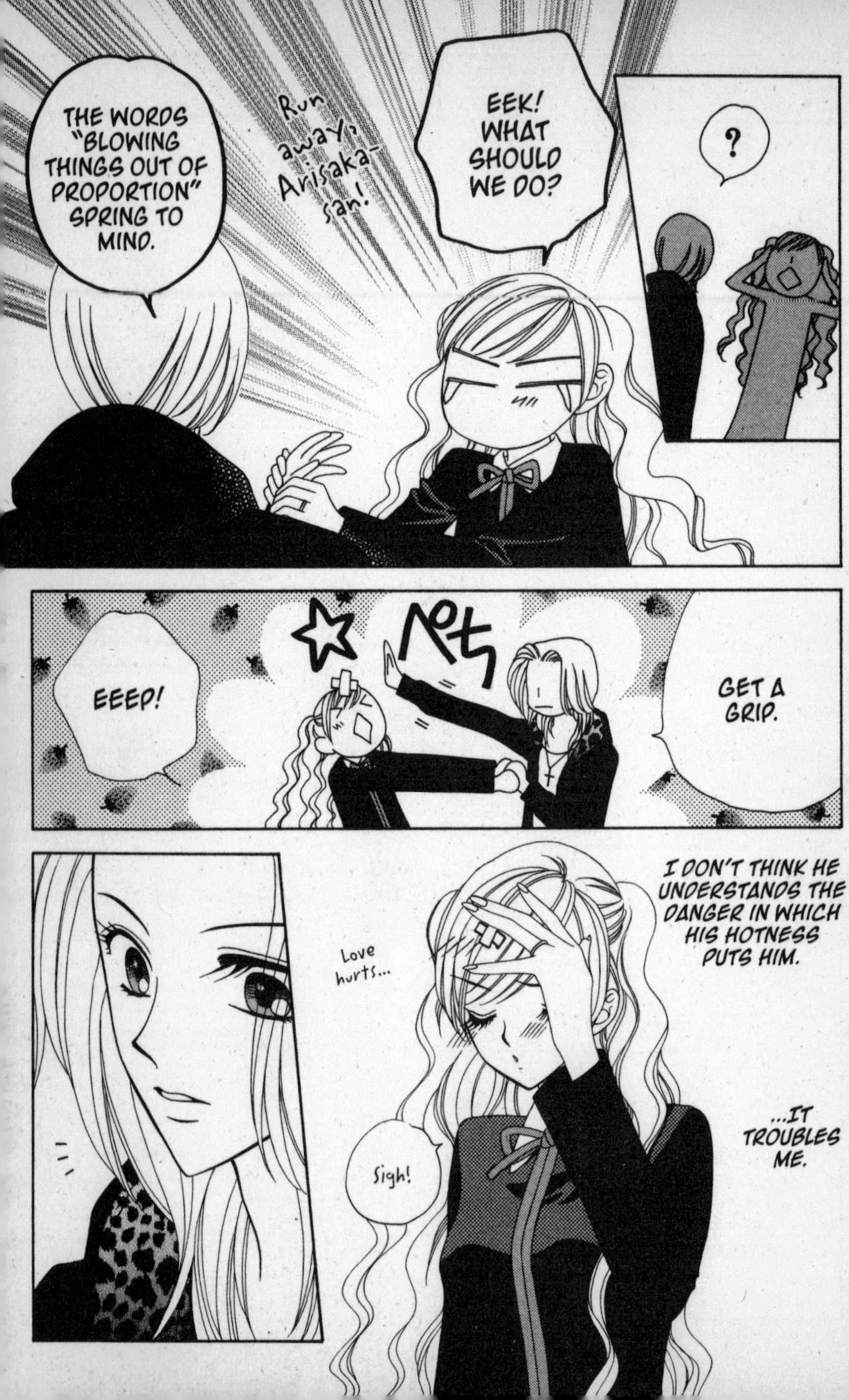
?
EEK! WHAT SHOULD WE DO?
Run away, Arisaka-san!
THE WORDS "BLOWING THINGS OUT OF PROPORTION" SPRING TO MIND.
GET A GRIP.
ぺち
EEEP!
I DON'T THINK HE UNDERSTANDS THE DANGER IN WHICH HIS HOTNESS PUTS HIM.
Love hurts...
...IT TROUBLES ME.
Sigh!

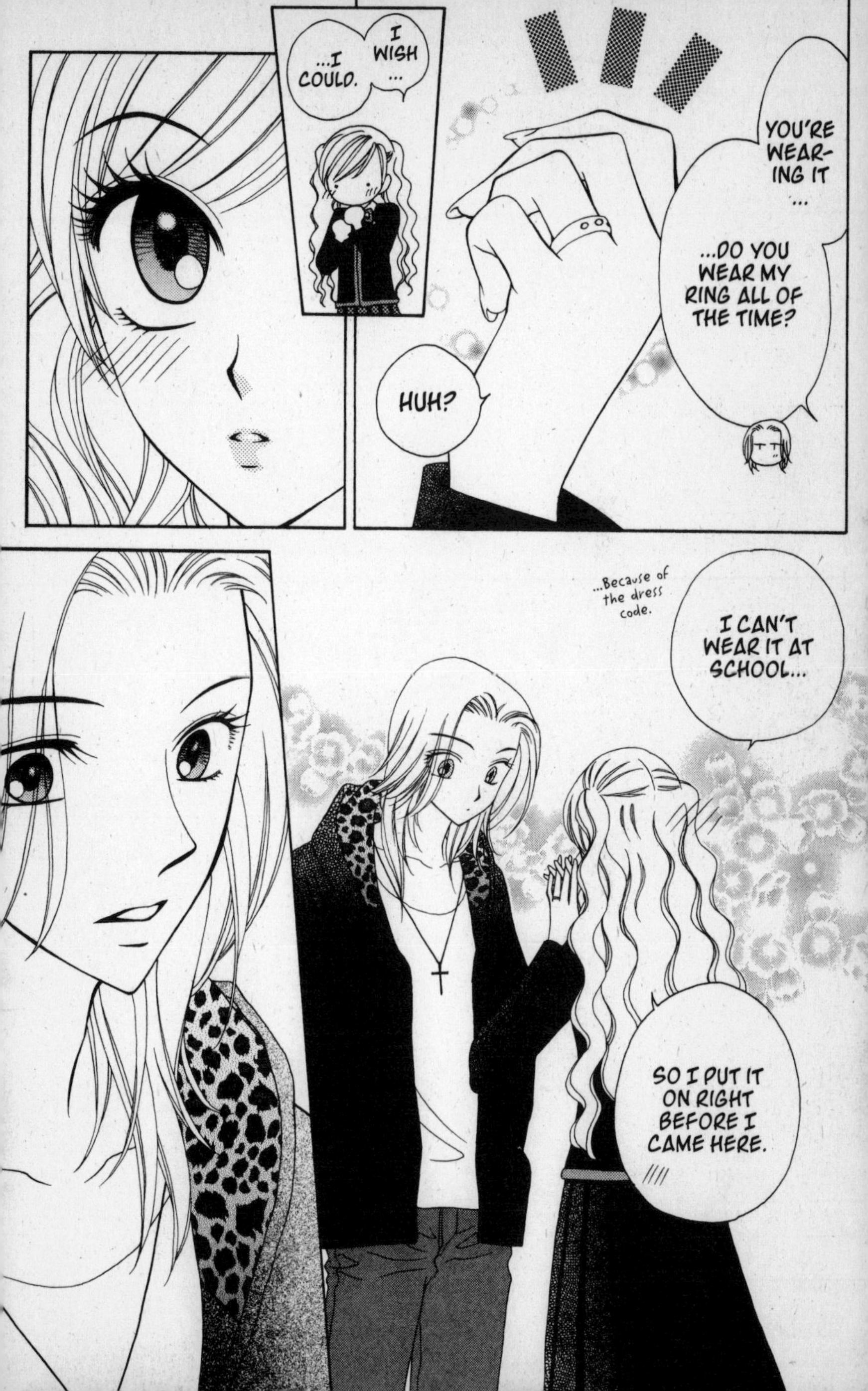
YOU'RE WEARING IT ...
...DO YOU WEAR MY RING ALL OF THE TIME?
HUH?
I WISH ...
...I COULD.
I CAN'T WEAR IT AT SCHOOL...
...Because of the dress code.
SO I PUT IT ON RIGHT BEFORE I CAME HERE.

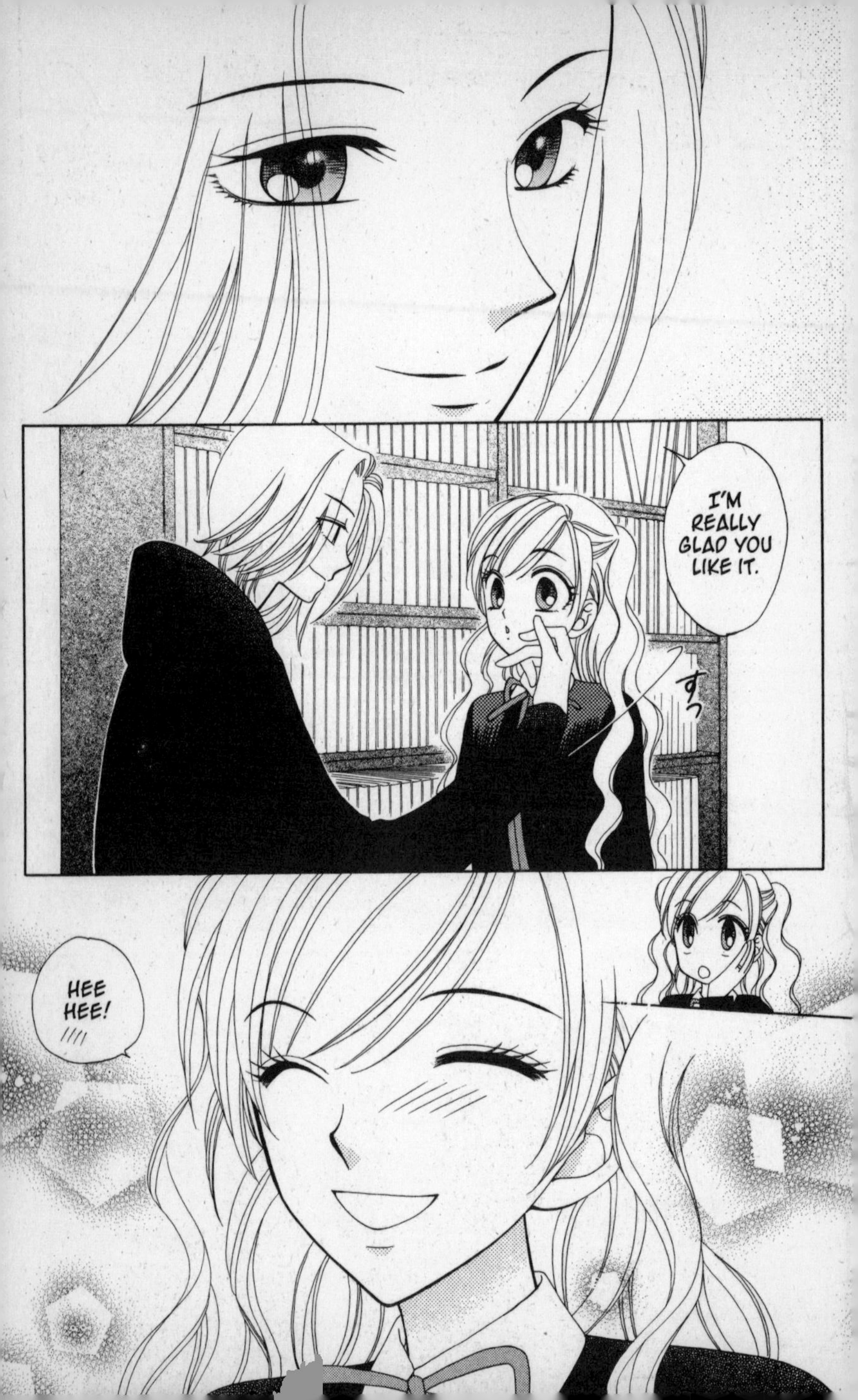
I'M REALLY GLAD YOU LIKE IT.
すっ
HEE HEE!

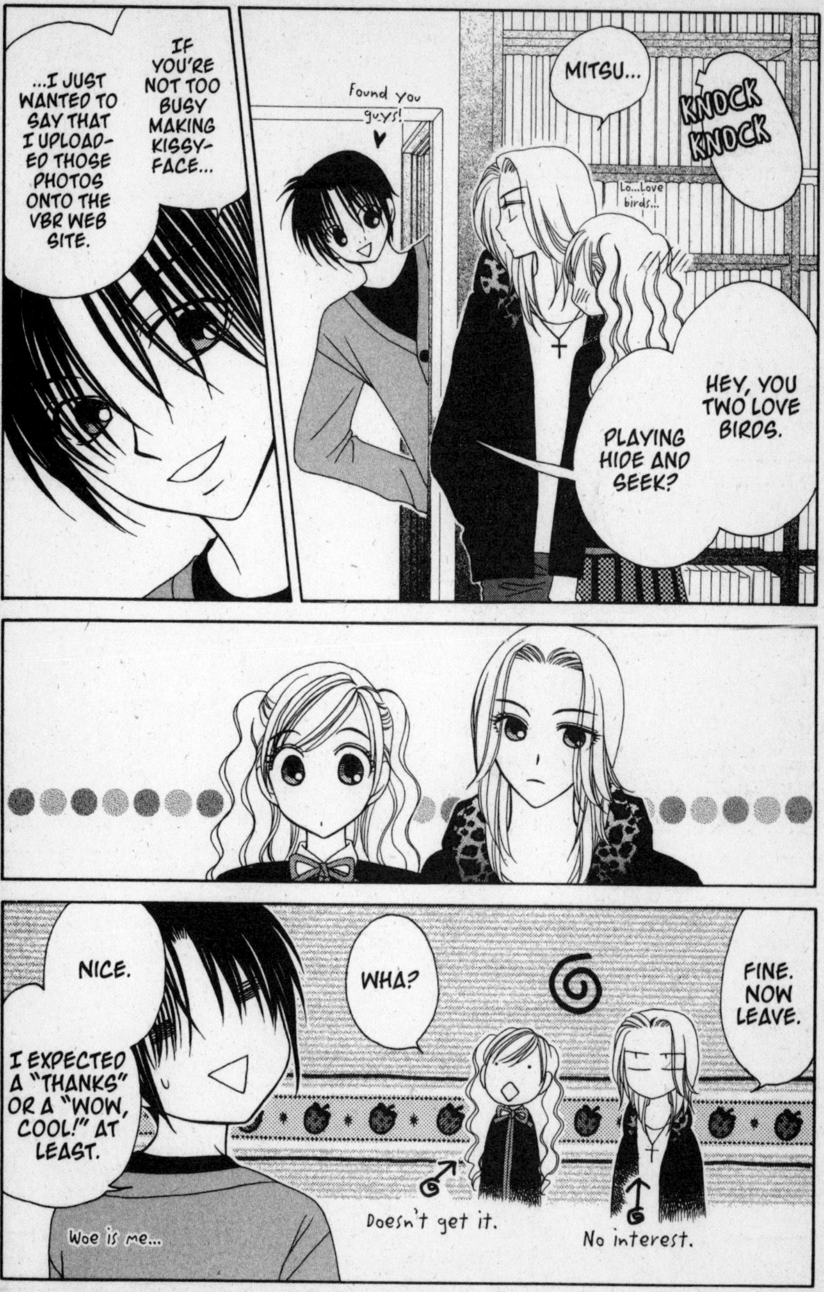
KNOCK KNOCK
MITSU...
Lo...Love birds!..
HEY, YOU TWO LOVE BIRDS.
PLAYING HIDE AND SEEK?
Found you guys!
IF YOU'RE NOT TOO BUSY MAKING KISSY-FACE...
...I JUST WANTED TO SAY THAT I UPLOAD-ED THOSE PHOTOS ONTO THE VBR WEB SITE.
FINE. NOW LEAVE.
No interest.
WHA?
Doesn't get it.
NICE.
I EXPECTED A "THANKS" OR A "WOW, COOL!" AT LEAST.
Woe is me...

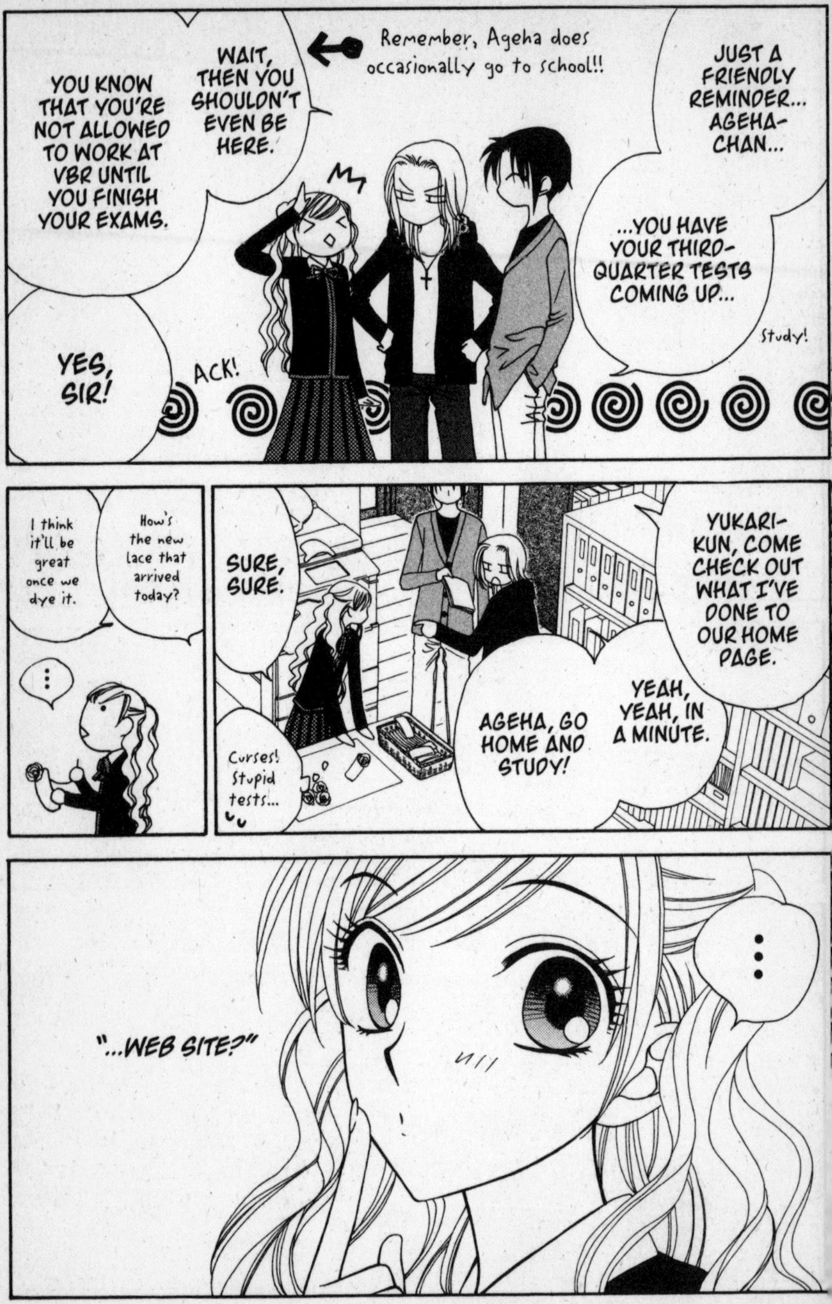
JUST A FRIENDLY REMINDER... AGEHA-CHAN...
...YOU HAVE YOUR THIRD-QUARTER TESTS COMING UP...
Study!
Remember, Ageha does occasionally go to school!!
WAIT, THEN YOU SHOULDN'T EVEN BE HERE.
YOU KNOW THAT YOU'RE NOT ALLOWED TO WORK AT VBR UNTIL YOU FINISH YOUR EXAMS.
ACK!
YES, SIR!
YUKARI-KUN, COME CHECK OUT WHAT I'VE DONE TO OUR HOME PAGE.
YEAH, YEAH, IN A MINUTE.
SURE, SURE.
AGEHA, GO HOME AND STUDY!
Curses! Stupid tests...
How's the new lace that arrived today?
I think it'll be great once we dye it.
...
...
"...WEB SITE?"

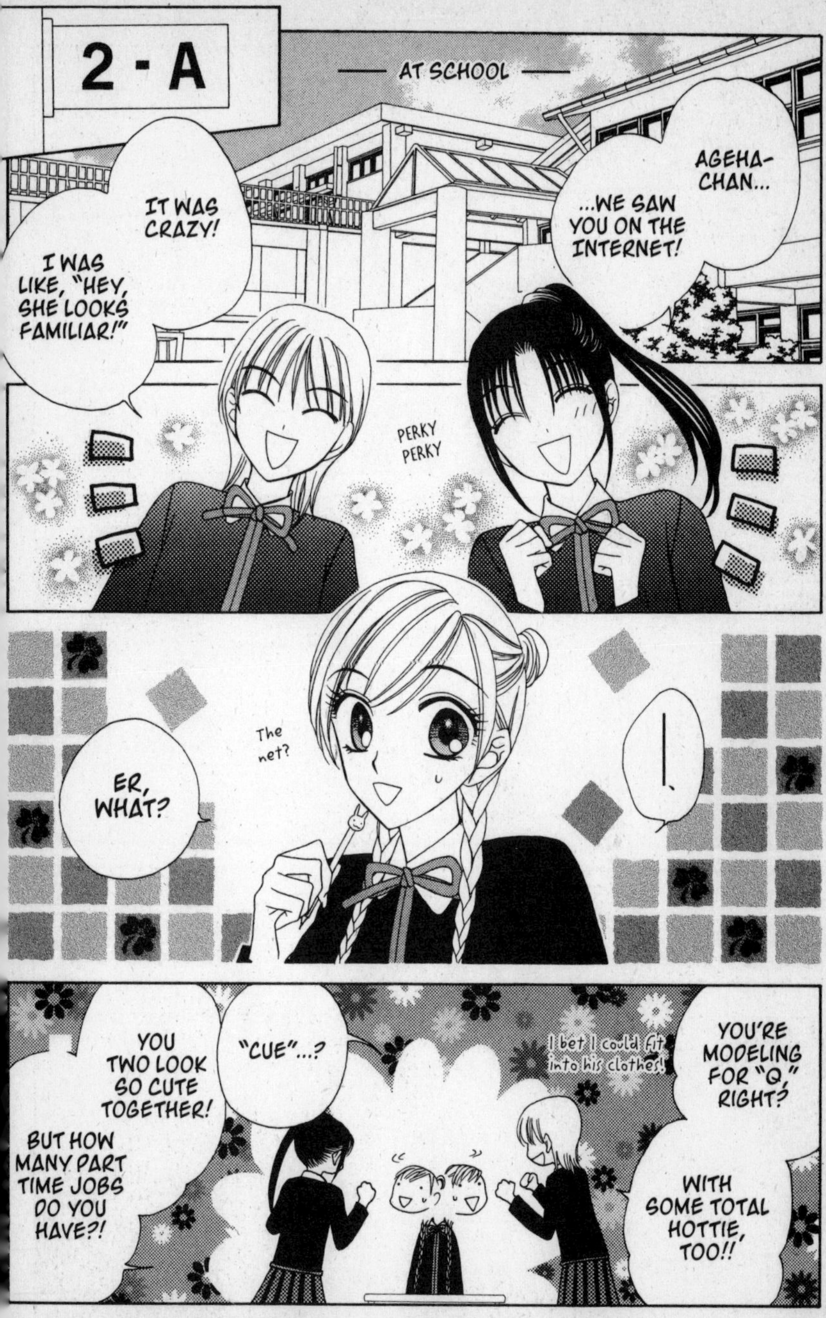
2-A
AT SCHOOL
AGEHA-CHAN...
...WE SAW YOU ON THE INTERNET!
IT WAS CRAZY!
I WAS LIKE, "HEY, SHE LOOKS FAMILIAR!"
PERKY PERKY
!
The net?
ER, WHAT?
YOU'RE MODELING FOR "Q," RIGHT?
WITH SOME TOTAL HOTTIE, TOO!!
I bet I could fit into his clothes!
"CUE"...?
YOU TWO LOOK SO CUTE TOGETHER!
BUT HOW MANY PART TIME JOBS DO YOU HAVE?!

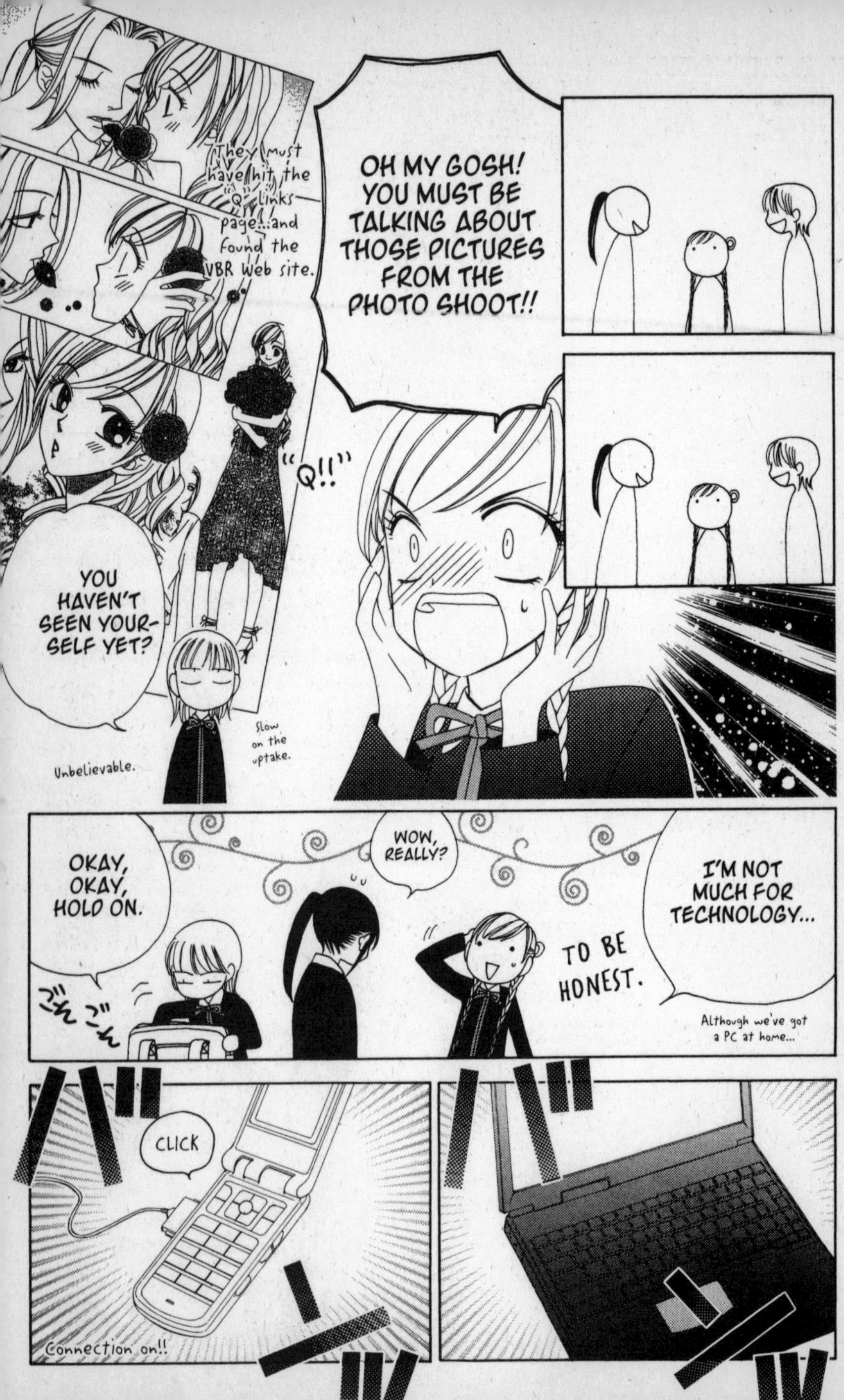
OH MY GOSH! YOU MUST BE TALKING ABOUT THOSE PICTURES FROM THE PHOTO SHOOT!!
They must have hit the "Q" links page...and found the VBR Web site.
"Q!!"
YOU HAVEN'T SEEN YOURSELF YET?
Slow on the uptake.
Unbelievable.
I'M NOT MUCH FOR TECHNOLOGY...
TO BE HONEST.
Although we've got a PC at home...
WOW, REALLY?
OKAY, OKAY, HOLD ON.
ごそごそ
CLICK
Connection on!!

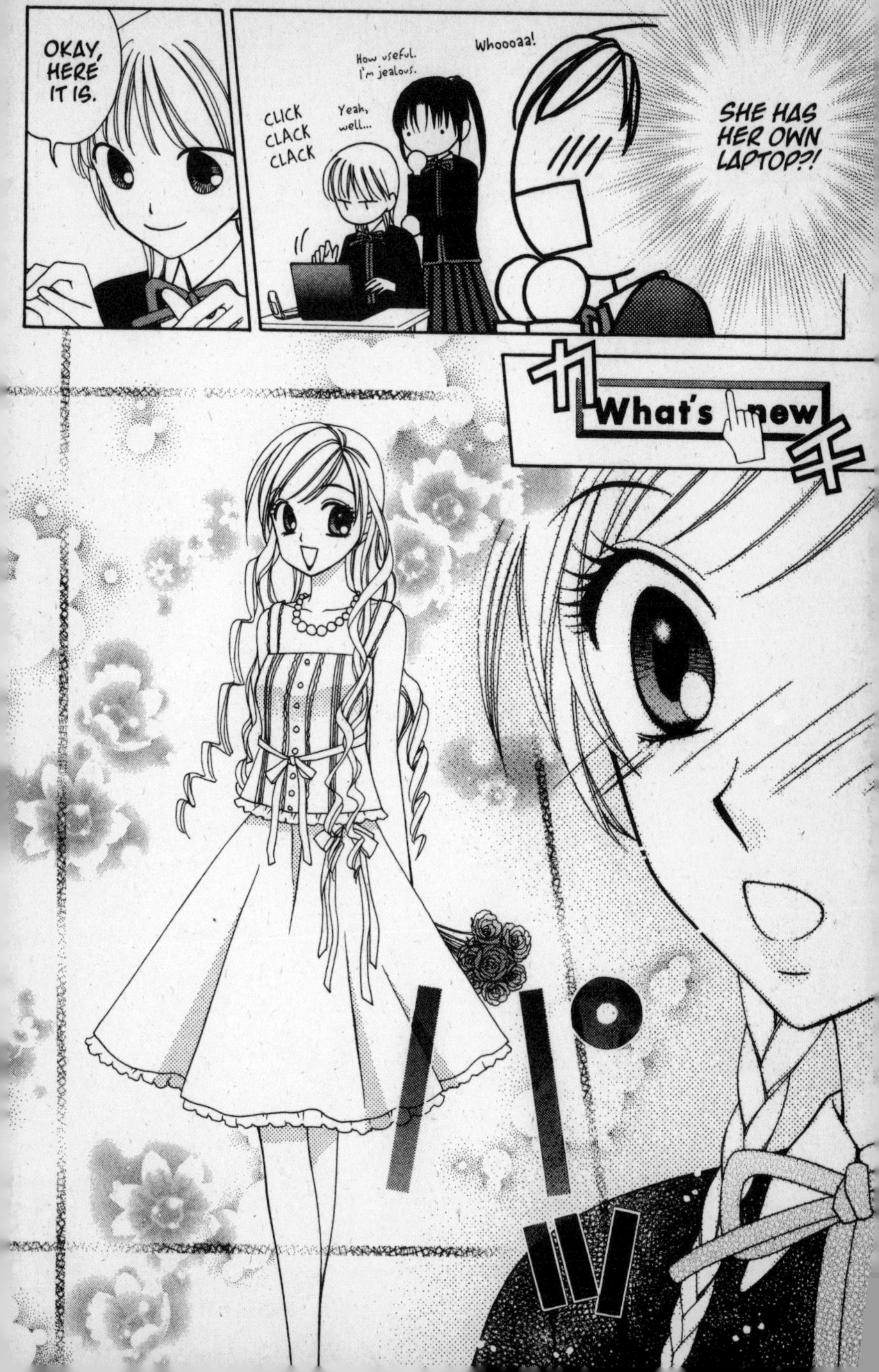
SHE HAS HER OWN LAPTOP?!
Whoooaa!
How useful. I'm jealous.
Yeah, well...
CLICK CLACK CLACK
OKAY, HERE IT IS.
カチ
What's new

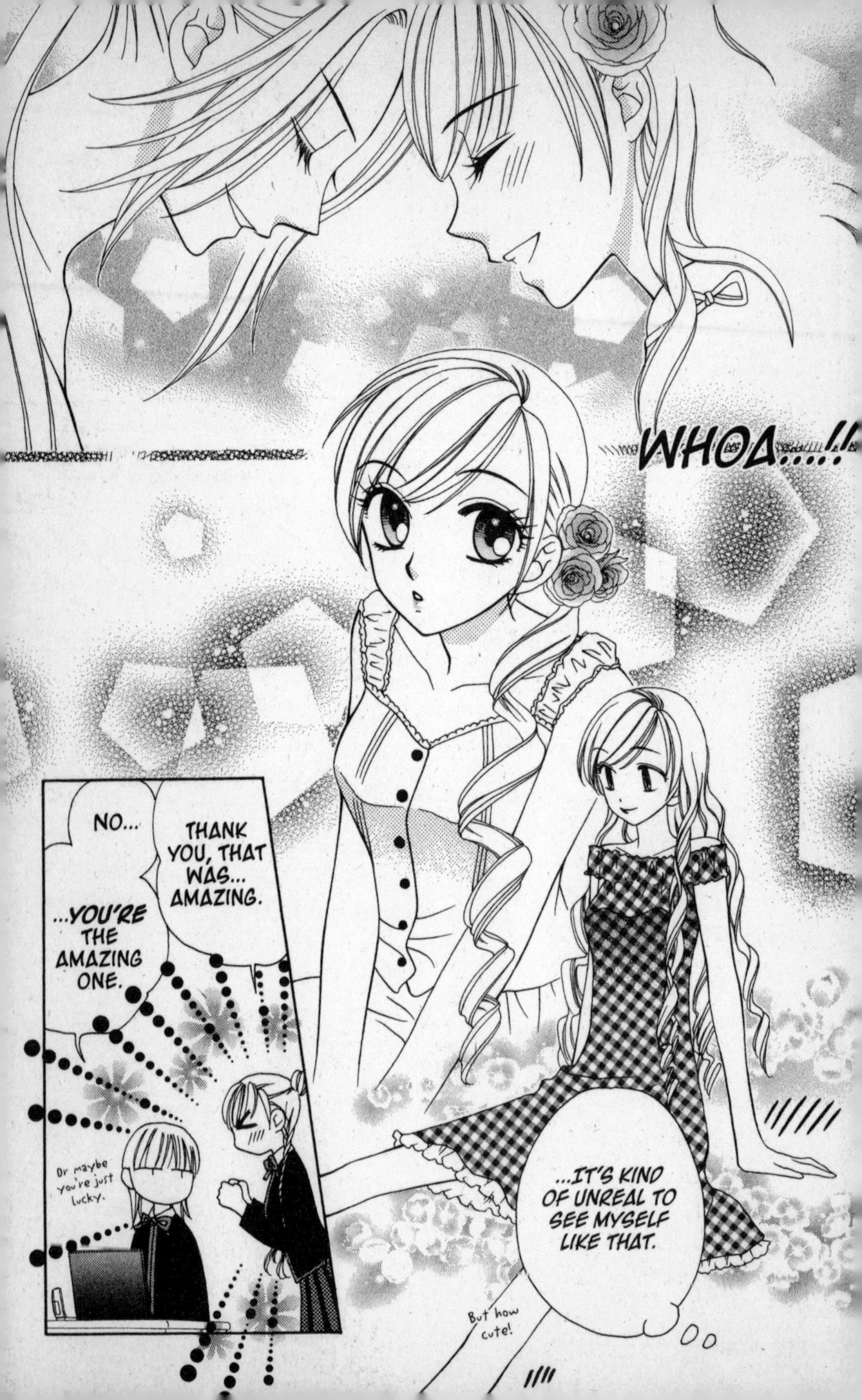
WHOA....!!
...IT'S KIND OF UNREAL TO SEE MYSELF LIKE THAT.
But how cute!
THANK YOU, THAT WAS... AMAZING.
NO...
...YOU'RE THE AMAZING ONE.
Or maybe you're just lucky.

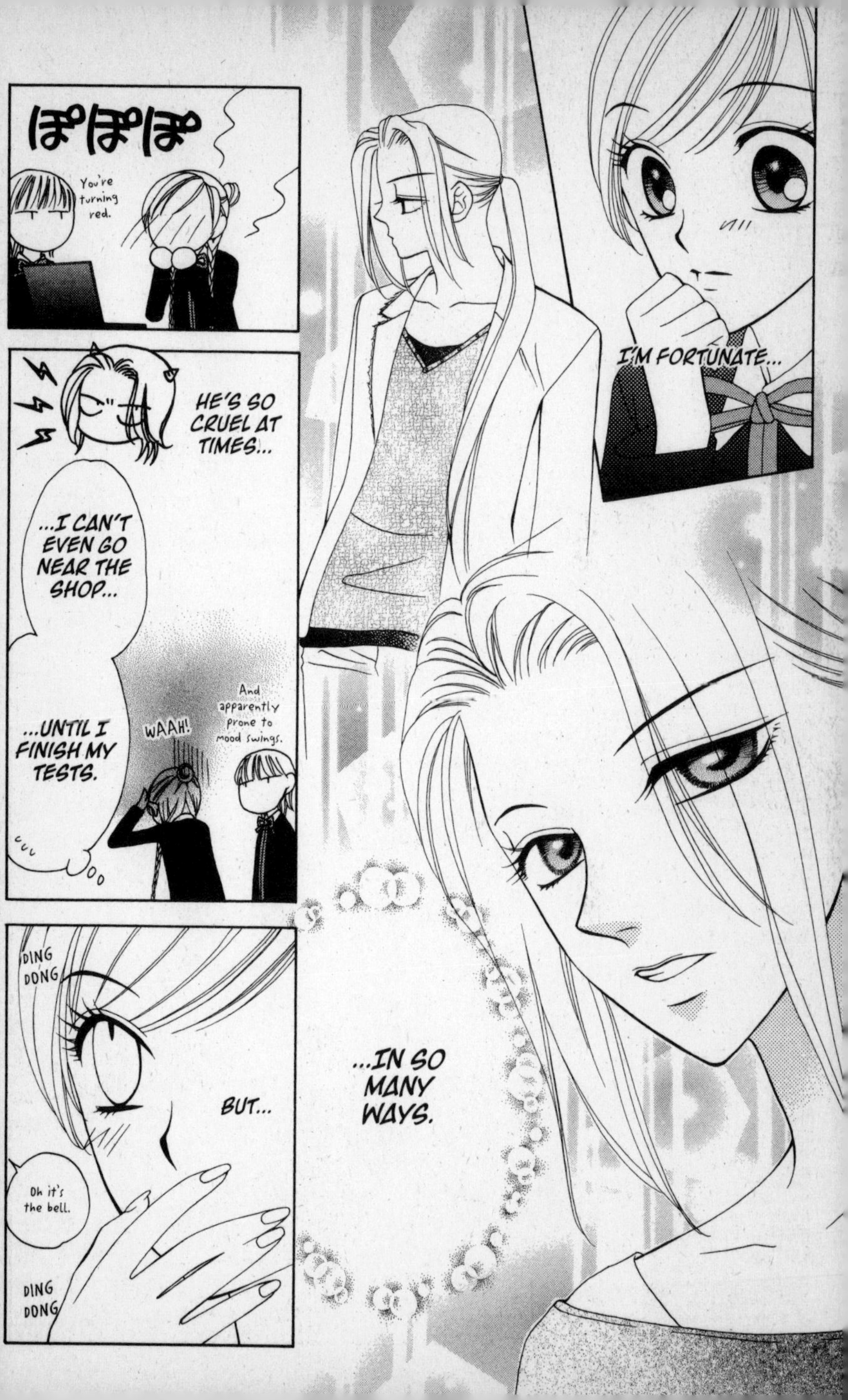
I'M FORTUNATE...
...IN SO MANY WAYS.
ぽぽぽ
You're turning red.
HE'S SO CRUEL AT TIMES...
...I CAN'T EVEN GO NEAR THE SHOP...
...UNTIL I FINISH MY TESTS.
And apparently prone to mood swings.
WAAH!
DING DONG
BUT...
Oh it's the bell.
DING DONG

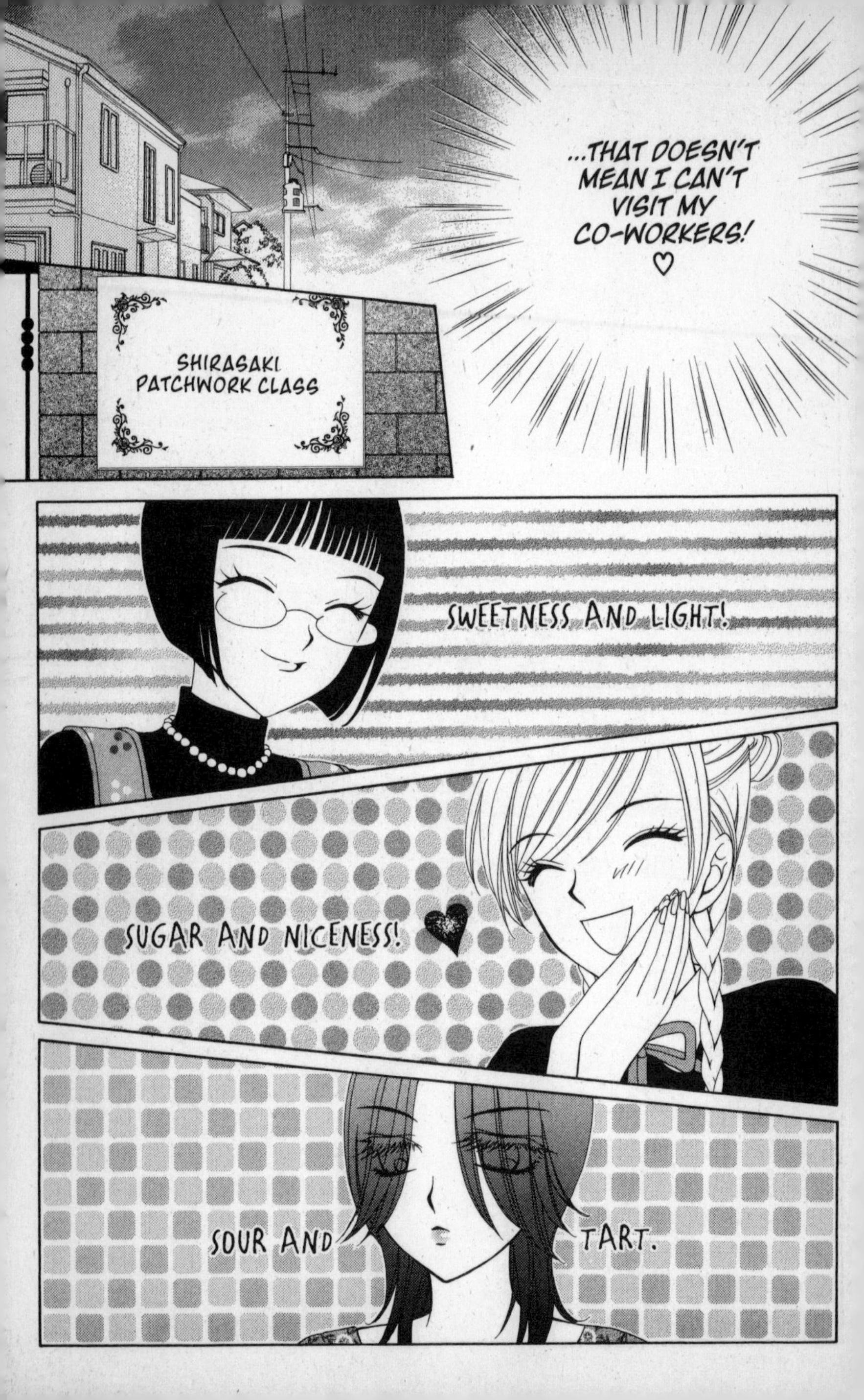
...THAT DOESN'T MEAN I CAN'T VISIT MY CO-WORKERS! ♡
SHIRASAKI PATCHWORK CLASS
SWEETNESS AND LIGHT!
SUGAR AND NICENESS!
SOUR AND
TART.

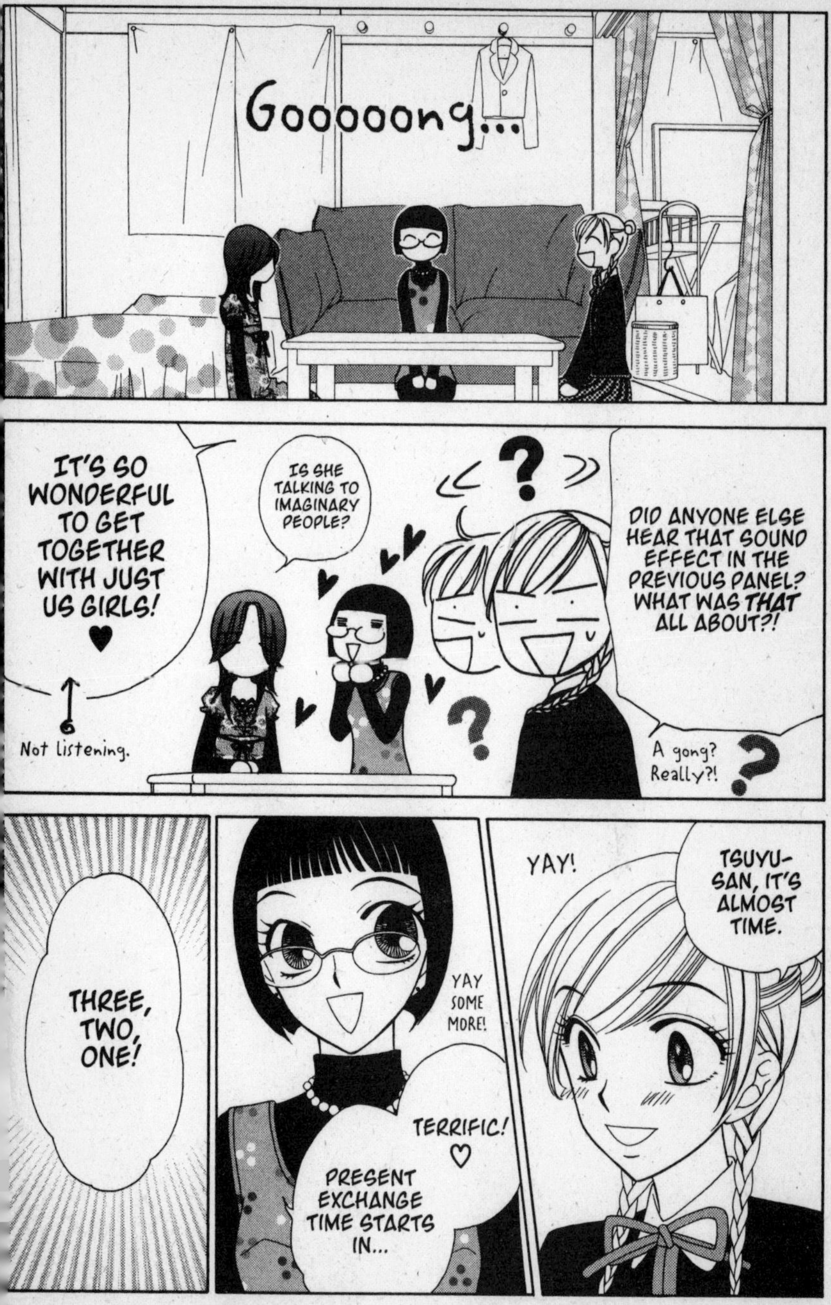
Goooong...
DID ANYONE ELSE HEAR THAT SOUND EFFECT IN THE PREVIOUS PANEL? WHAT WAS THAT ALL ABOUT?!
A gong? Really?!
IS SHE TALKING TO IMAGINARY PEOPLE?
IT'S SO WONDERFUL TO GET TOGETHER WITH JUST US GIRLS! ♥
Not listening.
TSUYU-SAN, IT'S ALMOST TIME.
YAY!
YAY SOME MORE!
TERRIFIC! ♡
PRESENT EXCHANGE TIME STARTS IN...
THREE, TWO, ONE!

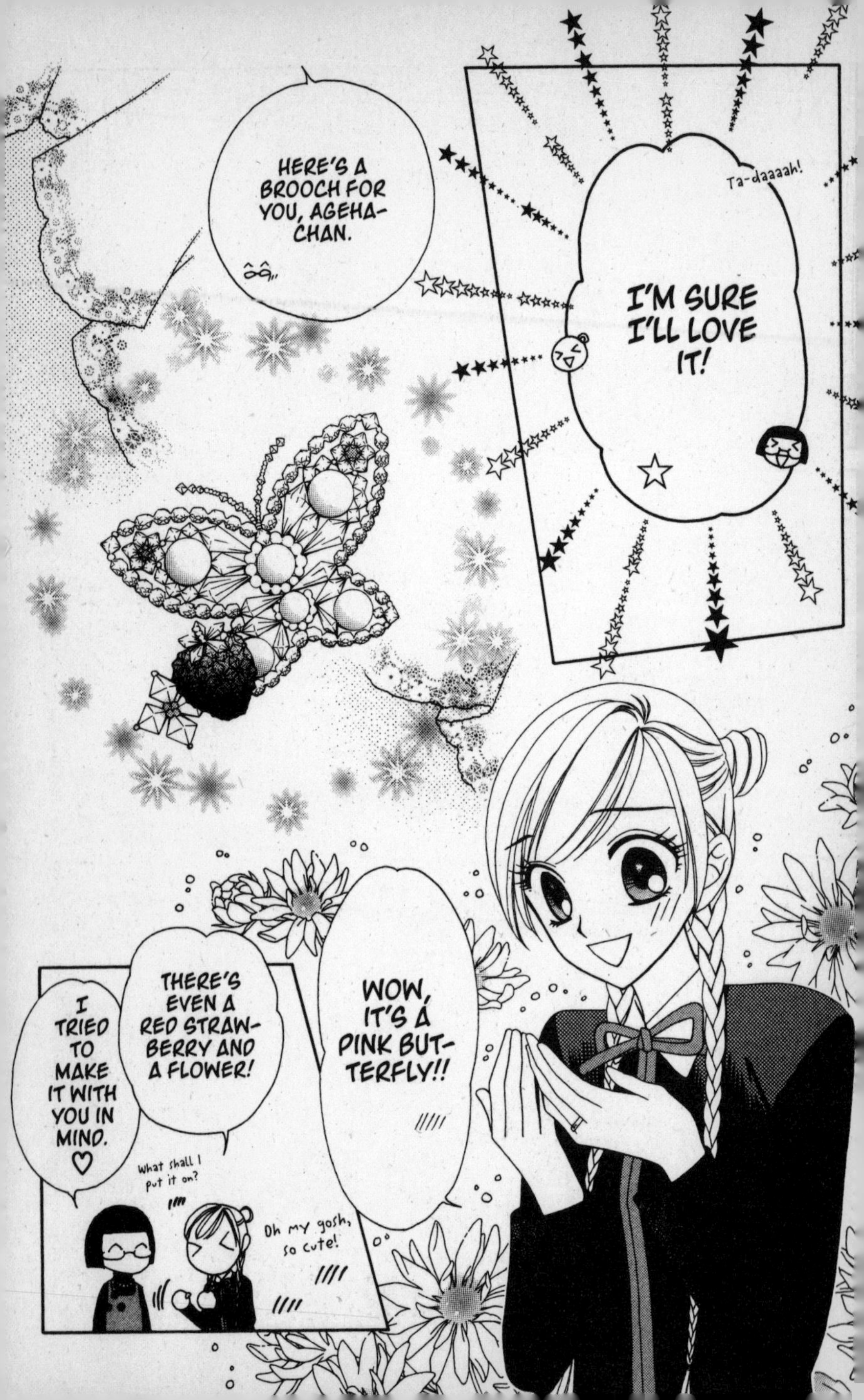
Ta-daaaah!
I'M SURE I'LL LOVE IT!
HERE'S A BROOCH FOR YOU, AGEHA-CHAN.
WOW, IT'S A PINK BUT-TERFLY!!
THERE'S EVEN A RED STRAW-BERRY AND A FLOWER!
I TRIED TO MAKE IT WITH YOU IN MIND. ♡
What shall I put it on?
Oh my gosh, so cute!

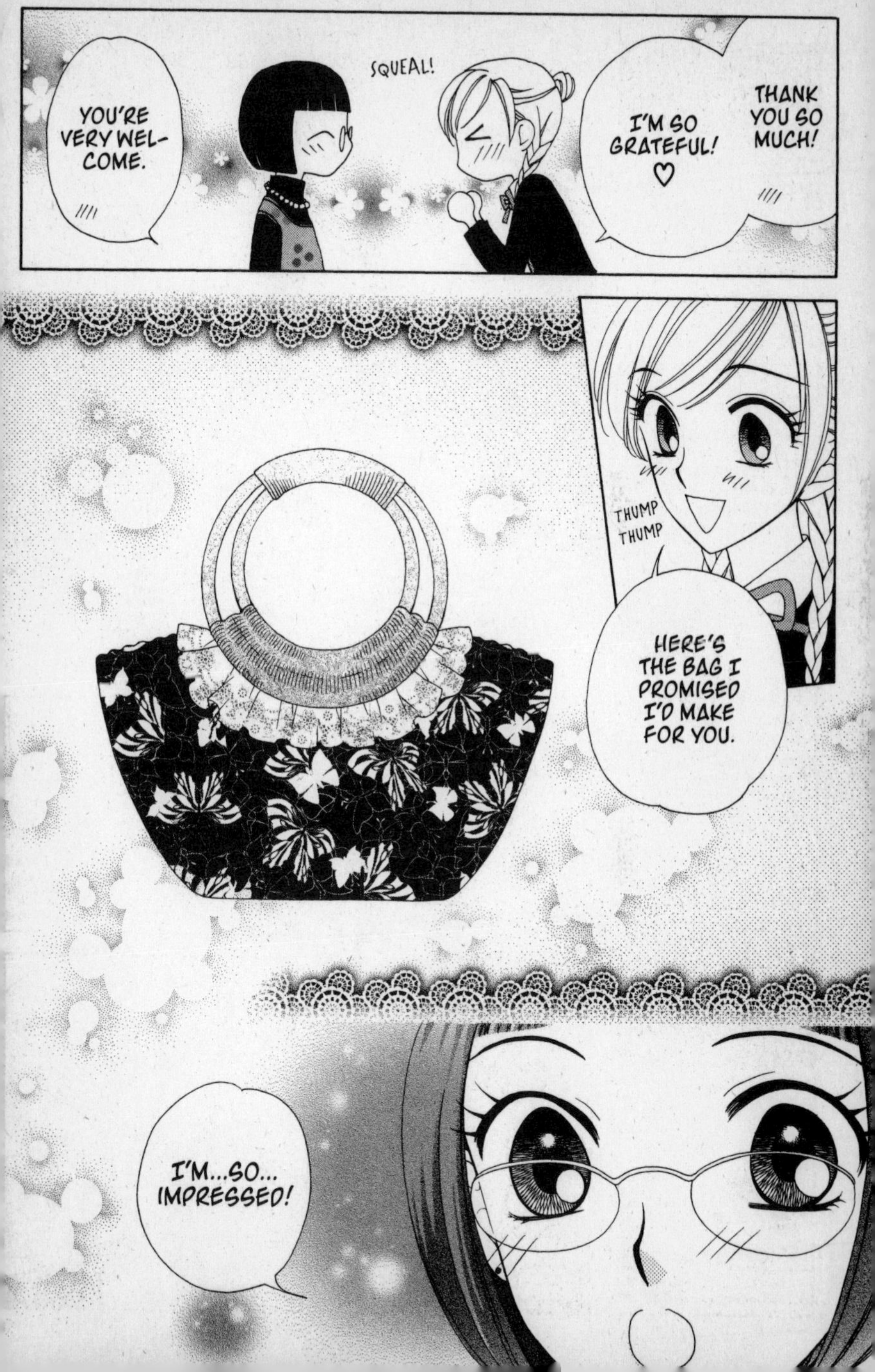
THANK YOU SO MUCH!
I'M SO GRATEFUL! ♡
SQUEAL!
YOU'RE VERY WEL-COME.
THUMP THUMP
HERE'S THE BAG I PROMISED I'D MAKE FOR YOU.
I'M...SO... IMPRESSED!

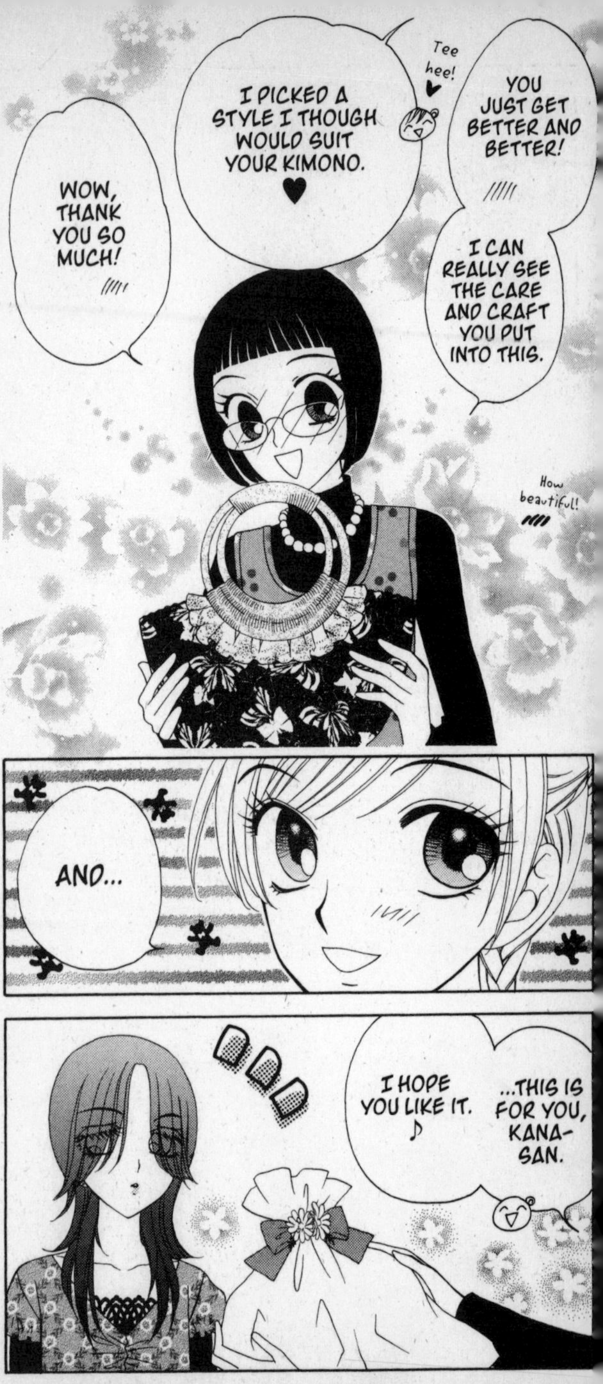
YOU JUST GET BETTER AND BETTER!
Tee hee!
I PICKED A STYLE I THOUGH WOULD SUIT YOUR KIMONO. ♥
WOW, THANK YOU SO MUCH!
I CAN REALLY SEE THE CARE AND CRAFT YOU PUT INTO THIS.
How beautiful!
AND...
...THIS IS FOR YOU, KANA-SAN.
I HOPE YOU LIKE IT. ♪

This is the last sidebar for this volume. Thank you very much for reading up until this point.

A great big thank you to everyone who helped out in the creation of this volume and to all of our readers! ♪

The Bridal Fair story is finally over! I hope you guys all liked it. I would be honored if you would read Volume 10 as well!

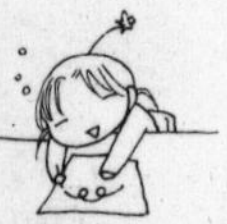

Volume 10 will be released in Japan sometime in the summer...I think. Feel free to send me your thoughts and comments about Volume 9. ♪

Banri Hidaka
c/o TOKYOPOP Inc.
5900 Wilshire Blvd.
Suite 2000
Los Angeles, CA
90036

Thanks! ♥

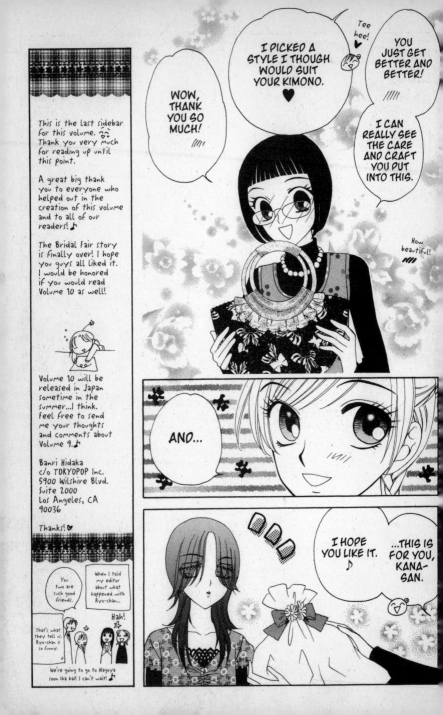

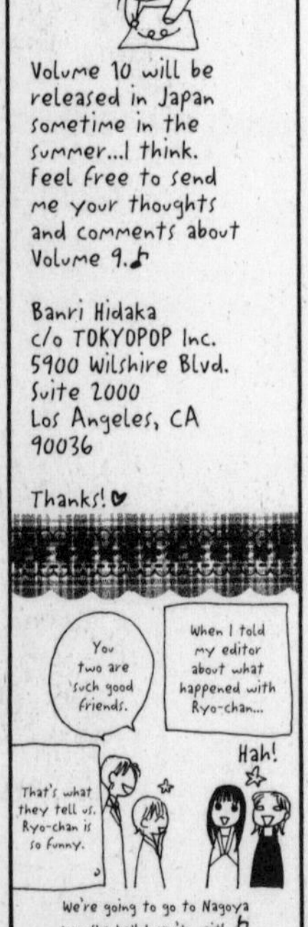
When I told my editor about what happened with Ryo-chan...
You two are such good friends.
Hah!
That's what they tell us. Ryo-chan is so funny.
We're going to go to Nagoya soon (ha ha)! I can't wait! ♪

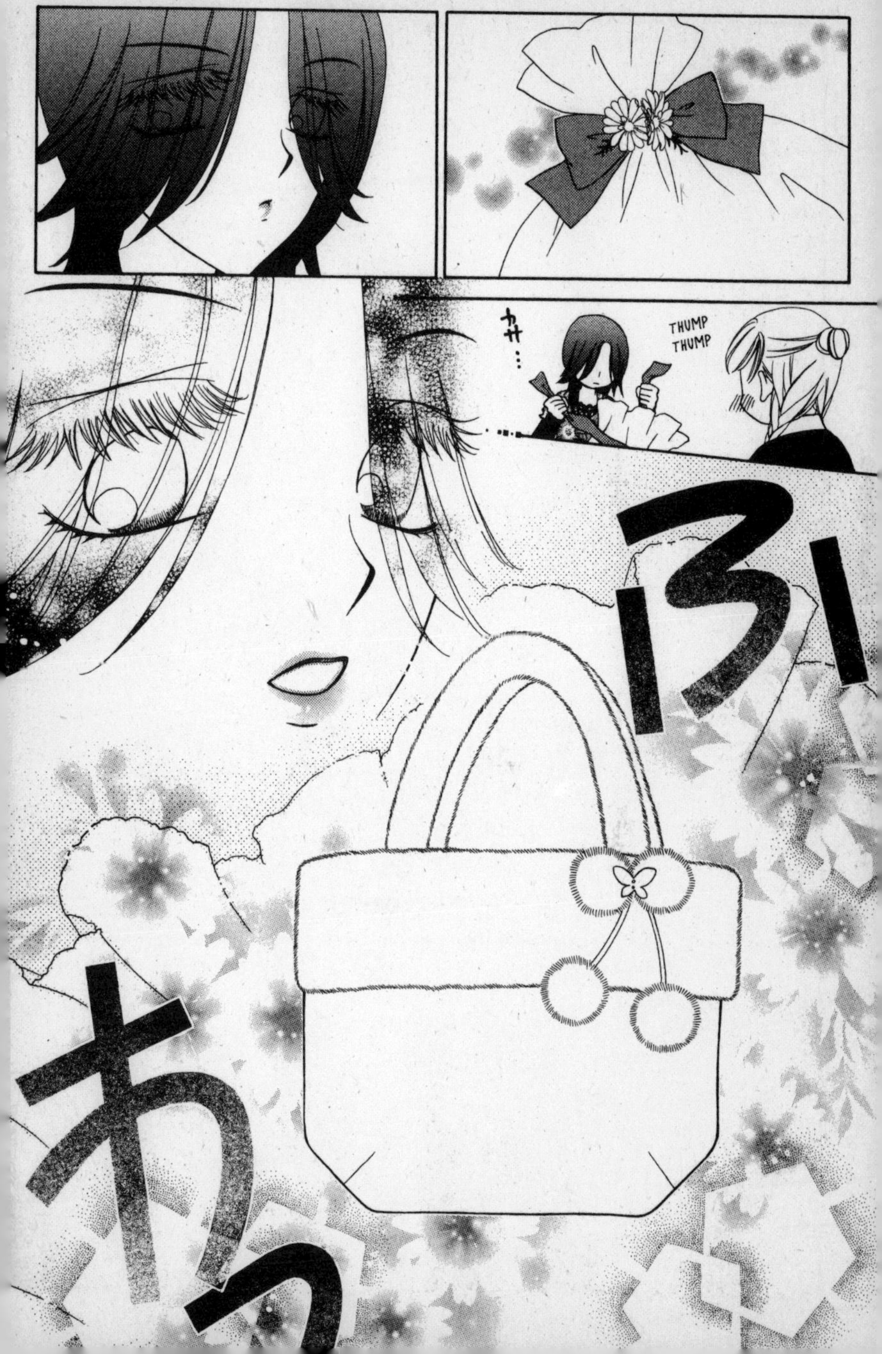

カサ…
THUMP THUMP
ふわっ

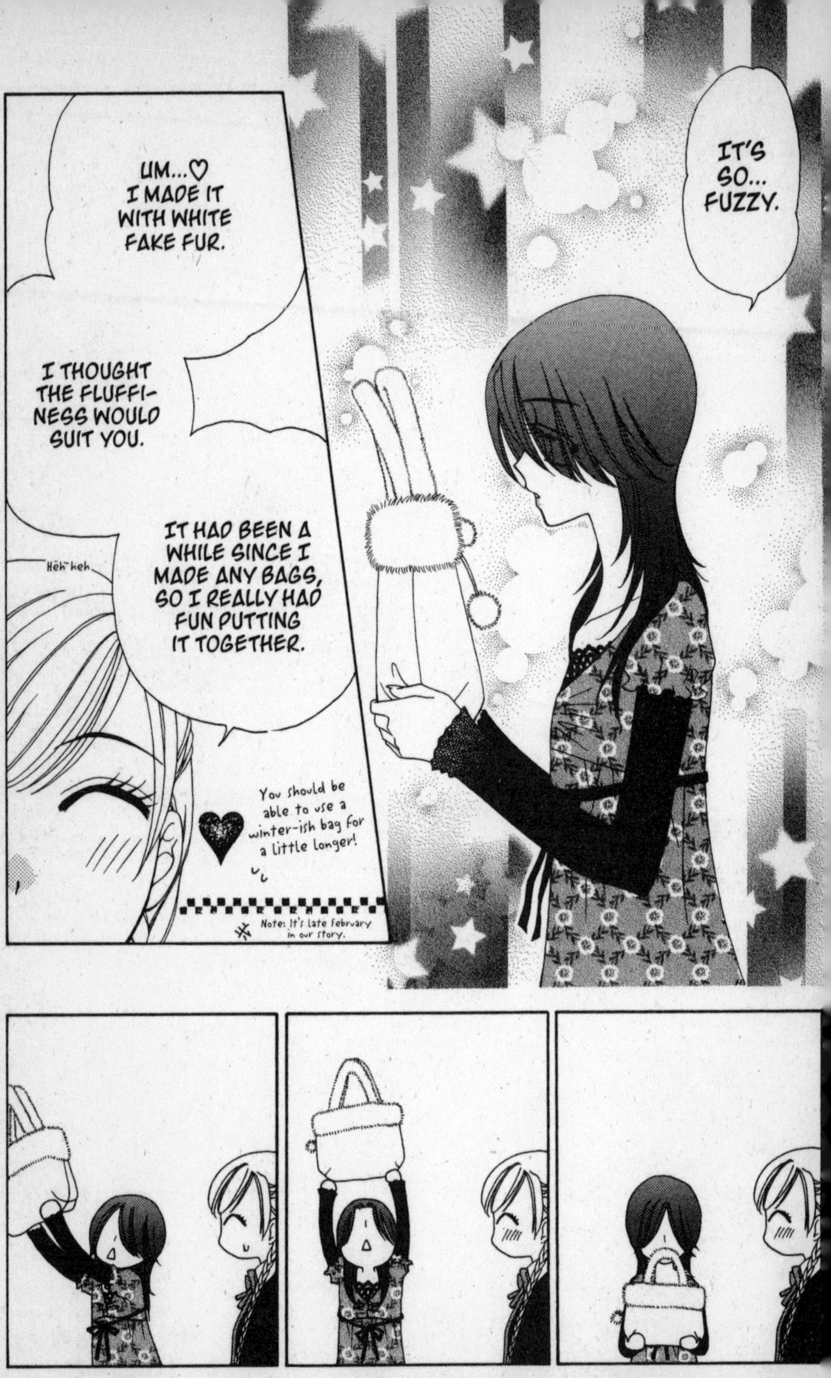
IT'S SO... FUZZY.
UM...♡ I MADE IT WITH WHITE FAKE FUR.
I THOUGHT THE FLUFFI-NESS WOULD SUIT YOU.
Heh heh
IT HAD BEEN A WHILE SINCE I MADE ANY BAGS, SO I REALLY HAD FUN PUTTING IT TOGETHER.
You should be able to use a winter-ish bag for a little longer!
Note: It's late February in our story.

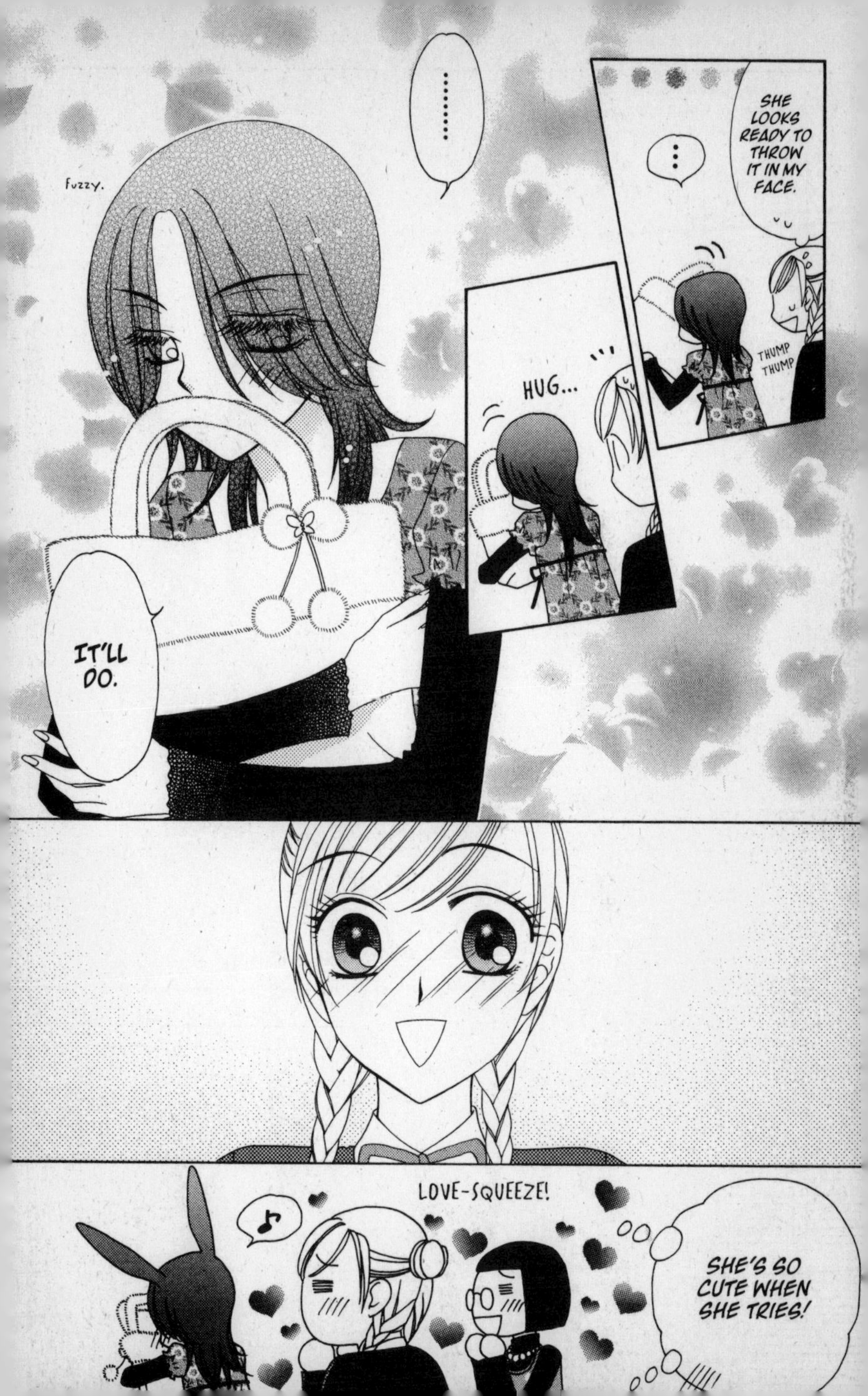

SHE LOOKS READY TO THROW IT IN MY FACE.
...
THUMP THUMP
HUG...
......
Fuzzy.
IT'LL DO.
SHE'S SO CUTE WHEN SHE TRIES!
LOVE-SQUEEZE!
♪

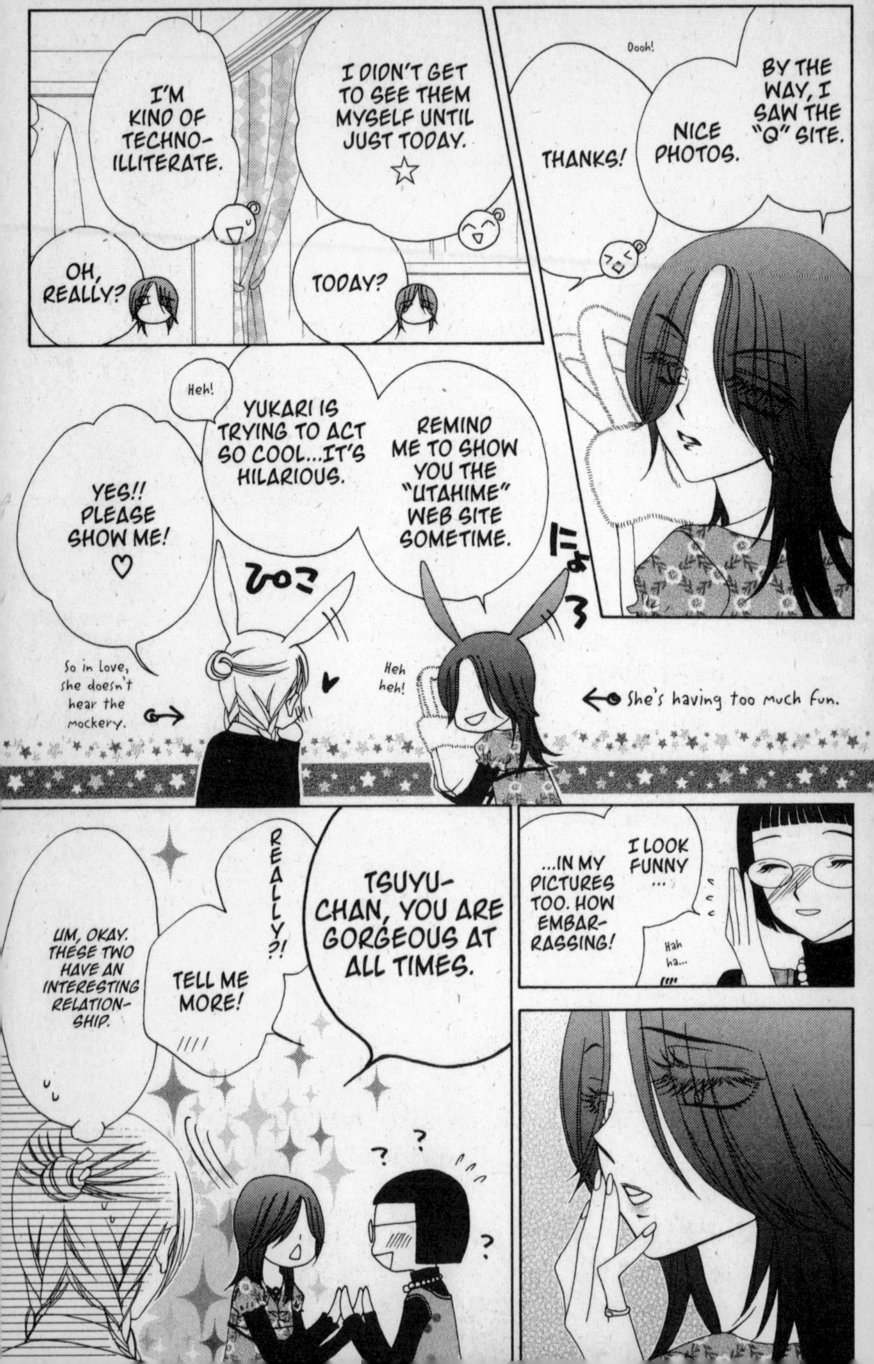
Oooh!
BY THE WAY, I SAW THE "Q" SITE.
NICE PHOTOS.
THANKS!
I DIDN'T GET TO SEE THEM MYSELF UNTIL JUST TODAY. ☆
TODAY?
I'M KIND OF TECHNO-ILLITERATE.
OH, REALLY?
にょろ
REMIND ME TO SHOW YOU THE "UTAHIME" WEB SITE SOMETIME.
Heh!
YUKARI IS TRYING TO ACT SO COOL...IT'S HILARIOUS.
ぴこ
YES!! PLEASE SHOW ME! ♡
She's having too much fun.
Heh heh!
So in love, she doesn't hear the mockery.
I LOOK FUNNY...
...IN MY PICTURES TOO. HOW EMBARRASSING!
Hah ha...
TSUYU-CHAN, YOU ARE GORGEOUS AT ALL TIMES.
REALLY?!
TELL ME MORE!
UM, OKAY. THESE TWO HAVE AN INTERESTING RELATIONSHIP.

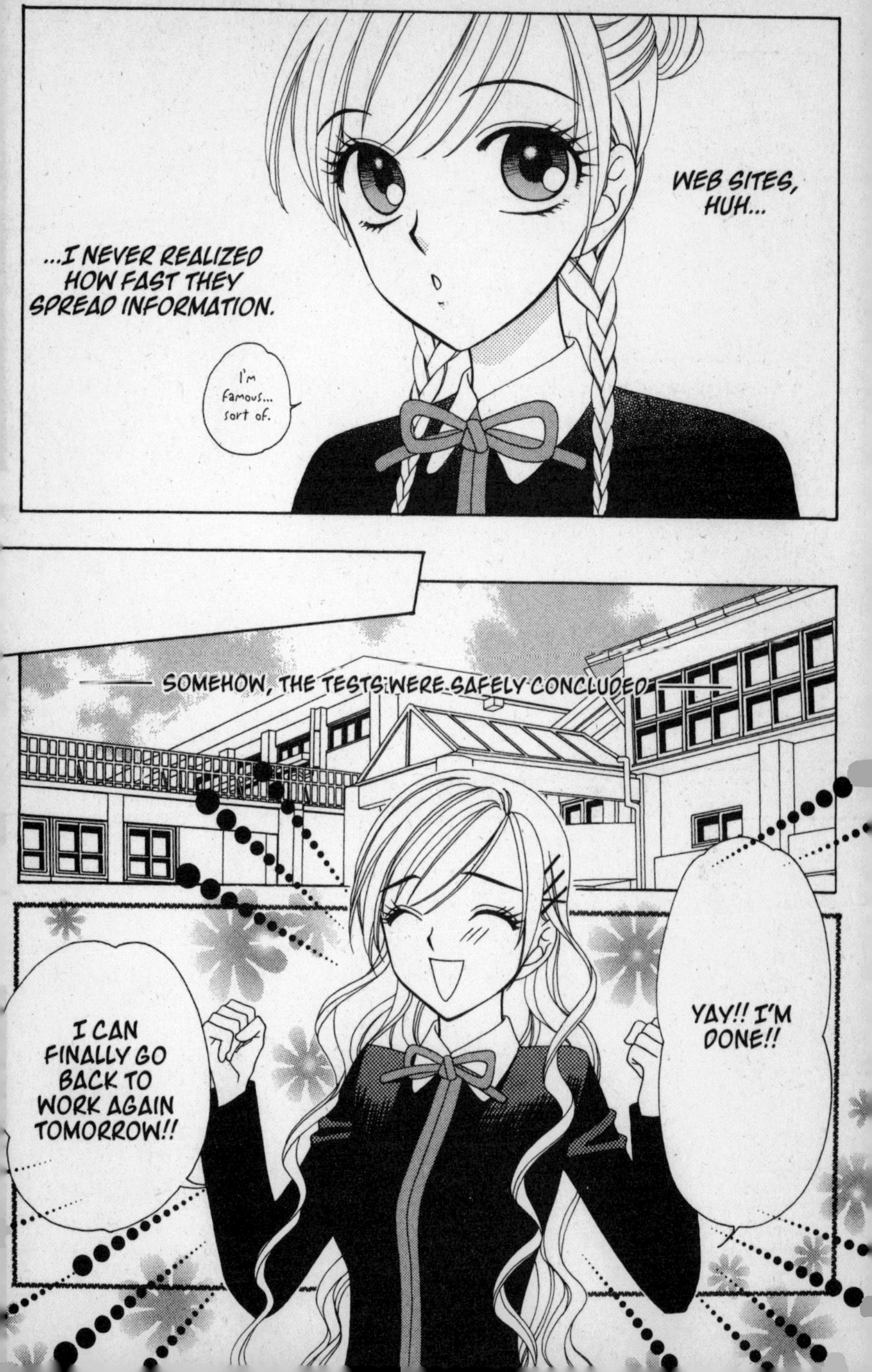
WEB SITES, HUH...
...I NEVER REALIZED HOW FAST THEY SPREAD INFORMATION.
I'm famous... sort of.
SOMEHOW, THE TESTS WERE SAFELY CONCLUDED
YAY!! I'M DONE!!
I CAN FINALLY GO BACK TO WORK AGAIN TOMORROW!!

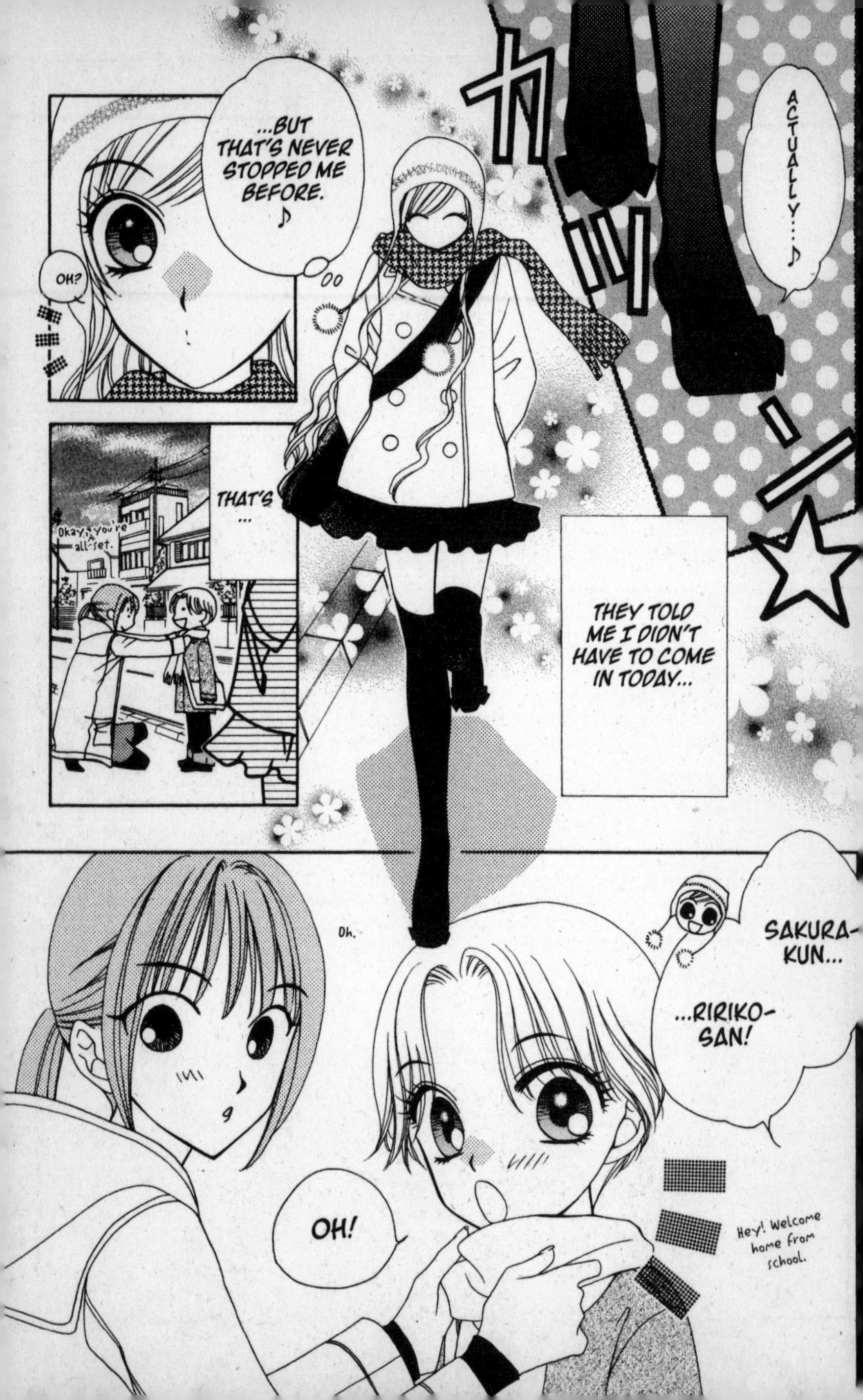
ACTUALLY...♪
THEY TOLD ME I DIDN'T HAVE TO COME IN TODAY...
...BUT THAT'S NEVER STOPPED ME BEFORE. ♪
OH?
THAT'S ...
Okay, you're all set.
SAKURA-KUN...
...RIRIKO-SAN!
Oh.
Hey! Welcome home from school.
OH!

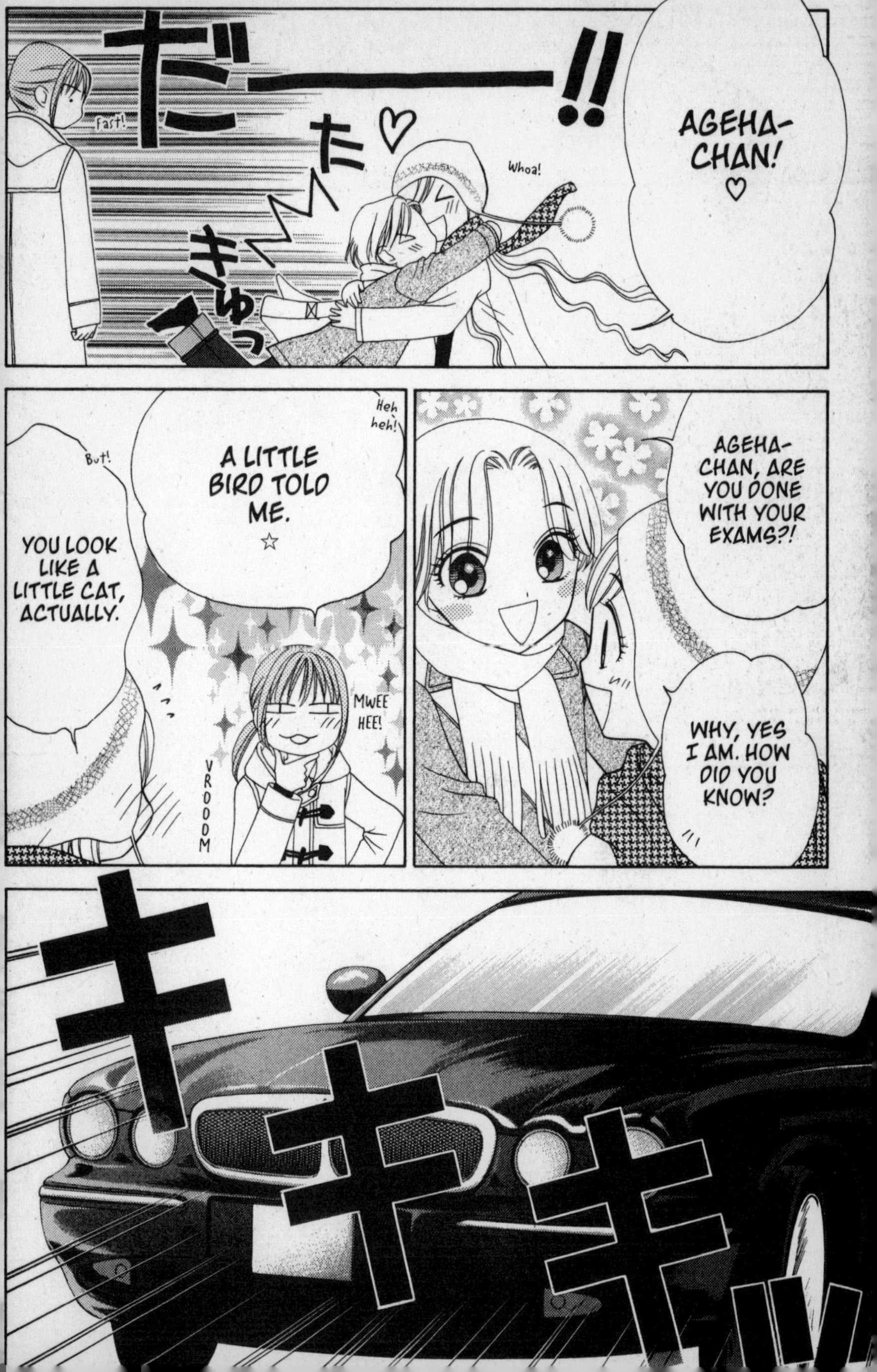
AGEHA-CHAN! ♡
Whoa!
だーー!!
♡
た
Fast!
きゅっ
AGEHA-CHAN, ARE YOU DONE WITH YOUR EXAMS?!
WHY, YES I AM. HOW DID YOU KNOW?
Heh heh!
A LITTLE BIRD TOLD ME. ☆
But!
YOU LOOK LIKE A LITTLE CAT, ACTUALLY.
MWEE HEE!
VROOOOM
キキキッ

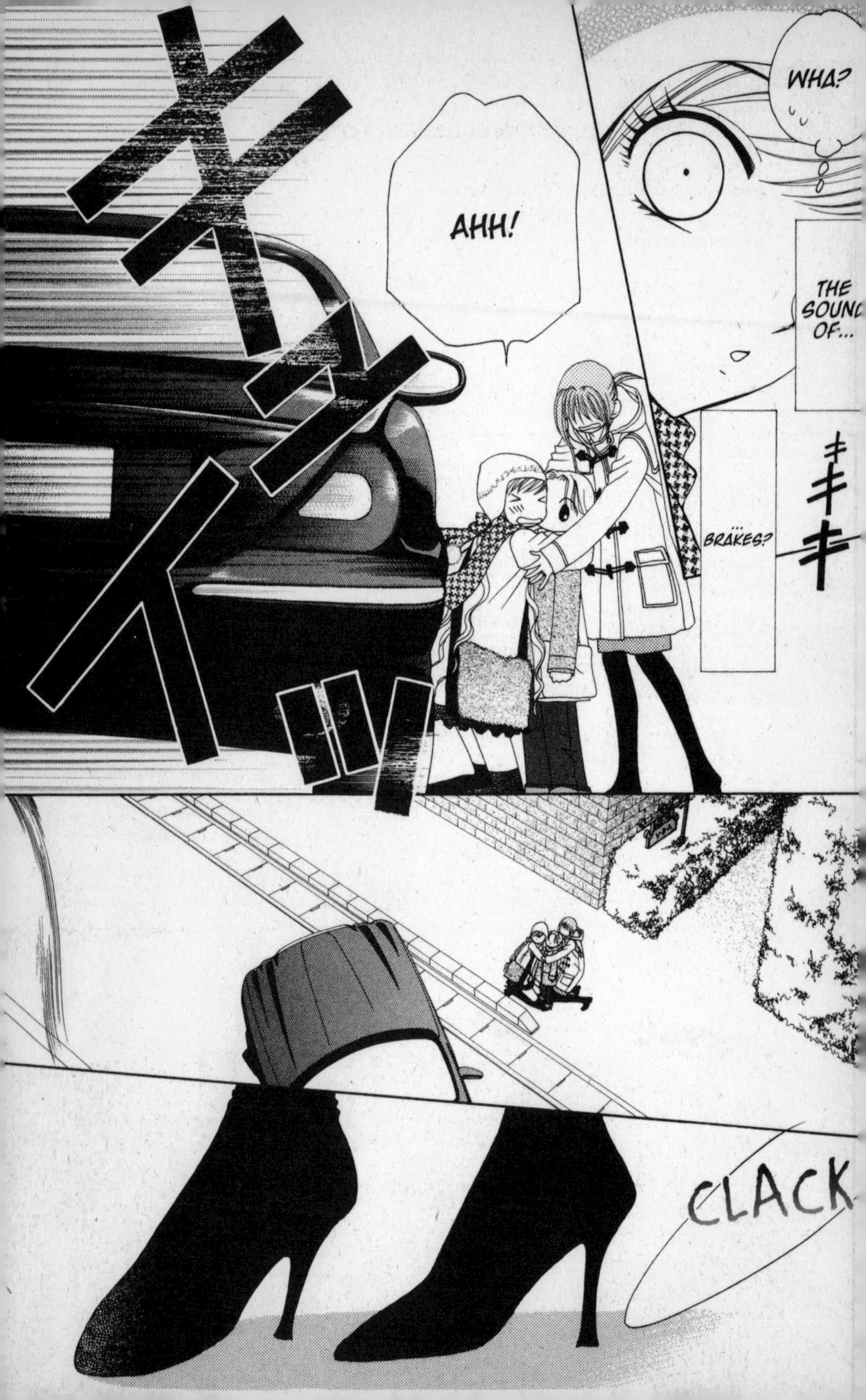
WHA?
THE SOUND OF...
...BRAKES?
AHH!
CLACK

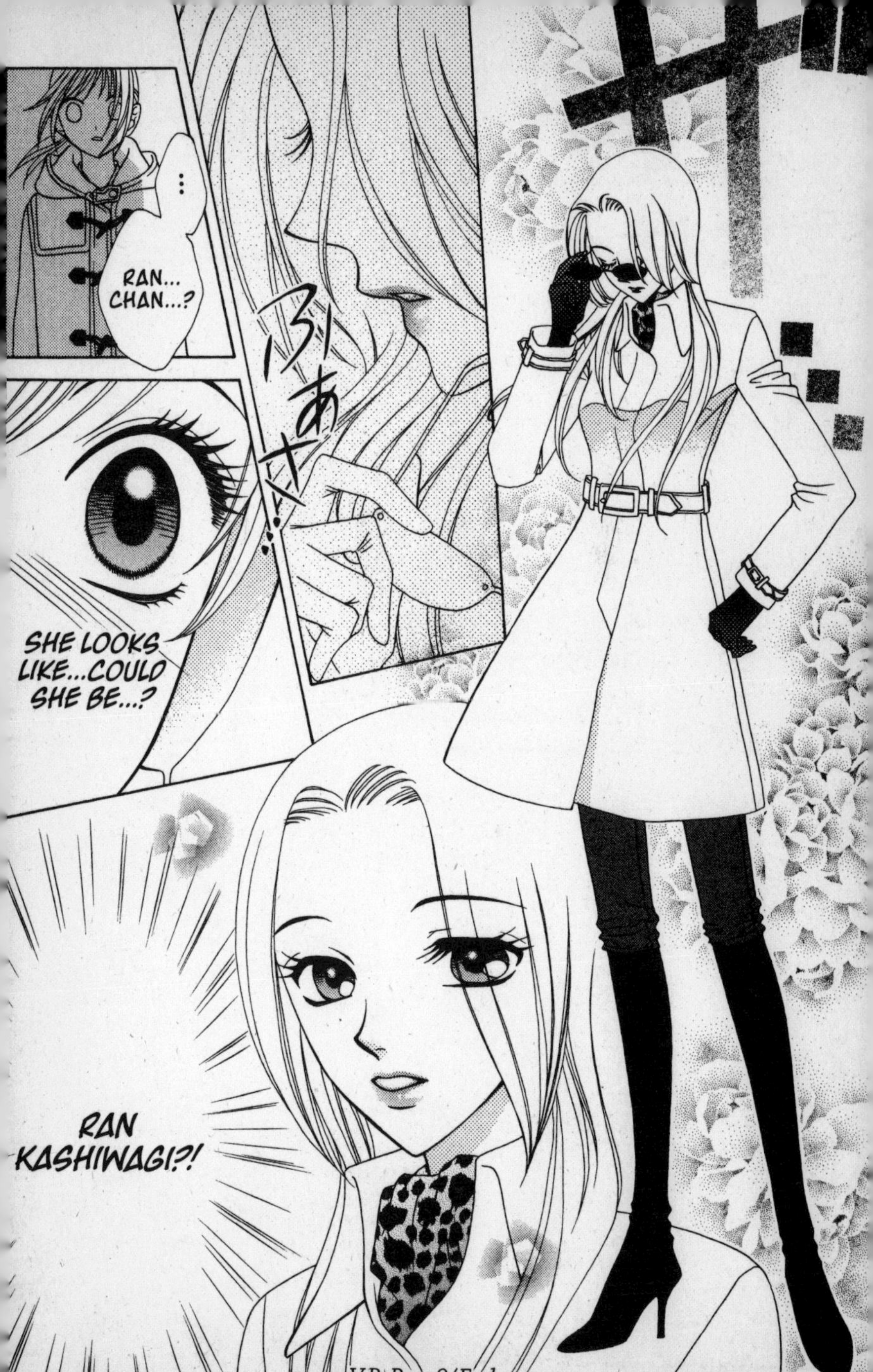
...
RAN... CHAN...?
SHE LOOKS LIKE...COULD SHE BE...?
RAN KASHIWAGI?!

V.B. Rose 9/ End

Banri Hidaka's Everyday Heaven.

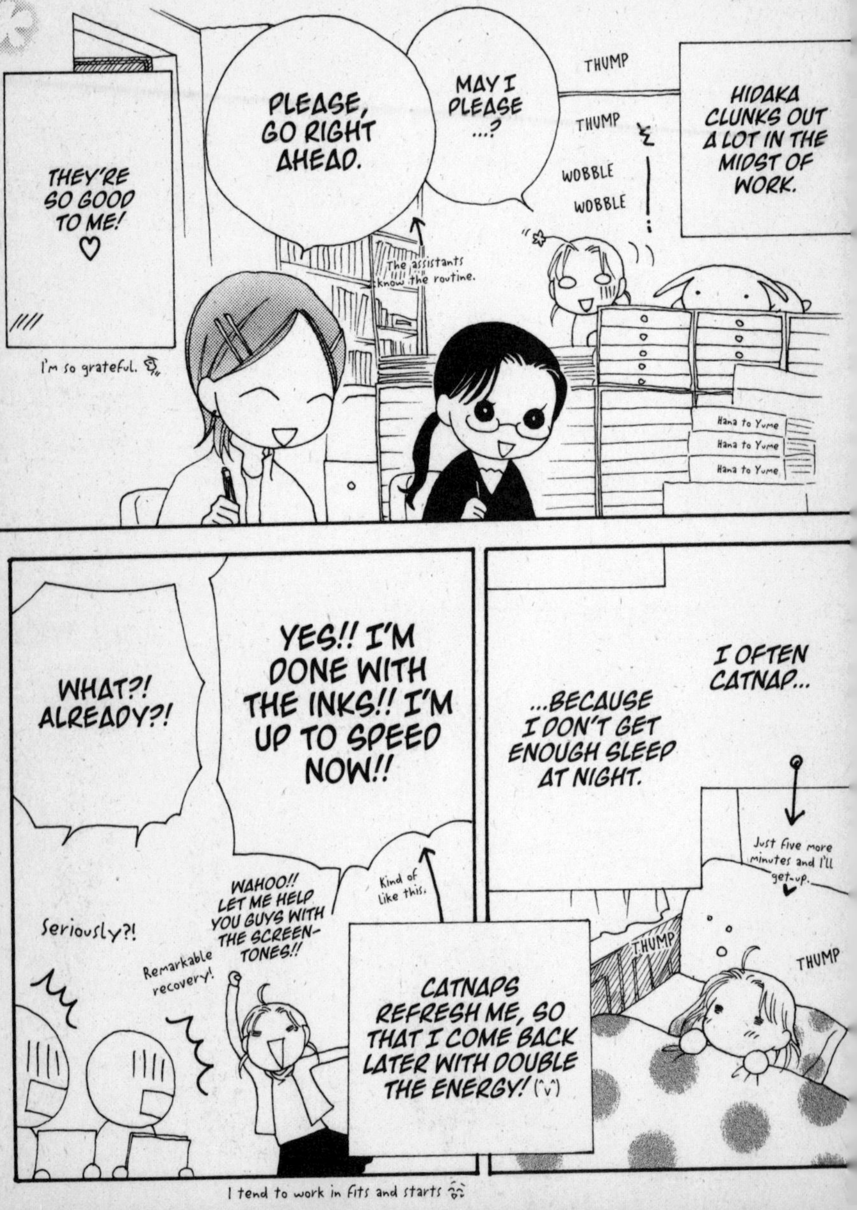
HIDAKA CLUNKS OUT A LOT IN THE MIDST OF WORK.
THUMP
THUMP
WOBBLE
WOBBLE
MAY I PLEASE ...?
PLEASE, GO RIGHT AHEAD.
The assistants know the routine.
THEY'RE SO GOOD TO ME! ♡
I'm so grateful.
Hana to Yume
Hana to Yume
Hana to Yume
I OFTEN CATNAP...
...BECAUSE I DON'T GET ENOUGH SLEEP AT NIGHT.
Just five more minutes and I'll get up. ♥
THUMP
THUMP
YES!! I'M DONE WITH THE INKS!! I'M UP TO SPEED NOW!!
WHAT?! ALREADY?!
CATNAPS REFRESH ME, SO THAT I COME BACK LATER WITH DOUBLE THE ENERGY! (^v^)
Kind of like this.
WAHOO!! LET ME HELP YOU GUYS WITH THE SCREEN-TONES!!
Remarkable recovery!
Seriously?!
I tend to work in fits and starts

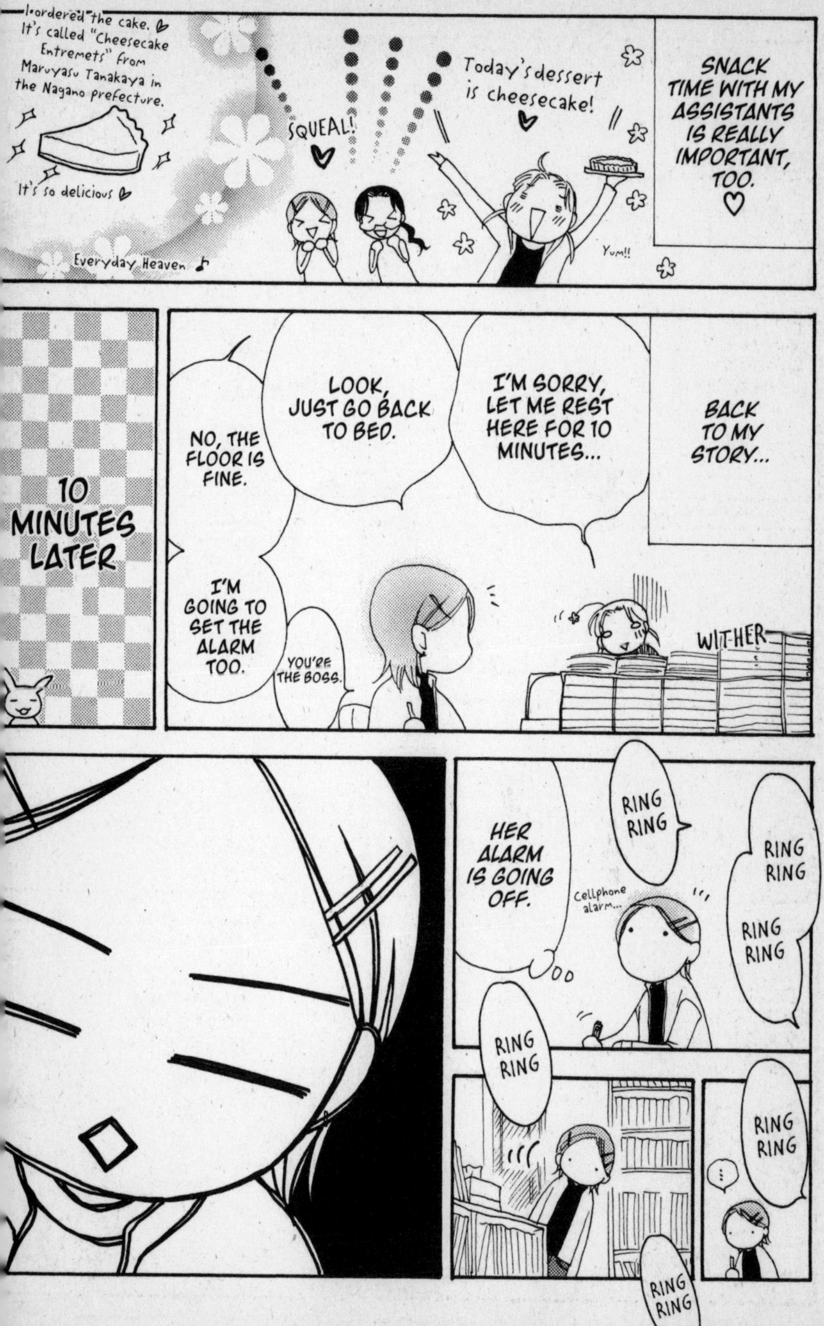
SNACK TIME WITH MY ASSISTANTS IS REALLY IMPORTANT, TOO. ♡
Today's dessert is cheesecake! ♡
Yum!!
SQUEAL! ♡
I ordered the cake. ♡ It's called "Cheesecake Entremets" from Maruyasu Tanakaya in the Nagano prefecture.
It's so delicious ♡
Everyday Heaven. ♪
BACK TO MY STORY...
I'M SORRY, LET ME REST HERE FOR 10 MINUTES...
WITHER
LOOK, JUST GO BACK TO BED.
NO, THE FLOOR IS FINE.
I'M GOING TO SET THE ALARM TOO.
YOU'RE THE BOSS.
10 MINUTES LATER
RING RING
RING RING
RING RING
HER ALARM IS GOING OFF.
Cellphone alarm...
RING RING
...
RING RING
RING RING

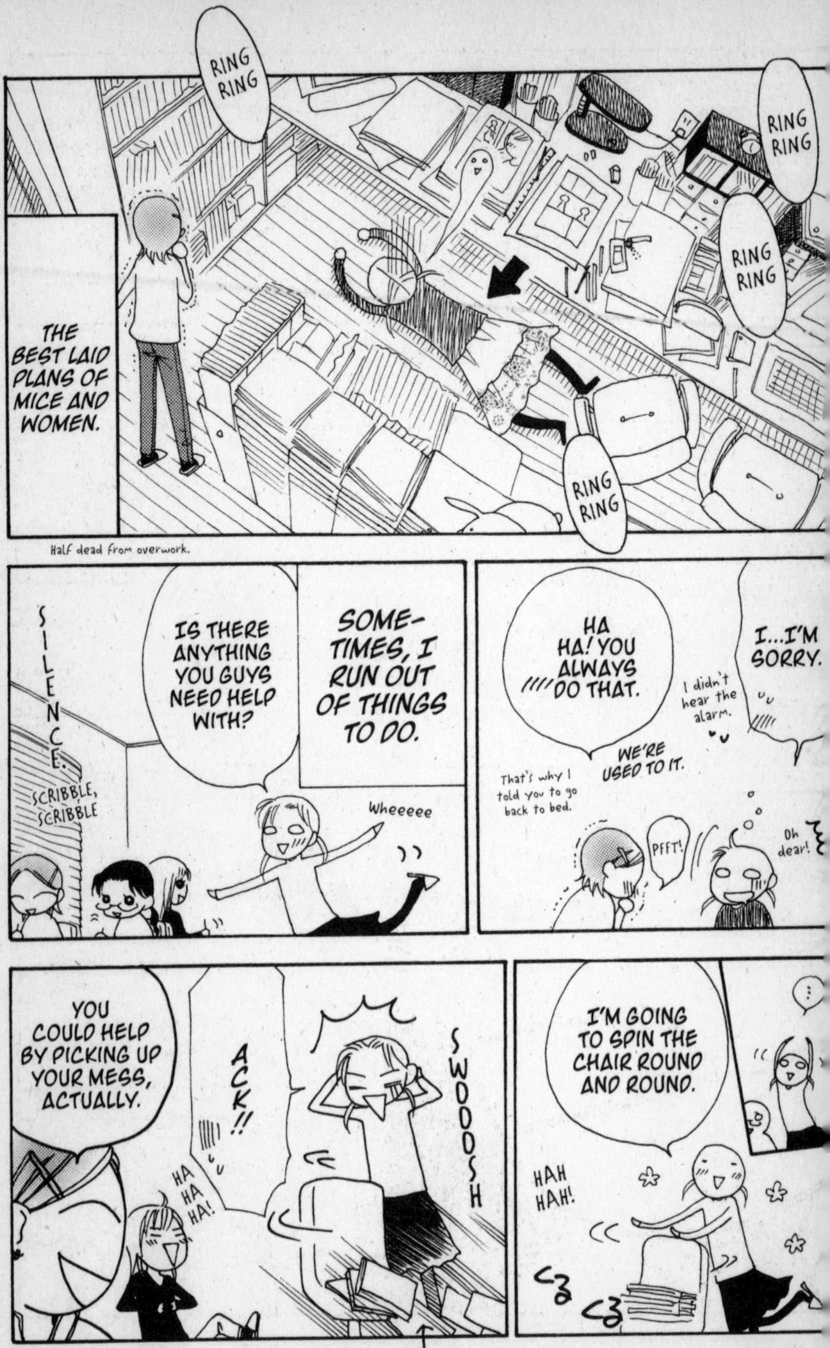
RING RING
RING RING
RING RING
RING RING
THE BEST LAID PLANS OF MICE AND WOMEN.
Half dead from overwork.
I...I'M SORRY.
I didn't hear the alarm.
HA HA! YOU ALWAYS DO THAT.
WE'RE USED TO IT.
That's why I told you to go back to bed.
Oh dear!
PFFT!
SOME-TIMES, I RUN OUT OF THINGS TO DO.
IS THERE ANYTHING YOU GUYS NEED HELP WITH?
Wheeeee
SILENCE.
SCRIBBLE, SCRIBBLE
...
I'M GOING TO SPIN THE CHAIR ROUND AND ROUND.
HAH HAH!
くる くる
SWOOOSH
ACK!!
YOU COULD HELP BY PICKING UP YOUR MESS, ACTUALLY.
HA HA HA!
Mountain of documents.

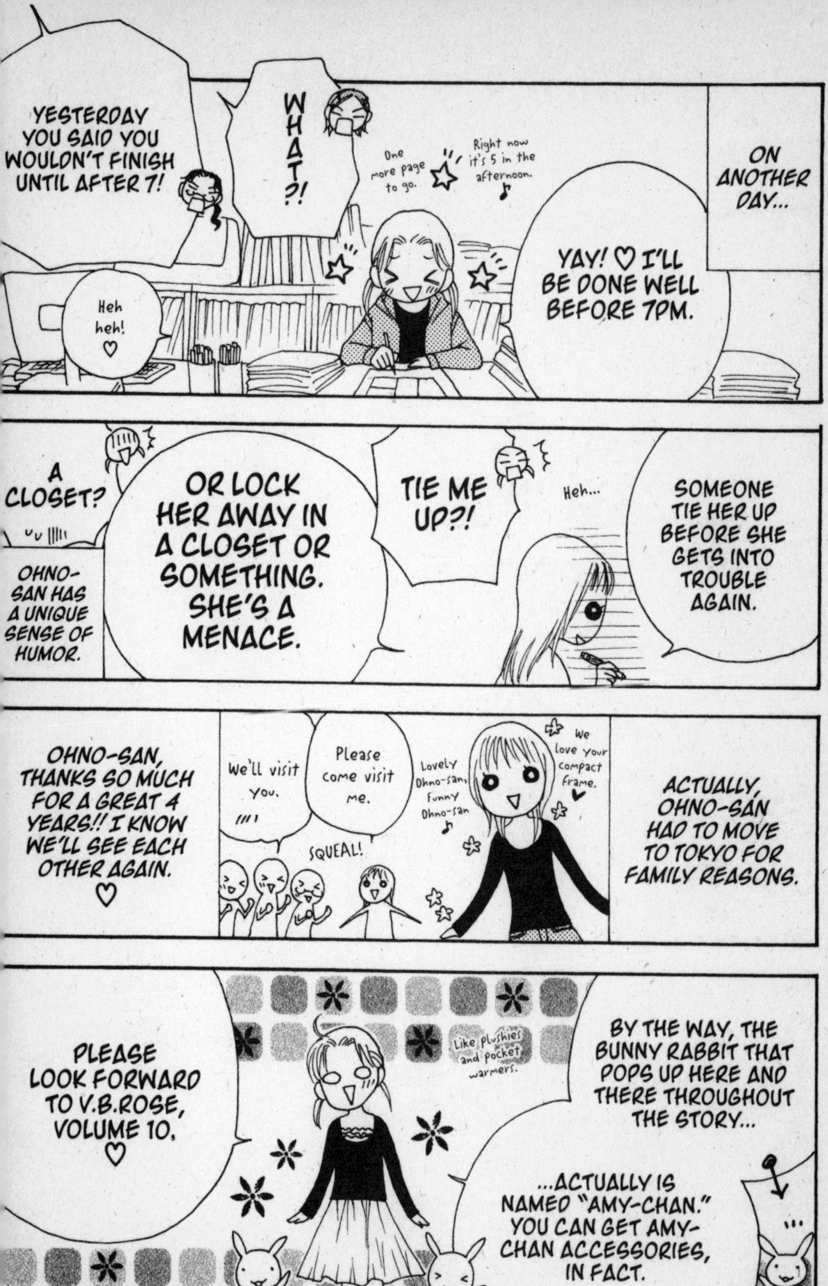
ON ANOTHER DAY...
YAY! ♡ I'LL BE DONE WELL BEFORE 7PM.
Right now it's 5 in the afternoon.
One more page to go.
WHAT?!
YESTERDAY YOU SAID YOU WOULDN'T FINISH UNTIL AFTER 7!
Heh heh! ♡
SOMEONE TIE HER UP BEFORE SHE GETS INTO TROUBLE AGAIN.
Heh...
TIE ME UP?!
OR LOCK HER AWAY IN A CLOSET OR SOMETHING. SHE'S A MENACE.
A CLOSET?
OHNO-SAN HAS A UNIQUE SENSE OF HUMOR.
ACTUALLY, OHNO-SAN HAD TO MOVE TO TOKYO FOR FAMILY REASONS.
We love your compact frame. ♡
Lovely Ohno-san, Funny Ohno-san
Please come visit me.
We'll visit you.
SQUEAL!
OHNO-SAN, THANKS SO MUCH FOR A GREAT 4 YEARS!! I KNOW WE'LL SEE EACH OTHER AGAIN. ♡
BY THE WAY, THE BUNNY RABBIT THAT POPS UP HERE AND THERE THROUGHOUT THE STORY...
...ACTUALLY IS NAMED "AMY-CHAN." YOU CAN GET AMY-CHAN ACCESSORIES, IN FACT.
...
Like plushies and pocket warmers.
PLEASE LOOK FORWARD TO V.B.ROSE, VOLUME 10. ♡

Banri Hidaka's Everyday Heaven./END

In the Next Volume of

V.B. Rose

Yukari's estranged mother finally makes her appearance! But the gorgeous Ran Kashiwagi is not at all what Ageha expected... and now she's got eighteen years of bad blood between mother and son to unravel. Even Ageha's eternal optimism and Ran's side of the story may not be enough to reconcile everyone's differences...

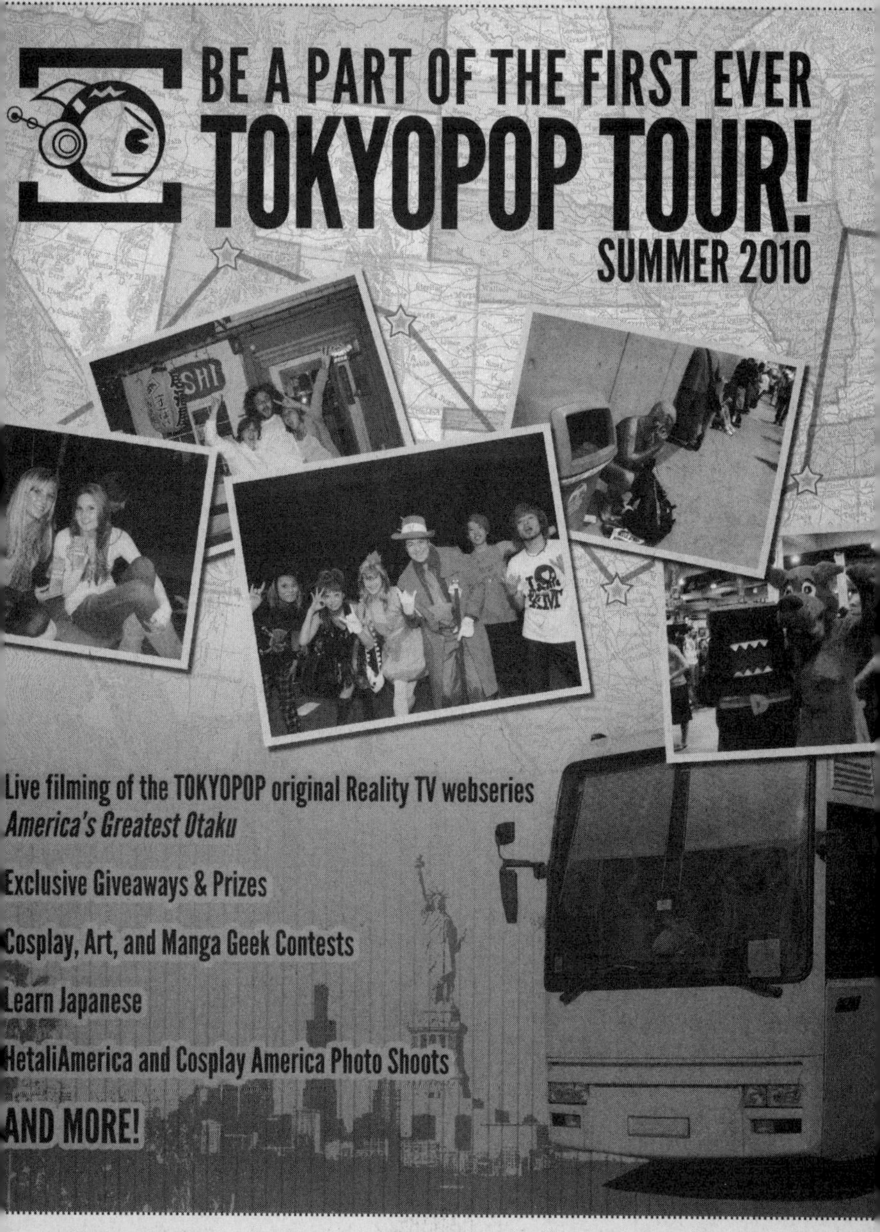
BE A PART OF THE FIRST EVER
TOKYOPOP TOUR!
SUMMER 2010
Live filming of the TOKYOPOP original Reality TV webseries
America's Greatest Otaku
Exclusive Giveaways & Prizes
Cosplay, Art, and Manga Geek Contests
Learn Japanese
HetaliAmerica and Cosplay America Photo Shoots
AND MORE!

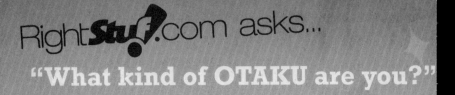

STOP!

This is the back of the book.
You wouldn't want to spoil a great ending!

This book is printed "manga-style," in the authentic Japanese right-to-left format. Since none of the artwork has been flipped or altered, readers get to experience the story just as the creator intended. You've been asking for it, so TOKYOPOP® delivered: authentic, hot-off-the-press, and far more fun!

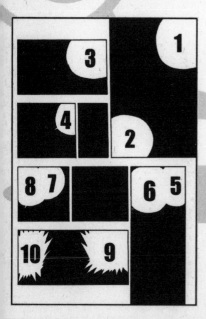

DIRECTIONS

If this is your first time reading manga-style, here's a quick guide to help you understand how it works.

It's easy... just start in the top right panel and follow the numbers. Have fun, and look for more 100% authentic manga from TOKYOPOP®!

漫画革命

THE MANGA REVOLUTION · LEADING · THE MANGA REVOLUTION · LEADING